WOMEN
IN SPORT

To the individuals involved in girls' and women's sport
who have provided the roots,
and to those who give it wings

WOMEN
IN SPORT
Issues and Controversies

GRETA L. COHEN
editor
Foreword by Jackie Joyner-Kersee

SAGE Publications
International Educational and Professional Publisher
Newbury Park   London   New Delhi

Photograph acknowledgments: page 1, Pam Mellor-Deslorieux; page 25, courtesy of Smith College Archives, Smith College; page 67, courtesy of Doris Corbett; page 117, Cameron C. Lynch; page 169, James Aulenback, Sport Graphics © 1991; page 215, courtesy of the Genuario Studio; page 249, courtesy of University of Iowa Sports Information; page 287, courtesy of Georgena Terry, Precision Bicycles for Women.

The quote from the *New York Times* on page 117 is from "College Sports and Motherhood," July 3, 1921. Copyright © 1921 by The New York Times Company. Reprinted by permission.

The quote from LaFerne Ellis Price on page 215 is from *The Wonder of Motion* (Reston, VA: American Alliance for Health, Physical Education, Recreation and Dance, 1970), p. 13. Copyright © 1970 by AAHPERD. Reprinted by permission.

For information address:

SAGE Publications, Inc.
2455 Teller Road
Newbury Park, California 91320

SAGE Publications Ltd.
6 Bonhill Street
London EC2A 4PU
United Kingdom

SAGE Publications India Pvt. Ltd.
M-32 Market
Greater Kailash I
New Delhi 110 048 India

Printed in the United States of America

Library of Congress Cataloging-in-Publication Data

Main entry under title:

Women in sport: issues and controversies / edited by Greta L. Cohen.
   p.   cm.
   Includes bibliographical references (p.) and index.
   ISBN 0-8039-4979-0. — ISBN 0-8039-4980-4 (pbk.)
   1. Women in sports—United States. 2. Women athletes—United
States. I. Cohen, Greta L.
GV709.18.U6W65 1993
796'.0194—dc20
                                    93-6510
                                      CIP

93 94 95 96 10 9 8 7 6 5 4 3 2

Sage Production Editor: Judith L. Hunter

Contents

100 Years in Women's Sports

1892   Senda Berenson is appointed instructor of gymnastics and director of physical training at Smith College

1895   Mountaineer Annie Smith Peck is first woman to climb the Matterhorn

1896   First women's intercollegiate sport contest is a basketball game between University of California, Berkeley, and Stanford University

1900   Twelve women compete in Paris at IInd Olympiad in the sports of golf and tennis

1901   Annie Edson Taylor, 43, is first person to go over Niagara Falls in a barrel and live

1904   Only women competing in the Olympic Games in St. Louis are American archers representing clubs from Cincinnati, Ohio, and Washington, D.C.

1908   Annie Smith Peck, 58, is first person to reach summit of 21,837-foot Huascaran South in Peruvian Andes

1916   The Amateur Athletic Union (AAU) holds its first national championship for women (the sport chosen is swimming)

The Women's International Bowling Congress (WIBC) is established

1917   Annie Oakley, sharpshooter and former star of Buffalo Bill's Wild West Show from 1885 to 1901, tours World War I Army camps, giving shooting lessons to the soldiers

1922   The Federation Sportive Feminine Internationale holds the first Women's World Games because the International Olympic Committee (IOC) refuses to include track and field competition in the Olympics for women

The Amateur Athletics Union sponsors a track and field team to the new Women's Olympic Games

1924	Golfer Glenna Collett Vare wins 59 out of 60 matches
	The first Winter Olympic Games are held
	Marion Hollins organizes the Women's National Golf Country Club on Long Island, financed totally by women for its all-women membership
1925	Gertrude Ederle becomes the first female to swim the English Channel, breaking the existing record by more than two hours
1926	Charlotte Shummel sets record in 150-mile swim from Albany to New York City
1927	Power boat racer Delphina Cromwell wins the President's Cup Race on the Potomac River in her boat *Miss Syndicate*
1929	Amelia Earhart founds an international organization of licensed women pilots called the Ninety-Nines (the number of charter members)
1932	Babe Didrikson sets world record in three track and field events in Summer Olympics, but her high jump record is disallowed because of improper technique
1934	The fourth, and last, Women's World Games are held in London, England
1937	Amelia Earhart disappears during her around-the-world solo flight
1938	Helen Wills wins her eighth singles title at Wimbledon
1940	Kathryn Dewey whizzes past the all-male competition to lead her four-man bobsled team to the National Championship title; the men are so irate they pass a rule to prevent women from further competition
1941	The Ohio State University women physical educators organize the first national collegiate golf tournament
1942	Edna Gardner Whyte sells her aviation school, hangars, and planes and moves to Texas to train Army and Navy pilots for World War II
1943	P. K. Wrigley forms the All-American Girls' Professional Baseball League
1949	The Ladies Professional Golf Association (LPGA) is established
1951	Associated Press votes Babe Didrikson Zaharias the "Woman Athlete of the Half Century"
1953	Maureen "Little Mo" Connolly becomes first woman to win the Grand Slam in Tennis
1956	Pat McCormick repeats 1952 feat by taking gold medals in both the springboard and platform diving events at the Summer Olympic Games
1957	Althea Gibson becomes the first black woman tennis player to win Wimbledon and Forest Hills
1960	Sprinter Wilma Rudolph wins three gold medals in the Olympics
1964	Volleyball is introduced as the first team sport for women in the Olympic Games

1967	Katherine Switzer is first woman to run the Boston Marathon, disguised as K. Switzer, wearing a baseball cap
1968	A sex chromatin test for women athletes is introduced as a prerequisite of Olympic competition
1970	Diane Crump becomes the first female jockey to race in the Kentucky Derby
1971	Five-person, full-court play is officially adopted in the sport of women's basketball, following a two-year experimental trial period
1972	Title IX of the Educational Amendments Act is passed by U.S. Congress
	Dorothy Harris organizes first National Research Congress on women's sports and becomes first person to conduct sports medicine research using women as subjects
1973	Billie Jean King defeats Bobby Riggs to win $100,000 tennis match billed as the "Battle of the Sexes"
	The Association for Intercollegiate Athletics for Women (AIAW) awards academic scholarships to women athletes at collegiate level
1974	The Women's Sports Foundation is established to foster development of women's sports in America
1976	Janet Guthrie is first female driver in Indianapolis 500
	Pitcher Joan Joyce leads Connecticut Falcons to World Series Championship in the International Women's Professional Softball Association
1977	Shirley Muldowney is named top drag car racer of the year
	Sheila Young repeats 1973 feat by winning the World Championships in two different sports: speed skating and cycling
1978	Mountain climber Arlene Blum leads first all-women's expedition up Annapurna
	Wade Trophy established by the National Association for Girls and Women in Sport (NAGWS) to honor basketball coach Virginia Wade; awarded annually to the top college basketball player in the country
1981	Kathy Whitworth becomes first female golfer to reach $1 million in earnings
	Women permitted membership to the former all-male IOC
	Edna Gardner Whyte, 80, considered the grande dame of aviation, enters the All Women's International Air Race (which she has won four times previously)
1982	The first time the U.S. Postal Service issues commemorative stamps to honor athletes, Babe Didrikson Zaharias and Bobby Jones are chosen
1984	The Supreme Court ruling in *Grove City v. Bell* is interpreted to mean that Title IX no longer covers sports
	Lynette Woodward becomes first woman contracted to play basketball with the Harlem Globetrotters
	Joan Benoit wins the first women's Olympic marathon in 2:24:52

1988   Congress passes bill to overturn *Grove City* decision and restore expansive interpretation of Title IX

Steffie Graf wins Tennis Grand Slam and exhibition gold at Olympics

Jackie Joyner-Kersee sets new heptathlon world record and surpasses old Olympic mark by nearly 1,000 points and wins her second gold medal in the long jump

Sarah Fulcher finishes the longest continuous solo run ever, certified by the *Guiness Book of World Records*, for her 11,134-mile run around the perimeter of the United States in 14 months, averaging a marathon every day

1989   Rock climber Lynn Hill captures women's championship title in World Cup Super Finals and third place in open competition for both men and women

Victoria Brucker of San Pedro, California, is first girl to play in Little League World Series, playing first base, batting in the cleanup position (fourth), and pitching in the final game

Paula Newby Fraser breaks the Ironman Triathlon World Championship record for the second year in a row and wins the World Biathlon Championships in same year

Martina Navratilova is named "Female Athlete of the Decade" by the National Sports Review

1990   Susan Butcher wins fourth Alaskan 1,049-mile Iditarod Trail Sled Dog Race

Ski racer Diana Golden retires after winning three gold medals at World Championships to continue promoting sports for disabled

Martina Navratilova wins record ninth singles championship at Wimbledon

1991   Judith Sweet becomes first woman president of the NCAA

The first World Cup Championships are contested in the sport of soccer and the U.S. team wins title

1992   The Supreme Court rules that Title IX plaintiffs may seek compensatory and punitive damages in sex discrimination cases

The Women's Antarctica Expedition begins historic trek across Antarctica

Foreword

I am very pleased to have this opportunity to endorse a textbook devoted entirely to the female sports experience. *Women in Sport: Issues and Controversies* is revolutionary. The comprehensive approach to women in sport explores issues that are relevant to *all* girls and women regardless of race, class, ethnicity, or handicap. The topics are "right on target" and reflect timely concerns. I look forward to the day when women are afforded the same opportunities and accolades for their sporting achievements as men are for their triumphs.

The sporting experience means many different things to different people. The chance to confront physical and mental challenges can be exhilarating. Women have fought long and hard for the right to engage in sport. The text recognizes these pioneers, their struggles, their accomplishments, and the goals yet to be realized. The opportunity to participate should be the right of all women.

While growing up, I never had the opportunity to read books about female athletes. Their struggles and accomplishments were hardly common knowledge. Female role models were at a premium. I was fortunate, highly motivated, and my efforts were nourished and encouraged by my parents and my brother, Al. Those early childhood struggles in East St. Louis, Illinois, serve as a reminder of how very far I have come. I competed in volleyball, basketball, and track and field at Lincoln High School, graduated in the top 10 percent of my class, and earned a basketball scholarship to UCLA. But it was the long jump and the heptathlon that became my passion. I have worked and trained exclusively for these events since 1981 and my dreams of victories, Olympic medals, and world records in these events have been realized.

Because of my athletic successes, I have had the chance to meet athletes throughout the world. The friendships developed are very important to me, and they are steeped in the common language of training, struggle, and the thrill of competition. I hope that the messages found in this book will provide insights that will impact positively on female athletes and increase the opportunities to experience the satisfaction and joy that can be gained through sport.

—Jackie Joyner-Kersee

Acknowledgments

This project, like most worthwhile endeavors, has been both exhilarating and frustrating. There were times when I never thought I would finish and other times when I just couldn't let it go!

I would like first to thank my contributors, without whom the text could never have been written. It has often been said that if you want a job done, you should give it to a busy person. The willingness of the chapter authors to take time from their incredibly full schedules to conduct research of this magnitude is commendable. Their receptivity to changes in both content and style, so that their collaborative efforts might appear more uniform, is genuinely appreciated. Collectively, they have created a real treasure and I am indebted to them.

I am grateful to the staff at Sage Publications, especially Christine Smedley, Judy Hunter, and Judy Selhorst. They believed in the merits of this project from its inception and skillfully edited and directed its progress.

In the initial stages, colleagues who provided insight that helped shape the development of the chapters included Stevie Chepko, Jan Felshin, Doris Hardy, Mimi Murray, and Carol Oglesby. I owe them my thanks.

As the chapters started to take shape, the process of validating research data, historical information, and what seemed like an endless parade of miscellaneous "facts" commenced. My appreciation is extended to the following individuals who provided that information: Sally Burke, Doris Corbett, Jeanette Crooker, Laurel Davis, Mary Jo Kane, Barbara Lubke, Don Sabo, Susan Shafer, Dana Shugar, Julien Stein, Victoria Tefft, Sue Tougas, and Susan True. My thanks also to the staff of the University of Rhode Island library, especially Vicki Burnett and Marie Rudd at interlibrary loan. I am most grateful to all the interns at the Women's Sports Foundation who researched endless questions and provided valuable resources, and to Kathy Cerra-Laquale, whose help as a research assistant in the final month before the text went to press was invaluable.

Special thanks go to Helen McCarthy and Stacia Peters, who convinced me that my computer was archaic, found a suitable upscale model for me to purchase, installed and programmed the machine, and showed me more than I ever wanted to know about computer technology! Thanks also to Lorna Prout, Nancy Meader, and Stephanie Champlin for their final corrections on disks not IBM compatible.

The search for appropriate photographs to accompany the text was exciting; however, the detective work needed to trace ownership soon lost its appeal. In my research, I contacted many individuals and was delighted to find so many people willing to assist me in supplying photos for consideration, taking pictures, tracking down photo sources, and contacting their legal departments to validate ownership. My genuine appreciation is extended to the following: Jim Aulenback, Alex Alexio, Rayla Allison, Lauren Anderson, Joe Caputo, Maria Cimino, Karen Congdon, Pam Mellor-Deslorieux, Sally Fox, Betty Hicks, Ellen Kaplan, Bettye Lane, Snooki Mulder, Dana Shugar, Lorraine Silver, Kathy Stilwell, Sue Weiner, and Jan Wilson, as well as Jan Armstrong at the Newport Tennis Hall of Fame Museum, Roseanne Bafundo at Wilson Sporting Goods, Jonathan Howard at PLAN International, Margery Sly at the Smith College Archives, Beth Weber at the University of Iowa Sports Information, and Wayne Wilson at the Amateur Athletic Foundation of Los Angeles.

My personal friends have humored me throughout this project, provided numerous distractions, and rescued me for brief snatches of time to enjoy an afternoon of kayaking or a good Sunday protest march. My gratitude is extended to many supportive friends, but especially to Judy Anderson, Marsha Blair, Rita Bugbee, Joan Clegg, Nancy Dowding, Bonnie England, Lorry Garvin, Michael Hamilton, Barbara Margolis, Jude Matteson, Dorrie McCaffrey, Helen McCarthy, Diane Seleen, and Marjorie Smit. They constantly remind me that there is a life beyond women in sport.

I am profoundly grateful to my family—my mother, Edna, and sisters, Joyce and Carol—whose continual support and encouragement is treasured. Lastly, I am indebted to Maryanne "Mac" Cunningham, who juggled all our collective responsibilities so I could devote all my time to this project, and then found time to assist me with everything from data collection to proofreading.

—Greta L. Cohen
University of Rhode Island

Introduction

My primary objective in putting together this volume is to provide a comprehensive textbook that includes a broad-based survey of issues relevant to girls' and women's participation in sport. As women enter the mainstream of American sport as athletes, coaches, and administrators, and as they take their place in sport-related businesses, the issues and controversies associated with their rights to equitable opportunities must be explored. The collaborative nature of this effort enabled me to choose leading feminist educators throughout the United States as participants. Inclusion of the works of such progressive educators and renowned researchers in a single volume makes the value of this collective endeavor immeasurable.

The book is divided into eight units covering political, economic, herstorical, psychological, and physiological perspectives, as well as sociological constructs—gender issues, the institutionalization of women in sport, and a contemporary look at our changing times. The configuration of an eight-unit structure with two to four chapters per unit can easily be adapted to most semester and trimester schedules at academic institutions. The accompanying 100-year time line provides a chronology of women's contributions to sport and the accomplishments that often go unheralded. The topics relate directly to courses in women in sport, gender issues, women's studies, sport in American society, and twentieth-century herstory. Anyone interested in the women's sports movement and issues related to women's opportunities for sports participation should find this text a valuable resource.

The foundational unit, Gender Issues, provides strong sociological constructs for the development of the text. In Chapter 1, Susan Greendorfer concentrates on the dynamics that create the process of gender role socialization and then discusses the likelihood of an individual becoming involved in sport. Her theory on the extent to which girls and women remain involved in sport is based on a parent-peer dialectic. Donald Sabo and Michael Messner, in Chapter 2, discuss deep-seated sex discrimination, male hegemony, and the sexual politics involved as women's participation in sport increases. The section in their chapter headed "The Locker Room and the Rape Culture" illuminates the sexual objectification of women by male athletes. This ideology is compared with a countertheory whereby women are viewed differently when they enter the world of sport as legitimate athletes.

Unit II, Herstory: A Legacy of Honor, functions like a pocket mirror, allowing us to reflect on the highlights of our more ambitious foremothers who redefined sporting opportunities for girls and women of all ages. The unit includes the stories of a unique blend of diverse personalities who paved the way for women in contemporary sport. In Chapter 3, Joan Paul provides an overview of early sports "heroines," and Betty Hicks shares memories of the legendary Babe Didrikson Zaharias in Chapter 4. The inclusion of a chapter devoted to the All-American Girls' Professional Baseball League, by a former player in that league, Mary Pratt, serves to illustrate the extent to which conformity to social protocol was necessary to ensure opportunity during an era when sports participation was much more restrictively defined. L. Leotus Morrison's chapter on the Association for Intercollegiate Athletics for Women documents the dramatic historical transition in collegiate politics.

In Unit III, Government and Policy, Paula Welch's chronology of the governance of women's sport in the educational arena bears witness to a unique transformation from the conservative philosophical ideologies of early leaders. As a result of pressure from an undercurrent of individuals and organizations who continually attacked the status quo, more liberal policies evolved. Linda Jean Carpenter vividly illuminates this struggle in Chapter 8, in which she effectively bridges the Title IX era to postmodern governance of girls' and women's sports. Mary Lydon's account in Chapter 9 reflects the backlash of the Title IX era at the secondary school level. In Chapter 10, Donna Lopiano shows how liberal and radical posturing at the collegiate level work as a catalyst for change in the 1990s.

Unit IV, Physiological Perspectives, develops a basic framework for understanding essential concepts in human physiology, nutrition, and care and prevention of sports-related injuries and eating disorders. The contributors to this unit—Carol Christensen, Helen McCarthy, Kathleen Cerra-Laquale, and Marjorie Caldwell—debunk the myths and provide the most current research available on the physiological impact of sport and physical activity on the health of girls and women. As females become more involved in health and wellness issues, physical fitness, and high-performance training, nutritional concerns become more acute. Similarly, the prevalence of eating disorders escalates.

The four chapters that constitute Unit V, Institutionalization of Women's Sport, focus on two primary themes. The first addresses the social construction of girls and women engaged in a world of sport shaped by a strong patriarchy. Chapters 15 and 16, by myself and Anita DeFrantz, respectively, examine how the existing power structure and hegemony are used to trivialize, oppress, and exclude females from the sporting arenas. The second theme of this unit concerns how prejudice and fear create social phenomena that are also institutionalized. As Pat Griffin (Chapter 17) and

R. Vivian Acosta (Chapter 18) show, homophobia is internalized, whereas ethnicity is racially defined. In both cases, girls' and women's entrance into sport and physical activity is marginalized. Throughout this unit, efforts to effect change are cogently articulated.

Unit VI, Psychological Perspectives, delineates the practical application of sport psychology as it relates to motivation, drive, and superior performance by the athlete. As Mimi Murray and Hilary Matheson make clear in Chapter 19, as long as girls' socialization differs from that of boys, the strategies used to motivate athletes must take the differences into account. In Chapter 20, Patricia Sullivan and Deborah Wilson describe various scenarios that distinguish coaches who contribute to the problems in this area from those who take on roles as part of the solution. Current research and anecdotal vignettes provide insights for both disabled and able-bodied athletes who strive to maximize performance. In Chapter 21, Claudine Sherrill addresses the subject of women athletes with disabilities and provides information on obstacles that able-bodied people may never even consider.

Sport is a multibillion-dollar industry. The economic impact of one-half of the population's access to that economy provides the focus of Unit VII, Economics of Sport. In Chapter 22, Christine Grant and Charles Darley use the parable of Persephone and Hades to illustrate the issues confronting women's participation in intercollegiate sport. In Chapter 23, Marjorie Snyder focuses on the job market and sports-related business opportunities. Christine Shelton, in Chapter 24, illuminates the strategies used by women in professional tennis to compete for their product.

The final unit, Changing Times, offers a contemporary look at some alternative models for the future development of sport. Mary Duquin's contribution in Chapter 25 is humanistic and introspective, whereas Chapter 26, by Nancy Bailey, is more politically motivated and action oriented. In the final chapter, I attempt to blend these two themes, devoting attention to girls' and women's access to sport in diverse cultures and to the cooperative model used by feminists working to promote sport worldwide.

Many of the issues and controversies raised in this text stem from the pervasiveness of sport in American society, the emergence of the female athlete, interest in health and fitness, and concerns pertaining to power and control. Educators contemplate the value of sports experiences to the overall mission of quality education. Owners of professional franchises and sports cartels envision sport as a product, the athlete as a commodity, and the relative value of each to fluctuate freely in the open market.

Is it unrealistic to assume that sport, as an American institution, and a relatively conservative institution at that, will suddenly cease to reflect our society at large and begin to lead the way by setting standards to diminish sexism, racism, and heterosexism? Sport is big business. How much corruption will be tolerated? Is the feminist perspective an essential component of the solution? Who will lead the way if the educators abdicate responsibility? It is my intent, and that of the contributors to this volume, that this text provide a starting point for just such an exploration.

—Greta L. Cohen

Gender Issues

Sport is for play, for the sense of competition, for recreation—certainly not to be used as some archaic form of gender role playing. Sport should be challenging, competitive, intense . . . whatever you want it to be. But in the end it has to be fun.

—Lisa Rubarth

If folks can learn to be racist, then they can learn to be antiracist. If being a sexist ain't genetic, then, dad gum, people can learn about gender equality.

—Johnnetta Betsch Cole

As far as I'm concerned, being any gender is a drag.

—Patti Smith

Gender Role Stereotypes and Early Childhood Socialization

SUSAN L. GREENDORFER

Title IX, which became a watershed in women's sport, seems to have ushered in significant social change in regard to women's roles in general and women's involvement in sport in particular.[1] On the surface, the fact that more females are engaged in sport and physical activity than at any other period in American history suggests that at long last women have achieved equal opportunity in sport. It would seem that society finally has accepted women's physicality and athleticism. Today approximately 2 million young women participate in interscholastic sports, compared with 300,000 before the passage of Title IX. More than one-third of all intercollegiate athletes are female, compared with 15% prior to Title IX. The amount and nature of change is suspect, however, because participation figures may be misleading. The significant question is whether or not a substantive shift in underlying cultural values and ideological beliefs has occurred. Alternatively, we should ask whether forced legislation, responsible for the increase in participation, has deceived us into believing that sport is no longer a male preserve steeped in a system of male values and male traditions.

Although some would argue that women's physical activity continues to be controlled by an ideological system of gender roles and values that dictate what a woman can and cannot do with her physicality, others would argue that times have truly changed and that this generation of females enjoys limitless opportunities to participate in physical activity. Pivotal to taking a position in this argument is the understanding that female interest and involvement in sport is not a chance occurrence that depends on legislation or on innate skill and motor talent. Rather, it is an outcome of a complex and systematic process called socialization. The purpose of this chapter is to discuss how this dynamic social process relates to gender roles and how gender roles influence the likelihood of who will and who will not become involved in sport and physical activity.

Socialization and Gender Roles

As previously indicated, the socialization process involves rather complex dynamics among psychological, social, and cultural considerations of learning and development. This process plays a key role in integrating individuals into society by transmitting cultural values and traditions from one generation to the next. The process connects the individual with society by imparting important knowledge that establishes social ties among individuals. Through socialization, individuals learn to behave in accordance with the expectations of others in the social order. This social learning is accomplished through a network of ideological beliefs that is socially agreed upon with respect to expectations pertaining to appropriate behaviors, attitudes, and values in a wide range of situations (Goslin, 1969). In addition, socialization is an influential process mediated by individuals, groups, and cultural practices; the outcome of socialization is the acquisition of an agreed-upon system of standards and values.

Often overlooked in attempts to understand this process is the fact that socialization would not be possible without an extraordinary degree of *conformity*, accomplished through the transmission of a consistent or dominant "set of learnings." Although socialization is an interactive process in which individuals can and do actively participate, societal expectations are a critical element, responsible for shaping behavior and conveying dominant beliefs, which often ultimately prevail.

Nowhere do we experience the potency of this process more emphatically or clearly than when we learn our most salient social roles—our gender roles. It is through the process of gender role socialization that we learn, from infancy, about the relationship between biological sex and behavior, mannerisms, dress, and activities. This learning is shaped by ideological beliefs pertaining to gender—namely, those that clearly distinguish what males are, do, and should be from what females are, do, and should be. Such beliefs dominate our adult behavior in child rearing and form the basis of what takes place in early infant socialization. Gender role socialization has two outcomes, produced by emphasis on differences between the sexes rather than on similarities: (a) Parents treat sons and daughters differently, and (b) we learn at a very early age to distinguish between male and female.

Although some assert that differential treatment in gender role socialization is essential for the maintenance of society, others argue that it is essential only for maintaining the gender inequalities that currently exist in the social order. Those who take the latter position believe that many child-rearing practices are discriminatory because they limit experiences of males as well as females simply because of children's biological sex. The argument is that differential treatment is tantamount to discrimination, and that gender role stereotyping, a specific form of differential treatment, is an extremely powerful and potent form of discrimination. Whenever we hold expectations that are *prescribed* according to biological sex, we are engaged in gender role stereotyping. Unfortunately, in many child-rearing practices the biological sex of a child frequently determines

In Texas, 5- and 6-year-old girls work on their cheerleading skills while the 5- and 6-year-old boys play flag football. (Photo by Pam Mellor-Deslorieux)

which activities he or she will or will not be exposed to or permitted to experience—in other words, biological sex determines opportunity and experience. Thus many socialization practices represent a type of systematic discrimination based on unfounded beliefs about gender.

Because we take these practices for granted and assume the outcomes to be "normal" (e.g., male behaviors and interests differ from female behaviors and interests), few of us ever question or challenge the reasons for or the validity of the underlying ideology that is embedded in such practices. The problem with not taking a critical look at early childhood socialization is that we tend not to challenge the basis for current child-rearing practices, and when we see superficial changes in behavior we assume societal change has taken place (for example, increased sport participation by females). Upon close examination, however, we note that underlying practices of gender discrimination continue to perpetuate themselves in the midst of outward shifts in patterns.

Early Socialization and Play Behavior

Family members, usually parents, are primarily responsible for early childhood socialization. They ensure that children are exposed to activities consonant with their gender roles; they reward the children for behaving "appropriately" and punish them for behaving "inappropriately."

Unfortunately, the argument that times have changed is not supported by research in child development that relates to sex differences, socialization, play behavior, gender roles, and behavior of significant others. Recent findings demonstrate that parents continue to treat sons and daughters differently (Power & Parke, 1986), that gender role stereotypes continue to be a dominant force in early childhood socialization (Fisher-Thompson, 1990), and that sex differences found in play styles of infants, toddlers, and older children are quite similar today to those found in research more than 40 years ago (Miller, 1987; O'Brien & Huston, 1985; Tasch, 1952).

Not only does this literature suggest how gender-stereotypic notions of masculinity and femininity continue to influence toy selection, play, physical activity, and sport behavior, but the amount of this evidence is overwhelming. In light of the fact that findings from the more recent research do not differ significantly or suggest different trends from those cited elsewhere (compare Greendorfer, 1983; Lewko & Greendorfer, 1988), I focus attention in this chapter primarily on the connection between gender role stereotyping (sex typing) and sport socialization. To achieve this goal I need first to establish some critical links among gender ideology, sex typing of toys, and precursors of physical activity.

Ideology, Sex Typing, Toys, and Play Behavior

Toys are potent mechanisms of socialization, and although the selection of boys' and girls' toys represents an overt aspect of sex typing, the subtle process of how values are inculcated is virtually invisible. For example, toy availability not only influences play experiences but also results in preferences and predispositions toward specific activities (Greendorfer, 1983). Regardless of how subtly the process operates, however, the ultimate socialization outcomes are clear: Most males become involved in sport, and most females do not. Unfortunately, too many of us consider this pattern to be a "natural" outcome of biological differences, which it most emphatically is not.

Toy, play, and sport behaviors are *learned*. They are explicit outcomes of differential treatment and discriminatory socialization practices that begin when we give infant males balls, bats, and blue items and females dolls, stuffed toys, and pink items. And these practices do not stop there; they extend beyond the delivery room and continue throughout early and late childhood. Unfortunately, the simple, subtle, everyday practices of child rearing become part of a system of structured discrimination that is never questioned or challenged, because our ideological system has taught us to believe that differential treatment is not discrimination. Gender ideology is involved when we attach color (pink/blue) to sex; when we consider design, style, and fashion as important elements when choosing "appropriate" infant clothing; and when we designate types of toys as "male," "female," or "neutral." The question is, Why should certain toys be considered better suited for boys and others better suited for girls? Why do parents select what they think is or is not an appropriate activity based on a child's biological sex? Why should a father show a son how to hold, throw, and catch a ball but not teach similar skills to his daughter? The answer is differential treatment, yet how often do we consider that by not exposing daughters to motor skill development, by not offering daughters a variety of sporting activities, by not encouraging daughters to develop motor skill patterns that allow them to move their bodies in the same way sons are allowed to move theirs, we discriminate? More significantly, how aware are we that by limiting opportunities in play and early motor skill development, childhood precursors to sport experiences, we impose limits on later sport skill development?

The implications of these socializing experiences are clear, as initial presence or absence of toys shapes play behavior of early childhood and influences preferences of later childhood. Many of the traditional sex differences in play styles and preferences seem to be influenced both *indirectly* by parental expectations and *directly* by parental toy choices (Fisher-Thompson, 1990). Parents, particularly fathers, reward or encourage sex-typed play and discourage cross-typed play. Moreover, fathers tend to buy sex-typed toys for their children more than do mothers (Thompson, Molison, & Elliott, 1988).

Girls who have brothers often have options to play with toys that otherwise may not have been available to them. (Photo by Pam Mellor-Deslorieux)

More important, through the years we have not seen major changes in the types of toys categorized as more appropriate for one sex than the other. For example, "female" toys include domestic toys (dishes, house), teddy bears, and dolls, whereas "male" toys include vehicles, construction toys, and sports equipment (Fisher-Thompson, 1990). Another form of sex typing occurs when we label toys as "masculine" or "boys' toys." An interesting chain of events occurs once parents initiate the sex typing of toys: Children begin to ask for certain types of toys. For example, boys develop preferences for trucks, guns, tractors, and manipulative toys. In addition, their play styles are shaped by specific types of toys; they spend more time with novel toys and tend to prefer toys associated with development of visual-spatial ability (Miller, 1987) and toys that encourage motor activity (O'Brien & Huston, 1985).

Sex typing in toy choices and play styles is evident by the age of 4, and throughout childhood further development of gender differences in play can be seen. Thus toys not only take on a reinforcement value—most likely emotionally toned by parents' initial selection—but they seem to be precursors to play activities. Moreover, research clearly demonstrates that play habits from one life-cycle stage tend to carry over to the next (Yoesting &

Burkhead, 1973). In short, most play behavior is an outcome of gender role stereotyping, which stems from deeply rooted cultural ideology. Most of our beliefs about boys' and girls' "natural" inclinations, skills, and capacities are based on erroneous meanings and beliefs that we attach to biological sex differences. Somehow sex (biological) and gender (behavioral) differences become gender hierarchy—a ranking system conveying meanings about power, worth, and value. This belief system leads us to perceive, falsely, that sexual and gender traits considered male are "better than," "more skilled than," and "of greater natural biological capacity" than those that are female. Once this translation occurs, a gender ideology system is activated and differential treatment of boys and girls—a pivotal mechanism of infant and childhood socialization—begins.

Although we cannot explain exactly how parents convey gender-stereotypic perceptions of play, games, and sports to their children, or how children read the messages when boys are rewarded for developing motor skills and girls are not, by the time children reach elementary school age, they have determined for themselves that active sports are masculine and not feminine (Greendorfer, 1983). Moreover, they perceive that masculine games and sports have a higher prestige value.

Sex Differences in Children's Games

As the above discussion suggests, by the time children reach middle childhood there are some striking differences in boys' and girls' games. And if boys and girls play different games, the social learning/social development outcomes of their games will be different (Harragan, 1977; Lever, 1978). Boys play in larger groups and in games requiring multiple and complementary (or interdependent) roles. For example, to play baseball, infielders and outfielders are needed, and these positions interact with each other in order to put batters or runners out. Second, boys' games have rules that can be adjusted according to group size without losing the spirit of the game. Third, boys' games can be adjusted according to skill level and allow for more progressive or complex forms as they grow older. For instance, after learning to bat, boys can learn to bunt or to "pull" the ball as well as to "hit behind the runner." Thus boys' games continually pose challenges of learning additional skills and strategies as well as learning to work toward specific goals. Boys also learn through their games how to negotiate and settle disputes over rule interpretations, and how to abide by compromise and majority rule.

Because girls' games do not provide experiences or opportunities that are similar to those found in boys' games, the potential outcomes for girls are not as rich. Girls tend to play indoors more, and this limits their experience with outdoor settings. Also, they tend not to play team or competitive games; girls' games consist more of turn taking and solitary, repetitive tasks (Lever, 1978). Because rules to girls' games are few, clear-cut, and explicit, they offer little room for negotiation or discussion when disputes arise. Generally, girls' games require less strategy than do boys' games. Further, girls' games do not provide for a progression of skill development, and do not incorporate levels that allow for greater complexity. As a result, girls' games are less challenging; frequently, they end because of loss of interest or at an arbitrary stopping point, rather than with clearly accomplished goals (Lever, 1978).

The above comparison suggests that males are provided with game experiences that can be applied to a variety of adult role requirements. In contrast, girls' game experiences do not provide them with skills for achieving goals or learning to develop strategies, nor do they expose girls to the value of cooperation or negotiation in competing or achieving an objective. Consequently, females are limited in the number of social outcomes they can possibly derive from their game playing, and they are not adequately prepared for a variety of adult social, political, or economic roles. In fact, Harragan (1977) argues that most females are not adequately prepared for leadership or managerial positions because of the games they played as children.

Socialization and Sport

Although large numbers of female children and adolescents continue to engage in various types of sport and physical activity, we are still relatively uninformed as to how various social forces shape their involvement. Given the current state of socialization research in general and sport socialization in particular, we have only just begun to unravel the processes by which females become active participants. Because reviews already exist relative to family influences and sex differences in children's sport socialization, and because recent research suggests that there have been no substantial changes in these patterns, I will devote the remainder of this chapter to a general overview of trends from socialization studies. (For more specific details and findings, the reader is referred to earlier reviews on this topic found in Greendorfer, 1983; Lewko & Greendorfer, 1988.)

Sport Socialization as Social Learning

Social learning theory is the framework that has been used most frequently in sport socialization research. In most instances the social learning paradigm has been conceptualized through the assumption that three clusters of independent variables constitute the primary influences on the dependent variable, active sport involvement: (a) personal attributes, (b) socializing agents, and (c) socializing situations. Among socializing agents, primary attention has been devoted to the influence of significant others—that is, people or groups who, because of their prestige, proximity, and power to distribute love, rewards, and punishment, either consciously or unconsciously influence the sport socialization process (McPherson, 1981). In most studies, family members, peer group members, teachers, coaches, and role models have been identified as major agents of sport socialization (Higginson, 1985).

Childhood and Adolescent Sport Socialization

During childhood the family and peer group are clearly more influential than the school; in fact, it seems there is an emergence of combined family and peer influence on girls as well as boys under the age of 12 (Lewko & Greendorfer, 1988). Then, between childhood and adolescence, the balance of influence shifts among peers, the school, and the family (Higginson, 1985; Yamaguchi, 1984).

As females become adolescents, the family seems to decline in influence while the peer group, particularly same-sex peers who may function as role models, becomes more significant (Higginson, 1985; McPherson & Brown, 1988). Most studies on female adolescents consistently support the emergent role of the peer group and possibly that of teachers and coaches (Higginson, 1985; Weiss & Knoppers, 1982; Yamaguchi, 1984).

These findings suggest that siblings may not play a major role in sport socialization of males, but may reinforce parental input to female sport socialization (Higginson, 1985; Yamaguchi, 1984). Parents seem to generate interest in traditional spectator sports, and the peer group provides social support and serves as a source of recognition and acknowledgment (McPherson, 1981). Although the provision of sport opportunities through the school still appears to be considerably greater for males (Greendorfer, 1983), it does seem that as sport becomes a more acceptable activity for adolescent females, the school may provide an even more conducive environment for their competitive sport experiences (Higginson, 1985; Weiss & Knoppers, 1982).

Whereas previous research focused on identifying *who* specifically was the most influential significant other, alternative approaches suggest that it may be more fruitful to examine the parent-peer dialectic. Obviously, socialization is an interactive and reciprocal process of multiple inputs, and more recognition of this dynamic could indicate whether or not parents are aware of how their daily activities and practices undermine the principle of equal treatment. Moreover, examination of the nature of infant and childhood play experiences with parents could determine whether or not trends in parental behavior have changed substantially. For example, research indicates that fathers continue to be more physically rough and to play more bouncing and gross motor games with male infants than with female infants (Frish, 1977); that parents continue to encourage more motor activity for boys, often punishing girls for engaging in active play involving gross motor skills (Frish, 1977); and that parents (as well as teachers) tend to engage in physically active play with boys but not with girls (O'Brien & Huston, 1985).

Given the recency of this research, it would seem that considerably more attention should be paid to the quality and types of interactions parents have with their children (Hasbrook, 1986). Relative to the issue of reciprocity, although very little is known about the ways parents influence sport behavior of their children, even less is known about the ways daughters who become involved in sport subsequently view their parents' sport behavior (Hasbrook, 1986; McPherson & Brown, 1988).

Further research pertaining to general social learning principles suggests a positive relationship between the amount and type of social support from significant others and the degree and type of participation in sport (McPherson & Brown, 1988). Thus children, especially females, who receive positive reinforcement for sport participation are more likely to become involved in sport than are those who receive neutral or negative messages (Greendorfer, 1987; McPherson & Brown, 1988).

Adult Sport Socialization

Early research on female sport socialization focused almost exclusively on college-age athletes and, although theoretical in conception, most of the findings reveal only descriptive general profiles. For example, unlike her male counterpart, the female athlete tends *not to be* the first-born—she seems to be a middle or the youngest child. Similar to male athletes, however, she begins her sport involvement at an early age—around 8 or 9 years old—and one or both of her parents were actively involved in sport during her childhood, which may be the reason her introduction to sport and physical activity is seen as a "normal or expected" family activity. In addition, the female athlete perceived at a very early age that she was well above average in skill level and ability. Her peer group influence is consistent through each life-cycle stage, and it is not clear exactly who in the family influences her initial sport involvement. Thus it seems that the likelihood of a female becoming an athlete is influenced by sport involvement patterns of the family she is born into (specifically, parental sport history), which is highly influenced by race and social class background (Greendorfer, 1979, 1987). Although school experiences seem to influence her sport involvement at some point (Weiss & Knoppers, 1982), it seems *not* to be a major influence in initiating the socialization process. Rather, the school merely reinforces performance and teaches skills previously learned elsewhere (Greendorfer, 1983).

Older Women and Sport Socialization

Research on the sport participation patterns of older women is virtually nonexistent, and the topic of sport socialization among these women has been all but ignored; research on this topic certainly is the exception (see Hasbrook & Mingesz, 1987). Although trends suggest increased interest and participation in healthful physical activity and sport among older women, the medical model of aging and notions pertaining to health limitations seem to have a direct influence on older women's physical activity patterns (Vertinsky, 1991). Older women are clearly underrepresented among the physically active, and the reason seems to be related to the strong beliefs they hold about potential risks of vigorous exercise (Ostrow & Dzewaltowski, 1986; Vertinsky, 1991). Ironically, these notions are contrary to current scientific findings that indicate both that women are more durable than men from a physiological standpoint and that one of the certain benefits of physical activity is health improvement (Vertinsky, 1991).

It seems that elderly women internalize perceptions that they are "too old" or are in poor or declining health, and these motivational factors influence their noninvolvement in physical activity (Vertinsky, 1991). Such beliefs can be traced to nineteenth-century ideas about menopause and related disorders of women's bodies. More significant, however, is the fact that several of these erroneous notions continue to play a role in older women's sport socialization. Evidence suggests that these beliefs affect women's personal definitions of old age and the aging process; thus, they may be strong factors in older women's disengagement from active pursuits and attempts to "preserve" their body machines (Featherstone & Hepworth, 1990; Vertinsky, 1991). Beliefs about older women's physical capacities not only influence these women's perceptions of the meaning of *health* and what it means to be an *older woman*, but seem to play a central role in societal definitions about "appropriate" types of physical activity for older women (Vertinsky, 1991). Thus, even during their older years, females are subjected to gender role stereotypes about physical activity—an outcome of a belief system that continues to discourage equality of opportunity.

Conclusion and Implications

Despite women's increased interest and participation in sport, we know very little about the nature and content of female sport socialization. If we take recent criticisms into account, we can conclude that the process of socializing women into sport is more complex than it might appear on the surface, and that several additional factors need to be taken into consideration. Unlike males, who receive strong, consistent influence from family, peers, and teachers/coaches, and whose sporting opportunities appear to be a birthright, females seem to have more general, diffuse, and subtle influences that socialize them into sport. Whether they become athletes or not, most females are subjected to gender role stereotyping and differential treatment. Although female athletes tend to come from backgrounds that positively sanction and encourage physical activity—most likely because such activity is perceived by the family as "normal"—their sport socialization may not be conscious or deliberate.

Future research in this area should focus on helping us to understand this complex and dynamic process, rather than on the generation of specific empirical facts that are only descriptive in nature. Sport socialization research needs to take a totally different direction from that pursued in the past. Immediate changes might include experimenting with different theoretical perspectives; approaches that take into account theories other than social learning may be fruitful (see Greendorfer & Bruce, 1991). In addition, alternative research designs could be applied; empiricist traditions and survey research could be replaced with naturalistic and ethnographic methods. Behaviorist and social psychological conceptions of the process might shift to more general sociocultural values; we could see greater interest in how political ideology and notions of hierarchy shape the content and nature of sport socialization. Notions from several disciplinary bases could be integrated and applied in the research. For example, it might be insightful to see how historical, cultural, and political forces influence ideas and beliefs about child rearing, gender, and sport.

Regardless of past or future research directions, the issue of female sport socialization has greater social and political implications than are suggested by the citation of research findings. Female participation in sport is related to core notions our society holds about gender, equality, hierarchy, and physicality. Although Title IX affords the legislative protection needed to bring an end to overt and blatant discrimination, we will be unable to eliminate discriminatory sporting practices until we look deep into the fabric of our society and begin to remove those covert forces that shape our gender ideology. Unless we discard the erroneous belief system that appropriates a woman's physicality and use of her body in sporting activities, we will never be free of discrimination, nor will we achieve equal opportunity. Female participation in sport is a political and ideological process as well as an outcome of individually acquired skills and predispositions.

Key Words

gender	sex differences
gender role	gender role stereotyping
sport	sex typing
physical activity	play behavior
socialization	gender ideology

Discussion Questions

1. What is sex typing or gender role stereotyping?
2. Explain how gender role stereotyping is related to toy and play behavior.
3. How is differential treatment related to discrimination?
4. How are males and females treated differently when it comes to opportunities to participate in sport?
5. How are gender, sport, and ideology related?

Note

1. Title IX, an extension of civil rights legislation, is part of the Education Amendments Act of 1972, which states: "No person in the United States shall, on the basis of sex, be excluded from participation in, be denied the benefits of, or be subjected to discrimination under any education program or activity receiving federal financial assistance." Interestingly, only 4% of the text of Title IX deals with athletics, yet the majority of comments and cases concerning Title IX have focused on sport.

References

Featherstone, M., & Hepworth, M. (1990). Ageing and old age: Reflections on the postmodern life course. In B. Bytheway, T. Keil, P. Allatt, & A. Bryman (Eds.), *Becoming and being old: Sociological approaches to later life* (pp. 144-156). London: Sage.

Fisher-Thompson, D. (1990). Adult sex typing of children's toys. *Sex Roles, 23,* 291-303.

Frish, H. L. (1977). Sex stereotypes in adult-infant play. *Child Development, 48,* 1671-1675.

Goslin, D. A. (Ed.). (1969). *Handbook of socialization theory and research.* Chicago: Rand McNally.

Greendorfer, S. L. (1979). Differences in childhood socialization influences of women involved in sport and women not involved in sport. In M. L. Krotee (Ed.), *The dimensions of sport sociology* (pp. 59-72). West Point, NY: Leisure.

Greendorfer, S. L. (1983). Shaping the female athlete: The impact of the family. In M. A. Boutilier & L. SanGiovanni, *The sporting woman: Feminist and sociological dilemmas* (pp. 135-155). Champaign, IL: Human Kinetics.

Greendorfer, S. L. (1987). Gender bias in theoretical perspectives: The case of female socialization into sport. *Psychology of Women Quarterly, 11,* 327-340.

Greendorfer, S. L., & Bruce, M. (1991). Rejuvenating sport socialization research. *Journal of Sport and Social Issues, 15,* 129-144.

Harragan, B. L. (1977). *Games mother never taught you.* New York: Warner.

Hasbrook, C. A. (1986). Reciprocity and childhood socialization into sport. In L. Vander Velden & J. H. Humphrey (Eds.), *Psychology and sociology of sport: Current selected research* (pp. 135-147). New York: AMS.

Hasbrook, C. A., & Mingesz, J. A. (1987, November). *Early socialization into and continuity of involvement in physical activity across the life cycle.* Paper presented at the Eighth Annual Conference of the North American Society for the Sociology of Sport, Edmonton, AL.

Higginson, D. C. (1985). The influence of socializing agents in the female sport-participation process. *Adolescence, 20,* 73-82.

Lever, J. (1978). Sex differences in the complexity of children's play and games. *American Sociological Review, 43,* 471-482.

Lewko, J. H., & Greendorfer, S. L. (1988). Family influences in sport socialization of children and adolescents. In F. L. Smoll, R. A. Magill, & M. J. Ash (Eds.), *Children in sport* (3rd ed., pp. 287-300). Champaign, IL: Human Kinetics.

McPherson, B. D. (1981). Socialization into and through sport involvement. In G. Lueschen & G. Sage (Eds.), *Handbook of social science of sport* (pp. 246-273). Champaign, IL: Stipes.

McPherson, B. D., & Brown, B. A. (1988). The structure, processes and consequences of sport for children. In F. L. Smoll, R. A. Magill, & M. J. Ash (Eds.), *Children in sport* (3rd ed., pp. 265-286). Champaign, IL: Human Kinetics.

Miller, C. (1987). Qualitative differences among gender-stereotyped toy choice in toddler boys and girls. *Sex Roles, 16,* 437-487.

O'Brien, M., & Huston, A. (1985). Development of sex-typed play behavior in toddlers. *Developmental Psychology, 21,* 866-871.

Ostrow, A., & Dzewaltowski, D. (1986). Older adults' perceptions of physical activity participation based on age-role and sex-role appropriateness. *Research Quarterly for Exercise and Sport, 57,* 167-169.

Power, T. G., & Parke, R. D. (1986). Patterns of early socialization: Mother- and father-infant interactions in the home. *International Journal of Behavioral Development, 9,* 331-341.

Tasch, R. G. (1952). The role of the father in the family. *Journal of Experimental Education, 20,* 319-361.

Thompson, D. F., Molison, K. L., & Elliott, M. (1988, April). *Adult selection of children's toys.* Poster presented at the annual meeting of the Eastern Psychological Association, Buffalo, NY.

Vertinsky, P. (1991). Old age, gender and physical activity: The biomedicalization of aging. *Journal of Sport History, 18,* 64-80.

Weiss, M., & Knoppers, A. (1982). The influence of socializing agents on female collegiate volleyball players. *Journal of Sport Psychology, 4,* 267-279.

Yamaguchi, Y. (1984). A comparative study of adolescent socialization into sport: The case of Japan and Canada. *International Review for the Sociology of Sport, 19,* 63-82.

Yoesting, D. R., & Burkhead, D. I. (1973). Significance of childhood recreation experience on adult leisure behavior: An exploratory analysis. *Journal of Leisure Research, 5,* 25-36.

Whose Body Is This?
Women's Sports and Sexual Politics

DONALD SABO
MICHAEL A. MESSNER

The congressional enactment of Title IX in 1972 made discrimination against girls and women in school athletics illegal. With the threat of lawsuits and the loss of federal monies, many school districts revamped their physical education and athletic programs. Given the chance, girls poured out of the bleachers onto the playing fields in unprecedented numbers. In 1972 about 294,000 girls (4% of the female school-age population) played high school sports. By 1987 their ranks swelled to 1.8 million, or 26% (Sabo, 1988). Public and parental attitudes toward female athletic participation are increasingly favorable. Today 87% of parents accept the idea that sports are equally important for boys and girls (Women's Sports Foundation, 1988). Researchers have showed that many girls derive social and academic benefits from athletic participation, just as boys do.

Despite these changes and two decades of struggle, today many high schools' male athletes get better uniforms, trophies, practice locations, and game times than do female athletes. Women coaches receive less recognition and lower salaries than do men coaches. Men's sports get top billing in school newspapers and on television, while women's sports are often overlooked. Faced with budget crunches, some school systems are dropping women's athletic programs in order to retain men's programs. Universities allocate disproportionately greater funds to men's sports than to women's sports. Leadership positions in university athletic administrations, the National Collegiate Athletic Association, and on the U.S. Olympic Committee are still for the most part filled by men (Birrell, 1987-1988).

And so we are faced with a paradox. On one hand, unprecedented numbers of girls are involved with athletics, parents overwhelmingly agree that sports are no longer just for boys, and we know that many women benefit from sports and fitness activities. Yet, on the other hand, sex discrimination in sports remains deep seated; men still get the gold mine and women get the shaft! Why? How can this paradox be explained? Why is it that men's domination of women in sports continues?

In this chapter we use a critical feminist perspective to explain why gender relations in sport often are defined and acted out in ways that reflect and reproduce men's domination of women in larger society. We view sport as a social and historical theater for feminist struggle in which traditional forms of gender oppression are being challenged. Our focus here specifically relates to gender issues in sports that are expressed in sexual politics, that is, the power struggles between women and men that unfold through or around sexual relationships.

Women's Sports as Challenge to Male Hegemony

Sport is one of many interconnected institutional sites (e.g., family, government, religion, and the health care system) where many women (and sometimes men) are challenging sexist attitudes and discriminatory practices. These efforts can be understood as part of feminism's historical struggle to bring about a more equitable and humane society. We realize that the term *feminism* resists handy definition, and that there is no single feminist school of thought but rather many feminist visions and practices. Here we use *feminism* generally to refer to a movement that seeks to end sexist oppression.[1]

Feminism is basically a movement to empower women by challenging male hegemony (Bryson, 1990). *Hegemony* refers to the influence of certain beliefs that overshadow public awareness in social and political situations and, in the process, help dominant groups to maintain their power over subordinate groups (Sage, 1990). During the nineteenth century, for example, the prevailing (or hegemonic) scientific and religious beliefs about blacks (e.g., that blacks were genetically suited to hard physical work, that blacks had lower intellectual capacities than whites) expressed and fostered stereotypes that helped elite whites maintain control of the slavery system. Likewise, the prevailing model of masculinity in our culture emphasizes aggressiveness, striving for dominance, competition, size, physical strength, and phallocentrism. The predominant model of femininity, in contrast, stresses passivity, physical frailty, dependence (on men), nurturance, cooperation, and sexual submissiveness. The maintenance of hegemonic "masculinity" and "femininity" has helped men collectively to maintain their control and domination of women.

The growing number and cultural presence of woman athletes represent challenges to hegemonic definitions of women as the "weaker sex" and men as the strong and powerful protectors or oppressors of women. At the level of the body, women's increased involvement in sports and fitness can be seen as a form of physical empowerment. At a psychological level, many women athletes are developing new strengths and elevated self-esteem. At a social level, by just living their day-to-day lives as

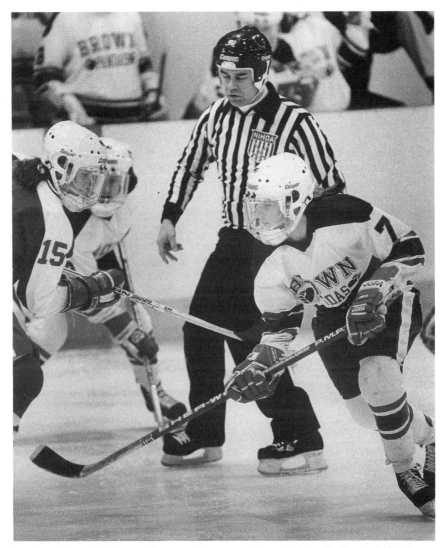

The physical empowerment of sport continues to challenge the male-dominated status quo. (Photo courtesy of Brown University Sports Information; photographer Thomas F. Maguire, Jr.)

athletes, many girls and women are facing up to and debunking the traditional gender stereotypes that have kept women down.

The empowerment of women through sports challenges the pattern of men's violence against women. Dominant groups maintain their control of subordinate groups through the threat or application of violence. Men's violence against women in our society is easy to find. Research indicates that one of three American women will be victimized by incest, rape, or battering in her lifetime (McBride, 1990). About 2 million women are physically abused by their male partners each year, about 1 every 18 seconds (Shapiro, 1987). Recent studies show that battery also occurs in about 12-22% of dating relationships (Bullock, McFarlane, Bateman, & Miller, 1989). Television programs, movies, written fiction, and pornography are riddled with images of male violence against women.

Though women's increased athleticism is confronting men's violence against women, it has by no means ended it. Mariah Burton Nelson (1991) writes:

> I'd like to think that women athletes are less violable, less vulnerable, than nonathletes. Athletes are stronger, generally. Athleticism builds self-esteem as well as muscles, so athletes may be better prepared than other women to think on their feet and, when wise, fight back. They walk and run with a pride that could deter attack. But in fact, most rape victims (84.6%) report that they fought back or tried to protect themselves in some way. (p. 129)

The struggle for empowerment of women through athletics will no doubt continue during the 1990s. On one side, women athletes are walking away from traditional gender expectations and challenging the male-dominated status quo. On the other side, however, women's quests for equal opportunity, physical empowerment, and respect are being resisted by many men and institutional forces. How is this struggle being played out in the sexual politics of sport?

From Able-Bodied Athletes to Sex Objects

The symbolic and physical empowerment of women through athletic participation and its concomitant challenge of masculine hegemony are being eroded by sport media. Sport media often imply women athletes' inferior status by portraying women as sex objects. For example, in their analysis of television coverage of women's and men's athletics, Duncan, Messner, Williams, and Jensen (1990) found that the longest television news segment featuring a woman was on Morgana, the Kissing Bandit, an extraordinarily buxom woman who runs onto baseball fields to kiss players. *Sports Illustrated* fully exploits the "tits and ass" motif of soft pornography to produce its annual swimsuit issue, where women models, not women athletes, make the sport scene. And perhaps most tellingly, after a decade of feminist protest against its publication, this issue remains the best-selling single magazine issue each year in the United States. Near-naked women posed languidly in faraway and exotic places do not challenge gender stereotypes and male dominance. This is no accident, Dyer (1982) notes, as it is in long-distance swimming where women hold most of the world records and where the mythos of male supremacy is most vulnerable to debunking. The sexualization of female athletes in sport media, such as the case of Katarina Witt's performances in figure skating in the 1988 Olympic Games, robs women of athletic legitimacy and preserves hegemonic masculinity.

Women's status is further denigrated in the beer commercials that are commonly grafted to athletic events. When women are represented at all,

Wenner's (1991) research shows, they occupy tangential and servile positions in the "sanctum sanctorum of male beer-and-sport commercials" (p. 405). Male viewers do not actually perceive the rituals of sport and beer as vestiges of male culture; ideology is safely dissolved within the suds. In the end, the juxtaposition of dominant males and subservient, sexy females reflects the unequal power balance between the sexes.

In short, the power and far-reaching presence of sport media expose children and adolescents to the illusion of a shared cultural consensus about the elements that constitute masculinity, femininity, and appropriate gender relations (Himmelstein, 1984). Prevailing notions of masculinity and femininity are portrayed as being "normal" or "natural." Male hegemony remains stable.

Homophobia and Women's Athletics

Homophobia is an irrational fear of and hostility toward homosexuals. Like other forms of prejudice, homophobia feeds on stereotypes and discriminates between who is afforded opportunity and who is not. Homophobia reinforces sex inequality and male hegemony in sports in several ways. First, homophobia obviously hurts gays in sports, who face the daily threat of stigma and discrimination. A woman basketball player who openly identifies herself as a lesbian or who is even suspected of being a lesbian may be ridiculed or ostracized by peers.

Second, homophobia in sports hurts many women, whether they are gay or not. Allegations of lesbianism and questions about women's sexual preferences are sometimes used on college and university campuses to intimidate female students and faculty members. Female coaches and athletic administrators are vulnerable to such rumor and innuendo. What is going on here? Is it that male coaches and athletic administrators are uptight about the "femininity" of their women colleagues? Not likely. Within the male-dominated hierarchy of sport, men hold most of the prestige, power, and resources. Accusations about the "masculinizing" effects of sports on women or rumors about female leaders, therefore, really serve to discredit *both* straight and gay women professionally so that men can retain their status advantage and maintain control of resources.

Third, homophobia serves to enforce conformity to traditional gender roles, thereby reinforcing male hegemony. For example, the powerful threat of being labeled a homosexual forces boys and men to behave in accordance with traditional masculine stereotypes. A young male who takes an interest in any nonsexual but culturally defined "feminine" activity, such as dance or nursing, is often considered "queer" and labeled a sissy or faggot. The girl interested in playing contact sports gets snickers from boys and cold shoulders from girls. The threat of homosexual stigma, therefore, serves primarily to maintain gender stereotypes and only secondarily as a vehicle for regulating sexual behavior. Hence *both* gay and straight athletes are victimized by constrictive gender stereotypes.

Finally, the moralizing and policing around homosexuality in sport distracts public awareness from more common sexual abuses. The heterosexual abuse of female athletes by male coaches is ignored and goes virtually undetected despite much anecdotal evidence indicating its prevalence. Until recently, the homophobia in traditional men's sport hid the connections between locker-room sexism and the sexual maltreatment of women.

The Locker Room and the Rape Culture

In boyhood, adolescent, and young adult male peer groups, especially on athletic teams, insults such as "fag," "girl," and "woman" are used almost interchangeably. Through this practice, males learn collectively to define masculinity through the denigration of homosexuality and femininity. One man, interviewed by Messner (1992) in his study of the lives of male former athletes, described how his high school male peer group helped to structure his own public presentation of his sexuality:

> I was shy [with girls]; I hung out more with guys. I never dated. I never was real intimate with anyone. It was kinda scary because I thought I'd get teased by my peers. [Interviewer: For not being involved with women?] For *being* involved! But you *gotta* be involved to the point where you get 'em into bed, you know, you fuck 'em, or something like that, yeah, that's real important [laughs]—but as far as being intimate, or close, I wasn't. And that wasn't real important. Just so I could prove my heterosexuality it was real important.

This use of women as objects of sexual conquest is important for gaining status in the male peer group, and it also tends to impoverish young men's relationships with females (Sabo, 1989). The link between young men's tendency to "tell (sexual) stories about girls" and their lack of intimacy with girls is an important one. While talk of sex with females, then, bonds males together, the specific form of sexual talk (sexual objectification and conquest of women) helps males deal with their terror of intimacy with women.

In a very real sense, young male athletes' attitudes toward and relationships with girls and women, whether sexual or not, are *constructed through* (indeed, are often distorted by and subordinated to) their relationships with their male teammates. Logical results include the kinds of attitudes toward and relationships with women that former pro football star Jim Brown describes in his book, *Out of Bounds*. When he played football for the Cleveland Browns, he explains, his male "partners started calling me the Hawk" because he was so successful in "chasing women" (Brown, 1989, p. 190). Now at age 53, Brown continues to view and relate to women primarily as young, sexual bodies and as objects of consumption: "My lady right now is nineteen. . . . When I eat a peach, I don't want it overripe. I want that peach when it's peaking" (pp. 183-184). Clearly, this attitude serves to preclude Brown's developing a long-term intimate relationship with one woman. After all, every woman eventually ages, her body changes, but she can be discarded and replaced by what Brown sees as an endless supply of younger, firmer bodies.

How are these attitudes toward women and sexuality shaped? Sociologist Timothy Curry (1991) found in a participant-observation study of two college male locker rooms that sexually aggressive talk about women usually takes the form of a loud public performance. Curry also observed that any "private" conversations between two men about actual relationships with girlfriends usually take place in hushed tones, and often at the edges of the locker room. If this sort of talk is discovered by the group, the speakers are often ridiculed and taunted to reveal details about the woman's body and whether or not she is sexually "putting out." The result of this kind of locker-room culture is that many men end up suffering from a kind of "sexual schizophrenia [through which] their minds lead them toward eroticism while their hearts pull them toward emotional intimacy" (Sabo, 1989, p. 39).

Some young men deal with this split by keeping their emotional attachments with females a secret while continuing to participate in locker-room discussions about sexuality with their male peers. Some young men object to and eventually reject the sexism of the jock culture, but for young men who are fully committed to athletic careers, this sort of rejection of one of the key bonds of the male peer group could amount to career suicide. So, whether they like it or not, most go along with it. And when it goes beyond verbal sparring and bragging about sexual conquests to actual behavior, peer group values encourage these young men to treat females as objects of conquest. This sort of masculine peer group dynamic is at the heart of what feminists have called the "rape culture" (Herman, 1984). Robin Warshaw (1988) concludes from her research on date and acquaintance rape that "athletic teams are breeding grounds for rape," because they are "often populated by men who are steeped in sexist, rape-supportive beliefs" (p. 112).

The sexual objectification of women that is an important basis of male athletes' friendships with each other is probably, in most cases, a "rhetorical performance" that does not necessarily translate into actual physical aggression against women. But the fact that the locker room is a key site in which male athletes use sexually aggressive talk about women to forge erotic bonds "safely" among themselves helps to explain the vehemence with which men often defend this "turf" against, for instance, women news reporters. The fragile basis of men's bonding in the locker room is potentially disrupted by the presence of competent, professional women (rather than debased, sexualized objects). Unless and until the kind of masculinity that is constructed in the locker room is radically transformed, girls and women will likely continue to face covert barriers and, at times, overt sexual harassment in the sports world.

Coed Sport: A Theater for Change?

Patriarchal customs and structural constraints in society have kept women and men from playing together and competing against one another on an equal footing. Just as the historical exclusion of women from sport grew out of male dominance and sexist prejudice, so also has the relative absence of coed sport been grounded in the underlying patterns of sex segregation and sexist ideology. The walls of sex segregation are crumbling, however, and greater opportunities for coed athletics have emerged in recent decades, such as coed Little League teams, softball teams, school intramural programs, racket sports, health club member- ships, running, weight lifting, and volleyball.

Despite these trends, many men resist the spread of coed athletics. One of the arguments against coed sports used by some school officials is that coed sports would eroticize male-female relationships. This line of think- ing is that coed sports would lead to sexual impropriety, especially where boys and girls are playing contact sports, such as basketball or wrestling, together. This position conjures up visions of sexually aroused adoles- cents spending their postgame hours in heated coital clinches. One reason to doubt the proposition that physical contact automatically leads to sexual arousal is that it assumes that the human sexual response is phys- iologically or instinctually motivated. This is not so. For humans, sexual behavior is orchestrated by the mind's capacity to internalize cultural meanings, rather than by some primeval or genetically triggered im- pulses. It is culture that establishes what is sexual and what is not; for instance, hand-to-genital petting in a movie theater is sexual and a gyne- cological examination is not. *Same-sex* contact in sport has not resulted in excessive amounts of homosexual arousal or behavior—is it not, therefore, theoretically inconsistent to assert that *coed* athletic activity will inflame heterosexual passion?

It is more likely that coed sport deeroticizes male-female relations. Furthermore, it is the very possibility of deeroticization that challenges patriarchal values and practices. Prevailing male definitions of sexuality emphasize the purely erotic dimensions of the sex act while reducing women to expendable objects. In contrast, feminists and women in general proffer a definition of sexuality that integrates greater sensual awareness with love and commitment. It is the former definition of sexuality that currently has the upper hand in American culture. At a time when hun- dreds of thousands of women are beginning to engage in fitness and sports activities, for example, corporate advertising and media are pushing a sleek and sexy image of women athletes. The message seems to be, Even though she's a gifted athlete or in fine physical condition, she's really "doing it" to please men and not for herself; the woman athlete remains a subordinate. Put more crudely, the message runs, She may have muscle and skill, but she can still be laid.

The grass-roots reality of women's sports, however, is that when women become athletes, it is more difficult for men to perceive them in traditionally erotic terms. Accomplished women athletes are too busy competing to pose; too caught up in the physical and mental demands of the game to engage in sexual innuendo; too independent, animated, and obviously three-dimensional for men to reduce them readily to sex objects. It is simple brain work for a traditional male to sexually objectify a wiggling cheerleader; a fully extended female smashing a volleyball does not erotically compute. It may be, therefore, that coed sport has a potential to liberate women from being narrowly defined as sex objects and to diversify and humanize men's understanding of women and sexuality.

Conclusion

Women's movement into sport represents a genuine quest by women for equality, control of their own bodies, and self-definition, and, as such, it represents a challenge to male hegemony in athletics and larger society (Messner, 1988). The creation of autonomous athletic spheres in which women can play and compete on their own terms is one way to erode male hegemony. Coed sport involvement may be another route to athletic equity. Yet, as we have seen, gender relations and the definitions of femininity and masculinity in sport remain in a state of flux. The liberating potential of sports to empower women's bodies and minds is in danger of being coopted by

When women become athletes, it is more difficult for men to perceive them as sexual objects. (University of Rhode Island Volleyball; photo by Bob Schneck)

the media, distorted by homophobia, and ignored by the sexist legacy of the men's locker room. As we move into the twenty-first century, the power struggles around sexual politics in sport will no doubt persist. Women will continue to ask, Whose body is this?

Key Words

gender	masculinity
sport	homophobia
feminism	sexuality
hegemony	sexual politics
empowerment	violence

Discussion Questions

1. Collect some pictures of women athletes from popular magazines. Discuss whether the pictures portray the women mainly as athletes or as sex objects.

2. Do you agree with the authors' suggestion that the traditional male locker room fosters rape-supportive beliefs and practices among young men? Explain your rationale.

3. Is athletic participation empowering women physically, psychologically, and politically? Does sports involvement help women to be more assertive? How is this accomplished?

Note

1. Although we are men, we adopt critical feminist perspectives in our work and lives. We think of ourselves as "profeminist men"; that is, we seek to end sexist oppression of women and, at the same time, to help men change some of the destructive aspects of their lives and identities.

References

Brown, J. (1989). *Out of bounds*. New York: Kensington.

Birrell, S. (1987-1988). The woman athlete's college experience: Knowns and unknowns. *Journal of Sport and Social Issues, 11*, 82-96.

Bryson, L. (1990). Challenges to male hegemony in sport. In M. A. Messner & D. Sabo (Eds.), *Sport, men, and the gender order: Critical feminist perspectives* (pp. 173-184). Champaign, IL: Human Kinetics.

Bullock, L., McFarlane, J., Bateman, L. H., & Miller, V. (1989). The prevalence and characteristics of battered women in a primary care setting. *Nurse Practitioner, 14*(6), 47-54.

Curry, T. J. (1991). Fraternal bonding in the locker room: A feminist analysis of talk about competition and women. *Sociology of Sport Journal, 8*, 119-135.

Duncan, M. C., Messner, M. A., Williams, L., & Jensen, K. (1990). *Gender stereotyping in televised sports*. Los Angeles: Amateur Athletic Foundation of Los Angeles.

Dyer, K. F. (1982). *Challenging the men*. New York: University of Queensland.

Herman, D. (1984). The rape culture. In J. Freeman (Ed.), *Women: A feminist perspective* (3rd ed., pp. 20-38). Mountain View, CA: Mayfield.

Himmelstein, H. (1984). *The television myth and the American mind*. New York: Praeger.

McBride, A. B. (1990). Violence against women: Implications for research and practice. *Reflections*, pp. 10-12.

Messner, M. A. (1988). Sports and male domination: The female athlete as contested ideological terrain. *Sociology of Sport Journal, 5*, 197-211.

Messner, M. A. (1992). *Power at play: Sports and the problem of masculinity*. Boston: Beacon.

Nelson, M. B. (1991). *Are we winning yet? How women are changing sports and sports are changing women*. New York: Random House.

Sabo, D. (1988). Title IX and athletics: Sex equity in schools. *Updating School Board Policies, 19*(10), 1-3.

Sabo, D. (1989). The myth of the sexual athlete. *Changing Men: Issues in Gender, Sex, and Politics, 20*, 38-39.

Sage, G. (1990). *Power and ideology in American sport*. Champaign, IL: Human Kinetics.

Shapiro, R. J. (1987, September 28). A frightening new numbers game. *U.S. News & World Report*, pp. 32-33.

Warshaw, R. (1988). *I never called it rape*. New York: Harper & Row.

Wenner, L. A. (1991). One part alcohol, one part sport, one part dirt, stir gently: Beer commercials and television sports. In L. R. Vande Berg & L. A. Wenner (Eds.), *Television criticism: Approaches and applications*. New York: Longman.

Women's Sports Foundation. (1988). *The Wilson report: Moms, dads, daughters and sports*. New York: Author.

Herstory:
A Legacy of Honor

*Like their personal lives, women's history is fragmented, interrupted;
a shadow history of human beings whose existence has been shaped by
the efforts and the demands of others.*

—Elizabeth Janeway

It is not I that belongs to the past, but the past that belongs to me.

—Mary Antin

*Each arc of colour may be lovely to behold, but it is the full spectrum of our
woman rainbow that glows with the brightest promise of better things to come.*

—Merlin Stone

3

Heroines
Paving the Way

JOAN PAUL

Jennifer Capriati and Monica Seles are examples of young professional tennis superstars, along with such veterans as Martina Navratilova, whose feats regularly make the sporting news headlines. In 1991, Pat Bradley, after 18 years as a golfing professional, became the first female player in history to go over the $4 million career mark on the Ladies Professional Golf Association (LPGA) circuit. Other modern women athletes make news as serious Olympians, as college/school athletic stars, and occasionally even as auto racers and jockeys. Although there are examples of current women athletes achieving "stardom" in sport, none makes the money or receives the recognition or the public adulation of a Magic Johnson, a Michael Jordan, or a Bo Jackson. It appears that the women who come closest to receiving adulation from the public for their sporting exploits are those who not only have exceptional skill, but also fit the model of femininity. It is your Chris Evert of modern vintage, and those such as Helen Wills, Maureen Conolly, and Wilma Rudolph of years past, who successfully competed with little criticism and enjoyed almost universal public favor for their victories. Regardless of obstacles imposed through sexist societal attitudes, there have been women—pioneer sports heroines—who have dared to defy tradition and perceived propriety to pave the way for greater acceptance of today's sporting women.

Sports have been viewed through the years as male-oriented activities that are serious when played by boys and men, but more social, recreational, and leisurely when played by girls and women. This double standard has historically been the primary obstacle to women's gaining public acceptance as athletes. Attitudes and social mores about femininity and masculinity continue to be major barriers to serious women sport competitors. Unwritten rules about social and moral gender expectations have led to blatant prejudices against women engaging in activities deemed inappropriate. Although there have been attempts in the United States to create professional leagues for women in baseball, volleyball, basketball, and even football, only tennis and golf have maintained interest at a level where financially viable careers exist for a proportionate number of out-standing women athletes.[1]

Using the term *heroines* to describe women sports participants is applying a late twentieth-century perspective. More often, when describing women athletes, late nineteenth- and early to mid-twentieth-century writers used such expressions as "inappropriate," "freakish," "manly," "unwomanly," and, at best, "tomboyish" rather than adjectives appropriate for heroines. However, those women who paved the course for the modern sportswoman were courageous in a way that is partially understood today because the veil of prejudice still shrouds women's sport to some extent. This is often evident in the lack of media coverage of women's sports and in charges of sex discrimination with regard to Title IX compliance.

Collegiate sports for men developed and grew in the nineteenth century as extracurricular activities, while women were first introduced to competitive sport through physical education classes. Intercollegiate sport for men and women developed very differently, with men's experiences first beginning in 1852 as a commercial enterprise. Women were first introduced to team sports in the 1890s, and their sporting experiences were controlled and promoted only as educationally healthful exercises. Women of the nineteenth and early twentieth centuries were never encouraged to be highly competitive in sport, and when winning was perceived as becoming a primary objective, sport for women became undesirable in most educators' minds. There have been women in every age who have withstood public criticism to engage in organized sport, making it possible for other girls and women to become athletes with less ridicule. The earliest pathfinders who opened the door to genteel sport were Victorian in their attempts, yet they were the precursors to making sports participation a competitive affair and a rewarding and pleasurable part of girls' and women's lives.

The Victorian Heroines

Acceptable sport for women in the United States began in the mid-nineteenth century with such recreational sports as croquet, archery, and skating. Late in the century, middle- and upper-class women began to engage moderately in tennis and golf. Basketball, invented in 1891 by James Naismith of Springfield College, was first played by women in 1892. This was the first team sport in which women engaged, and because it was a vigorous game with the potential for roughness, women's participation quickly became highly controversial. The two women who deserve primary credit for molding basketball into an acceptable game for women and thus introducing them to more highly competitive sport are Senda Berenson of Smith College in Northampton, Massachusetts, and Clara Gregory Baer of Sophie Newcomb College in New Orleans, Louisiana. Berenson and Baer both experimented with the game in its original male form before realizing that modifications were necessary to make it acceptable as an appropriate game for "ladies."

They trimmed the game's most vigorous features, and, by emphasizing the components that called for cooperation and reasoning, eventually sold the merits of the game to the more conservative.

Baer of the South

After completing her education at the Posse Normal School of Physical Education in Boston, Clara Baer returned to her hometown of New Orleans in 1891 to develop a physical education program at the new Sophie Newcomb College. She inaugurated the first physical education bachelor's degree program in the South in 1907, invented the game of Newcomb Ball in 1895, and was first to introduce the game of basketball to women in the South when she had her students play a demonstration game for a public audience in 1895 (Paul, 1985). Baer's 1895 basketball rules were the first published in the United States. These rules were also the most Victorian of any of the several versions of the game that were played by women in the 1890s. Baer's first set of rules, published under the "feminine" title *Basquette,* called for the court to be divided into 8 to 11 sections called "bases," with a player per team assigned to each section.[2] The players were not allowed to move outside their sections, nor could they move within their allotted areas except when the ball was in the air. It was illegal by Baer's rules for players to speak aloud, to guard their opponents, to dribble, to shoot or pass with two hands, or to fall down—each of these breaches resulted in a foul. These drastic modifications to the game were deemed necessary at that time and in that region of the country because of the dress code for women, the code of expected behavior for genteel ladies, and the fear of unhealthy activity (Paul, 1991).

Clara Baer's influence in Louisiana and the South in the promotion of physical education, basketball, and Newcomb Ball, as well as bicycling, makes her deserving of recognition as a heroine in the early development of sport for Southern women.

Berenson in the East

Senda Berenson first introduced basketball to women in the United States in 1892, and she edited the first official women's basketball rules published in 1901 in the Spalding Athletic Library Series. By the fall of 1892, she had made modifications in Naismith's game to eliminate rough and "vicious play" (Berenson, 1901). Berenson believed that the standards for behavior in sports should uphold the moral values thought important for everyday life. She felt sport should *never* overemphasize winning, as this would be the element most likely to bring out "unwomanly" behavior. To prevent roughness she eliminated snatching or batting the ball from another player's hand, divided the court into three sections, and allowed only three bounces to constitute a dribble. Although Berenson believed basketball should be a social affair as much as an athletic one, she also believed the game should be one of spirit and vigor.

Berenson was appointed by the American Physical Education Association (now the American Alliance for Health, Physical Education, Recreation and

Senda Berenson inspired creativity and spirit in her students, as demonstrated by these sophomores, the class of 1902. (Photo courtesy of Smith College Archives, Smith College)

Dance) to chair the National Women's Basketball Committee that was formed in 1905 to keep the rules revised in the best interest of women players, a position she retained until 1917. This kept her in the forefront of developments in women's basketball, and in 1985 her national contributions to the growth and development of basketball were recognized when she was one of the first three women voted into the Basketball Hall of Fame (Tynan, 1985).

Heroines Who Dared to Break Feminine Tradition: The Early Mavericks

Although many women dared to break Victorian tradition as sport competitors in areas previously unknown to women, a few became influential pathfinders through their own exploits. Most of these women were not seriously praised by society for their athletic endeavors, but without these pioneers, doors would have opened more slowly for women athletes.

Eleanora Sears

One of the most remarkable early female athletes was Eleanora Sears, the first woman to receive nationwide publicity for playing sports with abandon, who thumbed her nose at the Boston blue bloods and their staid ideas about women and propriety. The great-great-granddaughter of Thomas Jefferson, she was born into a wealthy Boston family in 1881. At a time when croquet was considered the most appropriate sport for women,

Sears was riding horses in steeplechases and hunting meets, driving automobiles and daring men to race her (though none are known to have accepted the challenge), sailing and racing yachts, canoeing, swimming long distances, skating, and playing golf, tennis, baseball, football, hockey, squash, and polo. She was one of the first women to fly in an airplane, was a crack pistol and rifle shot, and was a horse enthusiast until her death in 1968 at the age of 86. She was a race walker, called a pedestrian, who once covered 50 miles in less than 10 hours. She was four times national doubles and mixed doubles tennis champion and was twice a national singles finalist between 1911 and 1917. In 1928, at the age of 46, she won the National Squash Racquets Championships, and she continued to compete in the National Championships until she was 70.

Eleo, as she preferred to be called by her friends, would do almost anything on a dare, or just on her own whim for that matter. She adopted "shocking" outfits for figure skating, swimming, sailing, and tennis. She was the first woman publicly to ride a horse astride, which the newspapers referred to as "cross-saddle" because of the "coarseness" that the other term elicited. Sears attempted to play on an all-men's polo team, but later formed her own when rejected. "Her appearance on a polo pony in men's riding breeches caused Boston women's clubs to raise their eyebrows, . . . but [it was] when a California Mothers' Club passed a resolution against her conduct in 1912 that she really became a national celebrity" ("Sport," 1936). Eleo Sears won 240 trophies during her amateur sports career, which spanned approximately 70 years (Davenport, 1982).

There were sermons preached across the country condemning Sears's wickedness, which was thought to have a bad effect on "the sensibilities of our boys and girls" (Hollander, 1976, pp. 58-60). However, Sears probably did more to emancipate womanhood from the conservative shackles in which she had been bound than any other person. She dared to do what she thought was right when others in society felt she was utterly wrong.

Mildred "Babe" Didrikson Zaharias

Another athlete who shocked society with her sporting exploits was Mildred Didrikson, born on June 26, 1914, in Port Arthur, Texas. Where Eleanora Sears had had wealth, culture, and society on her side, Babe was born into a lower-middle-class family and shocked society with her crudeness in manner and speech as well as by devoting her life to sports in a way that few women had before. Didrikson knew from an early age that her major ambition in life was to be the best athlete in the world. She became an all-American in basketball, once won a track and field meet single-handedly against clubs with many members, won two golds and a silver medal in the 1932 Los Angeles Olympics, and was one of the world's greatest golfers. Like Sears, she was an exceptional athlete, excelling in softball, swimming and diving, rifle shooting, billiards, boxing, horseback riding, bowling, tennis, skating, and any other sport she attempted. She could throw a football accurately for 50 yards, her golf drives averaged well over 200 yards, and she could throw a baseball almost 300 feet.

Didrikson won the nickname Babe when she hit seven home runs in seven at bats in the Texas Twilight League in the early phase of her sporting career. Babe was immodest and appeared to need attention, and through her sports performances and accompanying antics, she got her share.

In December 1938, at age 24, Babe Didrikson married George Zaharias, a professional wrestler she had met when playing in a men's golf tournament months earlier. With George assuming the role of manager, Babe put all of her energies into golf. She was the first American to win the Women's British Amateur Golf Championship, won the Women's U.S. National Open three times, and once won 16 consecutive golf tournaments. She was voted the Associated Press Woman Athlete of the Year six times, and in 1951 was voted the Most Outstanding Woman Athlete of the Half Century.

Through Babe Didrikson Zaharias's efforts, golf tournament purses for women were improved. She did much for women in sport, but, paradoxically, her crude antics also helped reinforce and perpetuate the unfair myth that women athletes were not quite women. Because of the conservative attitude of the times, women athletes lived with that tag from the 1930s through the 1950s. Yet, until Babe showed that women could play with abandon, professional women golfers seldom demonstrated any aggression on the course.

Other Early Heroines

One of the greatest boons to women in sport was the bicycle fad of the 1890s, which helped emancipate women by precipitating dress reform and allowing women a new freedom that included athleticism. Although bicycling was still perceived as more appropriate for the "working girl" than for the socially elite, women in both classes became avid cyclists between 1895 and 1900. The bicycle gave women an independence they had never experienced, and the bloomers worn most often by the riders allowed them to engage in sport more vigorously and freely than ever before.

May Sutton

Born in England but raised in Pasadena, California, May Sutton, one of four tennis-playing sisters, showed her ability in tennis in 1900 when she won the Southern California Women's Singles Championship at the age of 13. She introduced vigorous play in tennis that included the net game and hard overhead smashes, play that was considered quite masculine in that day. In 1905 Sutton became the first American to win the singles title at Wimbledon; until Tracy Austin, she held the status of the youngest woman to gain this world title. Playing in an ankle-length dress with long sleeves, she shocked the staid London crowd when she pushed her sleeves up to the elbow during her match. Sutton won the Wimbledon title again in 1907. In 1928, after bringing up a family, May Sutton Bundy won the Southern California Women's Singles Championship again almost 30 years after that first victory, and was ranked fifth in the United States.

Early portrait of the grande dame of field hockey, Constance Applebee, in her teaching attire. (Photo courtesy of Bryn Mawr College Archives)

Constance M. K. Applebee

In 1901 Constance Applebee came to the United States to spend a week at Vassar College to introduce the college students to the game of field hockey. Five of the other "sister schools" also had Applebee visit for this same purpose. College and club teams were formed throughout the East, and these eventually spread to the South, North, and Midwest. Applebee started a summer hockey camp in the Pocono Mountains of Pennsylvania, edited and published the first women's sports magazine (the *Sportwoman*), coached at Bryn Mawr College, and taught thousands of girls the game of field hockey (Woolum, 1992). Because of her influence, field hockey became one of the leading sports for college women in the East at a time when few such opportunities existed. "The Apple" coached field hockey until the age of 95. She lived to be 107 years old, and 10 years after her death she was inducted into the International Women's Sports Hall of Fame (Woolum, 1992).

Heroines of the 1920s

In the 1920s, four outstanding and influential sportswomen made national headlines: Gertrude Ederle, Helen Wills, Glenna Collett, and Babe Didrikson Zaharias. Amelia Earhart also became a sport heroine of sorts by being the first woman to fly across the Atlantic Ocean in 1928. Women won the vote in 1920, and with that success they began to engage in activities with a new flair. They got short haircuts, wore dresses with hems up to the knees, smoked, and drove automobiles. With this new-found political and athletic freedom, real or imagined, women demonstrated courage in standing up to ridicule and harsh criticism as they entered the male work force and playing arenas.

Gertrude Ederle

At the 1924 Paris Olympics, 17-year-old Gertrude Ederle earned a gold medal and two bronze medals. One of the most publicized athletic feats of the 1920s was Ederle's 1926 record-breaking swim of the English Channel. She swam the 20.6 miles from France to England in 14 hours, 31 minutes. Only five men had ever accomplished this arduous swim, and Ederle, the first woman, broke the men's record by almost two hours. Ederle's feat received newspaper coverage worldwide and seemed to prove once more that women who dared could achieve success in the athletic world; her success was celebrated in New York with a prestigious ticker tape parade (Gipe, 1978).

Glenna Collett

Like Helen Wills Moody, Glenna Collett exemplified the expectations of the "lady" as a sportswoman. With the exception of Babe Didrikson Zaharias, most of the women golfers and tennis players from the earliest days until the 1950s were from upper-class families. Most had the financial means to devote themselves to their games, which meant they had country club memberships, domestic help to run their households, and freedom from pursuing a livelihood. Most of these women had been taught the social graces expected by those of their class, were well educated, and generally tended to live by the social code of the day.[3]

Prior to Glenna Collett, women golfers were generally viewed with amusement by men. Women were famous for their poor putting skills, and men of the day blamed this on women's flighty nature, which supposedly prevented them from concentrating on their green play (Hergesheimer, 1927). Glenna Collett began playing golf in 1917 at the age of 14 under the tutelage of her father, and soon developed into one of the finest women golfers of all time. At 17, Collett won the North and South Championship and the Metropolitan (Woolum, 1992), and at 19 she won the Women's National Golf Championship. She won the U.S. Women's Amateur Championship six times from 1922 to 1935.

Although Glenna Collett was a remarkable athlete, when commenting on women in sport she showed the influence of the social expectations of her day. She referred to golf, tennis, swimming, riding, and skating as more feminine sports, and considered running, jumping, vaulting, basketball, and hockey as "boys' sports." Collett also noted that selecting the fine "feminine" sport of golf had its drawbacks because it was so difficult for many girls and women to find places to play.[4] She also dispelled the common notion of the time that sport made a girl "masculine" and therefore "not attractive to men" (Collett, 1924). Collett stated that if an athletic girl took interest in her personal appearance and "natural good sense," the reputation of being "masculine" would not follow her.

Glenna Collett was one of the early golfing legends, and her name will always be connected with women's golf. In 1953 Glenna Collett Vare inaugurated the Vare Trophy under her married name; this prize is awarded annually to the woman with the lowest average score in official LPGA tournaments.

Helen Wills Moody

Helen Wills, a physician's daughter, was one of the greatest tennis players ever to grace the courts—proud, aloof, and icy. At the age of 15 she won the junior singles national title, and at 17 the national women's title. In 1924 Wills won a gold medal in the Olympics and the national title, and took second in women's singles at Wimbledon. Wills dominated U.S. women's tennis between 1923 and 1931 by winning the national title eight times. In 1929 she married Frederick S. Moody, Jr., son of a socially prominent Californian, but remained in the headlines as a tennis player. She was ranked number one for seven years, and won at Wimbledon eight times between 1927 and 1938. She won every set she played from 1927 to 1932! In the Associated Press poll for the Greatest Female Athlete of the First Half Century, Helen Wills Moody was second only to Babe Zaharias.

Heroines Who Changed Sport: Modern Mavericks

Billie Jean King

Of all the women tennis players of old or modern vintage, none has had a greater impact on the game than Billie Jean King. Besides being one of the game's greatest players (as demonstrated by her numerous victories, including the most Wimbledon titles won by any player—male or female), she influenced tennis both on and off the court. By helping to initiate a women's boycott of promoter Jack Kramer's Pacific Southwest tournament in 1970 over the disparity in prize money, which was more than eight times greater for men than for women, King eventually achieved near equality in future tournament winnings of women and men. Because of her daring crusade, women tennis players have a favored financial position today over all other sportswomen.

In 1973 Billie Jean King accepted a challenge from former triple Wimbledon champion turned hustler Bobby Riggs to participate in a public tennis match supposedly to demonstrate men's athletic superiority over women. Riggs had badly beaten Margaret Court of England in an earlier tennis match, much to the disappointment of millions of women across America. Billie Jean King was one of the most outspoken feminists on the tennis circuit, and of course Riggs knew such a match would draw great interest. Although Riggs was in his 50s and King was in her late 20s, her victory still prompted women to celebrate gleefully. The match, while certainly not proving superiority of one sex over the other, proved to be a tremendous stimulus to the growth of tennis across the nation.

Althea Gibson

Born in South Carolina in 1927 but raised in New York's Harlem, Althea Gibson blazed the trail for black athletes in a game dominated by the white upper-middle class. She was the first black to integrate tennis, and she became the first black tennis champion on the national and international levels.

Gibson, a highly skilled, street-wise young girl, learned to play paddle-ball in the Harlem ghetto, and rose from a truant youngster to master the best in the game of tennis. Because there were those who cared for her and promoted her efforts to achieve, she was able to overcome almost impossible social obstacles. By 1948, Althea Gibson was the best woman player in Negro tennis. In 1950, perhaps due to the efforts of Alice Marble, a white tennis champion, Althea was allowed to play in the Eastern Grass Court Championships at South Orange, New Jersey, and in the Nationals at Forest Hills.

After retiring from professional tennis, Althea Gibson recorded an album, had a role in a John Wayne movie, played exhibition tennis, took up golf, and served as New Jersey state athletic commissioner. (Photo courtesy of the International Tennis Hall of Fame and Tennis Museum at The Newport Casino, Newport, Rhode Island)

Gibson's first major tennis victory was the French National Championship in 1956. The next year she became the first black person to win Wimbledon and the U.S. Nationals at Forest Hills. She repeated both of these victories in 1958 and was named Associated Press Woman Athlete of the Year, the first black so honored. Then, surprising the sports world, she announced her retirement from tennis to go into business, saying, "One cannot eat a crown" (Gibson, 1958).

Conclusion

There have been many heroines in women's sports who were forerunners to the athletes of today. This chapter as well as the time line in this volume provide some insight into the incredible accomplishments of these foremothers. This discussion should dispel any notion that these women compromised their love of physical activity and sport simply because societal pressures dictated a more genteel, passive approach to exercise. All of these women paved the way for today's sportswomen, just as our present athletes' achievements are laying stepping-stones for future generations, not only to follow, but to use as they leap ahead to a new millennium.

Key Words

Victorian heroines

sport

women athletes

early mavericks

modern mavericks

Discussion Questions

1. Interscholastic and intercollegiate sport developed at different times and in different ways for men and women. How did they differ in the developmental stages, and why?
2. What evidence is there today that women do not receive the same degree of recognition for their sporting exploits as do men? Be specific.
3. What differences are there in women's participation in sport as it relates to race and/or class?

Notes

1. The All-American Girls' Professional Baseball League operated from 1943 to 1954.

2. Clara G. Baer has been erroneously credited with devising the three-division court for women's basketball, but Baer was never even familiar with the three-court system. The smallest divisions she ever advocated were seven for regular play.

3. Of course, Eleo Sears was an exception to living by the social code of her day, but she did attend the social parties of the elite and, based on her evening attire, was even voted one of the best dressed young women of Boston.

4. Historically, women either were not allowed to play at the "men's" country clubs or were allowed to play only at certain times of the day and on certain days of the week. Such restrictions still exist at many country clubs.

References

Berenson, S. (1901). The significance of basket ball for women. In S. Berenson (Ed.), *Spalding's basket ball for women* (pp. 20-27). New York: American Sports.

Collett, G. (1924, September). Sports for women. *Women's Home Companion*, p. 21.

Davenport, D. (1982). Eleanora Randolph Sears: Pioneer in women's sports. In R. Howell (Ed.), *Her story in sport* (pp. 266-272). West Point, NY: Leisure.

Gibson, A. (1958, August-September). I wanted to be somebody. *Saturday Evening Post*, pp. 11-13ff., 30ff.

Gipe, G. (1978). Breaking the sex barrier. In *The great American sports book* (pp. 331-345). Garden City, NY: Doubleday.

Hergesheimer, J. (1927, July 9). Charleston. *Saturday Evening Post*, pp. 12-13.

Hollander, P. (1976). *101 greatest women in sports*. New York: Grosset & Dunlap.

Paul, J. (1985, April). Clara Gregory Baer: Harbinger of southern physical education. *Research Quarterly for Exercise and Sport*, pp. 46-55.

Paul, J..(1991). Clara Gregory Baer: Catalyst for women's basketball. In J. S. Hult & M. Trekell (Eds.), *A century of women's basketball: From frailty to final four* (pp. 37-52). Reston, VA: American Alliance for Health, Physical Education, Recreation and Dance.

Sport. (1936, March 16). *Time*, pp. 38-39.

Tynan, T. (1985, April 7). Basketball Hall to induct women. *Sunday Advocate* (Baton Rouge, LA), p. 11-D.

Woolum, J. (1992). *Outstanding women athletes*. Phoenix, AZ: Oryx.

4

The Legendary
Babe Didrikson Zaharias

BETTY HICKS

It was at Dyche Stadium in Evanston, Illinois, in the summer of 1932 that some of the most prophetic cheers ever to echo into sports history built goose bumps on an 18-year-old girl from Beaumont, Texas. And those roars continued to reverberate through 23 more years of athletic dominance.

Dyche Stadium was the site of both the 1932 Amateur Athletic Union (AAU) women's track and field championships and the trials for the Olympic Games to be held that summer in Los Angeles. During the opening ceremonies, team after team was introduced, groups of 15 to 22 women sprinting out into the center of the jammed arena. Finally, the "team" from Employers Casualty Insurance Company out of Dallas was announced. Out of the tunnel there whooped one skinny kid, waving her arms as though to create more of her, and growing goose-bumpy from the crowd's roar. She was entered in every event except two sprints.

Two and a half hours later, Dallas's one-woman squad had won that AAU championship single-handed. Of the eight events she entered, she won five, tied a sixth, and placed in a seventh. Her individual total of 30 points was almost double that racked up by the 22 members of the second-place team, the Illinois Athletic Club, who had a 16-point total.

Thus launched on that day of phenomenal achievement was the athletic career of Babe Didrikson. She was destined to dominate the women's sports world for the next quarter of a century. In her years of athletic competition, she accumulated an unparalleled list of victories, records, and accolades. There is no question that hers was the most magnificent sports record to be compiled by any woman who has ever lived.

NOTE: This chapter is a condensed version of a two-part series that originally appeared in the November 1975 and December 1975 issues of *WomenSports* magazine. It is reprinted here by permission of *Women's Sports & Fitness* magazine.

The Early Years

The Babe was born Mildred Ella Didrikson in Port Arthur, Texas, on June 26, 1914, the youngest of Ole and Hannah Didrikson's seven children. She adored her Norwegian-immigrant "Momma" and "Poppa." Poppa's trade was cabinetmaking and furniture refinishing. As Babe recounts in her autobiography, "With seven kids to support, he generally didn't have any dimes or quarters to hand out to us for picture shows." So he determined, "I'll build good bodies for them." Ole Didrikson built a backyard gymnasium complete with weight-lifting equipment and chinning and jumping bars on which the Didrikson children could work out together.

It may have been the hedges of Beaumont, Texas, to which the family moved when Mildred was 3 years old, that fired Babe's dreams of roaring crowds. Babe admitted she was never very good at straightaway running. "I didn't seem to want to stay on the ground. I'd rather jump some obstacle." The hedges were two feet across, forcing her to develop her own unique style. "I had to crook my left knee or I'd scratch myself." Sister Lillie, who aspired to the Olympics as a sprinter, would race Babe on the flat pavement while Babe flew over the hedges. Babe later thwarted the efforts of Olympic coaches to change her Beaumont hedge-hurdling style, and proved the correctness of that refusal by setting a new world's record of 11.8 seconds in the Olympic Games' 80-meter hurdles.

A retired Army officer, Colonel M. J. McCombs, was responsible for the transformation of Mildred Ella Didrikson from a hedge-hopper into a track star. McCombs was director of the women's athletic program at Employers Casualty, a Dallas insurance firm. He had read newspaper reports of an all-city, all-state Beaumont female basketball star whose 30 to 40 points a game were wiping out the opposition. McCombs scouted 15-year-old Babe Didrikson, seeking a potential point maker for his Employers Casualty girls' team. He promptly put Babe on his company payroll as an office worker. Led by Babe, the team was runner-up in the national championships that year and came in first the following season, its all-American star scoring a record 100-plus points in one game en route to the title.

The Olympic year of 1932 was near, and among talented athletes Olympic fever was beginning to burn. Colonel McCombs sensed a restlessness in his fleet star at the conclusion of basketball season; it was a restlessness he believed he could channel. Babe Didrikson had never seen a track meet, a situation Colonel McCombs soon rectified. The Babe was hooked.

In 1930 and 1931, Babe labored at track and field. Out of that enthusiastic training, parlayed with almost unbelievable native ability, she began accumulating her vast collection of gold medals. She particularly excelled at throwing and jumping events. Altogether, she was to win 364 first-place medals in innumerable track and field events, basketball matches, and softball games during that vigorous early phase of her career.

Seven homers for seven at bats in the Texas Twilight League earned her the none-too-imaginative nickname of Babe early in her sports career, when Babe Ruth was the athletic world's idol. In the course of her life,

Early in her sports career, Babe excelled at basketball. She toured the United States with the Babe Didrikson All-American Basketball Team. (Photo supplied by Wilson Sporting Goods Co.)

Babe was a champion in running, swimming, javelin throwing, diving, high jumping, hurdling, baseball, boxing, rifle shooting, horseback riding, and billiards.

"She can throw a baseball 315 feet," Tony Cordaro of the *Des Moines Tribune* wrote, obviously open-mouthed, "which is on a par with any of the good outfielders. She can toss a football accurately 50 yards. Her golf drives average between 200 and 220 yards. She was chosen as the best basketball player in the history of the southwest."

Between the years of Olympic fame and golf greatness, Babe dabbled in many sports. She permitted herself to be exploited in gross promotional stunts; at one time she even considered an offer to sprint against a race horse. Then in 1933 she saw Bobby Jones play an exhibition match in Houston and her restlessness was once again channeled. "Seeing Jones sort of fired up my own golf ambitions," she was to write later.

Thus motivated by a game she had once denounced as "silly," Babe was determined to devote all her resources to learning golf. In California she met driving-range professional Stanley Kertes, who offered her free lessons. This chance meeting could well have been the most fortuitous in Babe's career. Kertes is one of golf's most talented teachers.

Equipped with the game's elemental techniques, Babe returned to Dallas from California in 1934, once again to work for Colonel McCombs and Employers Casualty. Realizing her golf potential, the company gave her a membership in the Dallas Country Club, where she dedicated all her limited leisure hours to beating on golf balls.

Babe entered her first golf tournament, the Fort Worth Invitational, in November of that year. Texas newspapers headlined her performance in the qualifying round: "Wonder Girl Makes Her Debut in Tournament Golf; Turns in 77 Score." Babe remembered jubilantly, "It was like 1932 all over again." Beaten in an early round in that effort, Babe next entered the Texas Women's State Championship in spring of 1935. "No prize I've ever won, either before or since, looked any bigger to me than the Texas state women's golf championship did when I took aim on it." She instituted a vigorous practice schedule, immersing herself in golf.

Earlier, Babe had been declared a professional by the AAU for allegedly endorsing an automobile in an advertisement, though Babe said she had not given prior approval for the ad. Since the U.S. Golf Association (USGA) had not yet agreed with the AAU that Babe had relinquished her athletic purity, she was still allowed to compete as an amateur.

She qualified for the Texas championship with an 84, fought through four rounds of match play, and then squared off against a fine player, Peggy Chandler, in the finals. Their 36-hole match is now legendary. The rough and tough underdog wonder woman of the Xth Olympiad was pitted against the lovely lady from Dallas, wife of a West Pointer, mother of two sons, and a stalwart of "Big D" society.

The gallery at Houston's posh River Oaks Country Club that day was overrun with burly and uninhibited Babe fans down from Beaumont. The boisterous fans thought stepping on Peggy Chandler's golf ball was the height of hilarity and their idea of fan etiquette was to hoot like a wild baseball crowd. All of this inspired Paul Gallico to write his riotous fictionalized account of the match, "The Lady and the Tiger," for the *Saturday Evening Post*. Babe Didrikson's two-up victory over Peggy Chandler for her first tournament win was thus assigned cultural as well as historical significance.

Two weeks later the USGA, possibly inspired by compelling feminine voices with Texas accents, declared Babe a professional in golf, no longer eligible for amateur tournaments. But the USGA, unlike most other sports organizations, has a reinstatement provision for professional golfers who are willing to don figurative sackcloth and ashes and repent their professionalism. After a designated period of competitive limbo, these penitents may regain their amateur status. Since the opportunities for women professionals in the 1930s were limited to two tournaments annually, Babe decided to reapply for amateur status under this system. If she was going to realize her dream of becoming a great golfer, this was the only path to follow.

"Hirsute" was the word sportswriter Paul Gallico had used to describe her in those days of her brilliant ascension. What impact that word had on me! Gallico sent me scurrying to the dictionary. With only Webster to guide me, the portrait my 11-year-old imagination created of Babe was of a totally furry creature. At our first meeting seven years later I marveled—Babe Didrikson was no more hirsute that the rest of us, and never had been!

Later, Babe made it a playful habit, as we sat on a tournament tee waiting to drive, to stroke one of my calves approvingly and rasp, "Shaved 'em this morning, didn't ya?" It was always in front of a gallery and embarrassed me enormously. But behind my flushed face I wondered if Babe, once she had learned that women usually shaved hirsute legs, had become obsessed with her startling discovery.

The men who swarmed the fairways in Babe's wake did not seem truly threatened by her. There were those rumors after the Olympics that she took testosterone, so it was not a castrating experience to be outdriven by her. Men could convince themselves that she wasn't quite all woman.

But to those of us who shared the country club locker rooms with her, Babe was conclusively female. She was not feminine by our culture's peculiarly warped definition of it, though she did develop the sensibility to acquire certain layers of the veneer of femininity. She painted her fingernails, curled her hair, put on high heels, and wore lace-trimmed dresses. But the Babe remained back-alley tough and barroom crude, seemingly with determined effort and obviously with the intent of delighting fans with her uninhibited repartee.

Striving for Attention, Thriving on Applause

Babe begged to be exploited by the image molders because exploitation, in her mind, was synonymous with attention. She boisterously protected her reputation as uncouth and rough, gloried in the gallery mirth at her primitive humor. "Man!" she'd protest loudly after a bad shot. "All that work and the baby's dead!" Gallery guffaws were symphonic to Babe. Her autobiography is repetitive with phrases such as "The crowd roared" and "The gallery went wild."

In 1950 several of us made the movie *Pat and Mike* with Katharine Hepburn and Spencer Tracy. "How'd it go today, you old son-of-a-bitch?" she once asked director George Cukor, leveling a flinch-producing whack

On the Riviera Country Club (Pacific Palisades, California) set of the 1950 MGM film Pat and Mike, *starring Katharine Hepburn and Spencer Tracy. Left to right: professionals Helen Dettweiler and Beverly Hanson, Tracy, Babe Zaharias, and pro Betty Hicks. (MGM photo, supplied by Wilson Sporting Goods Co.)*

at his thigh. "She's rawthah outspoken, isn't she?" was Ms. Hepburn's discreet appraisal.

Babe catered to her fans in the ways that came easiest to her—crudely, without rules of rhetoric fettering her quips, and without attempting to substitute country club-approved phrases for the vernacular with which she was more facile. "Couldn't hit an elephant's ass with a bull-fiddle today!" she'd complain publicly after a bad round.

"Babe, what do you think about when you hit the ball out in the woods?" asked one incredibly naive galleryite at one of the East's most fashionable clubs. "Just wish to hell George was there so we could . . . ," Babe replied, completing the expression with an explicit description that propelled the horrified fan off to gallery a more couth professional.

The "George" in the reference was Babe's husband, George Zaharias— "the Crying Greek from Cripple Creek" George Zaharias, marquee name for Theodore Vetayanis. The infamous professional wrestler was in fact Greek and was from Pueblo, Colorado, which was close enough to Cripple Creek to make the publicity valid. "He was husky and black-haired and handsome," Babe recalled, obviously smitten, since George was not by most standards an Adonis, even in his more slender days with his enormous cauliflower ears retouched for publicity photos. George was a grunting grizzly bear of a man, with a deep vein of tenderness permitted to surface only if it did not interfere with a business objective.

Babe and George were married in St. Louis on December 23, 1938. For the next 17 years George was Babe's devoted husband, manager, and golf coach, waiting in the wings throughout her career. In introducing her monstrous mate, Babe frequently quipped to galleries, "When I married George Zaharias, he weighed 250 pounds and looked like a Greek god. Now he weighs 300 and looks like a gawddamned Greek."

Shock techniques they were. "Just spell mah name right," she would growl at the press, and then give the syllables of Zaharias a lewd emphasis. Yet I wondered if Babe truly knew, deafened as she was by the gallery's huzzahs for her unwrought histrionics, how viciously contemptuous her followers turned in locker rooms and club bars.

Babe gave them the show they wanted, and she in turn was assured center stage. But by seeking the limelight in this way, she was helping to perpetuate a cruel myth about women athletes—the myth flourished in the 1930s and 1940s and was to become an enormous burden to those of us who were Babe's contemporaries in golf in the 1950s. How many years and how much energy has women's professional golf spent attempting to elude that shadow?

And yet professional women golfers owe Babe so much! The Babe metamorphosis turned women golfers into attacking hitters—still rhythmic and graceful, but hitters nonetheless. Scores in the low 70s became commonplace in Babe's era; rounds in the 60s ceased making sports-page headlines. Babe let us know that it was not merely possible but essential to break 70.

Riding High

In professional golf, as in amateur play, Babe continued to dominate the field. But by now her competition was more skillful and less inclined to play dead when confronted with Babe's brash boastfulness. So Babe no longer won all, or even a majority, of the open tournaments she entered. Her record, however, was still unmatched. Between 1948 and 1956 she won 34 of the 88 golf tournaments she entered, with 18 major titles interspersed among lesser tour events.

Material measurements were seemingly the only ones she could understand. "Listen," she would say, eyes narrowing, "Ah can remember them hamburger days in Beaumont. Ah want nothin' but filets now." She was obsessed with making money, money by the square of what her competitors made. "Ah'm makin' it faster'n Ah can spend it!" was her boast after she entered full-time professional golf in 1947.

"The Babe is here!" she would announce, poised at the locker-room threshold at almost any tournament site, Texas accent at its twangiest. "Are ya girls goin' home now, or are ya goin' to stick around to see who's goin' to finish second? Ah'm goin' to whup all of ya!"

Babe was chosen A.P. Athlete of the Year six times and was named to an impressive collection of halls of fame: those of the LPGA, PGA/World Golf, National Track and Field, and International Women's Sports, as well as the U.S. Olympic Hall of Fame. (Photo supplied by Wilson Sporting Goods Co.)

High decibels of applause, appearance money, engraved summonses to the White House, newspaper clippings—all of these were the corpuscles of Babe's lifeblood. She told the members of the LPGA at one particularly stormy meeting in the early 1950s: "Listen, ya girls. Ah don't go for this rule of no tournament appearance fees. Ah can't buy me them mink coats on just prize money, and where Ah go these days, Ah gotta have mink."

Babe's other side—her tender side—was actually very private to her, as though she feared one of the kids from Beaumont might suddenly reappear and screech "Sissy" at her. But her relationships with those of us who were her competitors ranged from vicious combativeness to feigned hostility to warm friendliness. At one time or another she engaged in open verbal warfare with all of us, since we occasionally had the audacity either to beat her or to threaten her ill-structured ego in an area other than golf.

When her winning streaks subsided, Babe feared that the end of her supremacy was imminent. So Babe and George made other plans for her. A sports promoter by primary occupation, George had said, "Women's golf belongs to me. Me and Babe can promote this thing right. It's a racket, golf is, just like the wrasslin' and the boxin' racket. And it's gotta be run the same way."

The LPGA was struggling organizationally at that time. Wilson Sporting Goods Company had given the fledgling association an economic and promotional assist in 1949, and for a short period was joined by other sporting goods companies. By 1953, however, all had withdrawn. The LPGA was cast adrift to do its own promotion and tournament contracting. I naively accepted the nonpaying assignment to rewrite the LPGA bylaws, and also agreed to a $200-a-month job as publicity director.

Babe and George had other ideas. They visualized Babe in a new starring role as our wheeling-dealing tournament director, with George as her ex officio adviser. The bylaws and a tournament-playing publicity director did not fit into their scheme. Then the bombshell that Babe needed to launch her plan exploded, with exquisite *Saturday Evening Post* timing, in the midst of the Tampa Open. In the *Post* issue was an article about the women's professional golf tour and the stars who constituted it. I was the author. This was all Babe needed.

"I'm resigning from the LPGA," she fumed. "The LPGA has fired Fred Corcoran." Since we had not hired Corcoran, we could scarcely fire him. But we had, for want of a treasury, been unable to contract his further services. Fred had been Babe's manager and doubled as our tournament director.

Several other pros were miffed about what I had—or had not—written about them. Rallying the malcontents around her, Babe promised: "You all come with me. I'll set up my own tour. Where I go, the galleries will go. Let the rest starve." Many of the tournament entrants were frightened, reasoning, We can't get along if Babe doesn't play tournaments. She's the whole show. They were too young to remember that golf writers had already written golf's obituary once, almost 25 years before, when Bobby Jones retired. Babe was a show, but she wasn't the whole show.

"Babe'll come back in the LPGA if you'll resign as publicity director," George Zaharias told me in an impromptu encounter at Tampa's Palma Ceia Golf Club. The essence of the discussion was, wrasslin' terms deleted, that the LPGA didn't need no rules, no bylaws, no publicity director. All we needed was Babe, and a minor supporting cast. And if Babe ran out of golf shots, I presumed, the hurrahs would still be hers as Babe Zaharias, LPGA president and tournament director.

A job paying just $200 a month was scarcely worth standing up to George Zaharias's hulk to retain. I resigned. As news of our donnybrook splattered onto sports section front pages, Babe and I drew the biggest galleries in the history of the Tampa Open. Three months later, once more playing winning golf, Babe announced she was quitting as tournament director. There was no one else in the LPGA who carried a typewriter on tour, so Babe selected me as tournament director, a job that also paid $200 a month. I ended up losing nothing but three months of dubious employment.

The End of an Era

Babe's succession of medical problems began in 1952, when she neglected an abdominal hernia to play "just one more tournament" after "just one more tournament." Surgery corrected that condition just prior to critical strangulation. But Babe failed to regain her strength. Though Babe was unquestionably heroic in the manner of her comeback after surgery, she was not exemplary in the acknowledgment of her symptoms. Between 1952 and the winter of 1953, she disregarded serious physical signs that would have sent anyone with a less highly developed illusion of physical invulnerability scurrying to the doctor.

"Aw, Babe," George would continue to reassure her, and probably himself, "it's just them hemorrhoids," and they would move on to the next tournament. Finally, even Babe had to face the reality that she needed a medical diagnosis. It was in Fort Worth in April 1953 that proctologist Dr. William C. Tatum quietly announced, "Babe, you have cancer." Colostomy surgery was performed on Babe in Galveston on April 17, presumably ridding her of the minuscule remnants of her malignancy of the colon.

Babe's widely publicized friendship with Betty Dodd, the gangly Texas redhead and long-ball hitter whom Babe called "the kid," emerged from these crisis years of 1952 through 1956. The companionship, competition, adulation, loyalty, and solicitude of Betty Dodd were deeply meaningful to Babe. But the relationship destroyed Betty as a golfer of promise. The Babe could not tolerate "the kid" escaping through her own talents from the Zaharias shadow.

Betty had a potentially great golf game; she could belt a tee shot out there with Babe, and she put together some fine rounds on the LPGA tour. One of these was at Sea Island, Georgia, in 1954, and it was good enough to lead the field in the first round. Beaming, tournament-leading Betty came off the eighteenth green, where the press awaited her. But so did Babe Zaharias, whose ego could not tolerate watching newsmen interviewing her protégé instead of herself. Babe grabbed Betty with the flimsy ruse, "C'mon, Betty, let's go get a sandwich," and strode off.

But Betty Dodd was largely undaunted. She had been beside Babe as always, playing in her threesome. Once more Babe heard the thunderously melodic roar of the crowd as she creamed a typical Babe Zaharias drive off the first tee in Chicago's All-American Open. "Man, they didn't cut that out!" she yelled to the hordes. But the laughter she shared with the gallery that July did not endure. Surgery as extensive as Babe's normally required a full recuperation period of many months. Not even the physical resilience of the Associated Press's "Greatest Woman Athlete of the Half Century" could cope with the demands she made on her body.

Few moments of true poignancy punctuated Babe's career. I shared one of these while playing with her in the first round of the Sea Island

Invitational on a bitterly cold January day. On the sixteenth tee she sagged wordlessly onto a bench, her scorecard, heavy with bogeys, speaking for her. I sensed the galvanic drama of the end of an era. Stunned, I realized that my passion for sports had made me the only witness to the now full circle of this incomparable athlete's career; from the anonymity of my seat in the Los Angeles Coliseum in 1932 to the lonely intimacy of a teeing ground bench in Georgia 22 years later, from watching her achieve immortality in the Olympics to sharing her depression over the only out-of-the-money finish in her entire professional golf career.

Yet Babe was not through as a professional golfer. She spurred her cancer-wracked, injury-beset body to seven more tournament victories before overwhelming illness finally forced her out of competition in 1956.

Her last tournament win came in the spring of 1955 at the Betsy Rawls-Peach Blossom in Spartanburg, South Carolina. This was to be her final round of competitive golf. "All Ah want now," she told me at that tournament, "is to have me a little country place near Beaumont, where Ah can have mah dogs and mah horse, and mah friends to come to see me."

"Yeah," rumbled George, "but it'll sure be funny not goin' down to the lobby to buy the mornin' papers."

Babe Didrikson Zaharias died in Augusta, Georgia, on September 27, 1956.

Key Words

Olympic track and field	uncouth and rough
gold medalist	primitive humor
AAU champion	LPGA
revolutionized golf	greatest woman athlete

Discussion Questions

1. What made the Babe such a great athlete?
2. The five Cs—crass, crude, colorful, competitive, and controversial—describe Babe. Compare and contrast her public life to other athletes with similar personalities.

Suggested Reading

Hicks, B. (1975, November). Babe Didrikson Zaharias: "Stand back! This ain't no kid hittin'." *WomenSports*, pp. 24-28.

Hicks, B. (1975, December). Babe Didrikson Zaharias: "Where I go, the galleries go. Let the rest starve." *WomenSports*, pp. 18-25.

Knudson, R. R. (1977, December). Babe Didrikson: No more Ms. Nice Guy. *WomenSports*, pp. 54-56.

Raque, S. (1990, May-June). You've come a long way, ladies. *Women's Sports & Fitness*, pp. 61-66.

Zaharias, M. D. (1955). *This life I've led: My autobiography.* New York: Barnes.

The All-American Girls' Professional Baseball League

MARY PRATT

In 1943, a World War II phenomenon made history. The All-American Girls' Professional Baseball League (AAGPBL) was conceived, financed, and organized by Philip K. Wrigley, the chewing gum magnate and owner of the Chicago Cubs, in collaboration with a group of colleagues in Chicago (AAGPBL Players Association, 1987). The establishment of this experimental league took place while men, including those in professional baseball, were being drafted. Phil Wrigley, Branch Rickey, and U.S. President Franklin D. Roosevelt were all concerned that major league baseball might have to be suspended (Taylor, 1987). The formation of the women's league, Wrigley believed, would serve as a viable substitute and keep the interest in baseball alive. The venture became both successful and popular in the Midwest.

It was Mr. Wrigley's policy that the league be organized and operated on a sound fiscal policy, with high moral and social standards. This concept was fostered during his association with the league. Although money became one of the contributing factors in the league's eventual demise, this was not the case at its inception. Kenneth Sells, an associate from Wrigley's Chicago office, was given $100,000 and the task of recruiting the best female softball players in the country. Scouting agents invited women to try out in Chicago, and the new league was composed of four teams: Rockford, Illinois; Kenosha and Racine, Wisconsin; and South Bend, Indiana. In future years the league would expand to include Fort Wayne, Indiana; Peoria, Illinois; Minneapolis, Minnesota; Milwaukee, Wisconsin; Battle Creek, Michigan; Chicago, Illinois; Grand Rapids, Michigan; Muskegon, Michigan; and Springfield, Illinois.

During those first years, the league was controlled by a central organization out of Mr. Wrigley's office. The financial support and organizational structure of each team was sound. Prominent people within the public and private sectors of each city involved formed a strong nucleus to ensure financial solvency. These groups were also very active in hosting the women at civic functions and in sponsoring special evenings at the ballpark. In later years, a decentralization of government occurred and individual towns and cities assumed control of their own teams.

A Professional League for Women

Because major rule changes were made in the game itself and a transformation took place in the governing policies of the league, it is easy to divide the life of the league into three eras: the early years (1943-1946), the transitional period (1947-1949), and the late era (1950-1954). Although more than 500 women participated in the league over its 12-year span, very few were active for that entire length of time.

The Early Years

When the league began in 1943, it consisted of the Rockford Peaches, the South Bend Blue Sox, the Racine Belles, and the Kenosha Comets. Each roster had 15 players, a chaperone, a manager, and a business manager. The distribution of players was under the control of Philip Wrigley's office in Chicago, and each team operated under a board of directors, who, for the most part, were men from local business and fraternal organizations.

Player contracts ranged from $60.00 to $85.00 per week. League officials had the authority to assign and trade players as they saw fit, as a method of assuring that all teams would remain competitive. Meal money supplied to each player when a team was traveling amounted to $2.75 a day, or $19.25 weekly. Transportation and hotel accommodations were provided when a team was on the road. When the teams were at home, players lived in private homes under arrangements made by the league, and the players were responsible for their own expenses. Room rental was usually $5.00 weekly, whether players were in town or on the road. On many occasions players' host families prepared meals and did the players' laundry. Many players returned year after year to these "homes away from home."

Consistent with the high standards that had been set, dress codes that stressed femininity were established for attire both on and off the playing field. The uniform was not even remotely related to the style

The first four players to sign with the AAGPBL. Seated: Shirley Jamison. Standing, left to right: Clara Schillace, Ann Harnett, Edie Perlick. (Photo courtesy of the Northern Indiana Historical Society)

usually associated with a game in which one was often required to slide. It resembled a tennis dress, with the hem approximately 4-6 inches above the knee. The pitchers folded over and pinned the flared part of the skirt on their pitching side, in order to avoid interference with their delivery. Tights and knee socks, caps, and the AAGPBL jacket completed the uniform. The red jacket with the AAGPBL emblem was common to all teams. The brightly colored uniforms came with accessories in contrasting colors.

During the early years, game rules were basically those of softball, with a few exceptions. Both pitching distance and baselines were longer, runners were allowed to take leads, and pitchers were allowed to develop a "semibalk" as a means of restricting the length of leads taken by base runners. Games were held at regular softball facilities reserved expressly for league play, except in Milwaukee and Minneapolis, where games were played on the baseball diamonds used by the men's minor league teams of those cities. These two teams joined the league in 1944. The playing season was divided into two halves, with the winners of the first and second halves competing in September for the league championship. The receipts from these playoffs were divided into winner's and loser's shares.

Players were recruited from throughout the United States and Canada. They demonstrated diversified talents.

> I guess my forte was stealing bases. My best year was in 1946. That year I stole 201 bases. (Sophie Kurys, second base, Racine; in Taylor, 1987)

During the war years, the patriotic tradition of forming a large V for victory on the playing field at the start of every game was established. The teams would run the base lines from opposing directions, alternating at second base and forming the apex of the V at home plate.

The managers were all men. Their backgrounds were in baseball, many having been former big league players, managers, and coaches. Max Carey, who had been known for his base stealing, had been a player, coach, and manager in the National League. He managed the Fort Wayne team for a number of years and also served as president of the league. Marty McManus, former manager of the Boston Red Sox in the 1930s, and Johnny Gottselig of the Chicago Black Hawks managed teams in the original league. Bill Allington joined the league in 1944, bringing many excellent players with him from his California homeland. He stayed to the very end. Jimmy Foxx, Bill Wambsganss, and Dave Bancroft arrived on the scene later.

The chaperones were all women. "It was the manager's job to make sure the women played like professionals. But it was the chaperone's job to look after the players' appearance and make sure they conducted themselves like ladies off the field" (Johnson, 1988). The chaperones were responsible for getting the players' paychecks, taking care of their uniforms, giving them their meal money, and making hotel reservations. They also approved the players' social engagements and looked after their adherence to curfew hours (Fidler, 1976). The chaperones always traveled with the teams, attended all team meetings and practices, were responsible

The Rockford Peaches dugout, 1943. Left to right: B. Fritz, E. Burgmeister, M. Pratt, A. Kerrar, M. Peters, H. Nelson, M. Timm (chaperone), M. Deegan. (Photo courtesy of Mary Pratt)

Kenosha Comets catcher Ann Harnett, 1945. (Photo courtesy of the Northern Indiana Historical Society)

for the first-aid kit, and even sat in the dugouts during games. The white dresses with red blazers worn by chaperones in the early years were replaced by 1947 with navy blue suits and hats (similar to the airline hostess uniforms of the time).

Transition Period

Between 1947 and 1949 the league blossomed. Ten cities competed and the league drew a million fans. Wrigley sold his interest to Arthur Myeroff, an associate from the Chicago office. It was becoming difficult to recruit a sufficient numbers of pitchers who could pitch "softball style." Players able to employ the sidearm technique began to take over some of the pitching chores. However, it was not too long before the pitching went completely to the overarm style; the distances were extended, baselines were lengthened, and the ball become regulation baseball size. The AAGPBL game became baseball.

Interest peaked! The league was attracting players such as Jean Faut, who had been pitching batting practice five days a week for a men's semipro team by the time she was 14 (Young, 1982).

> Jean had a fastball, a great curve and a screwball and could put them all just where she wanted. She pitched a no-hitter against us one night, the best game I've ever seen pitched. It was perfect, overpowering. (Dorothy Kamenshek, AAGPBL all-time batting leader; quoted in Young, 1982, p. 52)

The feminine angle continued to be stressed. Players' hair had to be a length that extended below the collar. They were not allowed to wear shorts or slacks in public, and both smoking and drinking in public were also prohibited.

Spring training sites differed from year to year. A league highlight occurred in 1947 when spring training was held in Havana, Cuba, a favorite resort and island paradise for tourists. The entire league trained on the island, enabling the teams to then barnstorm as they traveled north prior to opening the regular season.

> We played between 115 and 126 games per season. In a little over three months we played six nights a week and a doubleheader on Sunday. The league rivalry was fierce, the competition intense. The short skirts may have attracted the first audiences; let's face it, they came out for a laugh. What they saw were women baseball players and they kept returning because it was great baseball. (Dottie Collins, pitcher, Ft. Wayne Daisies, personal communication, August 1991)

Late Era

During the final years, league operation became decentralized. Myeroff resigned, and in 1951 independent team ownership took effect. Individual cities assumed responsibility for the governance of their own teams. With the adoption of a draft system, the practice of switching players during the playing season in an attempt to equalize teams came to an end. This greatly reduced intraleague squabbles (Fidler, 1976).

With the decentralized system, continuity began to wane. However, the league maintained a regular schedule for a period of time. As the game was more closely akin to baseball than to softball, recruitment of players became problematic. To alleviate problems with player shortages, various touring teams materialized to create interest in other parts of the country. Exhibition games increased in regularity. A rookie rule was adopted to ensure playing experience for the newcomers (Fidler, 1976).

> Following regular season play, the touring teams always played against men's teams, since women's baseball was nonexistent. (Wilma Briggs, 1950 Touring Team, personal communication, September 1991)

In 1952, All-Star Games were held at mid-season. Since there was only one league, the team that commanded first-place status by mid-season hosted the All-Star Team, which was "selected by the working press and radio" (Fidler, 1976). The event was an instant success.

Many efforts to economize were instituted during the final years, but by 1954 the league had folded. With the demise of the AAGPBL, an era in the history of women in sport had ended. Because baseball was America's "national pastime," the loss was even more profound.

Nostalgia Revitalizes the League

Since the late 1970s, interest has been generated by individuals intent on acquiring more historical information about the AAGPBL. Ironically, many of these projects were initiated concurrent with the passage of Title IX regulations. A parallel interest in our heritage and concern for the contemporary status of girls' and women's sports programs materialized. Researchers were surprised to discover that a venture such as the AAGPBL had existed in the 1940s.

Many former players were contacted by interested historians. Questionnaires formed the nucleus of information for many articles, studies, and books. Mary Fidler (1976) amassed a wealth of data for her master's thesis, a historical account of the league.

In 1975, Sharon Roepke's enthusiasm to learn more about the league set in motion a personal venture to uncover the story of the AAGPBL. Years later, she produced the first series of traditional-style baseball cards for the league. Through her efforts, she was able to retrieve all 12 seasons of the Howe News Bureau statistics for 500 ball players. The stats are displayed on the reverse side of each player's card. To date, four series have been printed. Roepke has presented her research to many groups, including the North American Society for Sports History, the Popular Culture Society, and the North American Society for Sports Sociology. Her initial contact with Clifford Kachline, the historian at Cooperstown in 1981, led to the eventual representation of the AAGPBL at the New York Baseball Hall of Fame.

Issues relating to the league's longevity and its eventual abandonment in 1954 were debated in conversations held during the first reunion in Chicago, July 8-11, 1982. (Enough interest had been generated over the 30-year hiatus to create a nucleus of 300 former players, fans, and sponsors to organize the first reunion.) The expressed opinions have subsequently been published in numerous articles; they focus on the following reasons for the league's demise:

1. The end of World War II brought the renewal of men's baseball to the homefront.
2. Television developed and improved steadily, offering more extensive mass entertainment.
3. The high standards originally set for the league declined in later years.
4. Government of the league's operation was decentralized.

Since that first reunion, additional gatherings have taken place in Indiana, in Arizona, and at Cooperstown, New York.

The groundwork for official recognition at Cooperstown was the result of continuous efforts of many former players, who contacted the authorities at the New York shrine and persisted in their desire to have the league recognized by the Hall of Fame. Information was forwarded to both the historian and the curator. "I had never heard of the AAGPBL until I came to work here," said Ted Spencer, who became the Hall of Fame's curator in 1983. "It's fascinating!" Spencer said he learned only recently, while researching the league roster, that a woman who had been his gym teacher had been a professional baseball player (*Women & Sport*, December 1988, p. 2).

The official unveiling of the AAGPBL display on Saturday, November 5, 1988, was cause for much celebration. The town virtually overflowed with former players, their families, and friends. Busloads of students arrived to honor their teachers who had played in the league. Included in the exhibit's memorabilia were uniforms, baseballs, gloves, pictures, trophies, and a plaque on which was engraved all the names and residences of the players who participated from 1943 to 1954. A formal banquet followed at the Sportsman's Tavern, extending the festivities well into the night.

Perhaps no project revived the history of the league and renewed as much interest as the publication of a league newsletter. This was accomplished by June Peppas, who had played in the league from 1948 to 1954. She was the owner of a small print shop and in 1981 she produced the first mailing, which was sent to former players in the United States, Canada, and Mexico. She encouraged players to forward information, and the newsletter became a source for locating other players. Two years later the project was taken over by Shirley Stovoff of Long Beach, California, and then assumed by Pepper Paire, another former California player. Mailing lists are continually updated, and they now include not only former players, but also friends and fans who have joined the recently created Players' Association as associate members. A league archives site has been established in South Bend in conjunction with the Northern Indiana Historical Society. A documentary film about the league, titled *A League of Their Own* (Wilson & Candaele, 1987), inspired director Penny Marshall's successful 1992 theatrical feature film of the same title. A children's book about the AAGPBL has been written by Sue Macy, the groundwork continues for the printing of a commemorative postage stamp, and many more projects are ongoing as the league approaches its fiftieth anniversary.

Political Savvy or Selling Out?

It is difficult to assess the viability of the AAGPBL without relating it to the status and plight of girls' and women's athletic programs in the United States. At the present time, many more opportunities to compete are being offered to females at the community, high school, collegiate, and Olympic levels. However, opportunities to compete in team sports at the professional level remain dismal. More diverse opportunities exist abroad.

This certainly raises speculation as to how a venture such as the AAGPBL survived for a period of 12 years in the 1940s and early 1950s.

The fact that the AAGPBL operated successfully in that era has given rise to a great deal of speculation as to why such a venture has never again been attempted in the years since. How was the league able to succeed for such a long period of time? What were the contributing factors? One issue surfaces repeatedly in this discussion: the concerted efforts made by Wrigley and continued by Myeroff regarding the high standards set for the league—the issue is *femininity*.

> Wrigley understood the importance of image. His league would have nothing to do with the kind of short-haired, mannish dressed toughies then touring the country on several all-girl barnstorming teams. As one of Mr. Wrigley's associates put it, the new league's athletes would be expected to epitomize the highest ideals of womanhood. At the league's tryouts in Chicago that spring, Mr. Wrigley expected to see nothing but healthy, wholesome, all-American girls. (Fincher, 1989, p. 92)

Mr. Wrigley was insistent that his demands be carried out. "Enforcement was provided by the chaperones who upheld Wrigley's decree that players not appear 'tomboyish'" ("Skirting a Forgotten Era," 1988). He never compromised his ideals. The charm-school lessons held at night were required of all ball players. They practiced everything from walking correctly and applying makeup to conversational techniques with fans and media personnel. Keep in mind that this was 1943, and traditional values regarding appropriate behavior were very much in vogue. Wrigley packaged the product so that it would sell. By conforming to the customs, values, and mores of the society, the novelty of women's professional baseball teams did not appear an anomaly.

The players who had the privilege of participating in the AAGPBL at that time were not overly concerned about the league's standards. The fun, enjoyment, and competitive experience were the top priorities.

> You can do a lot of things when you're young. You can get on that bus and sing all night after a ball game and have a great time, sleep a few hours, get up, eat, dress, and go out and play again. You could do this all the time; that's what we did. (Thelma ["Tiby"] Eisen, outfielder, Peoria; in Taylor, 1987)

It was only in later years that many players really became aware of the uniqueness of the venture and the many opportunities that materialized from their former playing careers. In 1940, who would have conceived of league competition at the professional level for women in a team sport? In retrospect, one might conclude that the efforts of the AAGPBL organizers to consider conformity to traditional values assured the success of the league.

The marketing of any product in a free-enterprise society is vital to its existence. But at what expense? What level of play were fans denied because some very tough-looking women did not fit the image of femininity and were prohibited from league play? What chances to develop even greater expertise as ball players were denied the players themselves? Was this justifiable? Would the charm-school lessons be considered illegal by today's standards, or would they be considered a "fringe benefit" for the Players' Association? Were the women being showcased in traditional, stereotyped ways, and were the incredible feats that they performed daily on the ball field being ignored?

In assessing this situation, one must reflect on the prevailing social ideology of the time. It was five years *after* the inception of the AAGPBL that Branch Rickey attempted his "noble experiment" with the men's league to break the color barrier by asking Negro ball player Jackie Robinson to join the all-white men's professional baseball league, signing him to the Brooklyn Dodgers.

Was Mr. Wrigley overly concerned about image? Was he paranoid, or was he a visionary? Was his femininity angle a brilliant tactical move that ensured success of the league, or was it another example of the packaging of women's sports to ensure that traditional stereotypes would remain intact?

Conclusion

Males and females have always competed in sports. Quite often in such competition the rules are modified to allow for differences in size and strength. But rules change and games evolve as the level of expertise increases. The original game played in the AAGPBL was a unique modified version of softball. The rules changed continually. The longer distance between bases and from the pitching mound to the plate did allow for a more active game. In the end, the game was baseball. And the women played the game well. We know that sport has no gender, but in the 1940s and 1950s that concept was not readily accepted in the United States. It is doubtful that the league would have received Hall of Fame recognition if the game had remained softball.

The All-American Girls' Professional Baseball League certainly represents a milestone in organized sports for women. The players were all pioneers in the development of women's sports in the United States. They were the stars and legends of the baseball diamond more than 40 years ago. This entire league of women baseball players provides viable role models for our youth, enriches our heritage, and adds nobility to our legacy.

Key Words

AAGPBL
Philip K. Wrigley
femininity
charm school
regulation baseball

centralized and independent
  team management
touring teams
Baseball Hall of Fame

Discussion Questions

1. Contrast the social, political, and economic factors responsible for the popularity of the AAGPBL with the comparable factors responsible for its demise.

2. Was Mr. Wrigley's femininity angle a brilliant tactical move for that era that ensured the success of the league, or was it another example of the packaging of women's sports to ensure that the traditional stereotypes would remain intact? Explain.

References

All-American Girls' Professional Baseball League Players' Association Inc. (1987). [Flyer]. Chicago: Author.

Fidler, M. (1976). *The development and decline of the All-American Girls' Professional Baseball League, 1943-1954.* Unpublished master's thesis, University of Massachusetts, Amherst.

Fincher, J. (1989, July). The belles of the ball game. *Smithsonian, 24*(4), 92.

Johnson, D. (1988, November 13). Fun and games. *Sunday Courier* (Evansville, IN), p. C-8.

Skirting a forgotten era. (1988, July 20). *Boston Herald*, p. 94.

Taylor, J. L. (Producer & Director). (1987). *Diamonds are a girl's best friend* [Documentary film]. Chicago: Independent Programming Association.

Wilson, K., & Candaele, K. (Producers & Directors). (1987). *A league of their own* [Documentary film].

Young, D. (1982, October). Seasons in the sun. *WomenSports*, pp. 48-52, 72-74.

6

The AIAW
Governance by Women for Women

L. LEOTUS MORRISON

The creation of the Association for Intercollegiate Athletics for Women (AIAW) in 1971 was a giant leap forward for girls and women. AIAW was to become the designer and creator of sport opportunities for college women, an advocate for equality in sport and athletics for all women, and a proponent of fairness in support of revenue and nonrevenue sports. In just one decade, AIAW became a success. Ironically, however, its accomplishments were perceived as a serious challenge to the power structure and status quo in collegiate and international athletics. Its success triggered opposition and led to its demise.

The Pre-AIAW Climate

To understand the accomplishments and the significance of AIAW, one needs to reflect historically. What was it like to be a girl or woman interested in sport from the 1940s through the 1960s? What events led to the creation of AIAW and to the development of the athletic programs of today?

In the 1940s-1960s a girl or woman who professed interest in sport would have been the exception rather than the rule, and her interest would probably have been pursued only with the understanding from parents and society that it was a fleeting preoccupation that she would abandon for homemaking, marriage, and motherhood. In those days, if a woman was interested in a career associated with sport, her only choice was to become a "gym teacher."

If a young woman was gutsy and chose to study physical education, she either went to a women's college or enrolled in a large university where there were separate men's and women's physical education departments. A third

alternative included small colleges where men and women studied together, but the men were athletes and played football, baseball, and
basketball, and perhaps ran track, while the women were encouraged to
take part in the intramural program, the dance club, or the synchronized
swimming club. Toward the end of this era it was possible for a woman
to select a college where a limited number of teams were sponsored by the
women's physical education department, with a season schedule of five
or six games. Players supplied much of their own equipment, shared team
uniforms with other teams, and on road trips paid for their own meals or
ate in the opposing college's dining room. On those rare occasions when
a team had to stay overnight away from home, everyone chipped in to pay
the cost of rooms.

The coach was probably a physical education teacher who volunteered
to take on the additional responsibility because she loved sport and
wanted students to have this opportunity. Incidentally, she paid her own
way, used her own car, and paid for additional auto insurance in order to
transport players.

Maybe some of the players' roommates came to see the games, but
spectators were rare. Players reported early to prepare the field and also
helped find volunteers to keep time or score. Perhaps the school newspaper reported on the games, especially at a women's college, where the
image of men's athletics was not of overshadowing importance.

Women's athletics were definitely not high in priority among the
programs of colleges and universities in those days. However, the women's
programs that were in existence, from the perspective of today, were
unique. The participants were students who tried out for the teams, and
most programs had junior varsities for those who did not make the first
team. Class attendance was required and academic work had priority. The
programs were controlled and conducted by women and provided many
leadership opportunities for students. The programs were competitive and
winning was important, but the greatest emphasis was on the sheer enjoyment of skilled participation and the challenge of trying to become better.

Interestingly, the majority of women educators accepted the status quo.
They were part of a culture that viewed women as physically weak, questioned the appropriateness of vigorous activity, and acquiesced to the idea
that girls and women had no need for strenuous exercise. With these limitations in mind, yet believing in the educational benefits of sport, the women
educators in physical education planned and conducted a variety of programs that had as a motto, "A sport for every girl and every girl in a sport."

For many women in physical education, life in the 1950s and 1960s
revolved around the Division of Girls' and Women's Sports (DGWS). In
addition to teaching, these women officiated, served as committee members, conducted training programs for officials, and wrote and rewrote
rules. These women were committed to increasing opportunities and
improving programs for students. This process stimulated the rethinking
of the entire competitive scene, including DGWS positions, with regard to
competitive opportunities.

Creation of the AIAW

In 1969, DGWS sponsored a National Workshop on Intercollegiate Sports in Estes Park, Colorado. Women physical educators represented every region of the country and various types of collegiate institutions. The discussions of the pros and cons of competition and types of programs were lively and thought provoking.

Later, DGWS and the Women's Board of the U.S. Olympic Committee, with money from the Doris Duke Foundation, sponsored a series of National Institutes on Sport. Each institute was concerned with several sports, and the participants included selected women from each of the states. The women learned the latest in teaching and coaching strategies and each individual promised to conduct at least two statewide workshops to pass on her expertise to other teachers and coaches. These workshops were a great educational endeavor and an important and critical turning point for women's sports. Many of the participants from the Estes Park workshop and the institutes were foremost among the leaders in developing AIAW and women's athletic programs in the 1970s.[1]

The institutes created a groundswell of interest in higher-level skill for girls and women, and additional schools and colleges began to provide programs. As the level of skill increased, these women wanted opportunities for competition. Thus DGWS created the Commission on Intercollegiate Athletics for Women (CIAW) in 1966 to conduct national championships. Almost immediately it was evident that a commission with four commissioners could not meet all the needs associated with championships.

In the summer of 1971 the commissioners, the DGWS Executive Board, and representatives from what became the nine regions met and designed an operating plan for an institutional membership organization to be known as the Association for Intercollegiate Athletics for Women to lead and conduct programs for women in colleges and universities.

The National Association for Physical Education of College Women, an organization made up of women physical educators who were teachers and administrators at colleges and universities, worked with DGWS in examining and reevaluating previously held beliefs regarding competition for women and in assessing the needs for change.

Goals and Objectives of AIAW

The following statements illustrate the underlying principles that gave form to the structure of the AIAW:

1. Women should have the opportunity to strive for excellence in sport.
2. Women should plan, administer, coach, and officiate sports programs for women and, in so doing, provide viable role models that will empower other women. Women should have power over their sports lives.

3. Programs should be designed for women and should be inclusive rather than exclusive, encouraging the growth of sport and the inclusion of many different sports and different levels of skill.

4. The system should provide many competitive opportunities on state, regional, and national levels in colleges, universities, junior colleges, community colleges, and public and private colleges.

5. Sport programs should be educational, not just athletic; they should be developmental, honoring the best but not negating the achievements of those who do not win.

6. The rights of the athletes should be considered, especially as they relate to students who transfer, who return to school after dropping out, or who are making an Olympic bid.

The first statement in AIAW's position paper on Intercollegiate Athletics (1974) sums it up: "The enrichment of the life of the participant is the focus and reason for the existence of any athletic program. All decisions should be made with this fact in mind." The leaders were successful in creating an organization that addressed these goals. In short, women wanted sports and physical activity as a part of their lives; they had the skill, desire, and stamina to compete; and they wanted to play, coach, and govern. Yes, they were successful, and athletics in this country would never again exclude female participants.

Critical Issues

One must remember that the AIAW leaders were educators first, and they were trying to develop a very different model to govern athletics. Every decision was critical. Each move set a precedent, and they wanted to be fair to all students, to each sport, to Divisions I, II, and III, to the junior and community colleges, and to the National Association for Intercollegiate Athletics (NAIA) institutions. The leaders were also concerned about the impact of their decisions on men's athletics on their own campuses.

Title IX was an extremely important piece of legislation, and it produced many dilemmas. AIAW was created in 1971 and Title IX was passed in 1972. AIAW helped define Title IX and was active in resisting the efforts of the NCAA to limit Title IX and defeat the adoption of the Title IX Regulations. But the AIAW women also had to struggle with issues relating to the definitions of *equality* and *equity*. In athletics, *equality*, to most women, meant the equal right to develop their own programs, but given that men's programs were already long established, the pressure was there to develop identical programs. So a big dilemma arose between the "right to become" and the "pressure to mimic."

Many women felt that "sameness" was not necessarily equality and that modeling women's programs after existing men's programs was not self-determination. The men in athletics perceived *equality for women* as meaning that women would be given the perks and the rewards that come from playing and winning. For the women, *equality* meant the right of self-determination.

With the pressure to be identical and the interest on the part of some to be different, women's programs and the AIAW were always compared with men's programs and the NCAA unfavorably, with the assumption that *different* means *inferior*. Since the structure of women's programs differed from that of the men's programs, it was perceived as inferior.

Many AIAW members did not want to adopt some of the practices and procedures found in men's athletics. If the programs had to be identical, the women felt, but were hesitant to suggest, that what might be *best* for student athletes, both men and women, would be the model AIAW was advocating. Because the women did not want others to tell them what women wanted, they were hesitant to suggest drastic changes for men's programs. The issue of financial aid (scholarships) is a good example of this dilemma. Many of the women in AIAW believed in financial aid based on need only. They believed that such a program would be best for both men's and women's athletics. They tried to legislate "need-only" aid, but it quickly became evident that the powerful football and basketball schools in the NCAA would block passage of that legislation. With that realization, AIAW members were torn between their beliefs regarding financial aid and the fact that no financial aid for women would be cheating women and would not be possible legally.

Perhaps the biggest frustration focused on ideological differences. The women were continually asked, What do you women want? When their answers did not agree with the men's philosophy of how athletics should be conducted, the reaction was, You women just don't understand athletics. This response left no room for intelligent debate. In actuality, the women in athletics were highly educated people; they possessed advanced degrees and represented diverse backgrounds encompassing a much broader spectrum of sporting interests than a concentration in football and basketball. The men's response was an insult.

How did it feel to be a part of the creation and growth of AIAW? For most of the 1970s, the development of AIAW was very exciting. However, the women were often torn. They did not want to hurt existing programs, although in actuality men's nonrevenue sports were "third-class citizens" in those days and have benefited since from the advent of women's programs and Title IX.

Feelings ran the gamut. There were moments of great elation and triumph, such as when AIAW successfully fought off the opponents of Title IX (the Tower Amendment), and finally the passage of Title IX and the dissemination of the Title IX Regulations. There was great pride and empowerment found in being a part of a women's organization that accomplished its goals and objectives. There was a wonderful camaraderie in working with creative women in collaborative efforts despite long and often soul-searching deliberations and debates among women. There were moments of depression. There were clashes and disagreements within the membership. There was the constant threat from other organizations to start competing championships. There were difficulties associated with efforts to meet the unique needs of various kinds of institutions. There were petty human struggles that sidetracked more important issues.

The NCAA Takeover

The greatest moment of depression came in Miami. Both NCAA and AIAW were institutional membership organizations, which meant that a college's vote at a convention represented the will of the institution. At the AIAW convention in Detroit in 1981, representatives overwhelmingly voted to urge the NCAA to postpone initiation of women's championships. The NCAA convention was held in Miami one week later. The atmosphere in Miami was hostile toward the women and particularly toward AIAW leaders and those women who tried to speak to the convention. There were boos, snide and sexist remarks, limits on speaking time for women speakers identified as AIAW followers, and orchestrated calls to end debate. Then came the vote on the addition of championships for women in Division I and a brief moment of elation when the membership voted to defeat. But then, within a minute, came an opportune and unusual recess for some "arm twisting," followed by an immediate call to reconsider, and the vote was overturned narrowly. After that crucial vote the other motions related to rules accommodations for the women passed quickly. It was difficult for the women to go to the NCAA meeting the morning after that loss—the men in NCAA were *not* gracious winners.

Within six months the implementation of the NCAA plan was detrimental to AIAW and to women's intercollegiate programs. The NCAA offered women's governance and women's championships without any increase in membership dues. The additional cost would be covered by a revision of the distribution formula for men's championships. In practical effect, the women at institutions where men's teams qualified for championships would receive appreciably less support for those trips and less chance to receive any profits from championships. In addition, the NCAA allowed members to choose to enter either AIAW or NCAA championships; to choose to follow any set of rules and regulations in existence prior to August 1, 1981; and to waive the requirement of numbers of teams to qualify for divisional membership. This "flexibility" led to chaos. By July, AIAW experienced a 20% loss in membership, a 32% drop in championship participation, and a 48% drop in Division I championship participation. In the fall, the NBC television network notified AIAW that it would not televise any championships and would not pay the monies due under its contract (approximately a half million dollars for 1981-1983).

Consequently, in 1982, the AIAW Executive Board determined that it could not accomplish its stated goals and, rather than jeopardize women's programs, voted to dissolve the association. Women created the AIAW, and women disbanded it in the interest of women's sports.

Conclusion

For women in athletics, this era represented a time of moving out of the women's gym and into the arena of life. The participants played a critical part in bringing about a fundamental change in societal attitudes

The evolution of the governance of women's sports is dramatically reflected in the playing styles of these college women. (Left photo, circa 1946, courtesy of the University of Rhode Island Archives; right photo, 1992, courtesy of the University of Rhode Island Sports Information)

toward the role of sport in the lives of women. Enduring friendships were formed; many women became feminists. The AIAW left a heritage and a legacy of women leaders who examined, created, controlled, and supported a critical decade of intercollegiate athletics. That decade was a period of great accomplishment for women and for women's athletics, and the AIAW's success was a threat to the athletic establishment and precipitated the takeover by NCAA.

Looking back to the days of AIAW, one must now ask, Who will act as watchdog for those accomplishments, and who will assure the continuation of opportunity for girls and women in sport and athletics? Any individual who has studied the history of the women's movement cannot help but be struck by the pattern of small surges forward followed by slips backward, and by the diminishing numbers of women found in particular professions once those professions begin to attract attention and respectable salaries.

The athletic power establishment is well entrenched, self-serving, generally insensitive, and extremely competitive, and thus it perpetuates exclusivity. Although there are individual exceptions, it is extremely difficult for women to effect change, achieve equity, and maintain equality within this environment. The price of freedom is eternal vigilance and attention by generation after generation of fair-minded women and men. No one is free until all men and women, regardless of color, creed, age, or class, are free. Sports participation and the opportunity to govern that participation are part of that freedom.

Key Words

women's athletics	scholarships
DGWS	philosophical issues
CIAW	legislation
goals and objectives	NCAA takeover
Title IX	

Discussion Questions

1. What was the prevailing philosophy that governed AIAW?
2. Contrast the governance of women's sports under AIAW with the present-day governance of women's sports.
3. What is the difference between the "right to become" and the "pressure to mimic"?
4. What led to the demise of AIAW, and how did it occur?

Suggested Reading

Boutilier, M. A., & SanGiovanni, L. (1983). *The sporting woman: Feminist and sociological dilemmas.* Champaign, IL: Human Kinetics.

Morrison, L. L. (1989). From the playing fields and courts. In C. S. Pearson, D. L. Shavlik, & J. G. Touchton (Eds.), *Educating the majority* (pp. 250-263). New York: Macmillan.

Nelson, M. B. (1991). *Are we winning yet? How women are changing sports and sports are changing women.* New York: Random House.

Slatton, B., & Birrell, S. (Eds.). (1984, July). The politics of women's sports [Special issue]. *Arena Review, 8*(2).

Note

1. Interested readers can find AIAW archival material at the following locations: the University of Maryland Archives; Eastern Kentucky University Archives (Region 2 materials); the University of Iowa (video collection of a four-day workshop featuring presentations from 10 AIAW presidents and discussions of the development of AIAW and women's intercollegiate athletics); and the National Association for Girls and Women in Sport in Reston, Virginia (records regarding the early history of sports leading to the creation of AIAW).

Reference

Association for Intercollegiate Athletics for Women. (1974). *Position paper on intercollegiate athletics for women.* Paper presented at the meeting of the Association for Intercollegiate Athletics for Women, Harrisonburg, Virginia.

III

Government and Policy

Complacency is a far more dangerous attitude than outrage.

—Naomi Littlebear

Women offer new leadership in an uninspired time, a new supply of energy in a void of scarcity, and the power of our collective spirit in a time of apathy.

—Yvonne Burke

A wild patience has taken me this far.

—Adrienne Rich

7

Governance
The First Half Century

PAULA WELCH

The origins of women's sport governance can be traced to basketball just prior to the turn of the twentieth century. Diverse women's basketball rules during the fledgling years of the sport signified the necessity to evaluate and establish uniform rules. Safe and appropriate rules for women were the paramount concerns expressed by the first generation of women who championed basketball. The National Women's Basketball Committee appointed during the June 1899 Physical Training Conference examined the numerous sets of rules and provided the foundation for the eventual governance of women's sports in the United States (Berenson, 1903). Senda Berenson, who pioneered the introduction of basketball for women, was the editor of the first guide, published in 1901. She continued to edit the official rule book, *Basket Ball for Women*, published by the American Sports Publishing Company, through the 1915-1916 edition.

The Early Years

Leaders in the American Physical Education Association (APEA) recognized the expansion of women's sports and replaced the National Women's Basketball Committee with the Committee on Women's Athletics (CWA) in 1917. By 1922 there were six committees functioning under the auspices of the CWA, concerned with basketball, field hockey, swimming, track and field, soccer, and publicity. The sports committees made, revised, and interpreted rules and set standards. Eline Von Borries (1941) notes that "from the beginning the work of the committee was of an investigating nature, although its ultimate aim was to formulate a comprehensive and varied program of athletic activities adapted to girls and women. It was neither a controlling nor legislative body" (pp. 8-9). Nevertheless, women in the physical education profession carefully orchestrated the development of women's sports and worked diligently to advance their philosophy, which emphasized sport for all.

Basketball initially gained momentum through limited interschool rivalry among schools and colleges, but competitive swimming and diving were promoted outside the context of educational institutions. Skilled swimmers and divers profited from the governance of their sport outside of educational environs. The Amateur Athletic Union of the United States (AAU), influenced by its authoritative president, James E. Sullivan, had blocked early attempts by women to gain access to AAU swimming and diving. Two months after Sullivan's death, a motion to sanction women's swimming was passed during the November 17, 1914, AAU meeting. Women first experienced preparation for national and international competition through swimming and diving. The Women's Swimming Association of New York (WSA) played a decisive role in organizing highly competitive sports for women. Charlotte Epstein invited swimming enthusiasts to a meeting, and on October 20, 1917, the WSA was officially established. The founding members agreed to promote interest in swimming, provide instruction, and offer opportunities for competition. The AAU's extensive network and its power to sanction meets increased aquatic opportunities and elevated competition to a national level.

The WSA's first athletes rose rapidly from novices to champions, bringing visibility to the club and respect for their dedication and accomplishments. The highly successful members of the WSA were the subjects of numerous newspaper articles in metropolitan New York City. Following unprecedented performances in the 1920 and 1924 Olympic Games, many of the WSA swimmers and divers toured resorts and attracted large crowds at aquatic exhibitions. National AAU swimming and diving competitions held in a variety of cities throughout the country advanced the sport. After the 1925 National AAU Indoor Swimming Championships, many of the participants remained in Florida and visited the state's resort cities. Sportswriter Ed Sullivan (1925) was impressed with the zealous reception of the 3,000 spectators who gathered at Ormond Beach, Florida, for a two-hour aquatic exhibition.

Sportswomen gradually gained acceptance through their involvement in country club sport. Their status was further abetted by columnists who chronicled women's sporting events in newspaper society columns. Beginning in the 1890s, tennis and golf became the prominent country club sports. As women excelled at the national and international levels in these country club-spawned sports, they gave even more credence to the role of women in sport. Furthermore, a fictitious paragon penned by the acclaimed illustrator Charles Dana Gibson brought the athletic young woman to the forefront. The Gibson Girl made her debut in 1890 and inspired women until World War I. She was the ideal American woman, personified as tall, beautiful, healthy, intelligent, and athletic. A Gibson admirer wrote: "He did more through his drawings to convince maidens East and West that they wanted to be athletic than any number of health crusades could do" (Downey, 1936, p. 25). The ubiquitous Gibson Girl was portrayed as a golfer, tennis player, cyclist, sidesaddle horseback rider, and swimmer. These independent factors gave rise to society's gradual acceptance of women in sports.

The Anticompetitive Era

Meanwhile, an international event in 1922 focused attention on the feud between women in the physical education profession and the AAU. Early in 1922, the AAU had declared interest in overseeing women's track and field. The AAU was not eager to expand its responsibilities by assuming such authority, but organization leaders recognized that the sport lacked supervision and direction and were concerned that no other group had organized the sport on a national level (AAU, 1922, pp. 25, 34). Objections from women physical educators had no effect when the AAU voted on the motion to sanction women's track and field; the AAU membership voted unanimously to assume jurisdiction over the sport ("Prout Again Chosen," 1922). Dr. Harry E. Stewart, a physiotherapist from New Haven, organized the American women's team that entered the 1922 Women's Olympic Games in Paris. Women members of the American Physical Education Association objected to the Paris meet on the basis that the sport lacked national-caliber status ("Report of the Business Meeting," 1922, p. 334). The meet amplified their growing skepticism that exploitation and elitism prevalent in men's sports would infiltrate women's sports programs. Nonetheless, Stewart's team sailed to Paris on the *Aquitania*. (The name of the Women's Olympics was later changed to the Women's World Games because of disapproval from the International Olympic Committee.)

The large number of draft rejectees during World War I prompted an evaluation of physical training in the armed services and physical activities among the nation's youth. Furthermore, there was growing dismay over the questionable practices occurring in men's intercollegiate athletic programs and what was perceived as an analogous trend in women's sports. Early in 1922, Secretary of War John W. Weeks and Secretary of the Navy Edwin Denby met with Lou Henry Hoover (Mrs. Herbert Hoover) to discuss the feasibility of establishing an organization that would set standards for girls' and women's sports programs. During the early discussions it was suggested that men and women should adhere to the same regulations. Mrs. Hoover consulted physical educators and determined that separate organizations were needed. The first meeting of the men's organization, the National Amateur Athletic Federation (NAAF), was held on February 21, 1923. Mrs. Hoover called a meeting of health, physical education, recreation, and YWCA leaders in Washington, DC, on April 6-7, 1923. Both men and women attended the conference. As a result of this Conference on Athletics and Physical Education for Women and Girls, the Women's Division was founded. The purpose of the Women's Division (WNAAF) was to offer ideas for others to implement. The field of membership included schools, colleges, and community organizations.

Among the original resolutions of the WNAAF were condemnations of highly organized and competitive sport for the select few. Furthermore, participation in international competition was deemed "inopportune." Special emphasis was placed on the involvement of competent women in administering, coaching, and teaching girls and women in sport. Women in the physical education profession greatly influenced the work of the Women's Division. The CWA and the WNAAF worked to oppose all forms of elite and varsity competition. These professionals operated in separate departments of physical education for women. Unencumbered by discrimination in leadership roles, they used their autonomy to shape collegiate sport. Many of the same women were members of multiple physical education and sport organizations.

By the late 1920s, women in the physical education profession considered the Committee on Women's Athletics an inadequate body to deal with athletics on a national level. As early as 1922, when Harry Stewart's team went to Europe, the CWA recognized the need to exert more control over women's sports. The committee became the Section on Women's Athletics and affiliated with the Council of the APEA in 1927. A section was more influential than a committee in that it was permitted to write a separate constitution, elect officers, and manage its own business. Following a process of reorganization, the body became the National Section on Women's Athletics (NSWA) in 1932. The NSWA gained representation on the Legislative Council of the APEA. The aims of the NSWA were to promote desirable athletic programs by (a) stating guiding principles and standards for administrators, leaders, officials, and players; (b) publishing an interpretation of rules governing sports for girls and women; (c) disseminating accurate information in periodicals and special publications, and through convention programs; and (d) stimulating and evaluating research in the field of women's athletics (Von Borries, 1941, pp. 10-13).

Another international track and field incident that drew the ire of physical educators occurred at the 1928 Olympic Games in Amsterdam. A controversy arose over the perceived lack of physical preparedness of finalists in the women's 800-meter run, which resulted in the elimination of the event. The "Olympic protest" was waged by women in an attempt to end women's participation in the Olympics. In January 1929, WNAAF inaugurated a crusade to end women's track and field in the Olympic Games. Olympic officials devoted nearly a day to deliberating the pros and cons of women's competition in international sport. A motion to end women's Olympic track and field was rejected. On May 25, 1930, a *New York Times* reporter credited the American delegates to the Olympic meeting, led by Gustavus T. Kirby, with the favorable outcome of the vote. Kirby was active in the Olympic movement and a prominent AAU leader.

The WNAAF merged with the NSWA in June 1940. Members of both groups believed the maintenance of sound program standards, as well as an expansion of services, was essential to the war effort (Waterman & Atwell, 1941). The NSWA became one of the largest and most active sections of the American Association for Health, Physical Education and Recreation (AAHPER) and, through its state representatives, formed a national network. Anyone could join the activities of the NSWA by paying membership fees to the AAHPER. Attendance at state, district, and national conventions, applying standards of the NSWA, and committee involvement constituted membership status. The extensive network established by sportswomen was effective in carrying out sports programs deemed appropriate for girls and women. Furthermore, rule revisions in official *Sports Guides* made available by the NSWA kept women apprised of the latest sports rules.

Women had greater success in reducing intercollegiate sport than in controlling counterpart programs in high schools. Interscholastic basketball for women was the bane of several generations of physical educators and by 1926 was considered a national problem (Coops, 1926). Many collegiate physical educators worked diligently to eradicate the negative aspects of interscholastic basketball. In 1927, Blanche Trilling, of the University of Wisconsin, delivered a speech at the annual meeting of the National Association of Deans of Women and specified the unacceptable practices rampant in interscholastic basketball. She condemned lengthy trips to contests, travel on school nights, male coaches, sending injured players into games, omission of physical examinations, general disregard of participants' well-being, play during menstrual periods, championship tournaments that produced nervous strain, overemphasis on winning and rivalry, derogatory comments from spectators, long seasons, involvement of only a small portion of the student body, and the neglect of other sports and school activities by basketball players (Trilling, 1930, pp. 11-12). Another practice that provoked considerable debate was the use of boys' rules by girls' teams. Physical educators were convinced that modified rules were the remedy for physical contact and serious injury. They maintained that the welfare of the participant was of paramount importance to women in sports leadership positions.

A national decline in women's interscholastic basketball was evident by the 1940s. Disciples of collegiate physical educators became convinced that interscholastic basketball was unacceptable, thus contributing to the curtailment of the sport. Their mentors had convinced them that "the evils of interscholastics far outweighed the values, and no good could ever come from girls participating in interscholastic basketball" (Hall, 1941, p. 27). The continuing existence of the competition was attributed to the prevalence of male coaches and officials. In small towns where there were few other diversions, townspeople supported teams. Josephine Fiske (1953), chair of the National Section for Girls' and Women's Sports (NSGWS), reported that qualified women physical educators were rarely hired in small schools, which constituted more than 60% of U.S. high schools. Principals were more inclined to hire men, who, because of their athletic experience, favored interscholastic sports.

Fighting Conventions

The 1948 Olympic Games revived the issue of international sport among NSWA proponents. The imminence of the 1948 London Olympic Games probably influenced the NSWA Olympic Study Committee's favorable

Field days, sports days, or class days usually involved a variety of sports rather than emphasis on one particular activity. Team composition was continually rearranged to foster social interaction. These events often commenced with a procession of the players. (Photo by Fred G. Chase; courtesy of Smith College Archives, Smith College)

report. The report was approved by the NSWA in April 1947. In general, the committee reiterated NSWA standards by calling for women coaches and emphasis on participants' health as primary considerations ("Participation in Games," 1947). The NSWA may have been persuaded to support women's participation in the Olympics not only because the organization could not prevent them from entering the Olympics, but also because of the participation standards.

The National Section for Girls' and Women's Sports continued publishing its motto: "The one purpose of sports for girls and women is the good of those who play." The motto, which was preeminent in the section's philosophy, inspired the work of its members. *Standards in Sports for Girls and Women*, published by the NSGWS in 1953, reaffirmed the social values of play rather than high performance in sport. The conservative approach to competitive sport was evident in the statement addressing "constructive competition," which called for equal opportunity for all participants and a variety of activities rather than emphasis on one activity. Moreover, the criterion that dealt with the effects of competition—"The goal of sports is not to find the 'best' team or player but to give opportunity and pleasure

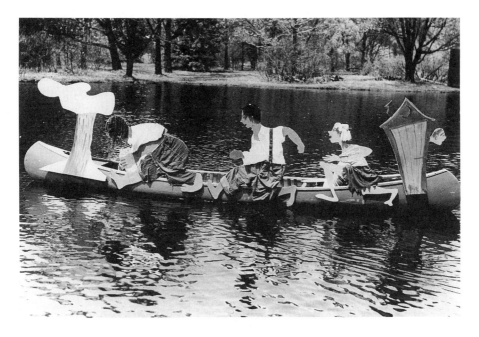

Using the theme of "Holidays," this winning float, titled "Sadie Hawkins Day," typified the activities that climaxed the Float Night segment of Smith College's Spring Field Day, 1947. (Photo by Fred G. Chase; courtesy of Smith College Archives, Smith College)

to all participating" (p. 24)—reiterated the philosophical position of sport for all.

The Legislative Board of the NSWA had appointed a committee in 1933 to write a statement on women's sports competition. The statement was revised in 1948 and again in 1953 by the Standards Committee. Specific standards were published in each *Sports Guide* and sold through AAHPER. The standards for acceptable competition published in the guides further solidified the women's network and were a source of revenue. Sportswomen became a part of the action, not only through committees, but also by contributing to the guides and revision of rules. Opportunities to suggest and place rule revisions on an experimental basis were hallmarks of the NSGWS.

Winds of Change

A 1954 NSGWS survey of attitudes toward competition, involving 813 women members of AAHPER, revealed a transformation from conservative views regarding competition at the national and international levels. The checklist, sent out by Naomi L. Leyhe of Indiana University, resulted in an 87.7% return. Survey respondents generally favored the involvement of young adult women in the Olympics. Opinions expressed by Leyhe's respondents regarding interscholastic and intercollegiate competition represented a partial departure from the traditional antagonism to high-performance sport. The survey showed that there was no majority opinion regarding team sport competition on either the interscholastic or the intercollegiate level. However, there was a definite swing toward acceptance of interscholastic and intercollegiate individual sports competition. Leyhe (1954) also reported that a large majority of the respondents were in favor of exploring the possibilities of AAU competition. The winds of change were apparent, but decisive action to establish high-performance sport was well over a decade away.

A New Beginning

In 1958, the NSGWS was officially elevated to division status and became known as the Division for Girls' and Women's Sports (DGWS). During the summer of 1958, a committee composed of representatives of the National Association for Physical Education of College Women (NAPECW) and the DGWS reported that there existed a consensus of opinion that sports programs did not meet the needs of highly skilled college women. The committee called for an expansion of sports into extramural competition (Jernigan, 1962, p. 26). By 1963 the DGWS, in its revised *Statement of Policies for Competition in Girls and Women's Sports*, offered more recommendations specifically calling for interscholastic and intercollegiate sport. While interscholastic competition was viewed more favorably, sweeping changes were in the future for college women. The 1963 publication cited the desirability of sport opportunities for highly skilled women that extended beyond intramurals. A committee was also established to study high-performance sport. Representatives of the DGWS, the Athletic and Recreation Federation of College Women, and the NAPECW formed the National Joint Committee on Extramural Sports for College Women (NJCESCW). The NJCESCW supported the DGWS sports standards but additionally called for specific involvement of women's physical education departments in scheduling, financing, and housing. Furthermore, the committee agreed that intercollegiate competition should not interfere with academic programs at institutions sponsoring competition and that excessive time demands should not be placed on participants.

The DGWS recognized the growing interest in highly competitive sport for girls and women and scheduled a study conference on competition in 1965. The purpose of the conference was to discuss problems and develop guidelines reflecting the best interests of girls and women (DGWS, 1965). Twenty men and women assembled for the conference. DGWS members from secondary schools, colleges, and universities were named to the committee. It should be noted that the National Federation of State High School Athletic Associations and the National Association for Intercollegiate Athletics were also represented at the meeting.

Intercollegiate athletics were still viewed as extensions of existing extramural programs. The report that came out of the conference focused on administration, leadership, and participants; it represented a radical change from previous DGWS philosophy, which had been steeped in a conservative form of competition. The major problems cited by the committee were philosophical differences concerning appropriate athletic competition for girls and women, provision of facilities, the financing of programs without gate receipts, and difficulty in finding competent women leaders, coaches, and officials.

While the guidelines of the committee were approved by the AAHPER Board of Directors and were a drastic departure from previous competition for girls and women, some of the earlier traditional practices were still strongly encouraged. For instance, informal social interaction for intercollegiate participants was recommended following competition. Furthermore, there was adamant opposition to athletic scholarships and regional and national tournaments.

Conclusion

The process of establishing governance of women's sports in the United States was set in motion by the National Women's Basketball Committee. During the first half of the twentieth century, women in the physical education profession operated comfortably with the doctrine of *in loco parentis*. Distinctly revealed in their standards for the conduct of sports programs was concern for the welfare of the participant and avoidance of the problems that had beset men's sports. These women believed that a focus on socialization and on participation by all in play days, sports days, intramurals, and interclass competition was the best approach for accomplishing their objectives. Attempting to combat the "evils in men's athletics" by designing their own prototype for girls' and women's sports, women in the physical education profession largely ignored the highly skilled woman athlete.

In contrast, AAU competition is well documented and launched American women into national and international sport. Industrial, community-based competition and the Young Women's Christian Association provided competitive experiences. There were some colleges and universities that offered intercollegiate sports for women but shrouded the competition by calling the events sports days or extramurals. Tuskegee Institute, now Tuskegee University, provided work-study scholarships for promising black female athletes. However, this was not a standard practice; it would be more than two decades before recruiting became commonplace and minorities were considered viable candidates.

Key Words

AAU

National Women's
  Basketball Committee

DGWS

Gibson Girl

participation versus competition

Sports Guide

sport governance

Discussion Questions

1. Contrast the work of the AAU and that of WNAAF during the anticompetitive era.
2. What function(s) did the *Sports Guides* serve? Does a comparable service exist today? Explain.
3. How did the new DGWS philosophy radically oppose the ideology that preceded it? How did it differ from current contemporary philosophy governing girls' and women's sports?

References

Amateur Athletic Union of the United States (AAU). (1922, November 20-21). [Minutes of the meeting held at the Hotel McAlpin, New York].

Berenson, S. (Ed.). (1903). *Basket ball for women*. New York: American Sports.

Coops, H. L. (1926). Sports for women. *American Physical Education Review, 31*, 1086.

Division for Girls and Women's Sports (DGWS). (1965). *Guidelines for intercollegiate athletics programs for women: Report of the DGWS study conference on competition for girls and women*. Washington, DC: American Association for Health, Physical Education and Recreation.

Downey, F. (1936). *Portrait of an era*. New York: Scribner's Sons.

Fiske, J. (1953, November). The Athletic Federation of College Women and the National Section for Girls and Women's Sports. *AFCW Sportlight*, pp. 1-3.

Hall, N. P. (1941). The swing of the pendulum. In *Official Basketball Guide 1941-1942* (p. 27). New York: A. S. Barnes.

Jernigan, S. S. (1962, April). Women and the Olympics. *Journal of Health, Physical Education and Recreation, 33*, 25-26.

Leyhe, N. L. (1954). *Attitudes toward competition in sports for girls and women* (Summary of NSGWS study). Washington, DC: National Section for Girls' and Women's Sports.

National Section for Girls' and Women's Sports (NSGWS). (1953). *Standards in sports for girls and women*. Washington, DC: Author.

Participation in games by women. (1947, December). *Sports Bulletin, 2*, 2.

Prout again chosen as head of AAU. (1922, November 22). *New York Times*, p. 25.

Report of the business meeting of the American Physical Education Association. (1922). *American Physical Education Review, 27*, 332-335.

Sullivan, E. (1925, February 17). Famous women aquatic stars please Ormond. *Florida Times-Union*, p. 10.

Trilling, B. M. (1930). Safeguarding girls' athletics. In B. M. Trilling, *Women and athletics* (pp. 11-12). New York: A. S. Barnes.

Von Borries, E. (1941). *The history and functions of the National Section on Women's Athletics*. Washington, DC: American Association for Health, Physical Education and Recreation.

Waterman, E. F., & Atwell, R. H. (1941). A merger of the Women's Division, NAAF. *Journal of Health and Physical Education, 12*, 36-37.

8

Letters Home
My Life With Title IX

LINDA JEAN CARPENTER

October 13, 1962

Dear Big Brother,

How's your first week of college going? As your sibling, I'm not supposed to say this, but I miss having you at home.

This week my PE teacher asked if anyone wanted to play Saturday in a volleyball sports day with eight other high schools. I jumped at the chance. You know how I like volleyball—how I play in the school yard every day during lunch hour. You should see the looks Mrs. Smith gives me every day when I come sliding into my 1 o'clock class just as the bell rings, all hot and sweaty with my smelly sneakers plopped on top of my books! Yes, there's still no locker room for girls, so we play in our street clothes. Think of those poor students who have to sit next to me in the afternoons! Ugh! At least they haven't started calling me "tomboy" yet.

Anyway, the sports day is something new. Instead of our annual play day, where we're put on teams along with girls from all the other schools, a sports day is a one-day tournament where we actually get to play as a school team. I wish we could use the gym so we could practice as a team, but the boys' teams have it scheduled. I guess the boys come first because they have a regular schedule of matches with other schools all semester long. They even have uniforms! I wish we did—we're supposed to wear white shirts and shorts so that we all look alike.

Mom has volunteered to drive us to the sports day. I don't think Principal Jones would let us use the school bus even if the boys' team didn't have it scheduled. We never get to use the bus—oh well. Guess what! I've been elected captain of the team, which is a bit scary. We won't have a coach so I'll have to be in charge. Wish me luck.

Love,

Little Sister

In 1962, the Division for Girls' and Women's Sports (DGWS) was the overseer of the nation's high school and college female athletes.[1] DGWS set the rules, trained the officials, and tried to protect the participants from potential evils. Any leadership, coaching, or supervision provided for female athletes by an individual school came almost universally from the ranks of female physical education teachers who, in large part, volunteered their services.

"Tomboy" was one of the kinder labels affixed to girls who participated in sports beyond the required physical education classes. A price was exacted by society in 1962 from those female athletes who sought excellence.

December 16, 1965

Dear Big Bro—

I'm enjoying college a lot. I'm captain of one of the 120 intramural teams here. Can you imagine 120 teams?! It's wonderful!

It's fun being on the varsity basketball team. This year we played five other schools and even had an overnight trip to one. You should have seen the old rattletrap school bus we rode in. Two flat tires and 13 hours later we arrived at our competition site—cold and very tired. The motel put a big dent in everyone's budget even though we split the room four ways. We all brought food from home so we wouldn't have to spend much on meals. Our uniforms consisted of white shorts and shirts and pinnies.[2] I thought we looked pretty good—AND we won our game, 35-27.

This year's new rules include two "rovers" out of the six players. The rovers play full court while the rest of us are either guards or forwards. When it's my turn to play the rover, I feel like a real klutz because I've never been taught how to be anything but a guard. So I don't shoot very much because I don't really feel comfortable shooting. Actually I'm not very good as a dribbler either because in junior high school the rules restricted us to one-third of the court and only three dribbles. They thought we were too fragile to move further than a third of the distance of the court. If the rover experiment is made permanent (the rule makers want to find out if we have the stamina), kids growing up playing the new rover rules will really have an advantage.

Tomorrow we start varsity tryouts for softball. I'm going to try for a spot on the team although I'm worried that the rough image softball has might rub off on me. You know what people say about softball players, and I don't want that said about me. We'll be playing six other schools this year, which sounds exciting. Hope all is well with you.

Love,

Li'l Sis

P.S. I was able to get season tickets for our men's basketball team for next year. Because they play 24 home games, whenever you decide to come for a visit it will most likely coincide with a game. The men play in the big 12,000-seat field house. The pep band, yell leaders, and mascot are there too, so even if the men's team continues to play poorly, it should still be fun. Maybe while you're here you'll have time to see one of our 5 women's home games. We play in the old women's gym, where there are no bleachers, no pep band, no yell leaders or mascot, but, unlike the men, we win our games. You'll have to bring an umbrella, because if it rains during our games the roof leaks (smile).

In the late 1960s considerable discussion was taking place within DGWS about the need for more competitive opportunities for females. Some feared that increasing college seasons beyond three to six games for the women would be taking a giant step toward the perceived excesses of men's athletics. Others felt that highly skilled women athletes were being deprived of opportunities to expand and test their talents. All were committed to the idea that on one basis or another, participation in sports helps females become more complete human beings.

May 29, 1971

Dear College Teacher Big Bro—

Thanks for your congratulatory note on our third winning season here at Urban U. I wish I got paid for coaching, but I don't. However, it is gratifying to see the impact on the team members' lives from their experiences together. I know it sounds corny, but even the traditional orange slices at half-time and the socials with the opposing teams after the games seem to bring a sense of camaraderie.

Thanks for your advice about remembering that my promotion will come not from coaching but from teaching and research-related efforts. I'm trying to keep a balance, but it's hard. I care very much about the team but I also have so many classes to teach and committee assignments that it's hard to do any research and writing.

The coach of the men's team receives seven release hours for coaching, while I receive none. His committee assignments are to "do-nothing" committees and his team has a much poorer record for the same length season as ours. My department chair is trying to get one release hour for me next season, but the chances don't look very good. I know it's not fair, but I guess that's the way the world is.

Love,

College Teacher Li'l Sis

In October 1971 the Association for Intercollegiate Athletics for Women (AIAW) was born as an independent child of its mother, DGWS. The AIAW expanded highly competitive opportunities for the nation's female college athletes. At the same time, Congress was being intensely lobbied concerning the passage of the anti-gender discrimination law called Title

IX. Some women felt that the proposed Title IX didn't go far enough; others were supportive but concerned about how it might be interpreted through regulations yet to be written. Still others believed that with the birth of the AIAW, opportunities would automatically expand for women and Title IX might cause a backlash against women, such as the refusal to promote female coaches and retrenchment of their programs.

It was a divisive, exciting, and unsettling time, filled with both promise and foreboding. Consciousness levels of women about the blatant and pervasive gender discrimination in society in general and sport in particular were quite diverse. For instance, many women were only beginning to realize that although there was hope for increased opportunities, equality was not a realistic probability. Others were perceived as radicals who had gone too far too fast in pursuit of feminist advocacy.

June 24, 1972

Dear Dr. Brother,

Congratulations on passing your Ph.D. orals. I'm proud of you, Doc. Where are you going to hang the diploma?

Today's newspaper included an article about yesterday's congressional passage of legislation called "Title IX of the 1972 Education Amendments." It has caused quite a stir here on campus. Some of the men's coaches were wringing their hands and grumbling that Title IX will mean the death of men's athletics. Some of my friends who have been lobbying for its passage say it is not as strong as they had hoped but it's better than nothing. Apparently the language of the legislation tracks similar civil rights legislation passed in the last few years for other areas of discrimination. Don't you think Congress could save time and paper by just passing legislation that says, "Don't discriminate based on any gratuitous classification" and be done with it? Let me know if you hear anything on your campus about what people think the impact of Title IX is going to be. I've read recently that this year over 90% of intercollegiate athletics programs for women are administered by females and that about 95% of the coaches of women's teams are females, too. I also read recently that this year women received only 1% of the budget of the nation's intercollegiate athletics budgets. Do you think Title IX will bring changes? It is a scary but exciting time.

Love,

Li'l Sis

Title IX says, "No person in the United States shall, on the basis of sex, be excluded from participation in, be denied the benefits of, or be subjected to discrimination under any education program or activity receiving federal financial assistance" (20 U.S.C. Section 1681 [a] [1990]).

The salient points upon which jurisdiction of Title IX rests concern (a) education programs, (b) discrimination based on sex, and (c) federal funds. Title IX applies to all *educational* programs within its jurisdiction (including private businesses that conduct educational programs funded by the federal government), but not to non-education-based business activities. Title IX protects against discrimination based on *sex*; it does nothing to protect against discrimination based on race, handicap, or age. Finally, it applies only to educational institutions that receive *federal* funding. Therefore, almost all public primary and secondary schools, and most colleges, are included. The inclusion of the reference to federal funding within the language of Title IX should not be taken to mean that Congress believed discrimination is acceptable at schools that receive no federal funding; rather, the reference is included to indicate the method of enforcement. A school that fails to comply with the requirements of Title IX risks the loss of its federal funding.

Title IX, passed by Congress on June 23, 1972, was patterned after the language in Title VI of the Civil Rights Act of 1964 (P.L. 88-352), which prohibits discrimination against students on the basis of race, color, or national origin. It is important to remember that Title IX applies only to sex discrimination and is gender neutral in its protection; it protects against discrimination based on a person's being male *or* female. Although proposed initially as an amendment to the Education Amendments of 1971, its successful proposal as part of the Education Amendments of 1972 came as a result of its reintroduction by Senator Birch Bayh. (For excellent and detailed historical reviews of Title IX as a tool for sports equity, see Harris, 1991; Heckman, 1992.) Congress built in a four-year period for elementary schools and a six-year period for secondary and postsecondary schools to arrive at Title IX compliance. Therefore, 1978 is referred to as the compliance date for colleges and universities.

The AIAW championed Title IX's application to sports. The National Collegiate Athletic Association (NCAA) adopted the opposite position. At the first AIAW Assembly, held in November 1973, an NCAA representative was invited in the spirit of collegiality, and he attended. The AIAW voted to have a joint meeting with the NCAA, the National Association for Intercollegiate Athletics, and the National Junior College Athletic Association to develop feasible working policies for the governance of athletic competition relative to the implications of Title IX. In early February 1974, NCAA leaders told the AIAW that they supported such a meeting, and one was scheduled. However, only a week or so later, the NCAA lost interest in meeting with the AIAW. Why? Well, in the interim, NCAA members learned of Washington's intent to include revenue sports within the jurisdiction of Title IX, and they were not pleased. So the NCAA canceled its meeting with the AIAW and announced plans to form its own NCAA Women's Committee, thus excluding the AIAW. The formation of this committee was politically significant because prior to this time the NCAA had demonstrated no interest whatever in taking responsibility for women's sports.

Other strategies were also being employed to limit the applicability of Title IX to athletics. For instance, in 1974 Senator John Tower of Texas authored, with the encouragement of the NCAA, the Tower Amendment, which, in its first version, excluded all intercollegiate athletics from the jurisdiction of Title IX. The amendment was later watered down to remove only "revenue" sports from Title IX jurisdiction, with language to be added to Title IX saying, "This section shall not apply to an intercollegiate activity insofar as such activity provides to the institutions gross receipts or donations required by such institutions to support that activity" (120 *Congressional Record* 15, 322[1874] and opposing statements in 121 *Congressional Record* 29791-95[1975]). The Tower Amendment, which made no requirement that a "revenue" program actually needed to provide any net revenue, was defeated by a joint Senate-House conference committee. The committee replaced the Tower Amendment with the Javitts Amendment, which, in very general terms, called upon the Department of Health, Education and Welfare to consider the nature of particular sports when developing its regulations for Title IX.

November 23, 1974

Dear Dr. Bro,

Thanks for your congratulatory note about my doctorate. It means a lot to me, coming from you.

Bad news at the college—the president came to our department meeting today and announced he is going to merge the men's and women's athletic programs "because Title IX requires it." Even though compliance with Title IX is not mandated until 1978, he said he was going to "start early." (I have my doubts whether mergers are required by Title IX.) Some of us tried to argue against merging, but the president's only "concession" was to appoint Jane, our current women's athletic director, as the new assistant athletic director reporting to Richard, the current men's AD (now titled THE athletic director!). I felt awful. I wonder what the future holds here at Urban U for our women's program of 17 varsities, JVs, and club sports.

I'll keep you posted.

Love,

Dr. Sis

In 1973, colleges averaged about 2.5 "varsity" (short seasons of 4 to 6 games) intercollegiate teams for women and 7.3 (full seasons of 20+ games in basketball, for instance) for men. During the 1972-1973 academic year about 700,000 girls participated in interscholastic athletics, compared with about 3.6 million boys.[3]

Pioneering research conducted by Carolyn Lehr and continued by Acosta and Carpenter demonstrated a continual decrease in the number of females serving as coaches and administrators of women's programs.[4] Other data, such as those gathered by Matheson (1980), demonstrate that even though it was neither required nor suggested by Title IX, previously separate men's and women's athletics departments were merged into single departments, with the head athletic director's position almost always being assumed by a male. Thus females were quickly losing control over their own programs.

The two situations found by Lehr and Matheson are not unrelated. The growth of participation opportunities for girls and women and the equal access to coaching jobs required by Title IX necessitated the hiring of coaches for new teams (as well as for many previously coachless teams). Because of the merging of departments, the person making the hiring decisions was more and more likely to be a male. The "old boy's club" often served as a hiring pool, and even when a woman learned of a job opening, her AIAW and DGWS experience was often discounted by the male athletic director, who could relate more easily to the NCAA experience of the male applicants.

Prior to the passage of Title IX, coaches for women's teams were paid very little, if anything, for their efforts. Coaching a girls' or women's team was truly a labor of love. In 1974, as schools began to move toward compliance, these coaching positions began to have greater remuneration attached to them, and therefore these same jobs began to be more attractive to males as employment options. Where women still served as administrators, fear of violating the spirit of Title IX often barred them from following any desire to hire only women to coach females.

Even though changes were taking place within athletics programs across the nation, the final nature of Title IX was still being questioned. In 1975, the regulations for Title IX were issued. They set out to expand on the meaning and application of the law. In mid-February 1976, after reviewing the regulations and finding they still included all of athletics within the jurisdiction of Title IX, the NCAA filed an unsuccessful lawsuit against the Department of Health, Education and Welfare, challenging the validity of the 1975 regulations (*NCAA v. Matthews*, 1976). The totally incorrect notion that Title IX's jurisdiction was restricted to nonrevenue sports continued to surface as a rationale to avoid gender equity within the entire program, or, in most cases, to avoid moving toward equity anywhere within the program.

July 30, 1978

Dear Dr. Bro—

The bad news here at Urban U seems to go on and on. The women's junior varsities in basketball, softball, and swimming have all been canceled for next season, and that's on top of last season's cuts. It saddens me to think of all the young women who won't have the chance for an intercollegiate experience. It seems ironic that the money saved from the canceled women's teams will go to feed the men's basketball and soccer teams. In addition, Jane, who used to be the women's athletic director when we had separate departments and then became the assistant AD when we merged with the men's department, will be replaced by a male next year. So, as of September, no women at all will be involved in the administration of our women's program. This is progress?

Love,

Dr. Sis

Although there was never any judicial, legislative, or administrative indication that the structure under which a school organizes its athletic programs needed to be merged, the NCAA seemed to encourage such a misunderstanding. At its August 1978 council meeting (following the June 1978 Title IX compliance date), the NCAA voted to offer technical assistance to the Department of Health, Education and Welfare in the implementation of Title IX Regulations. These were the same regulations that in 1976 the NCAA had claimed (via the *Matthews* case) to be invalid.

In 1979, the NCAA was again frustrated by the official interpretation of Title IX via the promulgation and adoption of the Athletics Policy Interpretation. The Policy Interpretation is the third main descriptive document for the meaning of Title IX, following, in relative order of power, the 1972 law and the 1975 regulations. The Policy Interpretation attempts to spell out, with some specificity, what is and is not allowed within athletics programs under Title IX jurisdiction.

The frustration of the NCAA at the specter of enforcement of Title IX's provisions was expressed by NCAA lawyers in a 1979 statement: "This whole Title IX effort can . . . be viewed as an attempt by the Federal government to take over control of higher education in America" (NCAA, 1979, p. 80). They went on to say that the proposed 1979 Athletics Policy Interpretation of Title IX was the result of "the entrenched thinking of HEW's cadre of young, female lawyers" (p. 64).

April 1, 1984

Dear Bro—

I wish things were going better for our athletics program here at Urban U. I find fulfillment in both my teaching and coaching but it sure seems to me that the athletics program has not done right by its women athletes in many years. Did you see a newspaper account last week of the U.S. Supreme Court's ruling in the Grove City v. Bell *case? The article said that, among other things, the Court defined the word* program *as found in Title IX to mean a subunit of the institution rather than the entire institution. This decision by the Supreme Court is not good.*

In effect, the case means that all college athletics programs are no longer under the jurisdiction of Title IX. Take, for example, our Biology Department. It receives a lot of federal research money, so if one of our students is discriminated against on the basis of sex by the Biology Department, the student could try to use Title IX to stop the discrimination. However, if that same student walks across campus and joins a team, the Athletics Department can discriminate against her all it wants to and get away with it because the athletic department does not receive federal funding. The federal money in the form of scholarships that comes to some of our athletes triggers jurisdiction over the Financial Aid Office but not over the Athletics Department. The result of the Grove City *decision makes no sense to me. I can't believe Congress intended to limit the effectiveness of Title IX to such an extent when they went to all the trouble of passing it in the first place.*

Unfortunately, the significance of the Grove City *case has not been lost on our AD. He has already canceled 10 of the women's athletic scholarships! Relying on goodwill for the achievement of equity is obviously foolhardy.*

There is talk of trying to get Congress to pass new legislation that would correct the problems brought by the Grove City *decision. How about joining the letter-writing campaign?*

Love,

Sis

The *Grove City* case involved a small private college in Pennsylvania that wished to remain free of any entanglement with the federal government. Therefore, when the government asked the college to sign a statement affirming the college's compliance with Title IX, the college refused to do so. The refusal was not based on a desire to discriminate, because there was no evidence that any gender discrimination was going on. Instead, the college's refusal to sign was a matter of principle—an expensive matter of principle, as it turned out.

The college's refusal to sign was, in itself, a violation of the Title IX regulations, and so the government decided to withhold any federal money going to Grove City College. The only federal funding in any way associated with the college was in the indirect form of Basic Education Opportunity Grants (BEOG). Student recipients, male and female alike, were deprived of their grants. It has always seemed odd that the government would take such an action at a school that was apparently *not* discriminating, while it totally ignored schools where gender discrimination was rampant.

In any case, Grove City College, on behalf of its students, sued for the reinstatement of the BEOG grants. The two main issues in the case were (a) Is indirect funding such as BEOG grants sufficient to trigger Title IX jurisdiction? and (b) Does the word *program* in the language of Title IX refer to the entire institution or only to the subunit actually receiving federal dollars? In the years the case took to move through the legal system, the government, originally in favor of enlarging jurisdiction, did a 180-degree turnaround, so that in the end the government *and* Grove City were basically arguing on the same side, for restricting Title IX's jurisdiction!

The Supreme Court decided that indirect federal funding such as BEOG grants is indeed sufficient to trigger Title IX jurisdiction. That was good news to the supporters of equity. But the Court defined the word *program* (undefined in the original legislation) to mean "subunit" of the institution, thereby effectively removing intercollegiate athletics, which, as a subunit, receives no federal dollars. Any federal scholarship money received by athletes triggers Title IX jurisdiction over an institution's financial aid office, but not over the athletic department. High school physical education and athletics still remained under Title IX because federal aid is typically poured into the central budget, tainting it all, and then is dispersed to individual subunits.

The Court defined the jurisdictional unit as only the specific program within the institution that actually receives federal funds. So college athletics and physical education programs were, in effect, removed from Title IX jurisdiction by the *Grove City* decision. This one decision accomplished what all the amendments and lobbying efforts of the NCAA had not. To this day, the name of Grove City College carries with it the negative image of being responsible for the loss of Title IX jurisdiction over intercollegiate athletics, even though the college itself was never accused of actual discrimination. It's odd how things turn out sometimes.

Within days of the *Grove City* decision, several colleges, no longer feeling the pressure to behave equitably, cut scholarships for their female athletes. Those coaches and athletes who had, prior to the decision, bravely filed intercollegiate athletics Title IX complaints with the Office of Civil Rights (OCR) against their schools saw their complaint files summarily closed. These closures included a number of cases in which investigations had already resulted in findings of discrimination and, most likely, also exposed those who had filed the complaints to unfettered retaliation.

For several years following the *Grove City* decision, Congress tried unsuccessfully to pass corrective legislation that would clearly state the definition of *program* to mean "entire institution." Then, in 1987, Congress finally passed the Civil Rights Restoration Act (CRRA) and all who cared about equity celebrated. When President Reagan vetoed the act, however, celebration ceased.

March 25, 1988

Dear Equitist Bro,

Guess what! Congress was able to override President Reagan's veto of the Civil Rights Restoration Act of 1987 yesterday. Finally, Title IX will apply on an institutionwide basis. It took Congress long enough to get its act together. Four years—a whole generation of college students—have come and gone since the Grove City *decision. Don't any of those guys in Congress have daughters?*

I surely hope that things will change quickly for the better here at Urban U now that Title IX's jurisdiction over athletics has been reinstated. I know you're glad the Civil Rights Restoration Act finally passed too—I know you were running out of paper to write your representatives with!

Thanks, Bro, for lending a hand. We've learned a lot through the four years of letter writing, haven't we—not the least of which is that inequity and discrimination diminishes us all.

Love,

Equitist Sis

When, on March 22, 1988, Congress passed the Civil Rights Restoration Act of 1987 over presidential veto, it corrected the Supreme Court's *Grove City* definition of *program* not only for Title IX but also for similarly worded legislation. The CRRA, in effect, redefined *program* to mean "entire institution," thus once and for all including athletics and physical education within Title IX's jurisdiction.

However, the four years from 1984 (*Grove City*) to 1988 (CRRA) were difficult ones for women in sport. Enforcement of Title IX had never really been allowed to flourish. From its 1972 birth, its application to athletics in general and to intercollegiate athletics in particular had been constantly under attack from the NCAA. In spite of valiant leadership, clear vision, and amazing growth, the female-led champion for gender equity in sports, the AIAW, succumbed in the early 1980s to NCAA attacks on its existence and its ability to direct women's intercollegiate athletics. Then the 1984 *Grove City* decision seemed like the last coffin nail for women in sport. By 1988, when the CRRA passed, some female sports leaders had lost heart in the struggle and had no faith in OCR's ability to effect change. From the 1988 passage of the CRRA to May 1990, only 35 intercollegiate Title IX complaints were filed with OCR. By February 1992 only 10 more had been filed, for a total of 45 in almost four years.

November 20, 1990

Dear Bro,

Happy Thanksgiving! Hope you have a festive and yummy dinner. Well, it's been over a year now that I've been telling the administration that Urban U is violating Title IX. I was astounded at the last meeting when the AD told me to "go ahead and sue because that will keep you and the women students out of the way for five or six years." So, after much thought and soul searching, I took his "advice" (don't think he expected me to) and I filed a Title IX complaint with the Office of Civil Rights on behalf of the students. Urban U's administration left me no choice. I will try to protect myself as much as I can because, from what I hear, fear of retaliation is one of the biggest reasons so few college athletic complaints have been filed since the passage of the Civil Rights Restoration Act. I sure hope I still have a job and that I will be strong enough to see this through. I know that I can count on your help. We've made a good team through the years, haven't we?

Love,

Sis

There are several ways to enforce the requirements of Title IX.[5] There is no required order to be followed, nor do plaintiffs/complainants have to give up any of the options just because they started with one and changed their minds. There is no need to exhaust in-house remedies before proceeding to an OCR complaint or lawsuit. However, there is a 180-day time limit for filing a complaint following a single act of discrimination. In the unusual situation in which only one specific act is being contested rather than a continuing pattern and practice of discrimination, the plaintiff/complainant should keep an eye on the calendar.

In-house complaints. Under the provisions of Title IX, each institution must have a designated Title IX officer. Often this responsibility is simply added to the job description of someone working in the college president's office, such as the affirmative action officer. The least threatening, least public way to try to enforce Title IX is to file an in-house complaint with the institution's designated Title IX officer. The officer is then required to investigate. This sounds friendly and easy and it may be so, but in the absence of goodwill on the part of the college administration, it is very seldom effective. The Title IX officer is usually someone whose job security is contingent on the goodwill of the president and therefore an unbiased, thorough investigation conducted by that person is unlikely.

OCR complaints. Anyone, regardless of whether he or she is directly connected to the athletics program, may file a Title IX OCR complaint. It is inexpensive (no lawyer is needed) and simple to file (a short letter will meet the basic requirements). The problem comes in OCR's ability to investigate and enforce Title IX issues. OCR is underfunded and, some would say, undermotivated by the executive branch. However, the enforcement of Title IX within athletics programs is one of the designated priority areas for OCR's 1991-1992 and 1992-1993 fiscal years. The small number of intercollegiate Title IX complaints filed with OCR since jurisdiction was restored by the Civil Rights Restoration Act lends credence to the belief that confidence in OCR's ability and will to enforce Title IX is not widely held.[6]

Once a complaint is filed, OCR has an internal, unenforceable proposed time line of 15 days to organize itself, followed by 120 days to investigate and develop a Letter of Findings. If the Letter of Findings includes a determination that the institution is failing to comply with a portion of Title IX, OCR will usually negotiate with the institution to develop a list of assurances and a time frame for their attainment. The assurances are promises made by the institution to OCR to the effect that specific steps to correct the inequities will be made, and it is the purpose of OCR to monitor these promises. In return for the assurances, OCR does not remove federal funding from the institution.

If the institution fails to keep its promises, OCR maintains its ability to cause federal funding to be terminated. OCR has never removed federal funding in an intercollegiate athletics case, so the threat is, to date, inconsequential, even though the amount of federal funding on most campuses is significant. Because there has been no real threat of losing federal funding, many colleges have chosen to delay action as long as possible, hoping the complainants will give up the struggle.

Title IX lawsuits. Unlike an OCR complaint, where the complainant can be anyone, a lawsuit requires the plaintiff to be someone with legal standing. Basically, this means that the person filing the lawsuit must have something to gain or lose from the outcome. Thus an athlete or coach would have legal standing, but a faculty member in a different department would not. The requirement of legal standing means that a lawsuit cannot be filed by a surrogate to protect the identity of the coach or athlete who is really the main actor. A coach can get someone outside the school to file an OCR complaint and officially appear to be uninvolved. A coach filing a lawsuit, however, would have to be named and known.

The lawsuit option needs an attorney's help and so the cost, even if an attorney will take the case *pro bono* (without charge), can be significant when transcripts, data gathering, and such are taken into account. An advantage to a lawsuit is that the plaintiff has the attorney's advocacy and thus does not feel as isolated as the filer of an OCR complaint. Remember, OCR is not an advocate; OCR looks at itself merely as an enforcement agency.

Following the February 26, 1992, U.S. Supreme Court decision in *Franklin v. Gwinnett County Public Schools* (90-918, U.S. Supreme Court, decided February 26, 1992, 911 F2nd 617, reversed and remanded), plaintiffs who select the lawsuit option may find attorneys more willing to take their Title IX cases. The unanimous *Franklin* decision makes it very clear that Title IX plaintiffs may seek compensatory damages and are not barred from seeking punitive damages as well for intentional discrimination. Because of the *Franklin* decision, it is no longer strategically sound for an institution to drag its feet when charged with gender-based discrimination. The *Franklin* case will probably lead to earlier settlements in discrimination cases because of the potential for punitive damages. Similarly, because of the potential for damages, and thus greater compensation, more attorneys are now likely to offer their services to plaintiffs.

March 15, 1992

Dear Brother,

This has been quite a month for our old friend Title IX. Did you see in the paper the article about the Office of Civil Rights finding in favor of the complainants at Brooklyn College? OCR issued the strongest Letter of Finding ever issued in an intercollegiate athletics case. The people at Brooklyn filed a month after we did so all of us at Urban U are eagerly awaiting our Letter of Finding. It should arrive any day now, don't you think? OCR certainly doesn't seem to follow the 135-day time line it sets for itself in Title IX cases, does it? Brooklyn's decision took 14 months! In addition, the assurances in the Brooklyn case will take another 7 months to all be in place. But at least they are moving in the right direction.

Also, did you see the summaries of the just-released NCAA Gender Equity Study? The NCAA undertook the study at the urging of the National Association of Women Collegiate Athletic Administrators. The summary says some major segments of the NCAA provide only 10% of the recruiting budget to women compared to their men's program. As they say, it doesn't take a rocket scientist to see that if the recruitment is so poor and the support for coaching, uniforms, equipment, scholarships, etc. is shoddy, it is understandable why only a third of the athletes are women even though more than half of the student body is female.

A friend was telling me that as bad as the NCAA study says things are, things might be even worse. Evidently, on a number of campuses the senior woman administrator, or SWA (the highest-ranking female—although the position is sometimes held by a male), never saw the data before they were sent to the NCAA. And when the SWA finally did see a copy, it painted a much more equitable picture than reality.

Anyway, after the study's release, Dick Schultz, the executive director for the NCAA, said that equity is a moral issue in addition to being a legal issue and can no longer be ignored. The NCAA has appointed a task force to decide how to move toward equity, and their first task is likely to be to define equity. I hope they don't spend years trying to define it. Equity is living up to the requirements of Title IX. Why not have the NCAA say that if your school doesn't meet those requirements, it can no longer compete in NCAA activities?

Some of the Policy Interpretations for Title IX are going to be reconsidered, according to Michael Williams, OCR's head. I hope they are rewritten so that the assignment of financial aid is not considered equitable unless it is proportional to the gender makeup of the student body instead of the athletic participation, as is now the standard. For instance, here at Urban U 56% of the students are female, but only 33% of the athletes are female. I think 56% of the financial aid should be used for female students, not just 33%. I feel certain that the reason only 33% of our athletes are female is that there have been so many years of discriminatory practices, including lack of financial aid. Such practices should not be rewarded with additional financial aid being given to the men. To do so seems to me to ignore the very basic fact that financial aid is, in reality, a recruitment tool.

Makes sense to me! Sorry for being on my soapbox, but I guess I'm just getting tired of waiting for OCR and the NCAA to do what has been mandated as the "right thing" for 20 years.

Thanks for the news clippings about the Franklin case. Yes, I agree, it is a very useful decision. It finally puts teeth into Title IX. Suddenly, it has become cheaper to be equitable than to discriminate. Moral pressure hasn't been persuasive in very many cases. Wallet pressure might make the difference.

As frustrating as it has been to see our students discriminated against over the years, I do think there will be changes. There seems to be a critical mass of people, men and women alike, who realize that 20 years is long enough.

Let's get together for dinner this June 23 to celebrate Title IX's twentieth birthday, as brother and sister, and as equitists who have fought together for a long time.

> *Love ya,*
>
> *Me*

Key Words

Title IX	*Grove City v. Bell*
sex discrimination	Civil Rights Restoration Act
equity	*Franklin v. Gwinnett County*
gender discrimination	*Public Schools*
gender equity	

Discussion Questions

1. What have been the positive and negative outcomes of Title IX? Do you think the positives outweigh the negatives?

2. Title IX has been in existence for more than 20 years. With the benefit of hindsight, how would you have altered the strategies and efforts of gender equitists in the past 20 years to achieve a swifter and more complete attainment of equity?

3. Title IX applies not only to students but also to employees of educational institutions. What do you think is the impact of the loss in female representation within the ranks of coaching and administering women's athletics and the absence of women in men's athletics?

4. Title IX requires every institution within its jurisdiction to have a Title IX officer on campus. Who is yours? What is the nature of this person's job?

Notes

1. DGWS was a subunit of the American Association for Health, Physical Education and Recreation (now the American Alliance for Health, Physical Education, Recreation and Dance), and is today the National Association for Girls and Women in Sport (NAGWS).

2. Pinnies were cloth minivests that had numbers printed on the back and front. They were used by all teams at a school so that a more official uniform was not needed.

3. The U.S. Commission on Civil Rights (1980) publication *More Hurdles to Clear* contains a variety of useful secondary statistics concerning the fiscal and participation data in interscholastic and intercollegiate athletics during the 1970s.

4. Carolyn Lehr, at the University of Georgia, Athens, conducted landmark surveys that provided a baseline for the status of women in intercollegiate athletics in the early to mid-1970s. Data for 1977 through 1992 on the status of women in intercollegiate athletics collected by R. Vivian Acosta and Linda Jean Carpenter, Brooklyn College, demonstrate a pattern of increased participation and decreased leadership by women in intercollegiate athletics. Acosta and Carpenter's (1992) data indicate that in 1992 only 48.3% of the coaches of women's intercollegiate teams were women (down from 90+% in 1972) and only 16.8% of women's programs were headed by women (down from 90+ in 1972). No females at all are involved in the administration of 27.8% of women's programs. Only 2% of men's teams are coached by women, and half of those are in sports where the men's and women's teams often practice together, such as swimming and tennis. For more information, contact Acosta and Carpenter directly at the Department of Physical Education, Brooklyn College, Brooklyn, NY 11210.

5. The NAGWS publication *Title IX Toolbox* provides a great deal of specific information about the methods of pursuing rights under Title IX.

6. Only 411 interscholastic athletics Title IX complaints have been filed in the past 10 years, according to Jay Goldman (1991).

References

Acosta, R. V., & Carpenter, L. J. (1992). *Women in intercollegiate sport: A longitudinal study—fifteen-year update 1977-1992.* Unpublished manuscript, Brooklyn College, Brooklyn, NY.

Goldman, J. (1991, December). Leveling the playing field for female athletes. *School Administrator,* p. 21.

Harris, C. J. (1991). The reform of women's intercollegiate athletics: Title IX, equal protection and supplemental methods. *Capital University Law Review, 20*(3), 691-721.

Heckman, D. (1992). Women and athletics: A twenty year retrospective on Title IX. *Entertainment and Sports Law Review, 9*(1), 1-64.

Matheson, M. C. (1980, February). *Selective study of women's athletic administrative settings involving AIAW Division I institutions.* Unpublished manuscript, University of Pittsburgh.

National Association for Girls and Women in Sport (NAGWS). (n.d.). *Title IX toolbox.* Reston, VA: Author.

National Collegiate Athletic Association (NCAA). (1979). *Convention proceedings.* Mission, KS: Author.

NCAA v. Matthews, Civ. Action No. 76-32-C2 (D. Kan.) (1976).

9

Secondary School Programs
Diversity in Practice

MARY C. LYDON

Throughout the United States, governance and policy-making practices at the secondary school level are quite diverse. The philosophy that dictates policy is only as progressive as the individuals in the decision-making positions. Of primary importance are issues related to gender equity, ethnic and racial sensitivities, ethics and morality in sport, and budgeting constraints.

Governing Policies

The governance of high school athletics is controlled at the local level by an organization that may be known by various names, including interscholastic association or activities association. Individual educational agencies may or may not be members of their local high school association. The decision as to whether or not to join is made by local school committees. The local governing agencies of all 50 states are members of the National Federation of State High School Associations (NFSHSA). Additionally, 10 interscholastic organizations from the Canadian provinces, the Canadian School Sports Federation, and the associations of Bermuda, Guam, Republic of the Philippines, St. Croix, and St. Thomas-St. John have nonvoting affiliations. Membership is by application, and agreement to comply with NFSHSA membership requirements is implicit.

One representative from each of the 50 states sits on the National Council, which functions as the legislative body of the federation. An executive committee is elected from the national council membership; it is required that at least one representative from each of the eight regions be included.

National Federation Programs

"The National Federation is both a service and regulatory organization . . . founded to provide service to individual state associations by controlling interstate athletic events" (National Federation of State High School Associations, 1991, p. 15). It currently serves 20,000 schools as it works to improve interscholastic athletic conditions. The services provided by the NFSHSA to the states include the following:

- publication of the *National Federation News*
- maintenance of national records and resource center
- training for athletic directors, coaches, and officials
- management of a chemical health program
- maintenance of national events such as the High School Activities Week, the Dreamers and Doers program, spirit activities, and interstate and international events
- study and authorization of rule changes in sports
- sports equipment testing for safety and protection
- administration of an awards program

High school athletics are controlled by local governing agencies that are designated to act on behalf of the secondary school principals. Great variance exists among the individual states. Governance may range from complete autocratic control to democratic representation. Autocratic governance gives all power and decision-making authority to one person. In situations such as this, women's programs are not represented and no voting power is allocated to women. Consequently, decisions earmarked to improve a specific boys' sport are frequently implemented with complete disregard for the impact they will have on the girls' program. Conversely, democratic governance affords equal representation from both girls' and boys' sports programs with full voting power. The backlash from Title IX has created a situation in which females in decision-making positions have decreased significantly, although the number of female participants has increased (see Figure 9.1).

Everyday Atrocities

The practices followed in hiring coaches remain problematic. Unfortunately, what has become standard practice in many athletic departments can be illustrated by the following examples.

Act 1, Scene 1 (setting: office of the athletic director of an urban school system). Vacancies have occurred in the athletic department: A boys' varsity soccer coach is needed and a girls' varsity soccer coach is needed. As the curtain opens, five interviewers are seated around a table, discussing the relative qualifications of the three male candidates who have just been interviewed for the boys' varsity soccer coaching position. Most of the conversation centers on one candidate who appears to be the favorite, and comments such as the following are heard.

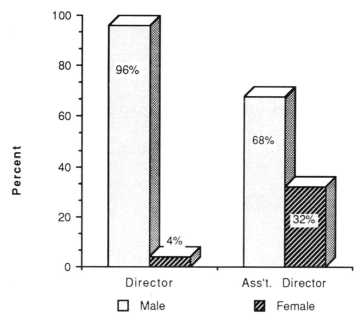

Figure 9.1. Administrators in High School Federations, 1991-1992
SOURCE: Data are from the National Federation of High School Associations (1991).

"He certainly has the qualifications for the position."
"His coaching background is extensive."
"He is a coach who makes demands on his players."
"He enforces the rules."
"He wants to win."
"He demands excellence."
"He is aggressive and demanding."

When the vote is taken, this candidate is approved unanimously by the screening committee. His name will be recommended to the superintendent, who will, in turn, submit his name to the school committee for appointment.

Act 1, Scene 2 (setting: same office, two hours later). Two candidates have just been interviewed for the girls' varsity soccer coaching position, one male and one female. As the curtain opens, five interviewers are seated around a table, discussing the relative qualifications of the two candidates, and the following comments are heard:

"He certainly has the qualifications for the position."
"She certainly has the qualifications for the position."
"His coaching background is extensive."
"She has good coaching experiences."

"He is a coach who makes demands on his players."
"She puts too much pressure on her players."
"He enforces the rules."
"She is inflexible."
"He wants to win."
"She pushes too much to win."
"He demands excellence."
"She is compulsive and demanding."

When the vote is taken, the male candidate receives three votes, the female candidate two votes. The name of the male candidate will be recommended to the superintendent, who, in turn, will submit his name to the school committee for appointment.

Such scenarios are repeated frequently in public school systems throughout the United States. Manipulation of the adjectives applied to male and female candidates for coaching positions results in women's being described in terms that imply or overtly state negative traits, whereas the very same attributes are described in positive ways when applied to male candidates. This is discrimination of the most insidious type. Ostensibly, everything is aboveboard. No one can deny that a woman has been interviewed, but she simply has not been found to meet the "qualifications."

Many individuals involved in sport have sat on screening committees in which male coaches have been rehired with the stipulation that they have one more year to "clean up their act." If they don't, their jobs will be reopened. Screening committees often give coaching jobs to untrained, unskilled, and inexperienced males because "they teach in the building," "they can learn the rules," or "they have families to support." Men hired to coach girls' teams have been known to call women physical educators before their first games, asking for a copy of the sport's rule book or for a crash course in how the game is played.

Women who have been candidates for these positions passively sit back and accept the hiring of male coaches for girls' teams without challenge or confrontation, even when they know that they are significantly more qualified than those who are hired. They refuse to demand that affirmative action policies be followed. They will not, for whatever reason, stand up and be counted. It goes on, ad infinitum. Participation by girls and women in sports programs has increased dramatically in the past 20 years. However, the number of women in coaching and administrative jobs associated with girls' and women's sports has plummeted.

Women Administrators and Coaches:
In Danger of Extinction

Administrative Positions

Have women left coaching, or are they being left out? The majority of administrators in education who are responsible for the hiring of sports

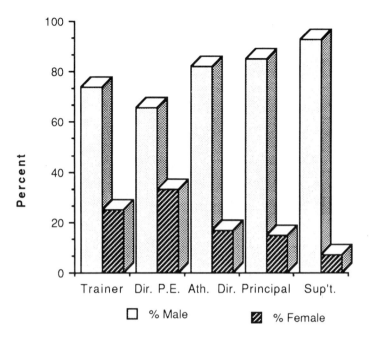

Figure 9.2. Decision-Making Roles by Gender
SOURCE: Data are from Clell Wade (1990-1991).

administrators, athletic directors, and coaches are men. As in other enterprises, they rely on their professional contacts when positions must be filled. The "old boys' network" assures that males are the first approached and the first considered for available sports administration and coaching positions. This is a situation that is replicated in high schools as well as in colleges.

Recent data comparing the number of male to female directors indicate that the situation has not improved since the enactment of Title IX. Men still outnumber women anywhere from 65% to 100%, even though women make up 57% of the work force. As Figure 9.2 shows, the ratio of male to female athletic directors does not even approximate equality. Males overwhelmingly control budgets, administrative positions, and power in high school athletic departments. Until more women move into administrative positions in high school athletic departments, little change will occur. Some 93% of superintendents, the CEOs of school districts, are males. They are the major power holders in public school systems throughout the United States, and they hire the principals, of whom 85% are males. Principals, in consultation with superintendents, hire the directors of athletics and directors of physical education (Clell Wade, 1990). Figure 9.2 illustrates gross gender inequities among administrative positions at the public school level. This is singularly significant when one remembers that more than 57% of our population is female, with very little representation in the decision-making arena of public education. The lack of viable female role models for our students is most apparent.

Recent reports and articles in trade magazines and journals indicate that women in business and industry are experiencing prejudice and shutouts as well. In a recent article in *Fortune*, Fierman (1990) noted that "only a minuscule number of women have top jobs at America's major companies" (p. 40). A *Fortune* survey of 4,012 people who were listed as the highest-paid officers and directors of their companies showed that less than 1% (19) were women. The major reasons cited for the lack of women in top administrative positions were "stereotyping and preconceptions" of women and their behavior by those holding hiring power.

We need females in leadership positions who believe they are competent and effective—and that includes coaching and officiating male and female sports teams. "The lack of female role models in leadership and decision-making roles is crippling the next generation of young women" (Carpenter, 1990).

Coaching Positions

Coaches of high school girls' varsity teams have changed significantly in the past 20 years. Unfortunately, situations still exist in which some women who are qualified or overqualified to coach girls' sport teams believe that they are not qualified, while exactly the reverse is true for some men. In American culture, some activities seem to carry gender designations—the assumption that biology is destiny. Some men tend to believe that their own Little League competition or other youth sports participation prepares them to assume any sport coaching position. Women, in contrast, tend to believe that they are not qualified to coach even when they have competed at the varsity level in both high school and college and hold degrees in physical education. This is true even among our young professionals in physical education who have benefited from the impact of Title IX. Many feel that they are not qualified to coach even though they have participated in extensive high school varsity programs, have gone to college (many on athletic scholarships), and have played at the varsity level at Division I, II, and III colleges. Somewhere the system is failing.

The coaching ranks of women in high school sports have decreased markedly since the much-heralded passage of Title IX. Those who fought so hard for this landmark legislation could not have foreseen that a significant majority of the power positions in women's sport—administrative, coaching, and officiating positions, as well as jobs as trainers, equipment managers, and sports information directors—would be held by males. Until 1972 and the passage of Title IX, the majority of decision-making positions in women's sports were held by women. They were not considered valuable positions because they involved *no money* and *no power*. Now, 20 years after the passage of Title IX, quite the reverse is true. Women are in the minority in the power structure of high school athletics, even though the number of high school female athletes has increased significantly.

A gender equity study conducted in 1985 for the National Federation of State High School Associations showed that 98% of the boys' teams were coached by men and that 58% of the girls' teams were coached by

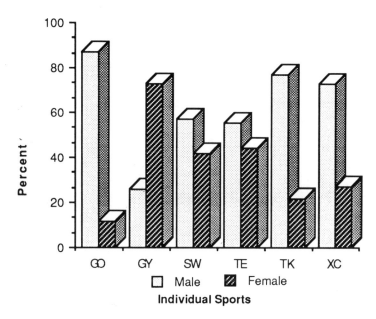

Figure 9.3. Percentage of Coaches by Gender: Individual Sports
SOURCE: Data are from True (1992).

women (Delano & True, 1986). When coed sports were examined, 84% of the teams were coached by men and 16% by women. The total averages show that 75% of all teams were coached by men and 25% by women—hardly equity. However, in some states, the number of women coaching women's teams has increased by a small margin.

Historically, approximately 90% of girls' and women's teams at the high school level were coached by women. Today the number of women coaches (and officials) of girls' varsity sports programs has decreased from the level it enjoyed in 1972. Figures 9.3 and 9.4 illustrate the proportion of male coaches of girls' varsity teams. A few sports—lacrosse, volleyball, and field hockey—still have at least 50% of teams being coached by women. However, unless action is taken on the local level to increase the pool of qualified female coaches, they may be headed for extinction.

Networking and Mentoring

Women need to extend their networks beyond local and regional borders. The feminist movement of the early 1970s created job opportunities in fields from which women were previously barred. Women are now in leadership positions where both networking and mentoring have commenced. This essential function provides stability to the infrastructure and assures the continuation of control and power.

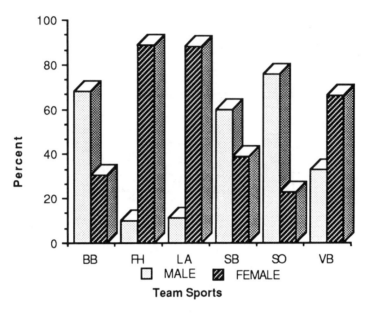

Figure 9.4. Percentage of Coaches by Gender: Team Sports
SOURCE: Data are from True (1992).

Women, however, are new to networking. Traditionally, women have been socialized to compete against other women and to assume subservient roles in all aspects of life. Their knowledge of financial strategies has been practically nonexistent. They have had no control over athletic budgets, and such control is generally equated with power and decision-making authority. We need women administering on the playing fields and in the gymnasiums, working with youth, mentoring and serving as role models, demonstrating that women are effective coaches, trainers, and officials. Women who are currently in the forefront of women's athletics must stand up and be counted. They have a responsibility to recruit, support, and empower other women, who, in turn, have the same responsibility. The women who have benefited from Title IX must come forward and pay back some of what has been given to them.

Key Words

policy-making   women coaches
board of control   women administrators
Nation Federation of State   networking
  High School Associations

Discussion Questions

1. What are the two most compelling problems facing girls' high school athletics today? How can these problems be addressed? What strategies would you employ to create change?
2. Compare the structure of governance for high school athletic programs to that of collegiate athletic programs.

References

Carpenter, L. J. (1990, September 14). Women participate more, missing from leadership roles. *USA Today*, p. 11C.

Clell Wade Coaches Directory. (1990). *Clell Wade coaches directory, 1990-1991*. Cassville, MO: Author.

Delano, L. C., & True, S. S. (1986). *Breakdown of the percentage of men and women athletic administrators and the percentage of women coaches at the high school level*. Kansas City, MO: National Federation of State High School Associations.

Fierman, J. (1990, July 30). Why women still aren't getting to the top. *Fortune*, pp. 40-62.

National Federation of State High School Associations. (1991). *National Federation handbook, 1991-1992*. Kansas City, MO: Author.

True, S. S. (1992, May). *High school coaching data*. Kansas City, MO: National Federation of State High School Associations.

10

Political Analysis
Gender Equity Strategies for the Future

DONNA A. LOPIANO

Gender Equity in Sport:
A Status Report

- Some 35% of all college athletes are women, but women constitute more than half of the college student population (National Collegiate Athletic Association, 1989).
- Some 36% of all high school athletes are women, but women constitute more than half of the high school student population (Mansnerus, 1992).
- Women still participate in only one-third of Olympic events (Murray, 1991).
- In 1972, 90% of all collegiate women's athletics programs were governed by women administrators; today the proportion is 16% (Acosta & Carpenter, 1990).
- Among the 106 NCAA Division I-A big-time football-playing institutions in 1991-1992, only one woman served as athletics director over men's and women's combined athletic programs (Lopiano, 1991).
- Among the other 192 NCAA Division I institutions in 1991-1992, only six women headed merged departments of men's and women's athletics (Lopiano, 1991).
- In 1991-1992 there were only nine NCAA Division I programs with administratively separate women's athletics programs headed by women (Lopiano, 1991).
- In 30% of our nation's collegiate athletics programs, there are no women athletics administrators (athletic directors, associate directors, or assistant directors) (Acosta & Carpenter, 1990).
- In 1990-1991 there were only 14 women among the 121 conference commissioners in the nation. Of these women, 13 served as heads of women's-sports-only conferences. Only 1 woman held a commissioner's position in a conference governing both men's and women's sports. Of the 19 major Division I conferences, there are no women serving as conference commissioners (Lopiano, 1989).

- In 1972, 90% of all women's collegiate teams were coached by women. In 1990, less than 48% of all women's teams were coached by women and less than 1% of all men's teams were coached by women (Acosta & Carpenter, 1990).
- Women athletics administrators' median salaries are $10,783 less than those of their male counterparts (Uhlir, 1987).
- On the average, a female head basketball coach in college earns $23,000 less per year than her male counterparts. In addition, *USA Today* reports that at many schools the women's head coach makes less than the men's assistant coaches (Goodman, 1989).
- The proportion of female minorities in college coaching and administration is only 5% (Women's Sports Foundation, 1991).
- Women's sports receive only 29 pages of coverage for every 527 pages of men's sports and only 1 newspaper photo for every 22 of men's sports. *Sports Illustrated* featured 173 men and only 8 women on its covers from 1954 through 1989 (not counting the annual swimsuit issues). Of the 8 women appearing on covers, 5 were athletes and 3 were models (Murray, 1991).
- Women receive less than 33% of the college athletic scholarship dollar (National Collegiate Athletic Association, 1988) and only 18% of the college athletics operating budget (Raiborn, 1989).
- Equal-opportunity employment laws appear to be virtually ignored in the hiring process experienced by female candidates for coaching and administrative positions (Delano, 1988).

Progress in the participation of female athletes in interscholastic and intercollegiate sport has been made in the 20 years since the adoption of Title IX of the 1972 Education Amendments Act (P.L. 92-318; Title IX—Prohibitions of Sex Discrimination, July 1, 1972, now codified as 20 U.S.C. § 1681[a]). However, despite the fact that girls and women constitute half of our secondary and postsecondary school populations, they are receiving only one-third of the total participation opportunities, and the benefits associated with those opportunities are far fewer than those afforded male athletes. At the same time, there has been a significant and steady decline in the percentage of women coaches and administrators involved in athletics programs. Something must be done to even the playing field for women in sport.

The Need for Both Liberal and Radical Feminist Strategies to Achieve Gender Equity in Sport

The distinction between liberal and radical feminism posits the liberal as believing the system is capable of change while the radical denies such a possibility and works to destroy the system, knowing that whatever arises from the ashes will be better. Radical feminists contend that the patient and compromised strategies practiced by most liberals work against revolution and significant change because these strategies result in extending the life of a system that effectively continues to discriminate against women. Liberal feminists condemn the efforts of radicals, contending that extremist efforts increase the resistance of the system to change.

It is ineffective to argue over which of these methodologies is better. In reality, both liberal and radical efforts are essential to the purpose of achieving gender equity in sport. The two approaches complement each other. The radical feminist makes the liberal feminist more effective by making possible the perception that the liberal is a comparatively "reasonable" person. The harder the radical works, the easier the job of the liberal, and the greater the possibility of real change. When the system must choose between the extreme and the more moderate solution, the moderate solution will prevail. If the moderate solution is the only choice put forth, it becomes the extreme, and the existing reality is perceived as more attractive. The odds for significant change are much better when both extreme and moderate choices are on the table.

Liberal and radical forces acting on the system simultaneously will change the system rather than cause its demise. This argument, of course, rejects the radical's contention that the system must be destroyed and supports the liberal's contention that the system can be changed. This process is based on the belief that it is impossible to imagine that all feminists would agree to be radical. Thus there will always be liberals within the system.

In sport, this process is supported by the belief that sport institutions, dominated by males, are huge, unyielding dinosaurs. The masculine culture of sport is slow to change and virtually impossible to destroy by virtue of its sheer bureaucratic form. Even in the face of the exploitation of student-athletes, continued cheating in the recruiting process, discrimination against blacks and women, and wasting of critical financial resources to feed the insatiable men's revenue sports of football and basketball, everyone is still both fearful and respectful of the dinosaur. The system would rather build it a larger, more cumbersome cage than kill it.

Another reason for promoting the "liberal" approach to sport reform is ultimately political and practical. Immediate attainment of gender equity in sport would require a massive redistribution of financial resources away from men's athletics and to women's athletics. As the support of men's programs was decreased and compromised with regard to the range of men's sports budgets among all institutions, competitive parity would be an inevitable result. It would be political suicide for college presidents to advocate to their alumni any change of college or high school sport that produces a perception of a "less successful" institutional male sports program. It would be foolish to expect 1,000 college presidents or even a majority of the same to stand up and commit mass suicide in the name of gender equity.

While there must be a redistribution of resources, parity must be approached in a very careful way. By pursuing parity under the guise of sport reform over time, there is a chance of maintaining the pecking order while compacting budgets. This alternative may be viewed as walking the tightrope of parity. Sport reformers push for legislation that makes the big spenders spend less. As the big spenders lose the sheer advantage of more money, their success more closely approaches the vast majority of programs in their class. What this really means is that the big spenders are still able to retain their superiority over those just below them, but the gap between the competitors closes. The reform process is not hurt as long as the big programs retain their relative status in the pecking order even if gaps are reduced. Over time, less successful win-loss records will be accepted as long as teams still win conference championships or make bowl appearances, and reform can continue as long as the pecking order is not harmed by movement toward parity.

The fate of radical feminists in sport is clear. They live the existential dilemma. They work incessantly for a result that is unachievable and suffer the despair of never being able to have the "clean slate" start that would produce a better result than what occurs under liberalism. The rewards of the radical are martyrdom (often in the form of termination of employment), knowing that one has tried to do the right thing and made a better life possible for others, and pushing the liberal feminist agenda further to the left than the liberal feminist would be able to achieve independently. However, the efforts of both liberals and radicals are essential to the purpose of achieving gender equity in sport.

Coordinating the Radical and Liberal Agendas

If radical and liberal strategies must be implemented simultaneously, is it possible or desirable to have coordinated leadership or a single organization that advances both agendas? The answer is clearly no. Even if the membership were agreeable, it would be difficult for a single organization overtly to advance both radical and liberal feminist strategies. To do so would lessen the effectiveness of the overall strategy of the organization. It is more likely that the outcome of this approach would be debilitating internal disagreements between competing factions. At best, the liberal feminists would seek to soften the radicals' stance and the radicals would urge the liberals to be more demanding. At worst, there would be an outright philosophical war. Such a process would waste the energies of both groups and would decrease overall the results of the organization.

A more effective concept utilizes both groups playing off one another. However, as is the case in all feminist organizations, communication links should be maintained. Organizational leaders may not agree on methodology or desired results, but all feminists must agree on direction. On questions of mutual interest where the organizations agree, coordinated action would always be desirable. Liberal and radical feminists can never lose sight of the fact that they have a common interest—gender equity. They may not agree on how to get there, but they must agree that the current reality is unacceptable and there is only one direction to move—toward more equitable opportunities for women in all areas of life, including sport.

It appears reasonable, then, to suggest that the radical and liberal agendas for sport equity proceed independently, although with overlapping areas of support. There will be numerous occasions on which it is perfectly reasonable for a liberal feminist to support the radical agenda "with some reservations" or simply to offer "no comment." Likewise, the radical feminist should support the liberal agenda "with disappointment that the position is not stronger."

Radical and Liberal Feminist Sport Agendas

What distinguishes the sport-related gender equity agenda of a radical feminist from that of a liberal feminist? Does it posit the demise of existing sport governance structures such as the National Collegiate Athletic Association (NCAA), National Association for Intercollegiate Athletics (NAIA), National Federation of State High School Athletic Associations, and the U.S. Olympic Committee (USOC) or the substructures of these organizations? Not necessarily. The radical condition is met as long as the position attacks a philosophical underpinning of the system that is imposing discriminatory treatment. It is acceptable to gut the structure and renovate the building—it can be less expensive than demolition and rebuilding. In addition, renovation gives the impression of less radical action, thereby inviting less resistance to change.

In developing the radical feminist agenda in sport, it is helpful to start by identifying the philosophical and structural appendages of the existing system that promote gender-discriminatory behavior. The proposition of antitheses to these tenets will identify the radical agenda. The liberal feminist agenda in sport then becomes all of those alternatives between the current reality and the radical posture. The following subsections focus on three major agenda items that are critical to gender equity in sport, regardless of whether the radical or liberal position is taken.

Change in Who Controls National, Conference, and Institutional Athletic Governance Structures

- *Radical agenda:* Establish separately administered programs for men's and women's athletics and support for federal and state intervention.
- *Liberal agenda:* Decrease the power of athletic directors or directors of the current structure (who are predominantly male) and increase representation of women and those sympathetic to the feminist agenda in all governance structures.

It has been said of women's sports that "the foxes are guarding the henhouse." The system of athletics governance at the secondary and postsecondary levels, which has either produced gender inequities or failed to correct them, has been controlled by athletics directors, close to 90% of whom are male (Acosta & Carpenter, 1990). Male athletic directors have been in control of the hiring process and have indicated that they have not been willing to share power with women by failing to practice the affirmative action necessary to increase the number of female coaches and administrators in the system. The number of women in these categories has steadily declined since 1972 (Acosta & Carpenter, 1990). In national governance organizations such as the NCAA and NAIA there has been no significant increase in the numbers of women participating on committees since women's championships were established in the early 1980s (Lovett & Lowry, 1989). The leadership of these systems must be replaced with a group that has more feminist inclinations.

There are four possible ways to bring about this change: (a) transfer of power to faculty athletic representatives, (b) transfer of power to chief executive officers, (c) transfer of power to senior women athletic administrators, and (d) separation of the governance of men's and women's athletics, which would invite senior women athletic administrators to achieve the same power role as that held by current male athletic directors. The last possibility is the antithetical position that should be taken by the radical feminist.

It makes sense, especially at the institutional level, to designate a special structure that has the sole purpose of remedying past discrimination against women in sport. Such action has precedent in academia. In our institutions of higher education it is common to find separate programs for women's studies, African American studies, and Hispanic studies and special people or offices, such as an equal-opportunity employment office, dedicated to affirmative action in areas that have previously been unfairly restricted. The existence of these special programs or efforts accomplishes two important functions: It focuses attention on the problem or issue, and it concentrates effort on the problem's resolution. An example of the success that can result from these special efforts can be found in separately administered women's athletic programs, which are few in number and a dying breed. These programs are six times more likely to produce 1 or more women's teams in the nation's top 10 than are administrative structures governing both men's and women's athletics (Zotos, 1989). In addition, compared with male-led merged programs, women's athletic programs administered by women hire twice as many female coaches (Sanders, 1985).

Is it possible for a radical push for separate governance of women's athletics to achieve results? Probably not. The radical feminist faces almost insurmountable odds with this position. The political game being played is "who controls the money." After a 10-year fight in the 1970s to gain control of women's athletics and achieving that end, male administrators are not about to hand over the spoils of war. Quite a few casualties of that battle are apparent. In 1972, 90% of all women's athletics programs were governed by women. In 1990, that figure was 16% (Acosta & Carpenter, 1990). The bottom line is that, as a result of Title IX, male athletic directors won total control of financial resources that were going to women's programs. They could not allow women into the athletics directors' club that controls that money, because they knew that money for women's athletics would be coming, to a large extent, from men's athletics. This control has continued because it is no secret that equity requires the reallocation of resources away from men's athletics and into women's athletics. Sufficient new economic resources are not available for the development of women's athletic programs that mirror the existing men's programs. Athletic programs with $5 million and $10 million budgets cannot double their participation to provide equitable opportunities for women and become $10 million and $20 million programs. The resources simply are not there.

However, the radical feminist position and those programs that are still separately administered perform an essential function. Separate programs realistically demonstrate what women's athletics are capable of achieving. Male athletics directors have always maintained that women's sports are nothing more than nonrevenue men's sports—programs that are a drain on the budget and have no possibility of fan support. Separately administered women's programs have demonstrated otherwise. The successful experience of the University of Texas at Austin has shown that women's basketball, a half-million-dollar budget item on many Division I campuses, can pay for itself. Separately administered and marketed women's sports programs are demonstrating that they can tap a new market for women's athletics that has never contributed to the support of men's athletics. As long as these programs are around to prove the "fox" wrong, the credibility of male-administered sport programs will be questioned and the gamekeepers, college and university presidents, may decide that there must be more objective control of athletic programs.

Liberal feminists believe it is totally unrealistic to expect the foxes to allow the hens to guard the henhouse or the foxhouse. Their position encourages a more influential role at the institutional level and within governance structures by faculty athletics representatives, chief executive officers, women athletics administrators, and others sympathetic to the need for gender equity. Liberal feminists also support efforts to take power away from Division I and disseminate this power more equitably to lesser competitive divisions. In addition, they support movements to give voice and power to student-athlete coalitions, because student-athletes will support gender equity and less exploitative, less commercial athletics programs.

The sport system that discriminates against women is built upon Division I institutions that spend more than half of their multimillion-dollar budgets on men's football and basketball and approximately 18% on women's sports. Sharing money with women's athletics and increasing parity in men's sports is not part of the Division I athletic director's agenda, and the power of Division I within the NCAA will not be easily diminished. Few people realize that NCAA regulations require Division I institutions to have twice as many representatives as Division II and Division III institutions combined on the most powerful executive boards (the Council and the President's Commission). The rationale for this advantage is that Division I produces more NCAA-shared revenue than other divisions.

Another issue in the control of governance structures is federal intervention, a relatively recent occurrence in postsecondary school athletics. Radical feminists support federal intervention in the athletics enterprise at every level with regard to legislation that intrudes upon the status quo control of intercollegiate athletics: (a) required publication of athlete graduation rates, (b) due process requirements, (c) full disclosure of financial information, (d) withdrawal of tax-exempt status to penalize excessive commercialization, and (e) granting of television antitrust exemptions as a reward for nondiscrimination, noncommercialization, and presidential control. Liberal feminists should not go so far as to be against federal intervention in an effort to align with their institutional positions. Rather, it would be less detrimental to the feminist agenda to adopt a position of polite indifference.

Although the redistribution of power is achievable at the postsecondary level, it is less plausible in secondary school athletics or open amateur sport. In secondary school sport, the position of athletic director is often filled at the district level; the athletic director reports directly to the superintendent, who is unlikely to have the time or the interest to become very involved in sport issues. However, many high school principals have real control over the hiring processes and supervisory structures on their individual campuses. The current education reform movement will give principals on individual campuses even more control. Thus increased power for high school principals and superintendents is the parallel to the collegiate position. The number of women currently in the governance structures at the state high school federation level is even smaller than what we see in the NCAA or NAIA, despite the fact that women's sport participation at the high school level is proportionally better. There are fewer intermediate and entry-level athletic administration positions at the high school level, and few women coaches hold the full-time positions and status of their male counterparts, who have preferential entry to the administrative ranks.

At the open amateur sport level, where single national sport governing bodies (commonly referred to as NGBs) exist in each Olympic and Pan-American sport, the situation is as problematic as the secondary school situation. The NGBs are overseen in a very loose structure by the USOC and Congress, despite the strict terms of the 1978 Amateur Sports Act, which requires equitable participation opportunities and representation of all constituencies, including women, at the executive board level within the NGB governance structures.

The increased distribution of this power can be achieved in the name of causes other than gender equity: the need for academic integrity, increased fiscal responsibility, ethical conduct, better graduation rates, concern over due process in enforcement and eligibility proceedings, and similar motives. The current leadership of athletic programs has failed in their charge in all of these areas. More responsible and accountable individuals must be given the power to steer athletics in a more positive direction.

In summary, liberal feminists believe that anyone other than the fox will be better for the cause of gender equity in sport and that there must be continual efforts to increase the number of women and sympathetic others in the governance structure at every level. Unfortunately, as long as the fox is in control of the hiring process, employment discrimination will work against this effort. Liberal feminists also understand that it is acceptable not to adopt or support a radical feminist position as long as one does not actively work against it. Radical feminists support separatism and federal intervention. The more energy is devoted to advancing both of these sport equity agendas, the sooner the feminist agenda in sport will be achieved.

Enforcement of Title IX

- *Radical agenda:* Work to encourage the filing of as many Title IX lawsuits and complaints as possible.
- *Liberal agenda:* Work to encourage OCR to enforce Title IX requirements more rigorously and for state, conference, and national governance structures to require Title IX compliance as a condition of membership or certification.

Title IX was adopted by Congress in 1972. Regulations promulgating the law as it applied to athletic programs in secondary and postsecondary institutions were not released until 1975. Institutions were required to appoint a Title IX compliance coordinator and to conduct self-evaluations; they were given three years to bring their programs into compliance. The Department of Education's Office of Civil Rights (OCR) did not issue its first Letter of Finding until 1981, and in the 20 years since the adoption of Title IX, no institution has been penalized for noncompliance.

In 1984, the Justice Department argued for limited application of Title IX. The Supreme Court agreed with the Justice Department position, finding in *Grove City v. Bell* that Title IX applied only to that program or department in the institution that was a recipient of federal funds. This decision virtually extinguished the application of Title IX to everything but athletic scholarships, which are administered through an institution's office of student financial aid. This decision was not overturned until the adoption by Congress of the Civil Rights Restoration Act of 1988, which restored the broader definition of *recipient*. Now, if any part of the institution receives federal aid, the entire institution must comply with Title IX. No program within the institution can practice gender discrimination—including athletics.

The radical feminist position on Title IX is obvious. OCR should be sued for nonenforcement of federal law, and girls and women suffering athletic program discrimination should be encouraged to bring suit against their institutions and school districts. Radical feminists should also use the Fourteenth Amendment and state equal rights laws as part of litigation strategies. In open amateur sport, national sport governing bodies and the USOC should be brought into federal court for failure to comply with the Amateur Sports Act of 1978.

Liberal feminists will, in all likelihood, continue their (to date) unsuccessful strategy of badgering OCR to "shape up" and "get its act together." Unfortunately, even if OCR does act, its investigatory process and findings will continue to be woefully inadequate. OCR is simply not holding educational institutions to the letter of the law. Liberal feminists must also continue to put pressure on educational institutions through formal complaints to Title IX compliance coordinators within their institutions. They must lobby for athletic governing body legislation that requires compliance with Title IX as a condition of membership or as an essential element of self-evaluation and certification programs. There is also a need to bring formal pressure to bear on OCR to make clear in its investigation procedure manuals exactly what is required under the law.

Attacking the Financial Underpinnings of Intercollegiate Athletics

- *Radical agenda:* Insist upon full disclosure of financial expenditures and income in intercollegiate athletics through the print and electronic media and state and federal law. Lobby for full taxation of intercollegiate athletic events, bowl games, and televised athletic events as unrelated business income.
- *Liberal agenda:* Work to promulgate legislation that initiates drastic cost-saving measures in athletics programs and distributes athletics program profits in a manner that will assist institutions in funding Title IX compliance.

Currently, 70% of all college athletics programs do not pay for themselves (Raiborn, 1989). They are being subsidized by state tax dollars, local institutional funds, or other discretionary institutional resources. In the vast majority of secondary and postsecondary institutions, coaches are directly subsidized by the paying of their salaries based primarily on their teaching responsibilities. The reigning mentality is to devote a disproportional amount of the dollars spent on athletics to men's football and basketball.

The radical feminist position is to bankrupt the system. Don't argue for cost reductions—if men's football players get chinchilla warm-ups, insist on chinchilla for women athletes. Only with a complete collapse of the financial underpinnings of intercollegiate athletics will the system be resurrected with greater gender equity in the distribution of its resources. While the system is collapsing, insist on full disclosure of how our educational institutions are throwing money down the drain. The resulting media attention and pressure will exacerbate the financial crisis. Better yet, encourage the federal government to remove tax-exempt status from athletics contributions and sponsorships and insist upon full taxation as unrelated business income of all commercial aspects of the athletics program—from television to bowl games to gate receipts to the sale of T-shirts and novelties. Keep the pressure on the system.

The liberal feminist agenda accentuates a slow but sure movement of the system toward fiscal sanity. It is important to understand that cost reduction requires conference-, state-, and national-level disarmaments of large groups of institutions that compete against each other, rather than unilateral disarmament of single institutions. If a single institution or school district reduces its expenses in order to redistribute resources to women's sports and its opponents do not, it is likely that its opponents will win on the playing field. Leaders of those institutions or school districts that unilaterally disarm will not be around for long. Those people who support fiscal sanity are friends of feminism and simply cannot be lost to the cause.

At the same time the superpowers of Division I-A are encouraged to disarm, there must be an expansion of championship opportunities for women at the conference, state, and national levels to accommodate increased participation resulting from the redistribution of resources to provide equity. Liberal feminists must make every effort to obtain widespread support for NCAA and NAIA national equity conventions. In the case of high school sports, there must be organized equity meetings of all state high school federations.

Full disclosure of athletics program practices. One of the reasons athletics programs have been so insulated from gender equity pressures is that they have grown into entities almost totally isolated from the rest of academia. Athletics structures have been highly politicized and controlled by relatively small numbers of institutions or alumni. Athletics directors and football and basketball coaches have had unquestioned power for a long time. They have abused that power by wasting money, giving themselves huge salaries and benefits compared with those of other teachers and professors, and bringing scandal and charges of unethical conduct down upon their institutions, which has, in turn, damaged public confidence in higher education.

The key to changing or overturning the system is exposure of athletic program practices and expenditures. Only when such exposure takes place will feminists be able to develop strong alliances with other groups that believe the current athletic system is unhealthy for both men and women. Radical feminists may use the "full disclosure" strategy via open records act requests or the subpoena of documents as part of lawsuits. Liberal feminists may slip some data to newspaper reporters or have committees within organizations gather such data for different purposes and then suggest to the press that interesting information is available through an open records request.

Creating alliances with other reformist groups. There are a number of factors that will assist in opening athletics programs for increased public scrutiny that will, in turn, increase the number of critics who will align themselves with those promoting more fair and equitable athletics programs. The print and electronic sports media, once the cheerleaders and promoters of sport, have reversed their approach and become investigative reporters. College faculties are becoming more outspoken in their criticism of athletic programs, especially as scandals and embarrassing graduation rates have challenged the academic and ethical integrity of their institutions. The American Association for University Professors has stepped up its formal national criticism of intercollegiate athletics and is actively encouraging faculty members on individual campuses to demand reform. Faculty athletics representatives on campuses are being charged with failure to fulfill their responsibilities as auditors of the academic integrity of athletics programs. These faculty representatives are rising to the occasion to prove their critics wrong.

The economic recession of the early 1990s has heightened public awareness of expenditures and educational priorities. Taxpayers are not anxious to subsidize athletics when classroom performance is at an all-time low, and misplaced priorities take the brunt of the blame.

Press coverage of athletic program scandals has created a reform alliance with the general public. This unfavorable media coverage, which questions the integrity of higher education by association, has brought college presidents out of their ivory towers and into the dangerous streets of alumni-supported athletics. Athletic programs have given presidents the ammunition for reform and a general public supportive of such efforts.

Developing active protected feminist groups. One of the problems facing women in sport who wish to be active in promoting gender equity is the fact that they fear such activity will have an adverse impact on their continued employment. Thus it is essential to identify "protected" feminist groups—groups that cannot be attacked by the male sports power structure. For instance, a growing number of retired men and women faculty and administrators are available who are capable of taking radical feminist positions. We must also encourage senior men and women faculty with tenure to play liberal and radical feminist roles in the quest. We should also explore the possibility of convincing student-athletes, open amateur sport participants, and professional athletes to pursue a reformist, athletes' rights agenda that should include gender and race equity in sport. Athlete groups hold a very powerful position by virtue of their visibility.

Women who are in fear of losing their positions cannot act as individuals. Women in athletics must join organizations in order to band together and show strength behind organizational action. It is easy to be a member of a women's organization such as the National Association for Collegiate Women Athletics Administrators (NACWAA), have that organization take strong positions, and then go back to your institution and explain that you really voted against that position—or you don't agree but the majority voted to adopt that position.

Perseverance. Feminists must know that there is power in longevity. The longer one remains in the system, the more friends and allies one gains, the more people are educated, and the greater the chance that major opponents will retire or pass away. Changing bureaucracies is a long-term task. The more constant pressure applied on the system over time, the more it will respond. On the other hand, those pushing on the system will feel pressure in response. If feminists feel such pressure, they should interpret this as an accomplishment. It is just the system rebelling against the inevitability of organizational change.

Key Words

gender equity	political agenda
liberal feminist	Title IX
radical feminist	financial disclosures
sports program reform	Office of Civil Rights

Discussion Questions

1. Why are both liberal and radical approaches essential components of the feminist agenda? Explain their interrelatedness.

2. Compare and contrast the liberal and radical approaches to sports reform for women as they affect (a) opportunities to compete and (b) program governance and control.

3. Why is it more difficult for women at the high school level to become involved in the governance of the school athletic experience than it is for women at the collegiate level?

4. How would the strategy to create Title IX compliance by "bankrupting the system" solve the gender inequity problem?

References

Acosta, R. V., & Carpenter, L. J. (1990). *Women in intercollegiate sport: A longitudinal study-thirteen year update, 1977-1990.* Unpublished manuscript, Brooklyn College, Brooklyn, NY.

Delano, L. C. (1988). *Understanding barriers that women face in pursuing high school athletic administrative positions: A feminist perspective.* Unpublished doctoral dissertation, University of Iowa, Iowa City.

Goodman, M. (1989, April). Where the boys are. *Washington Monthly,* pp. 18-20.

Lopiano, D. A. (1989, May 18). *Statement of Donna A. Lopiano, Ph.D., before the Subcommittee on Postsecondary Education of the Committee on Education and Labor, U.S. House of Representatives.* Washington, DC: Government Printing Office.

Lopiano, D. A. (1991, November 21). *Recruiting, retention and advancement of women in athletics coaching and administration.* Speech presented at the meeting of the Western Society for Physical Education of College Women, Pacific Grove, CA.

Lovett, D., & Lowry, C. (1989). Gender representations in the NCAA and NAIA. *Journal of Applied Research in Coaching and Athletics, 4,* 1-16.

Mansnerus, L. (1992, January 5). Women take the field. *New York Times Education Magazine.*

Murray, M. (1991). Media impact on women in sport and sport leadership. *Journal of Physical Education, Recreation, and Dance, 62,* 45-47.

National Collegiate Athletic Association. (1988). *Survey of NCAA member institutions on the elimination and addition of sports.* Mission, KS: Author.

National Collegiate Athletic Association. (1989). *Participation study, 1987-88: Men's and women's sports.* Mission, KS: Author.

Raiborn, M. H. (1989). *Revenues and expenses of intercollegiate athletics programs: Analysis of financial trends and relationships 1981-85.* Mission, KS: National Collegiate Athletic Association.

Sanders, M. T. (1985). *Comparison of various operation procedures in Division I women's athletics.* Unpublished manuscript, University of Tennessee.

Uhlir, G. A. (1987). Athletics and the university: The post-woman's era. *Academe, 73*(4), 25-29.

Women's Sports Foundation. (1991). *Did you know that . . . Clearing the hurdles: 20 years of Title IX* [Press release]. New York: Author.

Zotos, C. (1989). *Marketplace value and gender representation of successful coaches in women's intercollegiate athletics.* Unpublished manuscript, University of Texas, Austin.

IV

Physiological Perspectives

I wish to persuade women to endeavor to acquire strength, both of mind and body. Let us then by being allowed to take the same exercises as boys, not only during infancy, but youth, arrive at perfection of body.

—Mary Wollstonecraft (1792)

Every girl has a large store of vital and nervous energy upon which to draw in the great crisis of motherhood. If the foolish virgin uses up this deposit in daily expenditures of energy on the hockey field or tennis court, as a boy can afford to do, then she is left bankrupt in her great crisis and her children will have to pay the bill.

—New York Times (1921)

If the world were a logical place, men would ride sidesaddle.

—Rita Mae Brown (1984)

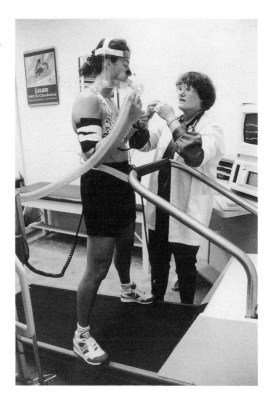

11

Basic Exercise Physiology
Myths and Realities

CAROL L. CHRISTENSEN

It has been said that "biology is destiny." If this is true, why was the first modern Olympic marathon for men staged in 1896 and for women in 1984? Why was the 10K race for women not an Olympic event until 1988? Why is weight lifting still not an Olympic event for women? Women have been performing in all of these events for many years, and their biology is not so different from men's as these Olympic delays and omissions would suggest. Despite women's recent sports successes, myths about women in sport persist. Some people still believe that women who engage in strenuous training will develop unsightly, bulging muscles and lose their femininity. It is also commonly believed that women should not exercise when pregnant or menstruating.

The citizens of ancient Sparta were more enlightened than modern societies; they encouraged women to engage in exercise. They believed that strong, healthy women would produce strong, healthy babies. This philosophy died with the Spartan civilization and was later replaced with the Victorian idea of womanhood, in which women were considered to be physically and intellectually frail. For reasons beyond the scope of this chapter, this idea persists today—even in the face of women's continued physical and intellectual accomplishments.

In analyzing world records set by men and women since 1900, Dyer (1982) concludes that in speed sports (such as running and swimming), women are catching up to the men. For example, in 1927 the men's record for 100 meters was 10.6 seconds and the women's record was 12.2 (a difference of 18.75%), and in 1977 the records were 9.95 and 10.88, respectively (an 8.55% difference). Dyer further observes that the top men's swimmers of the 1950s and 1960s would not have qualified for the women's Olympic teams in the 1980s. Whether women will continue to close the gap remains unknown, but the narrowing of the gap through improved women's performances demonstrates that women are not the weak and delicate individuals they were perceived to be in the Victorian era.

TABLE 11.1　Comparisons of Mean Aerobic Power and Relative Fat in Trained and Untrained Men and Women

Characteristic	Untrained		Trained	
	Females	Males	Females	Males
VO2max (ml/kg/min)	35-43	44-52	35-74	42-94
Body fat (%)	22-25	15-18	6-28	3-20

Women's world records in nearly all sporting events are proof that elite female athletes give superior physical performances. An examination of physiological characteristics and physical performances of athletes and nonathletes indicates that only a few men are superior to the best women athletes. In foot races of almost any distance (from 5,000 meters to the marathon) the first woman will cross the finish line before at least 66% of the men. This is also true in other events, such as swimming and cycling. An overlap of abilities exists for most physiological measures. Table 11.1 illustrates the overlap for aerobic power (VO2max) and relative (percentage) body fat. The highest recorded aerobic capacity (or VO2max) for a female is 74 ml/kg/min, while the average sedentary male reaches maximum at about 50 ml/kg/min. Most people would suggest that women are fatter than men, and in general they are. However, whereas the average young adult male has approximately 15-18% body fat, many female long distance runners have 12-15% body fat (the lowest value reported for a woman was 6% body fat; Wilmore & Brown, 1974). These two examples suggest that female athletes are superior to the average male and more similar to trained males in physiology and performance than to untrained females or males.

Men and women are often described as opposite sexes. This is a convenient but sexist means of separation for a variety of purposes, none of which is supportive of women. Observe the men and women around you. You will note that within each sex there is great variation in measures such as height and weight, shoulder and hip width, and muscular development. In fact, if physiological measurements were made you would find more variation within each sex than between the sexes (Harris, 1973). Great variation within a sex is also true of physical performance measures. If anything about men and women is "opposite" it is their reproductive organs; the uterus and ovaries are internal and well protected, whereas the testes are external and quite vulnerable to injury—a fact ignored by early physicians, who suggested that women's sports participation would result in damaged organs and inability to bear children. Males and females are not even at opposite extremes in sex-related hormones, given that members of both sexes have the same hormones, with differences in the levels of testosterone (men having high levels and women low) and estrogen (women having high levels and men low).

In most aspects of physiology and performance, males and females fall along a continuum of personal characteristics and physical performance.

There seems to be an athletic body type, which is the male type of body (this is perhaps because most athletic events were originally designed for men to play and therefore designed for their body type). Women who excel in athletics tend to have this "athletic" body type, with narrow hips and low percentage of body fat. While low testosterone levels hinder the development of muscle mass and therefore muscle power, strength, and speed in women, this does do not prevent women from considerable development of these characteristics. Women are represented throughout the continuum of performance and physical characteristics, not just at the low end.

Physical performance differences can be related to sex differences (primarily hormonal differences); however, sociological and cultural differences (e.g., clothing, less active life-style, lack of opportunities for women, social expectations for women, lower monetary rewards for women) also contribute to performance differences between males and females.

Physiology Related to Physical Activity

Prepuberty and Puberty

Prior to approximately 12 years or age, the average age of puberty for girls, there are virtually no sex-related differences in physiological abilities or physical performance. Differences observed between boys and girls at this time are the result of training and skills, not physiology.

Females mature two to three years before males, giving males more years to grow larger bodies (Wells, 1991). In addition, starting at puberty, hormone differences (estrogen for women and testosterone for men) have indications for sports performance. Relatively high levels of estrogen in women are responsible for the development of secondary sex characteristics such as deposition of fat in the breasts, buttocks, hips, and thighs. High levels of testosterone are responsible for the greater muscle mass that males possess. The higher amount of muscle mass makes a significant contribution to strength, power, and speed. The larger body, the result of the later growth spurt and longer developmental period, also provides an advantage in many sports.

Aerobic Capacity

An individual's aerobic power or capacity is best described by maximum oxygen consumption (VO2max) or the ability to use oxygen to provide energy for physical tasks. Aerobic power depends on the ability of the cardiorespiratory system (heart, blood vessels, blood, and lungs) to deliver oxygen to the working muscles and the ability of muscles to extract and use that oxygen. Thus the more oxygen an individual can deliver and use, the greater the VO2max or aerobic fitness. Many factors determine an individual's maximum ability to deliver oxygen to the muscles, including lung size, maximum cardiac output (the amount of blood pumped by the heart each minute), hemoglobin levels, and muscle mass.

TABLE 11.2 Comparison of Selected Performance and Physiological
Characteristics

Physiological Function of Women Compared With Men	Physiological Characteristics of Women Compared With Men
Lower maximum aerobic capacity	Fewer RBCs and lower hemoglobin levels; smaller heart and lungs; less blood volume
Lower absolute strength	Less muscle mass (fewer and smaller fibers); greater relative (%) body fat; no difference in quality of muscle; no difference in distribution of muscle fibers (slow and fast twitch)
Lower anaerobic power	Less muscle mass; no difference in anaerobic power per unit of muscle

In general, females function at a disadvantage in aerobic activities; this is in part due to their generally smaller size (see Table 11.2). Women, on the average, are 3 to 4 inches shorter and 25 to 30 pounds lighter than men; they possess 10 to 15 pounds more body fat and 40 to 45 pounds less fat-free weight, which is made up primarily of muscle, bone, and other organs (Fox, Bowers, & Foss, 1991). It is important to keep in mind that not all women are smaller; for example, the tallest living woman in North America stands 7 feet, 7¼ inches tall (McFarlan & McWhirter, 1989) and female volleyball and basketball players generally stand 6 feet and taller. However, smaller size gives females smaller hearts (with which to pump blood), smaller lungs (with a smaller surface area for intake of oxygen), and less muscle mass (with lower potential to utilize oxygen). The blood chemistry of women is also to their disadvantage; they have fewer red blood cells and lower hemoglobin concentration, which decreases their ability to carry oxygen in the blood. It has been said that women have a 15-20% handicap in aerobic activities. Most current world records in track and swimming events show an 8-10% difference in performance (Dyer, 1986), suggesting that much of this handicap disappears with proper training.

Anaerobic threshold (AnT) is related to aerobic power. It determines the percentage of aerobic capacity that can be sustained for a long period of time without any substantial increase in lactic acid, a fatiguing product of nonaerobic metabolism. Athletes who excel in endurance sports have high VO2max and high AnT. Anaerobic threshold, or the point where a person switches from aerobic to anaerobic energy sources, usually occurs between 40% and 70% of VO2max. Outstanding endurance athletes may not reach AnT until 90% of VO2max. Men and women with similar training reach AnT at the same percentage of VO2max (Pate & Kriska, 1984). However, women reach AnT at a lower absolute work rate because of their lower VO2max. Since performance in endurance events must be at or near the AnT (to avoid increases in lactic acid and early onset of fatigue), women cannot maintain as fast a pace (or absolute work rate) as men.

Anaerobic Capacity or Power

Anaerobic capacity or power is reflected in an individual's ability to give high-intensity short-term effort. Sports that rely primarily on anaerobic power are those that require bursts of speed and/or high levels of strength, such as basketball, volleyball, soccer, and the 100-meter dash. Muscle concentrations of enzymes responsible for anaerobic power are equal in men and women (i.e., each kilogram of muscle has the same amount of enzymes), but, because women generally have less muscle mass, they have lower anaerobic power (i.e., smaller muscles mean fewer enzymes available) and therefore they operate at a handicap when competing against equally trained men in sports requiring anaerobic power.

Muscle Strength and Physiology

Strength differences between males and females are greater than the differences in aerobic and anaerobic power. There is a large overlap in strength between men and women, but, in general, women have 66% of the strength of men (Holloway & Baechle, 1990). The greatest difference is in upper-body strength, where women are 50-60% as strong as men, and the least difference is in lower-body strength, where women may have 70-80% of the strength of men. The primary reason for this difference is the disparity of muscle mass (National Strength and Conditioning Association, 1989a). Compared with women, men have less body fat and more muscle mass because of their greater body weight and lower relative body fat. It should be noted that the quality of muscle is identical in men and women; that is, the strength per unit or cross-sectional area of muscle is the same. This means that, given muscles of equal size, men and women would be equally strong. Despite these differences and generalities, women who strength train and compete in power lifting "have achieved weight lifting feats which would be beyond the ability of most men" (Dyer, 1982, p. 57).

The distribution of muscle fiber type is the same for men and women. There are two basic types of muscle fibers: fast twitch (FT), utilized in rapid, strong movements, and slow twitch (ST), utilized in slower, more prolonged, endurance activities. The distribution of these fibers varies from muscle to muscle: A muscle may contain 30-70% FT fibers or 70-30% ST fibers. Endurance athletes (men and women) tend to have a higher percentage of ST fibers, and athletes in sports requiring strength and power tend to have a higher percentage of FT fibers. Differences in fiber types are more apparent between athletes who engage in different types of training (e.g., strength trained versus endurance trained) than between men and women (Drinkwater, 1984).

Body Composition

Relatively large stores of body fat (and, by implication, lower amounts of muscle) are a disadvantage in sports that rely on strength and power, or where the athlete must carry (as in running) or lift (as in high jump) his

TABLE 11.3 Average Percentage Fat for Untrained Persons and Athletes in Selected Sports

Sport	Females	Males
Average for untrained	22-25	15-18
Baseball/softball	14-18	12-16
Basketball	12-16	7-11
Swimming	14-17	8-12
Long-distance running	6-19	4-13
Tennis	15-20	12-16

SOURCE: Data are from Wells (1991) and Wilmore (1983).

or her own body weight. Table 11.3 contains some comparisons of percentage body fat of untrained females and males and athletes in selected sports. It is clear that female athletes tend to have body composition more similar to their male counterparts than to the average nonathletic female. The average young adult woman has 22-25% body fat, 5-10% more total body fat than the average female athlete. The lowest value reported for women athletes was 6% fat (Wilmore & Brown, 1974).

Some people suggest that when corrections are made for percentage fat and amount of muscle mass, differences in strength, speed, and power virtually disappear or that men and women are nearly equal in strength. This, however, is a moot argument, given that in a sporting event women cannot leave their fat in the locker room.

Heat Tolerance

A final area of physiological comparison is response to heat stress or hot environments. Early researchers observed that women were less able to tolerate hot environments than were males. Reexamination of the results of these studies revealed that random selection of men and women as subjects resulted in the selection of men who were moderately active and women who were inactive. In other words, the men and women were not equally trained. Later research demonstrated that fitness level, not gender, has a great effect on an individual's heat tolerance, and that men and women with similar aerobic fitness levels tolerate heat equally well (Drinkwater, 1984). Women's responses to heat may be different (women have a lower sweat rate and later onset of sweating than men), but they do not suffer any greater number of heat injuries or thermal regulation problems than equally trained men.

Response to Exercise and Training

Physiological responses to exercise are generic; they may be altered by disease or substance use (i.e., drugs and alcohol), but otherwise they are the same for all individuals. Responses include increases in heart rate, cardiac output, ventilation, and metabolism. The magnitude of the response (e.g., how high heart rate goes) depends on the intensity of exercise relative to the individual's capacity, body position, type of exercise, and fitness level among other factors. For a given level of work (e.g., jogging at a pace of 9 minutes per mile), women tend to have higher physiological responses than men because of their lower VO2max. However, if aerobic power were equal, responses would be equal.

A regular exercise program, or physical training, can be expected to produce physiological adaptations that result in increased VO2max, strength, power, and/or speed. The specific response to training depends on the type of training completed; that is, individuals who lift weights will gain strength, but will have no improvement in aerobic capacity, and individuals who engage in endurance training will improve their aerobic capacity, but will not increase their strength. Considerable evidence indicates that women's responses to training are similar to men's responses (Drinkwater, 1984). Depending on the type of training, a woman can expect to increase her aerobic and anaerobic capacity, strength, speed, and muscle mass and to decrease her body fat. The primary difference between male and female responses to training is the absolute amount of change; that is, after following an appropriate training program, men will be stronger or faster than women who follow a similar program.

One gender difference that has been observed is the initial response to weight or strength training. For women, initial increases in strength are the result of neural changes (that is, strength is increased by recruiting a greater percentage of muscle fibers rather than by increasing the size of muscle fibers); for men, initial increases in strength are the result of hypertrophy (or increase in muscle fiber size). Women will also show hypertrophy, but this occurs after several weeks of training. In addition, women have lower testosterone levels, which inhibits the development of excessively large muscles. A comparison of male and female bodybuilders shows that, although women can develop large muscles, women's ability to develop excessive muscle is quite limited. Some women, in their drive to win bodybuilding competitions, utilize anabolic steroids and are able to develop very large muscles because their testosterone (steroid) levels are similar to those of men. They also expose themselves to the risks of steroid abuse, such as liver and kidney damage and coronary heart disease.

It is clear that training programs should be based on the capacities, skills, and abilities of an individual, not his or her sex (National Strength and Conditioning Association, 1989b; Wells, 1991). Women should engage in lower-intensity workouts *only* if they possess low strength or low aerobic capacity. Highly trained women might work out with trained men, but they should be advised to avoid working out with poorly trained men, because this will impair the women's training.

Special Concerns

Menarche

The mean age for menarche (the onset of puberty and menstruation) in the United Stated is 12.8 years (Wells, 1991). It has been reported by several researchers that girls who begin training at a young age experience delayed menarche. Trained females begin menstruation from 0.5 to 2.5 years later than untrained females. The length of the delay appears to be related to the number of years of training prior to menarche. However, there is no evidence that this delay adversely affects later menstrual or reproductive function. The reason for the delay has not been discovered, but it is not necessarily a result of the training per se. One theory suggests that early maturing girls drop out of sport as they lose their athletic figures (the slim hips) and gain fat weight.

Menstruation

The menstrual cycle can enhance, impair, or have no effect on performance. While there are changes associated with menstrual function that might affect performance (increased breast size, increased body weight, and increased temperature at ovulation), research has provided conflicting results about the effects. For the majority of athletes, menstrual function does not enhance or impair performance. According to Wells (1980), "Individual variability obscures any patterns of performance differences caused by the menstrual cycle" (p. 143). Survey studies have noted that women have won Olympic medals in all phases of the menstrual cycle, even while menstruating. These same surveys also show that although many athletes feel their performance is not affected by their cycles, they stop or reduce training during their menstrual periods. It is important to remember that physical and mental changes associated with the menstrual cycle vary greatly from woman to woman and from cycle to cycle.

Although some evidence suggests that regular exercise decreases the incidence of dysmenorrhea (painful menstrual periods), most athletes report no change in menstrual function while training and/or competing. Recent research has focused on oligomenorrhea (menstrual periods occurring every 39 to 90 days) and amenorrhea (menstrual periods occurring more than 90 days apart) in athletes. Various researchers have suggested that these conditions exist in as little as 3% or as many as 80% of athletic women (Ruffin, Hunter, & Arendt, 1990). It is impossible to determine the exact percentage of athletes who have oligo- or amenorrhea from existing studies because of such research problems as (a) use of different definitions of the terms, (b) use of subjects of different ages, and (c) comparisons of athletes in different sports. After a thorough review of the literature, Wells (1991) concludes, "There is a notably higher incidence of menstrual disruption in younger, highly motivated athletes . . . ; intensively training athletes . . . ; and in athletes whose sports demand a particularly lean body type" (p. 94).

Many factors have been linked with "athletic amenorrhea," but none has been singled out as the primary mechanism or cause. While low percentage of body fat is often targeted as the causal factor, such designation is premature. Numerous other factors have been identified that might contribute to this condition, including prior menstrual irregularities, hypothalamic imbalance, stress, low body weight, high training mileage, age at menarche, diet low in protein, and nutritional status. Much is unknown about the etiology of this condition, and further investigation is needed.

Originally, athletic amenorrhea was not considered a health risk because most women who decreased their training gained weight and resumed regular menstrual function, and some became pregnant. Then, in the early 1980s, one study found noted that the bone mineral density of several young amenorrheic women, all members of a collegiate track team, was much lower than that in age-matched controls (Cann, Martin, Genant, & Jaffe, 1984). The medical condition of low bone mineral is known as osteoporosis, a condition where bones fracture easily, height is lost, vertebrae are crushed, and the individual suffers greatly. This finding of low bone mineral density spurred further research and concern for the bone health of young athletes who were amenorrheic (see the section below on osteoporosis for further details).

Menopause

Another type of amenorrhea is menopause, the natural or surgical cessation of menses. A precipitous drop in circulating hormones (particularly estrogen) occurs and is responsible for the hot flashes experienced by about 80% of postmenopausal women. These are not pleasant, but they leave no lasting impairment of function. However, does menopause affect the individual's ability to exercise? Very few researchers have studied exercise capacity and capabilities in postmenopausal women. The sparse evidence available suggests that, although exercise capacity declines with age (in part due to changes in activity level), menopause itself does not impair the ability to exercise. Postmenopausal women show the same ability to improve exercise function as premenopausal women of the same age (Wells, 1991). Exercise is recommended for postmenopausal women as an important factor in osteoporosis prevention; it is further important for prevention of loss of physiological functions often associated with age, particularly strength, that can impair the activities of daily living for many elderly persons.

Pregnancy

In addition to obvious changes in body and fat weight and distribution of that weight, pregnant women experience changes in most physiological systems. These changes include increased blood volume, cardiac output, ventilation, heart rate, and metabolic rate. In addition, the early stages of pregnancy are often accompanied by nausea and vomiting. The effects of these changes on exercise and the effects of exercise on pregnancy and the outcome of pregnancy have been the subjects of numerous studies.

In the early 1900s, when women were considered fragile and advised to refrain from strenuous physical activity (even when not pregnant), exercise was thought to be hazardous to reproductive function. Medical doctors suggested that women who participated in sports would suffer from ruptured or sagging organs. Survey studies from the 1950s and 1960s suggested that the occurrence of major disorders during pregnancy was no greater in athletes than in nonathletes. In addition, it was noted that athletes often had shorter periods of labor and fewer complications of pregnancy (e.g., cesarean section, forceps use). In short, these surveys demonstrated that strenuous exercise had no detrimental effects on pregnant women.

During the past two decades, researchers have noted that exercising pregnant women, when compared with nonpregnant women, have higher ventilation volumes, higher ratings of perceived exertion (the subjective evaluation of the stress of an exercise task), and increased energy expenditure (which is related to their higher body weight). Work capacity is probably reduced because the added body weight would add to the exercise effort, but, for safety reasons, researchers have been hesitant to conduct maximum-effort testing, so this awaits confirmation. Finally, it has been demonstrated that temperature regulation is not impaired during pregnancy. It appears that women who are pregnant can exercise and improve their fitness level with little risk to themselves or the fetus. However, some cautions must be observed.

Several authors and organizations have published exercise guidelines for pregnant women. All agree on two things: (a) If the pregnancy is high risk or complicated, exercise should be avoided, and (b) exercise should have physician approval (that is, the woman should inform her obstetrician of her intent to exercise and ask if exercise is contraindicated).

In general, concerns focus on the fetus, which is dependent on the maternal internal environment for protection and nutrition; if this environment is disturbed, the fetus may also be disturbed. The three main concerns are fetal hyperthermia, hypoglycemia, and hypoxia (Wolfe et al., 1989). Hyperthermia (elevated body temperature) is a normal response to exercise. It is theorized that if the fetus is exposed to a hot environment for a prolonged period of time (especially during the first trimester), neural development may be impaired or retarded. Another theory suggests that if the fetus is repeatedly deprived of glucose (hypoglycemia), upon which it relies heavily for nourishment, it may be undernourished. Exercise increases the maternal demand for glucose, which might result in fetal hypoglycemia. And finally, prolonged fetal hypoxia (or lack of oxygen) may affect development. During exercise the maternal demand for oxygen increases and this could reduce the oxygen available to the fetus. However, fetal blood has a higher affinity for oxygen than maternal blood and it is thought that this probably compensates for any reduction in blood flow to the placenta during exercise.

Published guidelines are meant to protect the health and welfare of mother and fetus. However, lacking solid research evidence for what is hazardous, guidelines are somewhat arbitrary and quite conservative— aiming at prevention of prolonged hyperthermia, hypoglycemia, and hypoxia. Thus, although it is generally agreed that exercise should be of low to moderate intensity (not requiring high levels of oxygen or glucose) and relatively short duration (so that body temperature will not be elevated for long periods of time), there is no agreement on how moderate the exercise should be or how long it should be engaged in (see Table 11.4).

TABLE 11.4 Guidelines for Exercise Intensity and Duration During Pregnancy

	American College of Obstetricians and Gynecologists[a]	*American College of Sports Medicine (1991)*	*Sady & Carpenter (1989)*
Intensity			
Heart rate (beats/minute)	≤140	not stated	≤150
Rating of perceived exertion	not stated	12-14	not stated
Duration (minutes)	≤15	15 to 30	≤30

a. Cited in Wolfe (1989).

Women are also advised to avoid contact and high-risk sports that might injure the fetus. Furthermore, increases in body weight and changes in center of gravity may change a woman's balance, making other sports unsafe also. Most women can benefit from an exercise program while pregnant; the form a program takes should be individualized for the woman's abilities, fitness level, and attitude toward physical activity.

Osteoporosis

Osteoporosis affects women about four times more frequently than it affects men. It is a condition in which bones lose calcium, becoming porous (riddled with holes) and quite fragile. An individual with osteoporosis generally loses height and is at high risk for fractures of the wrist, hip, and vertebrae. In the United States in 1990, more than $10 billion was spent for health care costs of osteoporotic hip fractures.

The major risk factors for this condition are low calcium intake, low levels of estrogen, and lack of physical activity. Other risk factors include family history, low body weight, cigarette smoking, excessive use of alcohol, and high intake of caffeine, protein, or fiber. It is apparent that most of these risk factors are the result of an individual's life-style and therefore can be changed to lower the risk of osteoporosis. There is no known cure for osteoporosis, so prevention is vital. Prevention (in the form of exercise and diet) should start in the early teen years and continue throughout the individual's lifetime.

For the athlete who is amenorrheic and the postmenopausal woman, estrogen replacement therapy (ERT) is commonly prescribed. Prior to 10 years ago, ERT consisted of high doses of estrogen. A high incidence of endometrial and breast cancer was observed in women on this regimen of ERT. During recent years it has been discovered that adding progestin to the prescription and lowering the amount of estrogen virtually eliminates a woman's risk of endometrial or breast cancer while providing protection against bone mineral loss.

Since lack of physical activity is a major risk factor for osteoporosis, it is sensible to theorize that engaging in physical activity would help prevent this condition. Research in this area is equivocal at best. Certainly if exercise alone were sufficient to prevent bone loss, the college runners mentioned earlier would not have low bone mineral density. Some research

TABLE 11.5 Selected Women's World's Records

Sport/Event (year record set)	Record
Bench press (1978)	107.5 kg (237 lb.)
500-meter speed skating (1988)	39 min. 10 sec.
Marathon, 26.2 miles (1985)	2 hr. 21 min. 6 sec.
50-meter freestyle swim (1988)	24.98 sec.
1,500-meter freestyle swim (1988)	15 min. 52.10 sec.
100-meter run (1988)	10.49 sec.
1-mile run (1985)	4 min. 16.71 sec.
High jump (1987)	6 ft. 10.25 in.

SOURCE: Data are from Dyer (1982) and McFarlan and McWhirter (1989).

suggests that exercise, along with proper calcium intake and ERT, can stop progressive bone loss. There is no evidence that exercise will reverse osteoporosis, but it appears that some physical activity (such as aerobics, jogging, or weight lifting) in combination with estrogen and calcium will help prevent osteoporosis (Drinkwater, 1990). It is prudent for the older woman to look at her risk factors for osteoporosis and cancer before deciding to begin ERT.

Conclusions

The special concerns women have generally do not limit their ability to participate and train, except for rather limited time periods (e.g., athletes may choose not to train during their menstrual periods, and during pregnancy they may decrease training intensity). Most of the old beliefs about exercise hazards to reproductive function are myth. Evidence suggests that it is not harmful to exercise, train, and compete in any phase of the menstrual cycle and that the menstrual cycle neither impairs nor enhances performance. Exercise during pregnancy, if not contraindicated, can have many benefits for the pregnant woman. The decision to exercise during menstrual periods and/or during pregnancy needs to be made on a case-by-case basis.

It has been shown that women have some physiological disadvantages (when compared with men) for sports performance: smaller hearts, less muscle mass, less hemoglobin, and more body fat, to name a few. These contribute to their generally lower VO2max, speed, and power disadvantage in sports and physical competition. However, it would be wrong to conclude that all women are weaker and slower than men, because many highly trained women athletes exceed the abilities of most men. Table 11.5 reports women's world's records for several selected activities, performances that many men only dream of.

Men's world's records would exceed these in speed, time, or weight lifted; clearly, in head-to-head competition women would not fare well, but then most men would not fare well either. One must ask, How important are the physiological differences? In head-to-head competition they may help determine the winner of the contest, but the differences should not keep women from being active and developing their physical capacities to the fullest. The record books show that women can excel and can beat most of the men. Cultural biases are more of a hindrance to women in sports than is their physiology.

Will men maintain their superior sports records? They would if sports performance were based solely on physiological differences. However, it is important to keep in mind that inherited physiology accounts for only 80-90% of sports performance; the remaining 10-20% is made up of training, diet, and motivation. In their analysis of past performances and improvements in performance since 1895, Whipp and Ward (1992) note that women's performances are improving at a faster rate than men's and project that women will run as fast as men (in events from the 200 meter to the marathon) during the next quarter century. While this seems unlikely in view of physiological differences, it should not be ruled out.

Cultural practices, biases, and expectations exert great influence on women, pushing them toward being homemakers and mothers, not athletes. This socialization starts very early in life. One example of the low expectations for physical performance on the part of females can be found in the fitness standards for prepubescent girls; these are lower than the standards for boys, even though there is very little difference in physiology. Rozdilsky, Wilkinson, and Williamson (1992) report that 88% of all 10-year-old girls they tested achieved the boys' standard for fitness as measured by the one-mile run. Yet the standard for girls, and therefore the expectation, was lower.

The sports performances of highly skilled women can be as exciting to watch as the men's, but we see them less often because the prevalent cultural sexism promotes men's sports, not women's. Title IX has helped equalize sports opportunities, but they still are not equal. In a nonsexist nation, the opportunities to excel in sports would be based on athletic potential, not sex. Girls and women would have equal opportunity to achieve their athletic potential: early training, high expectations, ample opportunity for participation, excellent coaching, and adequate awards. Women's sport performance records might then reflect a new reality.

Key Words

aerobic capacity or power	relative (%) body fat
VO2max	heat tolerance
anaerobic threshold	menarche
anaerobic capacity or power	athletic amenorrhea
strength	osteoporosis
muscle mass	pregnancy
body composition	

Discussion Questions

1. What physiological factors contribute to performance differences between men and women?

2. Are the observed performance differences between men and women the result of gender, genetics, or behavioral traits?

3. What are the pros and cons of males and females competing directly against each other? Indicate appropriate and inappropriate sports, if applicable.

4. Should youth sports (those for prepubescent children) be coed?

References

American College of Sports Medicine. (1991). *Guidelines for exercise testing and prescription* (4th ed.). Philadelphia: Lea & Febiger.

Cann, C. E., Martin, M. C., Genant, H. K., & Jaffe, R. B. (1984). Decreased spinal mineral content of amenorrheic women. *Journal of the American Medical Association, 251,* 626-629.

Drinkwater, B. L. (1984). Women and exercise: Physiological aspects. *Exercise and Sport Science Reviews, 12,* 21-51.

Drinkwater, B. L. (1990). Physical exercise and bone health. *Journal of the American Medical Women's Association, 45*(3), 91-97.

Dyer, K. F. (1982). *Challenging the men: Women in sport.* St. Lucia, Queensland: University of Queensland Press.

Dyer, K. F. (1986). The trend of the male-female differential in various speed sports 1936-1984. *Journal of Biosocial Science, 18,* 169-177.

Fox, E. L., Bowers, R. W., & Foss, M. L. (1989). *The physiological basis of physical education and athletics* (4th ed.). Dubuque, IA: William C. Brown.

Harris, D. V. (1973, March-April). Women in sports: Some misconceptions. *Journal of Sports Medicine,* pp. 15-17.

Holloway, J. B., & Baechle, T. R. (1990). Strength training for female athletes: A review of selected aspects. *Sports Medicine, 9,* 216-228.

McFarlan, D., & McWhirter, N. D. (Eds.). (1989). *1990 Guinness book of world records.* New York: Sterling.

National Strength and Conditioning Association. (1989a). Strength training for female athletes: A position paper, Part I. *National Strength and Conditioning Association Journal, 11*(4), 43-55.

National Strength and Conditioning Association. (1989b). Strength training for female athletes: A position paper, Part II. *National Strength and Conditioning Association Journal, 11*(5), 29-36.

Pate, R., & Kriska, A. (1984). Physiological basis of the sex difference in cardiorespiratory endurance. *Sports Medicine, 1,* 87-98.

Rozdilsky, R., Wilkinson, S., & Williamson, K. (1992, April). *The perpetuation of sexism through physical fitness testing.* Paper presented at the annual meeting of the American Alliance for Health, Physical Education, Recreation and Dance, Indianapolis.

Ruffin, M. T., Hunter, R. E., & Arendt, E. A. (1990). Exercise and secondary amenorrhoea linked through endogenous opoids. *Sports Medicine, 10,* 65-71.

Sady, S. P., & Carpenter, M. W. (1989). Aerobic exercise during pregnancy: Special considerations. *Sports Medicine, 7,* 357-375.

Wells, C. L. (1980). The female athlete: Myths and superstition put to rest. In E. J. Burke (Ed.), *Toward an understanding of human performance* (2nd ed.). Ithaca, NY: Mouvement.

Wells, C. L. (1991). *Women, sport, and performance: A physiological perspective* (2nd ed.). Champaign, IL: Human Kinetics.

Whipp, B. J., & Ward, S. A. (1992). Will women soon outrun men? *Nature, 355*(6355), 25.

Wilmore, J. B. (1983). Body composition in sport and exercise: Directions for future research. *Medicine and Science in Sports and Exercise, 15*(1), 21-31.

Wilmore, J. B., & Brown, C. H. (1974). Physiological profiles of women distance runners. *Medicine and Science in Sports, 6,* 178-181.

Wolfe, L. A., Hall, P., Webb, K. A., Goodman, L., Monga, M., & McGrath, M. J. (1989). Prescription for aerobic exercise during pregnancy. *Sports Medicine, 8,* 273-301.

12

Nutrition and the Female Athlete

HELEN T. McCARTHY

The nutritional needs of women engaging in sport are not greatly dissimilar from those of their male counterparts. Women and men both have the same nutrient requirements and possess the same physiological mechanisms for processing nutrients. Any differences that do exist are probably related to quantity, with men and women needing more or less of particular nutrients. For example, during the years when a woman menstruates, her iron needs are greater than those of a man.

Until recently, there was little interest in studying the nutrient needs of physically active women. This began to change when the numbers of women involved in vigorous exercise programs rapidly increased. To date, those who advise physically active women about their nutrient needs do not have any large data base of published research to draw upon. However, although the research is scanty, some initial studies began to emerge in the 1980s. Several of these preliminary dietary surveys of physically active women have reported intakes of some vitamins, minerals, and macronutrients well below the amounts recommended by the Food and Nutrition Board (1989). Of notable interest are low intakes of total kilocalories, iron, calcium, zinc, and folacin (Deuster et al., 1986; Keith, O'Keefe, Alt, & Young, 1989; Kleiner, Bazzarre, & Litchford, 1990; Tilgner & Schiller, 1989). Interpretations of these observations and their practical implications await further research. We can only conjecture as to the significance of these initial findings, perhaps providing a direction for the ongoing research in this area.

Low nutrient intakes are indicative of an individual's not eating enough or eating the wrong foods. In the case of kilocalories, blame is laid on not eating enough overall. In a society obsessed with physical appearance, the female athlete is tempted to restrict her intake of kilocalories. It is generally acknowledged that exercise increases the amount of energy needed, and intake below what is recommended would put an athlete at heightened risk of not getting enough energy to support exercise at an optimal level. Judging from the available reports of low kilocalorie intakes, many female athletes fit into this risk group. Thus, when advising female athletes of their nutritional needs, it is essential to know the minimal number of kilocalories necessary to sustain optimal performance without compromising the physical image of the female athlete. Since we do not know how many kilocalories an individual actually uses during training (overall energy needs are estimates), we do not know the accurate number of kilocalories needed to replace the energy expended. The number of kilocalories needed by an athlete may not increase as much as has been assumed; aerobic training may increase the efficiency of the body in using energy, allowing the athlete to perform optimally on fewer kilocalories. There are other times when the body can adapt by lowering its energy need. For example, chronically malnourished subjects need fewer kilocalories (Bruce et al., 1984).

The decreased intakes of some minerals and vitamins among female athletes, as reported in the literature, can be caused by (a) decreased food intake, as discussed above; (b) increased need for these nutrients resulting from the stress of the exercise; or (c) a combination of decreased intake and increased need. The American Dietetic Association (ADA, 1987) takes the position that although extended physical activity may increase the need for some nutrients, increasing consumption of kilocalories along with a balanced diet will meet this extra need. This line of thought, although valid, does not really address the needs of female athletes, who are often reluctant to increase caloric intake due to concern for physical appearance. For female athletes, this type of advice can result in a balancing act between getting enough vitamins and minerals and having enough energy to perform. The obvious consequence is the use of low-calorie diets and vitamin/mineral supplements.

Research is needed to determine the minimal energy needs necessary to obtain maximum performance output, at the same time not compromising the availability of necessary vitamins and minerals. This task is formidable and not likely to be achieved soon. In the meantime, each woman engaged in any physical activity must take control of her own nutritional needs, and taking control is contingent on an understanding of current knowledge of nutritional principles. The more valid information each individual has of her own nutritional needs and the implications of decreased or excessive intakes of certain nutrients, the better she will be able to mold herself, without compromises, into a healthy and successful competitor.

Successful athletes at any level are the product of three factors: heredity, hard work, and nutrition. Heredity is outside our control; the six-foot, large-boned woman most likely will be more successful engaging in a sport in which height and size are maximized. On the other hand, participation in a comprehensive physical and mental training program is undoubtedly the most effective way of enhancing athletic performance. Combined with training, the practical application of sound nutritional knowledge can and will enhance sports performance.

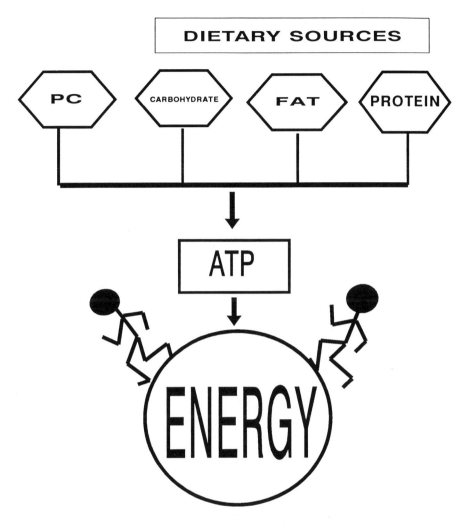

Figure 12.1. The Sources of ATP

The Fuels of Exercise

ATP and Phosphocreatine

There are two chemical compounds that fuel the muscles: adenosine triphosphate (ATP) and phosphocreatine (PC). When muscle is called into action, it is ATP that spontaneously supplies the energy that allows the muscle to contract. The supply of ATP in the muscle is enough for only several seconds. Therefore, the ATP must constantly be *resupplied* if the muscle is to continue to work (see Figure 12.1). Phosphocreatine, the other high-energy compound in the muscle cells, can be activated instantly to replenish ATP. The initial burst of energy from ATP and phosphocreatine can last about one minute.

Carbohydrates, Fats, and Proteins

Carbohydrates. When the level of ATP declines in the muscle tissue, carbohydrates are coaxed into action to supply ATP to continue exercise. Carbohydrates are the body's prime energy source during exercise, and glucose is the most important carbohydrate used by the body. Glucose is available to all cells in the body via the bloodstream and is stored in limited amounts in the liver and muscle cells as *glycogen.* Glycogen is made up of a long chain of joined glucose molecules.

Fats. In contrast to the limited carbohydrate storage in the body, fat storage is unlimited. Fat provides more than twice as much energy as carbohydrate. Fat supplies 9 kilocalories for each gram; carbohydrates supply 4 kilocalories/gram. In comparison with glycogen reserves, which are enough to fuel a runner for fewer than 20 miles if all of the glycogen could be used (which it cannot), fat reserves can fuel a runner for several hundred miles. The problem with fat is that it is harder to mobilize. Fat is stored in the form of triglycerides, which in turn are composed of fatty acids. During exercise, it is mainly the fatty acids that supply the energy by generating ATP.

Proteins. Protein's main function is to build and maintain body tissue, although as a secondary function it can serve as a fuel source. A fuller discussion of protein is offered below.

Commonly Asked Questions
About Fuel Sources and Exercise

What happens when muscle glycogen is depleted? When glycogen in the muscle tissue is depleted, the muscle tissue will take glucose from the bloodstream. The liver will try to replenish the supply of blood glucose. A continued reliance on blood glucose will eventually deplete the liver stores, resulting in the risk of hypoglycemia (low blood glucose). This affects the central nervous system because the cells of the central nervous system and brain rely primarily on blood glucose for proper functioning. When nervous system function comes almost to a halt, the continuation of exercise is all but impossible. This is often described as "hitting the wall."

Can the body conserve its glycogen? The human body can conserve its glycogen reserves by using fat as its primary fuel for regenerating ATP. In fact, the body would prefer to draw upon its fat reserves for its steady source of ATP. Fat burns in an oxygen environment, so the body can burn fat as its major source of fuel when an individual exercises at low intensity and has time to breathe in enough oxygen. Glycogen is always being used as a fuel; even if the muscles could use 100% fat for their energy source, some organs must rely on glucose to function properly.

What can the athlete do to conserve glycogen? There are several strategies for conserving glycogen. One is to coax the body into using its reserves of fat. Training, by increasing the amount of oxygen being delivered to the muscles, sets up an aerobic environment that allows fat to be used as fuel. The well-trained athlete can engage in longer-duration and higher-intensity exercise than can a less trained athlete. Training increases blood volume; expands the heart size, allowing more blood to be pumped per contraction of the heart muscle; and increases lung capacity, allowing more oxygen to be taken in.

The second strategy for conserving glycogen stores is to slow down the pace of exercise, increasing the time for the oxygen to reach its destination and for the muscle cells to use it. The faster one goes, the sooner one runs out of glycogen.

The third strategy is to increase reserves of carbohydrate. In the late 1960s, Scandinavian researchers reported a method to increase muscle stores of glycogen (Åstrand, 1967; Bergström & Hultman, 1972). Their technique, known as "classic carboloading," required that the muscles initially be stripped of their glycogen stores through heavy depletion exercise accompanied by a low-carbohydrate diet. The depleted muscles were then packed with glycogen through a high carbohydrate diet and reduced exercise. This regime, while substantially increasing muscle glycogen stores, caused problems such as weakness, lack of energy, dizziness, lack of interest in training, abnormal electrocardiograms, and increased water retention that resulted in a feeling of stiffness at the onset of an athletic event. Today, a "modified carboloading" plan is advised in place of the classic approach (Thornton, 1989). Beginning six days before an event, the athlete consumes a normal diet consisting of 50-55% carbohydrate, and training is gradually tapered. Three days before the event the amount of carbohydrate is increased to 70%. The day before the event is a rest day. The best foods for carboloading are pasta, rice, potatoes, whole-grain cereals and breads, dried fruits, and fresh fruits (see Figure 12.2).

There is little evidence that increased glycogen stores will improve performance in every sport, but some athletes in some sports may benefit, such as those participating in long-duration, high-endurance events and tournament events.

How much carbohydrate is recommended for training? The recommended amount of total carbohydrate is 50-55% of total kilocalories, with an emphasis on complex carbohydrates (pasta, whole-wheat breads, rice, potatoes, and the like). Athletes who train exhaustively over many days or who are involved in very grueling endurance events are encouraged to follow a diet of 65-70% carbohydrate (ADA, 1987).

Carbohydrate loading drinks: Do they work? Carbohydrate loading drinks contain 19-24% carbohydrate. High-carbohydrate drinks are not intended for consumption during exercise; rather, they are meant to supplement the carbohydrates from the diet. Athletes who find it difficult to follow a high-carbohydrate diet as suggested by the ADA (1987), or who train two or more times a day, may find these drinks beneficial. High-carbohydrate

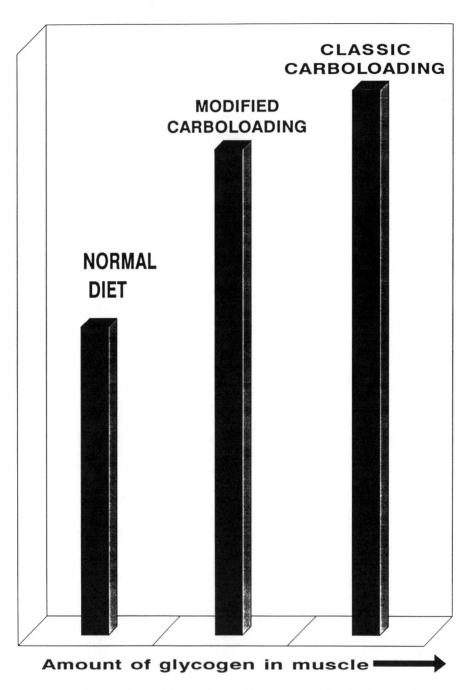

CLASSIC CARBOLOADING

MODIFIED CARBOLOADING

NORMAL DIET

Amount of glycogen in muscle ➡

Figure 12.2. Comparison of the Amount of Glycogen in Muscle Tissue Following Carboloading Diets Versus Normal Diet

drinks may also help replenish glycogen stores within the first two hours after an event, when the restoration of glycogen stores is most effective.

What should one eat on the day of competition? It is the diet one has followed during training that is crucial. No type of competition-day meal will make up for not eating well during training. A light meal (300 calories) should be eaten two to four hours before an endurance event to top off muscle and liver glycogen stores (Clark, 1990). The meal should consist primarily of carbohydrate and should contain little fat and fiber and include a little protein. Good choices are cereals with low-fat milk, bagels, muffins, or toast with jam.

Proteins

Protein Functions

Proteins, which are made up of amino acids, are the building blocks of muscles. Because proteins are the substance of muscles, and muscles are integral to exercise performance, athletes in the past have been taught that protein was the "stuff" of winners. Believing that the more protein one ate the more muscle one built up, athletes devoured large amounts of steak, hamburgers, eggs, and dairy products. It is true that the body uses proteins primarily to build cell structures, but it is not extra protein that builds muscle mass; exercise is primarily responsible for building muscles, and exercising the muscle requires energy. Supplying energy is a secondary function of protein. It is estimated that proteins contribute 4-10% to exercise energy expenditure (Brotherhood, 1984). Diets rich in carbohydrates will spare protein from being used as an energy source, because the body will draw upon the carbohydrate for energy. High-carbohydrate diets, therefore, will allow the protein to be used for its primary function of building and maintaining body tissue.

Commonly Asked Questions About Proteins and Exercise

What amount of protein is recommended for the athlete? The official recommended dietary allowance (RDA) is 0.8 g/kg body weight/day (Food and Nutrition Board, 1989). For a woman weighing 120 pounds this translates into 44 grams of protein/day (1 kg = 2.2 pounds), the equivalent of 2 cups of skim milk and a 3-ounce serving of chicken without the skin. The conventional scientific view has been that athletes do not need any extra protein, although some newer research has challenged this position (Brotherhood, 1984; Lemon, Yarasheski, & Dolney, 1984). At present, a consensus has not been reached. The ADA (1987), recognizing that the RDA may not be adequate for all athletes, advises an intake of 1.0 g/kg/day. Other researchers recommend values up to 2.0 g/kg/day for athletes involved in endurance sports and for strength-training athletes. In practical terms, the issue of how much extra protein is required may be largely an academic one. Average intakes for American women in general are already 144% above the RDA (U.S. Department of Health & Human Services, 1988).

Who might be at risk for developing a protein deficiency? Protein deficiency can result if an athlete does not take in enough kilocalories. Reduced caloric intake can be a problem for female athletes and may put these women at risk of inadequate protein intake. Women who experience problems with eating enough kilocalories should concentrate on eating high-density foods such as skim milk, nonfat yogurt, legumes, whole-grain breads and muffins, skinned chicken, and low-fat fish, such as cod, sole, and haddock.

Can too much protein be harmful? Ingesting only high-protein foods or protein supplements is not a good idea for several reasons. Excess protein replaces the high-carbohydrate fuel that is more beneficial for working muscles. Further, most high-protein foods are also high in fat (e.g., greasy hamburgers, steaks, cold cuts). High intakes of protein are also not advisable because the body has no way of storing excess protein as protein. Any extra protein that is ingested is modified and stored as fat. In the process of converting the excess protein to fat, urea is produced. Urea, a waste product, is eliminated thorough the kidneys via urine. Too much protein can increase the risk of dehydration, already a potential problem for athletes involved in some endurance sports. Amino acid supplements are also unnecessary and can be dangerous (Benevenga & Steele, 1984). The body best handles proteins in foods. The individual amino acids of amino acid supplements can overwhelm the absorption process in the body and result in imbalances and even toxicities.

Fluids

The Importance of Being Hydrated

Fluids in the body transport glucose to working muscles. They also carry away wastes and control body temperature. During exercise, the rate of heat production increases. To prevent an excessive rise in body heat (hyperthermia), the body copes by sweating. The evaporation of sweat from the surface of the skin cools the body. Care must be taken to ensure that dehydration does not impair this process. As one exercises, one's body loses water and the blood thickens. Consequently, the heart has to work harder to pump the more viscous blood around the body. As dehydration occurs, sweating is reduced and the body's inability to lose heat causes the temperature to climb steadily toward the danger zone (105°F). If this situation is not corrected, performance drops off and heat exhaustion, with potentially fatal consequences, can result.

There is a myth circulating among some athletes and coaches that withholding water during practice will allow the body to adapt to using less water. This is a false and dangerous idea. The body does not adapt to decreased intakes of water. It is imperative for individuals to be fully hydrated before exercising and that they not wait until they are thirsty to drink. The thirst mechanism is unreliable. By the time one is thirsty, the loss of fluid can be irreplaceable for any benefit to occur in exercise.

Commonly Asked Questions About Fluids and Exercise

How much fluid is necessary? Fluids should be taken before, during, and after exercising. Approximately 20-40 minutes before exercise, 1-2 cups of fluid should be ingested. During exercise, small amounts of fluid should be taken often. If an event lasts longer than 30 minutes, 1-1.5 cups of fluid should be taken every 15 minutes. As this may not always be practical, it is essential to be fully hydrated before exercising. Following exercise, rehydration should start immediately.

Does one need to replace electrolytes? Electrolytes are the minerals, such as sodium and potassium, that help the body function properly. Few electrolytes are lost in sweat. The athlete is rarely faced with a challenge to the body so severe as to induce electrolyte-associated problems. As more fluid is lost, the concentration of electrolytes in plasma increases.

Water or replacement sports drinks: Which is better?
    As the primary purpose of drinking while exercising is to replace water lost through sweat, water will always be the fluid of choice. Any commercially available sports drinks must also ensure maximum absorption of fluid to replace water lost. Water is cheaper, of course, but some athletes may prefer the taste of the sports drinks.
    For endurance athletes (those whose sports involve durations of more than 60-90 minutes), the carbohydrates found in some sports drinks have been found to delay fatigue. Carbohydrates improve performance by either preventing great drops in blood glucose levels or providing an outside source of glucose for muscle use. Until several years ago, most authorities would not advise anything more concentrated than a 2.5% carbohydrate solution. Current research suggests that the ideal concentration should be between 5% and 10% carbohydrate (Coleman, 1991; Davis, Burgess, Slentz, & Bartoli, 1990).

Vitamins

Definition and Functions

    Vitamins are substances needed in small amounts by the human body. Vitamins cannot be made by the body in sufficient quantities, so they must be supplied by the foods we eat. Vitamins function essentially as regulators for a wide variety of processes that occur in the body. Although vitamins do not contain energy, they do play special roles in the body's release, storage, and use of energy. The belief that excess vitamins will produce energy is not valid.

Vitamins come in two forms: fat soluble and water soluble. Fat-soluble vitamins (A, D, K, and E) remain in the body for long periods of time. Water-soluble vitamins (the B vitamins and C) leave the body more rapidly through the urine.

Commonly Asked Questions About Vitamins

Are vitamin supplements useful? Some people believe that, as certain vitamins are involved in energy metabolism, consumption of these vitamins in the form of supplements will improve performance by providing extra energy. Manufacturers of vitamin supplements, some coaches, and athletes themselves attest that vitamin and mineral supplements help boost performance. However, supplementation has no significant effect on performance and is of little benefit for the well-nourished athlete. Studies have shown that vitamin supplements help sports performance only if nutrient deficiencies existed initially.

Can vitamin supplements be harmful? Excessive intakes of vitamins can cause bodily damage from overload. It is relatively difficult to overdose on vitamins through food intake, but it is very easy to consume intakes in tablet form that are 10-1,000 times what could be consumed in food. The use of megavitamin preparations can expose the body to doses it cannot handle. This is especially true for fat-soluble vitamins, which can easily accumulate in the body. For example, excessive amounts of vitamin A can cause liver damage.

Are vitamin supplements ever warranted? Some young female distance runners, gymnasts, and dancers may continually restrict their food intake to maintain low body weight. It may be justified for such athletes to take a single daily multivitamin-multimineral supplement. It is preferable to improve or correct eating habits that are responsible for the shortage; then, if one elects to take supplements, megadoses will not be required.

Minerals

Definition and Functions

Approximately 4% of the human body is composed of minerals, which are inorganic substances. Minerals are found in soil and in water, and are absorbed into plants and further passed along the food chain as animals ingest plants. Minerals are necessary for the basic structure of bones, for the maintenance of nerve and muscle function, and for a host of other functions in the body. The most important minerals in relation to the athlete are iron and calcium. Consuming adequate amounts of these two minerals is often difficult for many women athletes.

Iron

Iron plays a vital role in carrying oxygen around the body and in the capacity to perform muscular work. Many studies have identified women athletes as at risk for iron deficiency (Deuster et al., 1986; Keith et al., 1989; Welch, Zager, Endres, & Poone, 1987). At particularly high risk are vegetarian women athletes. Iron deficiency anemia can cause marked impairments in physical performance: loss of strength, tiredness, and shortened attention span.

Sports anemia. Sports anemia is a temporary condition defined as low hemoglobin levels associated with strenuous athletic activity (Williams, 1985). Sports anemia may result from heavy sweating, heavy menstrual blood flow, increased destruction of red blood cells, insufficient intake of iron in the diet, a natural response to endurance training that results in an increased blood volume, and dilution of red blood cells. Sports anemia usually goes away by itself.

Young menstruating women often border on iron deficiency even without additional iron losses from exercise. The body conserves much of its iron by recycling, but small losses of approximately 1.5 mg per day do occur. Because only about 10% of the iron we consume is absorbed, a women needs to take in 15 mg daily from her diet. The average American diet supplies 0.6 mg/1,000 kilocalories, so to provide 15 mg a women must ingest 2,500 kilocalories per day. Since many women eat less than this amount, they fall short of consuming the necessary iron.

A moderate iron supplement may be recommended. However, blood levels should be checked before iron supplements are prescribed.

Calcium

Calcium is the most abundant mineral in the human body. The concern with adequate calcium intakes is linked with the concern for osteoporosis, a condition of decreased bone mass resulting in thin bones with the associated risk of bone fractures and bone breaks. Osteoporosis is mainly a problem for postmenopausal women. Estrogen deficiency and inadequate calcium intake are the two most probable causes of osteoporosis. Cessation of menstruation with corresponding low estrogen can be a side effect of intensive and/or extensive physical training for some women. This condition, known as *athletic amenorrhea*, is characterized by low estrogen levels. If calorie intake is also low, there is a greater likelihood of an inadequate calcium intake and an increased risk of losing calcium from the bones. In the case of amenorrheic athletes, supplements in the form of calcium lactate, calcium gluconate, or calcium carbonate may be needed. Women with normal menstruation cycles are advised to obtain calcium by eating calcium-rich foods (ADA, 1987). Those women who are concerned

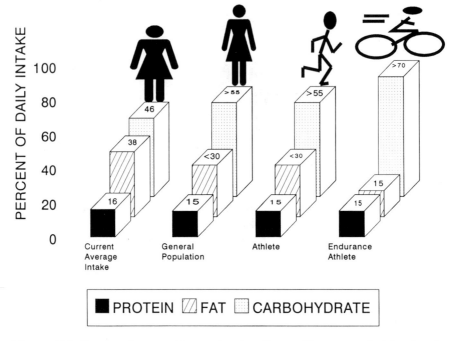

Figure 12.3. Current Average Energy Intakes Versus Recommended Intakes for Other Populations

about high-calorie foods can choose skim milk, nonfat yogurts, and low-fat cheeses (although these are still loaded with fat). Other sources of calcium include dark green leafy vegetables (broccoli, spinach, collards), tofu that has been processed with calcium sulfate, bok choy, and sardines with bones (one must eat the bones to get the calcium benefit). There is reason to be concerned about calcium in American women's diets. Although the recommended daily intake of calcium is 1,200 mg for adolescent women to the age of 25, the average calcium intake for women in the United States ranges from 500 to 650 mg/day.

Summary

It is incumbent upon all of us to take responsibility for our own health. The dearth of nutrition information available does not make this task easy for the female athlete, for whom it is all the more imperative. The basic truths held today are often contradicted tomorrow. It would be difficult and foolish to modify one's diet for every new piece of research reported. The best procedure is to follow a basically healthy diet now. An athlete must eat for energy and adequacy, and this means eating as close to natural as possible. This includes eating unprocessed foods (such as whole grains, legumes, fresh fruits and vegetables, and dairy products) that supply maximum vitamins and minerals. In addition, for those concerned about calorie intake, nutrient-dense foods supplying large amounts of minerals and vitamins relative to calories should be emphasized. Overall, an athlete should consume a diet that is high in carbohydrate (60-65% of total kilocalories or more), low in fat (20% or less), and moderate in proteins (12-15%) (see Figure 12.3).

Key Words

adenosine triphosphate (ATP)	electrolytes
phosphocreatine	sports anemia
carbohydrate	iron
glycogen	iron deficiency anemia
fats	calcium
fatty acids	osteoporosis
amino acids	vitamins
protein	minerals

Discussion Questions

1. Give examples of sports that would rely mainly on glycogen as their energy source. Why would fat not be used for regenerating ATP in these sports?
2. Although the human body can use protein as a fuel source, under normal conditions the body does not use a large amount of its protein for energy. Under what conditions would the body use protein as a source of energy?
3. What is the difference between sports anemia and iron deficiency anemia?
4. How are calcium, estrogen, exercise, and osteoporosis related?
5. Why are supplements of vitamins, minerals, proteins, and amino acids generally not advised? When might a female athlete be advised to take a supplement?

References

American Dietetic Association (ADA). (1987). Position of the American Dietetic Association: Nutrition for physical fitness and athletic performance for adults. *Journal of the American Dietetic Association, 87,* 933-939.

Åstrand, P. (1967). Diet and athletic performance. *Federation Proceedings, 26,* 1772-1777.

Benevenga, N. U., & Steele, R. D. (1984). Adverse effects of excessive consumption of amino acids. *Annual Review of Nutrition, 4,* 157-181.

Bergström, J., & Hultman, E. (1972). Nutrition for maximal sports performance. *Journal of the American Medical Association, 221,* 999-1006.

Brotherhood, J. R. (1984). Nutrition and sports performance. *Sports Medicine, 1,* 350-389.

Bruce, V., Crosby, L. O., Reicheck, N., Pertschuk, M., Lusk, E., & Mullen, J. L. (1984). Energy expenditure in primary malnutrition during standardized exercise. *American Journal of Physiology and Medicine, 63,* 165-174.

Clark, N. (1990). *Sports nutrition guidebook: Eating to fuel your active lifestyle.* Champaign, IL: Leisure.

Coleman, E. (1991, March). Sports drink research. *Food Technology,* pp. 104-106, 108.

Davis, J. M., Burgess, W. A., Slentz, C. A., & Bartoli, W. P. (1990). Fluid availability of sports drinks differing in carbohydrate type and concentration. *American Journal of Clinical Nutrition, 51,* 1054-1057.

Deuster, P. A., Kyle, S. B., Moser, P. B., Vigersky, R. A., Singh, A., & Schoomaker, E. B. (1986). Nutrition survey of highly trained women runners. *American Journal of Clinical Nutrition, 44,* 954-962.

Food and Nutrition Board. (1989). *Recommended dietary allowances* (10th ed.). Washington, DC: National Academy Press.

Keith, R. E., O'Keefe, K. A., Alt, L. A., & Young, K. L. (1989). Dietary status of trained female cyclists. *Journal of the American Dietetic Association, 89,* 1620-1623.

Kleiner, S. M., Bazzarre, T. L., & Litchford, M. D. (1990). Metabolic profiles, diet, and health practices of championship male and female bodybuilders. *Journal of the American Dietetic Association, 90,* 962-967.

Lemon, R. W., Yarasheski, K. E., & Dolney, D. (1984). The importance of protein for athletes. *Sports Medicine, 1,* 474-484.

Thornton, J. S. (1989). Carboloading and endurance: A new look. *Physician and Sportsmedicine, 117,* 149-156.

Tilgner, S. A., & Schiller, R. M. (1989). Dietary intakes of female college athletes: The need for nutrition education. *Journal of the American Dietetic Association, 89,* 967-969.

U.S. Department of Health and Human Services. (1988). *The surgeon general's report on nutrition and health.* Washington, DC: Government Printing Office.

Welch, P. K., Zager, K. A., Endres, J., & Poone, S. (1987). Nutrition education, body composition, and dietary intake of female college athletes. *Physician and Sportsmedicine, 15,* 63-74.

Williams, M. H. (1985). *Nutritional aspects of human physical and athletic performance* (2nd ed.). Springfield, IL: Charles C Thomas.

13

Athletic Training
for the Female Athlete

KATHLEEN CERRA-LAQUALE

During the ancient Olympics, females were not even permitted to observe the athletic events. History discloses how one woman, costumed as a man, attempted to view her son competing in the all-male Olympic Games. She was exposed and knew her fate was death. Caesar, however, impressed by her courage, saved the woman's life, but he did not alter the rule forbidding women to view the competition.

Secretly, the women of that time decided to have their own games, called the Heraea, in honor of Hera, the wife of the god Zeus. What types of injuries could these athletes have received? The clothes they wore for sport were far from protective: "It is known that females wore a high waisted, short tunic that ended between the hips and knee. The right shoulder and breast were bare" (Pike, 1988, p. 55). Undergarments were not available to support the breasts. They also ran barefooted. The sneaker as we know it today was unavailable and could not protect the foot from plantar fasciitis or shin splints.

Male athletes of ancient times had ample assistance in the care of injuries. Physicians and professional trainers such as Galen and Herodicus, along with the Paidotribai and Aleiptes (student trainers as we know them today), used various oils, massage, and hydrotherapy to service the athletes (Arnheim, 1988). Perhaps the first female athletic trainer may have been an athlete herself, competing in the Heraea.

Shamans were the world's first healers, diagnosticians, and psychotherapists (Doore, 1988, p. 101). For centuries the healing powers of herbalists, shamans, and medicine women have guided these women toward an understanding of the sacred stories and prophecies of medicine power, transmitted from the world of the supernatural to help and heal tribal members (Allen, 1991). In modern times, the physician provides care for the female athlete. Not until the early 1960s were women allowed to enter the private profession of sports medicine. In 1970, the first female was permitted to take the National Athletic Trainer's Association certification exam. By 1991, 43% of the certified trainers in the United States were female.

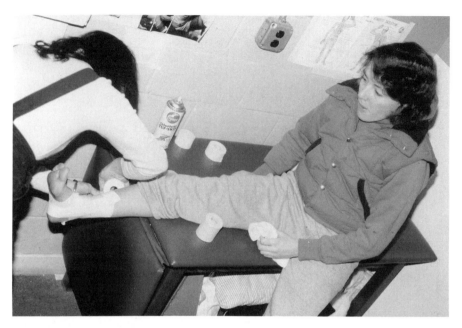

Although athletic trainers often develop their own style of a closed basket-weave pattern for the common ankle sprain, they should be able to justify the need for every strip of tape used. (Photo courtesy of Kathleen Cerra-Laquale)

Common Injuries in Female Athletes

In general, females are subject to the same types of injuries incurred by males. However, in some instances females are more vulnerable to certain injuries or conditions. The sprained ankle is by far the most prevalent injury in sports that involve jumping and lateral movements. The higher incidence of sprains in females can be attributed to a smaller proportion of muscle to adipose tissue and delicate ligamentous and tendinous structures.

Some females are at greater risk of heat prostration due to larger deposits of adipose tissue. Precautions such as adequate hydration and well-ventilated clothing can curtail the onset of heat illness.

Females have been plagued by upper-body injuries owing to muscular weakness in the shoulder girdle. Sharkey (1990) reports that because women use their legs in the same manner as men (walking, running, and cycling), a measurement of leg strength per unit of lean body weight (LBW) indicates that women have slightly stronger legs than men do. However, female arm strength is 30% below male scores. As conditioning programs address this issue, perhaps the incidence of shoulder injuries will also decrease.

The lower extremity is a source of potential injury in the female. Patellofemoral malalignment syndrome is very common among teenaged female athletes. Two familiar conditions are chondromalacia (the wearing away of the underside of the patella caused by improper patella tracking) and patella subluxation (displacement of the patella that returns to alignment unassisted). Both conditions are thought to be caused by external tibial torsion and a Q angle greater than 20% (Otis, 1986). Treatment of these conditions by strengthening the quadriceps and stretching the hamstring has been shown to minimize the pain and discomfort that accompany them.

Stress fractures, common among female athletes (especially runners), have been treated in an assortment of ways; however, the jury is still out regarding the causes of these debilitating injuries. Excessive rotation of the femur and malalignment of the patella, along with excessive foot pronation, can cause stress fractures. Repetitive movement combined with hard surfaces has been shown to yield a high rate of injury (Ritchie, Kelso, & Bellucci, 1985). Shock reduction (with shoe inserts designed to cushion impact) has proved to be ineffective in some cases, whereas improving the stability of the foot has helped to reduce the incidence of stress fractures.

Stress fractures develop over long periods of time, caused by small repeated microtraumas to the injured area. Many athletes experiencing these microtraumas tend to minimize the pain and attribute it to lack of training. Usually, the pain is not intense when the injury begins and the athlete "plays through the pain," hoping it will disappear.

The most common site of stress fractures is the tibia. A familiar name for pain in this area is *shin splints*; occasionally, such pain is the precursor to stress fractures. Shin splints are described by athletes as pain along the anterior border of the tibia beginning at the top of the tibia and reaching as far down as the ankle. Causal factors range from improper conditioning prior to activity to ill-fitting and poorly supported footwear. Improper biomechanics of the athlete's gait, a foot that has a high arch (pes cavus), and muscle imbalance between the anterior tibialis (usually weak) and the gastrocnemius (usually very strong) are typically the principal offenders.

If the pain persists, diagnostic tools such as X rays and bone scans are performed to determine the presence of a stress fracture. Observations of female athletes demonstrate a correlation between menstrual irregularities and bone disorders. Barrow and Saha (1988) report that "female distance runners who have a history of irregular or absent menses and who never used oral contraceptives (which alters estrogen balance) may be at risk for developing stress fractures" (p. 211).

Nutrition can play an important role in prevention of and recovery from injuries. Poor nutritional habits may lead to a decrease in percentage of body fat, which may affect the estrogen level. As percentage of body fat decreases, menstrual cycles can become sporadic and in some cases cease altogether. According to Solomon and Michelli (1990, p. 136), when the menstrual cycle decreases along with the decreased estrogen level (called hypoestrogenism), stress fractures can occur. Previous research contradicts this premise. Earlier studies found that the only area of diminished bone concentration in these women was the cancellous bone of the vertebral bodies; no change in density of cortical bone was found. As stress fractures occur just proximal to metaphysis, in the area of cortical bone, it was believed to be doubtful that the incidence was related to the low estrogen levels.

Menses should not prohibit the female from participating in athletics. Participation for the female during menses is not discouraged, for the benefits certainly outweigh any potential hazards. Two areas of concern include (a) the female's susceptibility to bruising during menses because of a decrease in estrogen and (b) increased laxity of the lower back (the female should try to avoid heavy intense lifting during that period).

The bunion (abnormal prominence of the inner aspect of the first metatarsal head accompanied by bursal formation that results in lateral displacement of the first toe) has been shown to be more prevalent in females than in males. According to Bruce Werber, D.P.M., females experience more painful bunions as opposed to bunions in general. He attributes this to the types of shoes worn by females and possibly to an inherited genetic factor (personal communication, December 8, 1991). Conservative treatment of bunions includes taping the first toe to minimize displacement of the colateral ligament and the use of orthotics. Radical treatment (bunionectomy) is commonly postponed to a time when the athlete is not in season to allow for full recovery. Both frequency and severity of this condition are more noticeable among relatively mature athletes.

Spondylolysis (defect in the pars interarticularis in the lower back) is an injury most often afflicting female gymnasts and some dancers. It is not clear whether this defect is a stress fracture resulting from repetitive hyperextension and flexion activity of the area or a developmental abnormality. Once the diagnosis is established and the spondylolysis has been shown to be indicative of an older injury, the athlete can return to activity after rehabilitation.

Breast problems are not considered injuries but can create annoyance. A good supportive bra, with nonelastic straps, that limits breast motion and reduces friction is recommended for large-breasted female athletes. Lycra or Spandex half T-shirts can lend support for smaller females. Runners can minimize "runner's nipple" by using something as small as a Band-Aid.

Exercise during pregnancy does not necessarily increase the incidence of injuries. Studies have demonstrated repeatedly that if a woman is in good health and physical conditioning prior to her pregnancy, a program of exercise is not detrimental. During pregnancy, the woman is at risk for sprains because of an increase in joint laxity as the body prepares for childbirth. However, with proper precautions, this risk can be minimized.

The more mature athlete participating in an exercise program should be aware of physical changes taking place. The Running and Fitness Association recommends that any athlete over 40 years of age have a maximal exercise stress test to determine how intensely she can train. More important, the test will show any underlying heart disease that could be aggravated by exercise. The symptoms of arthritis can be reduced in some athletes who exercise, but in such cases treatment of aching joints must be sure to differentiate between sports injuries and arthritis. It appears that older athletes tend to have fewer injuries than do younger athletes, but once older athletes are injured, they take longer to heal (Gundling, 1991).

In general, women need no different protective equipment from men except that the equipment should be manufactured to accommodate the size of the female. Athletes and coaches should understand the purpose of protective equipment and be able to evaluate its effectiveness during use. Once equipment has been issued to the athlete, it should be monitored periodically for defects. It is also important to remember that protective equipment should not be altered in any manner.

In all of the studies completed thus far on the incidence of female injuries, it has been concluded that the major cause of injuries is lack of proper conditioning—this is true for the male athlete as well.

Prevention of Injuries

Prevention of injuries should be of paramount interest to every athlete. Although a total prevention program is made up of many components, six factors are considered essential:

1. *conditioning:* aerobic and anaerobic training, flexibility, strength training, kinesthetic sense, and vision training (depth perception and eye-hand coordination)
2. *balanced nutrition:* adequate hydration and a combination of high-carbohydrate, low-fat, and low-protein diet
3. *proper equipment:* protective and supportive
4. *preseason physicals:* medical and orthopedic history
5. *screening protocols:* general physical fitness and anthropometric measurements
6. *common sense:* well-planned and properly executed practices

Conditioning programs help to prepare the athlete for the stress incurred in the activity, adaptation to the skills, and acclimatization to the environment. It is a systematic process of repetitive progressive work or exercise involving the learning process. When beginning a conditioning program, it is important that the trainer realize the strengths and weaknesses of the athletes, have knowledge of the injuries that are common to the sport, and prepare the athletes properly to prevent these injuries.

A trainer conducting a conditioning program should build on each session by steadily increasing intensity. *Activities should be sequenced to prevent injuries.* An overtrained athlete is typically not recovered enough to continue training intensely. Trainers should instruct athletes to "listen to their bodies" so that they will know when to slow down and when to put on the brakes. Athletes typically tend to overlook microinjuries, thinking them insignificant. They continue to work out and their injuries worsen, becoming macroinjuries that sideline them for weeks instead of days. Repeatedly, athletes use the sport to get in shape rather than get in shape for the sport.

The acronym SAID means specific adaptation to imposed demands. The SAID principle applies to the development of strength, cardiovascular and muscular endurance, and flexibility. When considering specificity of training for a muscle to increase strength or endurance, the training program must be specific to obtain the desired effects. Athletes should train the way they perform, with muscle groups working together, not separately. Weight training can be an essential aspect of the conditioning program; however, proper supervision and a controlled, progressive program are crucial. The type of equipment used should coincide with the size and shape of the female somatotype. Any adjustment in a beginning weight training program should meet individual strength capacity and training skill needs.

A sport skill training program deals with a set of nuances indigenous to a particular sport. The mode of the exercise should be the same as the skill performed and the same muscle group should duplicate the movement pattern of the skill. In this age of specialization, an individual may be well conditioned for one sport but not at all "in shape" for another sport.

Clearly, training is an adaptive process. Physical conditioning programs should match the physiological demands of the activity. The type of conditioning method should match the energy source and pathway required by the athlete to meet the demands of the sport involved. Thus the type of training used in the conditioning drill should duplicate the energy demands involved in the sport. Some sport skills require bursts of energy lasting merely a few seconds, whereas endurance sports require sustained energy pathways. Coaches theorize that, given the aforementioned, athletes should train aerobically for endurance sports and anaerobically for the other sports. Repeated research in exercise physiology suggests the contrary: Athletes in both types of sports must train both aerobically and anaerobically to achieve an optimal effect.

Cross-training has become quite popular as a way to encompass many different components in a conditioning program. This is a method of training that involves three or more complementary activities during one workout. A training period may be designated as one day or several sessions per week. Cross-training activities should incorporate skills that relate to the individual's specific sport. For example, a basketball player may choose to jump rope to enhance rebounding skills, engage in distance running or cycling for endurance, and play racquetball to develop quickness. Advantages of cross-training are that it allows the athlete a respite from the day-to-day routine of repetitive training and usually decreases injuries because it utilizes different muscle groups. The primary disadvantage is that some individuals dislike it; they do not respond to the variety provided by cross-training. Overall, the cross-training concept is gaining in popularity, especially for individuals who enjoy working out every day.

MMIs

When planning a specific drill or station (as in a circuit program), knowledge of the specific muscles that cause or control joint motion through a specified plane of motion in that skill or action is critical. The coach or trainer who understands the MMIs (muscles most involved) can design drills for a given sport that will benefit the athlete. Further, the coach will be able to develop proper stretches specific for the sport by determining which muscles actually do the "work." For the athletic trainer, this knowledge will facilitate proper evaluation and rehabilitation of any injury sustained in that sport.

Stretching

Which activity should come first, the warm-up or the stretch? An easy way to remember the sequence is $(WS)^2$: warm-up, stretch, workout, and stretch. The warm-up should include activities similar to those that will be performed, but without intensity. An increase in body temperature should occur to "oil" the musculotendinous units to be stretched in the next phase. It is important to remember that the athlete should never do any jumping during this phase. Heel-toe jogging or riding a stationary bike can be done to achieve a proper warm-up. The stretch phase must incorporate these important guidelines:

1. Stretches should be sport specific.
2. A muscle must be relaxed in order to be stretched.
3. Ballistic or pulsing actions tighten a muscle.
4. Static stretching (holding a stretch for a minimum of 10 seconds) allows the muscle fibers to lengthen.
5. Proper body alignment during the stretch is imperative to prevent injury and to allow for elongation of the muscle.
6. The musculotendinous unit, not the ligaments, should be stretched.
7. A stretch should not be painful.
8. When tension is felt at the beginning of a stretch, the athlete should back off the stretch slightly and hold that position for 10-20 seconds.
9. It is important to breath during stretches. The athlete should begin a stretch by inhaling, exhaling slowly while moving into the proper position.
10. Counterirritants and saunas are no substitute for stretching the muscles.

The workout phase will vary to accommodate individual needs. Finally, the stretch at the end of the workout is just as critical as the first stretch phase. The large muscle groups utilized during the workout should be stretched. Level of flexibility increases following workout activity; thus, the second stretch period is just as important as the first. Also, if the second stretch phase is performed with a group, such as with a team or in a class, the closure helps to promote unity and allows the coach or teacher time for final instructions.

Conditioning

Conditioning programs are very beneficial, and most coaches follow a certain preseason program. The intensity with which individuals approach preseason training will diminish as the season progresses. One factor affecting the conditioning level is a decrease in the muscle's stimulation of the motor unit. A common mistake by most coaches is to abandon some aspect of the conditioning program during the season; thus, some aspect of the practice drills should incorporate conditioning drills.

The objective of a conditioning program is twofold: to enhance the athlete's performance and to prevent injuries commonly caused by improper condition and incorrect body mechanics. Athletes should be trained specific to their individual needs for their sports. Coaches and trainers must be aware of new research findings and the latest in physiological and biomechanical analysis. General guidelines for coaches and trainers conducting a conditioning program are as follows:

1. *Educate the athletes.* Explain why a particular skill or action is a part of the conditioning program.
2. *Add variety to the program.* Use jump ropes, bench aerobics, Hula Hoops, plyometrics (athletes with knee injuries should avoid plyometrics), swimming and aerobics.
3. *Be culturally aware when motivating individual athletes.* The uniqueness of an individual will affect motivational technique.
4. *Have frequent water breaks.* Hydrating athletes will increase the length and quality of their performance.
5. *Sequence activities in a progressive fashion.* Try to give instructions during the stretch phase of the workout. Do not expect athletes to perform sprints after they have been seated for a length of time, especially in a cold environment.
6. *Include fitness screenings, preseason physicals, and medical histories.* These provide the physician, athletic trainer, and coach with information regarding athletes' health and injury status prior to the start of any conditioning program.

Anabolic Steroids and Medroxyprogesterone

Sadly, sports enhancement drugs have become part of the athlete's overall training and conditioning program. Anabolic steroids are used to enlarge musculature, and drugs such as medroxyprogesterone are used to diminish the size of the body or curb the maturation process.

For years, women avoided weight training for fear of "bulking up." The myth that musculature would increase regardless of the type of exercise persisted. Contemporary women now realize the importance of muscle tone and work to achieve a healthy, strong physique. Females cannot attain the immense musculature found in males because of their lower levels of testosterone and an additional 10% adipose tissue, which result in smaller muscle mass relative to total body weight. However, the female athlete of today possesses greater hypertrophy. This can be generated by two factors: (a) decrease in percentage of body fat, which allows muscles to appear larger, and (b) the genetic composition that demonstrates a larger somatotype. For the female who desires additional bulk and does not possess either factor, steroids provide an effortless shortcut. Muscle size is increased chemically through the systematic use of anabolic (growth-promoting) steroids. These drugs are illegal if not prescribed by a physician, and, as with many drugs, numerous side effects can be expected. When a female uses an anabolic steroid (which contains testosterone, a male hormone), her female characteristics diminish and male characteristics become more prominent, resulting in such changes as smaller breasts, enlarged clitoris, deepened voice, and growth of facial and body hair. When a male uses a steroid, the brain responds to the increase in testosterone by decreasing the release of testosterone and increasing the estrogen (female hormone) level. Thus a male will have larger muscles accompanied by an increase in female characteristics: increase in breast size, shrinkage of the testicles, and loss of body hair. In addition to these changes in external characteristics, many internal physiological processes take place. Individuals may experience an increase in blood pressure and increased incidence of cancer of the liver, because the steroid is filtered through the liver. Although muscle size increases, the tendon that attaches the muscle to the bone does not increase in size. When the larger muscle contracts, it stresses the smaller tendon; if the contraction is strong enough, the tendon will tear away from its attachment to the bone.

Athletes should avoid the use of anabolic steroids because of their many demonstrated deleterious physiological and psychological effects. Many sports federations have banned steroid use, and governing bodies conduct routine random drug testing procedures on athletes to deter cheating. Steroid abuse is still prevalent among recreational athletes who are being identified as "reverse anorexic." Instead of viewing themselves as fat, they view themselves as thin and use the drug to become larger. Some athletes are being lured toward amino acids as a safe alternative to the use of steroids. These amino acids are extremely expensive, and their effectiveness has not been conclusively validated.

Medroxyprogesterone is one of the hormones used to diminish growth. Young females just beginning puberty may use this type of drug to control maturation. Some females who have become elite gymnasts at an early age may be distressed at experiencing the increase in body fat and breast and hip size that accompanies the onset of menstruation. These athletes may view such changes as a detriment to their talents, and they may attempt to use the hormone to minimize the process of maturation.

> The theory of giving medroxyprogesterone to young gymnasts is that it will delay puberty by suppressing ovulation and menstruation in the same way it does during pregnancy. When ovulation is suppressed, there is also suppression of the hormones that are responsible for physical changes in the body. (Goldman, 1984)

Parents, coaches, and the athletes themselves are often very willing to sacrifice the athlete's health and future well-being to enhance that athlete's potential success. What price does the athlete pay for glory? Athletes must be educated regarding the ramifications of substance abuse and, more important, the values of self-reliance, self-esteem, and self-respect.

Conclusion

For most of our recorded history, limited knowledge has been available regarding the female athlete. While there have always been examples of daring individuals defying convention, these women were still the exception rather than the norm. It was not until the 1970s that opportunities mushroomed and serious training in events requiring strength, power, and endurance involved large numbers of girls and women of all ages.

It has been difficult to amass detailed sophisticated research related to performance of the female athlete. Researchers have been reluctant to engage in studies using women as subjects for scientific investigation. However, the increase in numbers of women entering programs in sports medicine and exercise physiology has resulted in the first wave of scientific data now available to athletic trainers for the care and prevention of athletic injuries.

Further investigations are necessary, especially research scrutinizing the specific causes of isolated injuries to females. A sizable pool of subjects is now available. The long-term effects of competition can now be analyzed. Although a great deal of investigative work remains, the prospects are encouraging. As women continue to participate in sports and exercise programs, they become keenly aware of the challenges, fulfillment, and enjoyment that participation can provide. Although injuries may occur, it is possible to reduce their probability through proper conditioning and training.

Key Words

shaman	stretching
common injuries	plyometrics
injury prevention	cross-training
conditioning programs	medroxyprogesterone
SAID	anabolic steroids
$(WS)^2$	

Discussion Questions

1. As the coach of a sport, plan a one-week conditioning program for your team. Include warm-ups, stretches specific to your sport, specific drills and aerobic and anaerobic energy pathways, and a cool-down session. You have one hour per day to work with the team and each segment of the hour must be organized.

2. There have been rumors spreading about your top shot-put athlete with regard to her use of steroids. How would you approach this issue? What substance abuse guidelines have you established for your team? What advice would you offer to this athlete if the rumors were true?

References

Allen, P. G. (1991). *Grandmothers of the light: A medicine woman's sourcebook*. Boston: Beacon.

Arnheim, D. (1988). *Modern principles of athletic training* (7th ed.). St. Louis: Times Mirror/Mosby.

Barrow, G., & Saha, S. (1988). Menstrual irregularities and stress fractures in collegiate female distance runners. *American Journal of Sports Medicine, 16*, 209-216.

Doore, G. (1988). *Shaman's path*. Boston: Shambhala.

Goldman, B. (1984). *Death in the locker room*. Tucson, AZ: Body Press.

Gundling, L. (1991, October 1). Smart training for older athletes. *American Running and Fitness* [Insert].

Otis, C. (1986). Female athletes: Special concerns. *Sports Medicine Digest, 8*(10), 4-5.

Pike, L. (1988, August-September). Olympic countdown. *Women's Sports & Fitness*, 54-55.

Ritchie, D., Kelso, S., & Bellucci, P. (1985). Aerobic dance injuries: A retrospective study of participants and instructors. *Physician and Sportsmedicine, 13*, 209-216.

Sharkey, B. (1990). *Physiology of fitness*. Champaign, IL: Human Kinetics.

Solomon, R. M., & Michelli, L. (1990). Stress fractures in dancers. In R. M. Solomon & J. Solomon (Ed.), *Preventing dance injuries* (p. 136). Reston, VA: American Alliance for Health, Physical Education, Recreation and Dance.

14

Eating Disorders and Related Behavior Among Athletes

MARJORIE CALDWELL

The eating disorders anorexia nervosa and bulimia have been the subject of considerable discussion in recent years. Reports of an increase in their prevalence in both athletes and nonathletes, coupled with a growing awareness of the detrimental effects of these disorders on health and well-being, have stimulated research into their etiology, treatment, and prevention. It is now apparent that, in addition to those who are anorexic or bulimic, a relatively large number of people practice some of the behaviors associated with eating disorders. These behaviors may have a negative impact on health and performance.

Anorexia nervosa is self-induced starvation characterized by excessive weight loss, preoccupation with body weight, and an intense fear of becoming fat. Body image is distorted so that, even though clearly underweight, anorexics view themselves as being too fat. While severely restricting food intake, anorexics often engage in excessive physical activity; running is usually the exercise of choice. Most anorexic women have prolonged amenorrhea.

The bulimic is also preoccupied with body weight and fears becoming fat. In contrast to the anorexic, however, the bulimic's body weight is usually within normal range. Bulimia is characterized by secretive and recurrent binge eating, which may be repeated several times per day; intakes of several thousand calories per day have been reported. Binge eating is followed by an attempt to prevent weight gain.

Self-induced vomiting, laxatives and diuretics, vigorous exercise, and strict dieting are commonly used to counter the excess caloric intake resulting from binge eating. The binge and purge cycle may cause rapid fluctuations in body weight. Typically, bulimics feel unable to control

AUTHOR'S NOTE: Preparation of this chapter was supported in part by the Rhode Island Agricultural Experiment Station.

TABLE 14.1 Diagnostic Criteria

Anorexia Nervosa	*Bulimia*
Intense fear of gaining weight or becoming fat	Regular use of self-induced vomiting, laxatives or diuretics, strict dieting or fasting, or vigorous exercise to prevent weight gain
Seeing oneself as fat even when clearly underweight	Constant concern with body weight
Body weight 15% or more below standard	Feeling unable to control eating
Amenorrhea in females	Recurrent episodes of binge eating, a minimum of twice a week

SOURCE: Adapted from American Psychiatric Association (1987, pp. 67-69).

binge eating, resulting in low self-esteem and feelings of shame and guilt. Bulimics may also have a history of other impulsive behaviors, such as drug or alcohol abuse.

Anorexia nervosa and bulimia are considered separate disorders; however, individuals with anorexia may, at times, exhibit bulimic behavior. Similarly, bulimics may pass through a phase of anorexia. The social consequences of both disorders are similar and are characterized by lack of interest in social activities and preoccupation with food.

Prevalence of Eating Disorders

There is a general belief that the prevalence of eating disorders in the United States is increasing, and it has been suggested that bulimia is endemic among college women today. However, studies concerning eating disorders often produce conflicting results, making it difficult to determine the extent of the problem and to document changes in prevalence over time. Study results vary because of real differences among the population groups surveyed, differences in data-collection methods, and, most important, differences in criteria used to establish the presence of an eating disorder. Early studies suggested that 15-30% of college women suffered from bulimia or . anorexia. However, when stricter criteria are used, the prevalence of these disorders appears to be much lower. It is now estimated that 1-5% of female adolescents are anorexic, and the prevalence of bulimia in college-age women appears to range from 5% to 10% (Katz, 1988). Overall, approximately 1% of women aged 15 to 40 are anorexic, and approximately 2-3% suffer from bulimia (National Institute of Nutrition, 1989).

There is considerable disagreement about the appropriate criteria to use in determining the presence of anorexia nervosa and bulimia. Although not uniformly accepted, the criteria most commonly used are based on those proposed by the American Psychiatric Association (1987), which are summarized in Table 14.1.

Adolescent or young adult females are at highest risk of developing anorexia nervosa and bulimia. Traditionally, anorexia and bulimia have been considered disorders of young Caucasian women of middle to upper income levels. There is now some evidence that differences in prevalence by race and income may be diminishing (Katz, 1988). The onset of anorexia tends to be in adolescence, whereas bulimia occurs more frequently in late adolescence and early adulthood. These disorders do occur in males, but about 90-95% of cases involve females.

Although the prevalence of eating disorders in the general population is relatively low, specific behaviors associated with these disorders, such as binge eating, vomiting, and severe food restriction, occur in a larger percentage of women than men in the United States. Attitudes associated with eating disorders, such as fear of becoming fat and dissatisfaction with body weight, appear to be widespread. These behaviors and attitudes are of concern because they increase the risk of developing eating disorders. In addition, these eating disorder-related behaviors may affect health and well-being.

Consequences of Eating Disorders

Eating disorders are potentially life threatening. Major causes of eating disorder-related deaths are suicide and cardiac arrest (U.S. Olympic Committee, 1989). Mortality rates of up to 22% have been reported for anorexia nervosa, however, most studies find mortality rates of 4% or less (Herzog, Keller, & Lavori, 1988). There is little information available regarding mortality rates associated with bulimia.

Medical complications associated with eating disorders result in high morbidity. With anorexia nervosa, complications are usually related to the effects of starvation. Body fat and protein are lost; there is a significant decrease in muscle function. Severe bone loss, characteristic of aging, has been reported in young women with anorexia nervosa (Rigotti, Nussbaum, Herzog, & Neer, 1984). The function of the thyroid gland is decreased, resulting in a decreased ability to tolerate cold, low heart rate, dry skin and hair, and decreased reflex time. There is decreased motility of the gastrointestinal tract,

Collegiate runner with anorexia nervosa.

gastric emptying is slowed, and constipation is a frequent complaint. Psychological changes accompany starvation and include preoccupation with food, sleeplessness, irritability, and decreased libido. Depression and other consequences of anorexia nervosa may increase the risk of suicide (National Institute of Nutrition, 1989).

Medical complications of bulimia result from binge eating and from techniques used to prevent weight gain. Repeated vomiting and abuse of diuretics and laxatives lead to fluid-electrolyte imbalance. Of greatest concern are low blood potassium levels, which affect the heart and can be life threatening. Vomiting may result in tooth decay, enlargement of the salivary glands, and irritation of the esophagus. As with anorexia nervosa, depression and feelings of social isolation increase the risk of suicide.

Etiology of Eating Disorders

The etiology of eating disorders is not known. Their causes are complex and multifaceted. Biological, sociocultural, and psychological factors seem to interact; however, the relative importance of these factors appears to vary from individual to individual. The concentration of these disorders in young white women from affluent backgrounds suggests that sociocultural factors are highly influential. It is widely accepted that the high value placed on thinness in women in the United States is an important sociocultural factor in the development of eating disorders and may explain the fact that most cases are female. The widespread acceptance and approval of weight loss and of dieting in American women probably contributes as well. However, these cannot be the only factors, as a large percentage of American women view themselves as being too fat, but only a small percentage of women actually develop eating disorders. The prevalence of these disorders in adolescents and young adults suggests that factors such as concerns over autonomy and separation from family and avoidance of physical maturation influence their development. Individual personality traits such as drive for perfection and low self-esteem may also be contributing factors. A biological or genetic susceptibility has been implicated in development of both anorexia nervosa and bulimia.

Treatment of Eating Disorders

Because eating disorders are multifaceted in etiology, treatment must be comprehensive. Intervention may require a combination of cognitive and behavioral therapy, medical monitoring, and nutrition counseling. Psychopharmacological agents may also be used.

Before treatment can begin, the individual must admit the presence of an eating disorder. Anorexics tend to deny their condition and are reluctant to seek treatment. Bulimics may be more likely to seek help, but may not remain in treatment.

In general, treatment is similar for both anorexia nervosa and bulimia. In early stages of eating disorders, individual or group therapy may be sufficient treatment. In severe cases, however, therapy is best provided by a multidisciplinary team experienced in treatment of eating disorders. In general, treatment takes place on an outpatient basis. Hospitalization may be necessary in cases of severe weight loss, life-threatening metabolic changes, severe depression or suicide risk, or family crisis (American Dietetic Association, 1988).

No one type of treatment is universally effective. Selection of the most appropriate treatment requires careful assessment of the individual, including the severity of the condition, medical state, eating patterns, and personality disturbances. Intervention involves therapy to address individual traits and family relationships that may contribute to development of the disorder. A variety of therapeutic techniques have been used, including psychotherapy, family therapy, behavior modification, and self-help groups.

Medical and nutritional problems must also be identified and corrected. A short-term goal of treatment in anorexia nervosa is to prevent further weight loss. A decrease in physical activity as well as an increase in food intake may be necessary to accomplish this goal. In severely malnourished patients, some weight gain may be required to correct psychological changes that accompany starvation and limit the individual's ability to respond to psychotherapy. If a patient is hospitalized, tube feeding or intravenous feeding may be used to initiate weight gain. However, these techniques are reserved for individuals who are at medical risk and in whom weight cannot be stabilized by other means. A longer-term goal of nutrition intervention for both bulimics and anorexics is to bring about gradual changes in food patterns and eating behavior and to develop realistic goals for body weight.

Response to treatment of anorexia nervosa and bulimia is variable. Herzog et al. (1988) found in their sample that at least one-third of people with eating disorders were still ill several years after follow-up. In addition, there was frequent crossover—that is, anorexics developing bulimia and bulimics becoming anorexic. The longer the duration of the disorder, the poorer the response to treatment. Thus early identification and intervention are of utmost importance.

Pharmacological treatment most often involves the use of antidepressants. With their use, significant reductions in the frequency of binge eating have been reported. However, opinions vary as to the effectiveness of drugs in treatment of eating disorders (Katz, 1988).

Eating Disorders and the Athlete

Weight control is an important part of the training and conditioning of an athlete. However, excessive concern about body weight, attempts to maintain a body weight that is too low, and the use of inappropriate and potentially detrimental weight control practices are of concern. In attempting to improve performance by reducing body weight, athletes may

Prevailing norms among choreographers and dancers place these athletes in a high-risk category for eating disorders. (Photo courtesy of Kathleen Cerra-Laquale)

use techniques that are, in fact, detrimental to their performance. When such techniques are carried to the extreme, an athlete may develop an eating disorder.

It has been reported that athletes, especially female athletes, are at high risk of developing eating disorders. Athletes are subject to the same societal pressures concerning body weight as are other Americans. In addition, there may be pressure from coaches and peers because (a) low body weight is considered to improve performance in some sports; (b) in some sports, for esthetic reasons, athletes are expected to maintain very low body weight; and (c) in some sports, such as wrestling, athletes are encouraged to compete in as low a weight class as possible. While it is clear that some athletes do suffer from anorexia nervosa or bulimia, the actual prevalence of eating disorders in athletes is unknown, and whether athletes are more likely to have eating disorders than their nonathletic peers has not been established.

Diagnosis

Diagnosis of eating disorders is more difficult in athletes than in the general population because athletes who do not have eating disorders have some characteristics in common with anorexics. Body weight is low, activity levels are high, and amenorrhea is common in some women athletes even in the absence of eating disorders. In addition, in the athlete with anorexia nervosa, increased muscle mass may initially mask the signs of weight loss and excessive physical activity may not be noticed. Indications that an eating disorder may exist in an athlete include excessive concern over body weight, physical activity beyond that required to be competitive in the sport, weight below that considered necessary or desirable for the sport, weight loss that continues in the noncompetitive season, and secretive eating, extreme weight fluctuation, and other signs of bulimia (U.S. Olympic Committee, 1987).

Eating Disorder-Related Behavior

In addition to those individuals who actually have eating disorders, a significant number of athletes appear to use some of the weight control methods associated with anorexia nervosa or bulimia. In a study of female collegiate athletes, 32% of those surveyed reported that they used at least one eating disorder-related behavior, such as self-induced vomiting, laxative abuse, or routine use of diet pills (Rosen, McKeag, Hough, & Curley, 1986). In another study, 62% of the competitive gymnasts questioned reported the use of at least one type of eating-disordered behavior. Most common behaviors were self-induced vomiting, use of diet pills, and fasting (Rosen & Hough, 1988). Severe food restrictions appear to be common among ballet dancers, and the weight control practices of wrestlers have long been a matter of concern. Wrestlers often use a combination of dehydration and severe food restriction to "make weight."

It has been assumed that eating disorders and eating disorder-related behaviors are most common among athletes who participate in sports where low body weight is emphasized. However, this assumption has not been well documented, and eating-disordered behaviors have been reported by athletes participating in sports in which low body weight is not typical, such as field hockey, softball, tennis, and volleyball (Rosen et al., 1986). Researchers have also found that swimmers are likely to use these behaviors to control weight. Although women are most frequently studied, behaviors related to eating disorders are also practiced by male athletes. In a survey of almost 700 college athletes, more than half reported using excessive physical activity to lose weight. Males were more likely to use this technique than were females. Both males and females reported use of severe caloric restrictions to control weight (Black & Burckes-Miller, 1988).

Consequences of Eating-Disordered Behavior

Controlling body weight to enhance performance is a reasonable goal for the athlete. However, the majority of athletes do not recognize that the weight-loss techniques they use are potentially detrimental to their performance.

Athletes and coaches usually monitor body weight. Body weight, however, reflects fluid and protein as well as body fat. Controlling weight by decreasing body water or body protein is not advantageous and may be detrimental to performance. Decreasing excess body fat may be desirable for some athletes, but reducing body fat below the level of that considered essential may have a negative impact on performance. The optimum body fat for various sports has not been established, and a wide range of body fat may be found in competitive athletes. For example, body fat ranging from 6% to 36% has been reported in elite runners (Brownell, Steen, & Wilmore, 1987).

Weight control techniques such as repeated vomiting, abuse of laxatives and diuretics or exercise, and fluid restriction lead to a rapid weight loss largely due to a loss of body water. Water loss can inhibit performance and, when severe, is life threatening. Fasting or severe food restriction may also be used to bring about rapid weight loss. An immediate effect of inadequate food intake is a depletion of glycogen stores, which may lead to muscle fatigue during endurance exercise. In addition, rapid weight loss from fasting or very restricted energy intake results in loss of body protein. The combination of restricted food intake and dehydration in trained athletes has been shown to result in decreased physical performance, and the psychological state of the athletes is also affected adversely (Horswill, Lohman, Slaughter, Boileau, & Wilmore, 1990).

When energy intake is too low, the body adapts in order to prevent excessive weight loss. The resting metabolic rate falls in response to a low energy intake. Thus energy requirements decrease, making it more difficult to lose weight or to maintain an extremely low body weight. In some people, decreased caloric intakes are associated with binge eating (National Institute of Nutrition, 1989) and with a preoccupation with food (Johnson & Tobin, 1991), making the restriction of food intake more difficult.

The effects of more prolonged dietary restriction depend upon the amount and type of food consumed, the duration of the food restriction, and the rate of weight loss. Low energy intake is associated with an inadequate intake of essential nutrients, potentially reducing strength and performance. A chronic lack of dietary protein leads to a loss of body protein, with most of the loss coming from skeletal muscle. Iron intakes low enough to cause anemia are associated with decreased aerobic capacity and early fatigue. In addition, calorie-restricted diets are frequently low in calcium. Low calcium intakes during adolescence and early adulthood may lead to lower bone mass, increasing the risk of osteoporosis in later life.

Amenorrhea or irregular menstruation is often reported in female athletes such as runners, gymnasts, and ballet dancers. The cause of menstrual dysfunction in these athletes is unclear; however, low body weight and severe food restriction may be contributing factors. Menstrual dysfunction, in turn, may be related to an increased risk of athletic injury (Myburgh, Hutchins, Fataar, Hough, & Noakes, 1990).

Weight cycling refers to multiple cycles of weight loss and gain. Athletes such as wrestlers may gain and lose weight many times during a season. Other athletes maintain weight throughout the competitive season, but gain weight out of season and thus, over a period of years, experience multiple weight loss-weight gain cycles. Researchers are still studying the effects of weight cycling in humans. However, preliminary data indicate several potentially harmful effects. Metabolic rates may decrease. People who weight cycle may find it more difficult to lose weight and may regain weight more readily than people who do not weight cycle. In addition, weight cycling may promote fat storage in the abdominal region of the body, a pattern of fat deposition related to an increased risk of diabetes and heart disease. Thus the information currently available on weight cycling in humans suggests that this practice may result in an increased health risk as well as greater difficulty in maintaining a low body weight.

Treatment and Prevention of Eating Disorders

The options for treatment of eating disorders in athletes are the same as those for the nonathlete. Nonathletes may be asked to curtail physical activity to gain body weight. However, athletes will need to continue with an exercise program, if possible, in order to maintain their competitive abilities (Johnson & Tobin, 1991). The appropriate level of physical activity and the appropriate body weight will need to be determined for each athlete. As with nonathletes, early identification of eating disorders is important in order to improve the response to treatment.

To decrease the risk of eating disorders, athletes and their coaches need to set weight goals appropriate to each athlete's size and sport. Athletes need to understand the potentially detrimental effects on performance of such weight-loss methods as severe food restriction and dehydration. The inclusion of instruction in appropriate weight control methods as part of training may encourage the athlete to achieve and maintain body weight in a manner compatible with good health and optimum performance.

Summary

Anorexia nervosa and bulimia are serious conditions that threaten health and well-being. The etiology of these disorders is incompletely understood, but sociocultural, psychological, and physiological factors are involved. Whether the prevalence of these disorders has increased in recent years and whether athletes are at higher risk than nonathletes is not yet clear. Although most athletes do not have actual eating disorders, a high percentage of female and male athletes appear to use weight control practices that may have detrimental effects on performance. There is a need for athletes to set goals for body weight that are compatible with health and optimum performance and to learn appropriate weight control techniques.

Key Words

anorexia nervosa	weight control methods
bulimia	college athletes
eating disorders	

Discussion Questions

1. What are the differences and the similarities between anorexia nervosa and bulimia?
2. What factors contribute to the development of eating disorders in the general public? What additional pressures do athletes face?
3. How do eating disorders and related behaviors affect athletic performance? How can these behaviors be prevented or controlled in athletes?

References

American Dietetic Association. (1988). Position of the American Dietetic Association: Nutrition intervention in the treatment of anorexia nervosa and bulimia nervosa. *Journal of the American Dietetic Association, 88,* 68-71.

American Psychiatric Association. (1987). *Diagnostic and statistical manual of mental disorders* (3rd ed., rev.). Washington, DC: Author.

Black, D. R., & Burckes-Miller, M. (1988). Male and female college athletes: Use of anorexia nervosa and bulimia nervosa weight loss methods. *Research Quarterly for Exercise and Sport, 59,* 252-256.

Brownell, K. D., Steen, S. N., & Wilmore, J. H. (1987). Weight regulation practices in athletes: Analysis of metabolic and health effects. *Medicine and Science in Sports and Exercise, 19,* 546-556.

Herzog, D. B., Keller, M. B., & Lavori, P. W. (1988). Outcome in anorexia nervosa and bulimia nervosa: A review of the literature. *Journal of Nervous and Mental Disease, 176,* 131-143.

Horswill, C. A., Lohman, T. G., Slaughter, M. H., Boileau, R. A., & Wilmore, J. H. (1990). Weight loss, dietary carbohydrate modifications and high intensity physical performance. *Medicine and Science in Sports and Exercise, 22,* 528-532.

Johnson, C., & Tobin, D. L. (1991). The diagnosis and treatment of anorexia nervosa and bulimia among athletes. *Athletic Training, 26,* 119-128.

Katz, J. L. (1988). Eating disorders. In M. M. Shangold & G. Mirkin (Eds.), *Women and exercise: Physiology and sports medicine* (pp. 248-263). Philadelphia: F. A. Davis.

Myburgh, K. H., Hutchins, J., Fataar, A. B., Hough, S. F., & Noakes, T. D. (1990). Low bone density as an etiological factor for stress fractures in athletes. *Annals of Internal Medicine, 113,* 754-759.

National Institute of Nutrition. (1989). An overview of the eating disorders anorexia nervosa and bulimia nervosa. *Nutrition Today, 24*(3), 27-29.

Rigotti, N. A., Nussbaum, S. R., Herzog, D. B., & Neer, R.M. (1984). Osteoporosis in women with anorexia nervosa. *New England Journal of Medicine, 311,* 1601-1606.

Rosen, L. W., & Hough, D. O. (1988). Pathogenic weight-control behaviors of female college gymnasts. *Physician and Sportsmedicine, 16*(9), 141-146.

Rosen, L. W., McKeag, D. R., Hough, D. O., & Curley, V. (1986). Pathogenic weight-control behavior in female athletes. *Physician and Sportsmedicine, 14*(1), 79-86.

U.S. Olympic Committee. (1987). *Sports nutrition: Eating disorders.* Omaha: University of Nebraska Medical Center, Swanson Center for Nutrition.

V

Institutionalization of Women's Sports

The Olympic Games must be reserved for men. . . . we must continue to try to achieve the following definition: the solemn and periodic exaltation of male athleticism, with internationalism as a base, loyalty as a means, art for its setting, and female applause as its reward.

—Pierre de Coubertin (founder of the modern Olympic Games)

If you're going to hold someone down, you're going to have to hold onto the other end of the chain. You are confined by your own repression.

—Toni Morrison

The most notable fact that culture imprints on women is the sense of our limits. The most important thing one woman can do for another is to illuminate and expand her sense of actual possibilities.

—Adrienne Rich

15

Media Portrayal of the Female Athlete

GRETA L. COHEN

Mass media is a "popular culture" term for all widely disseminated nonprint (television, radio, and movies) and print media (primarily newspapers, magazines, and books). The mass media are the creation of a technological society in which availability of information is essential. They provide two valuable services: the timely reporting of current events and entertainment for the masses. Responsibility for content is inherent in the very nature of the media's job. The selection process is critical; the decisions are vital to the culture. As Boutilier and SanGiovanni (1983) note, "Regardless of what is actually happening, it is the media's interpretation of that event that shapes our attitudes, values and perceptions about the world and about our culture" (p. 184).

Receiving the news "live via satellite" from remote locations is already commonplace in many parts of the world. In the near future, computer chip technology will allow viewers to select a particular country's interpretation of events as the global community tunes in. Everything—from political rhetoric, economic scandals, and environmental disasters to live-action broadcasts from war zones—is being interpreted by the media.

In the United States we have the impression that the mass media afford us expansive opportunities to ingest stimuli from every conceivable source. However, given that 87% of television stations are owned by three corporations (Downing, Mohamnadi, & Sreberny-Mohamnadi, 1990), this is largely an illusion. The three newspaper companies with the highest daily circulation rates own 136 daily newspapers (American Newspaper Publishers Association, 1991). Are consumers getting what they demand? Corporate executives tell us that they supply what the public wants (Powell, 1987), but the diversity of perspectives is far more compressed than might originally be assumed. As Jencks (1987) notes, the media are "in the business to make money and advertising revenue accomplishes that goal. Therefore, the media work endlessly with the format and substance of the news in order to attract the largest and most affluent audience possible" (p. 564).

In the field of entertainment, media power is no less apparent. Although the business of entertaining is far more subjective, the culture is reflected by the images the media portray. Content is constructed to conform with what a particular society finds entertaining. The potential to manipulate reality is relegated to an industry that does not always demonstrate a high degree of integrity. Vigilance often becomes the responsibility of the viewer.

Sport and the Media in U.S. Society

The institution of American sport has developed a unique relationship with the media industry. In many cases a symbiotic relationship has evolved, so that sport is used to sell newspapers and magazines, to boost television ratings, and to attract corporate sponsors at the same time sports coverage serves to create interest in and demand for sport. During the past 20 years, women have revolutionized their performance records and developed incredible skill and expertise in competitive sports. However, the media have barely acknowledged the existence of female athletes; they remain for the most part myopically focused on male athleticism.

Sport and the media have both served society as conservators of convention. They function to reinforce traditional values rather than to challenge or lead in the transformation to more enlightened thinking. This is especially interesting because these are the same mass media that sometimes choose to challenge convention, raise questions, and take on the power elite over issues of social consequence and political and economic hegemony.

Sexism and Racism Perpetuated, Overtly and Covertly

In the past, women's sports were virtually ignored by the media. When female athletes were featured, traditional stereotypes were on parade. Elaborate descriptions were provided of the women's physical appearance, dress, style, and even sexual preference. Commentary related sexuality directly to body type and overall appearance. Occasionally, comments about women athletes' sexuality were offered up as comic relief.

In recent years, ambivalence toward women athletes has taken the form of symbolic denial of power to women through exclusionary and denigrating tactics (Duncan & Hasbrook, 1988). The power, strength, and endurance factors related to drive, struggle, and strategy in competition are rarely mentioned. Positive images of sportswomen are combined with negative suggestions or innuendo that serve to trivialize or undercut their performance (Duncan & Hasbrook, 1988). Sexist references remain problematic, but the new brand of sexism is more covert.

Sports commentators have been notorious for creating artificial, ambivalent, sexist, and racist references. For example, a few years ago, completely unfounded references were made repeatedly concerning the "cattiness" and "animosity" that allegedly existed between top-seeded figure skaters Debi Thomas and Katarina Witt. Reporter Margot Adler has indicated that the feud was a media invention (Halpert, 1988). At the 1988 Olympics, ABC's Al Trautwig, while waiting for the women's downhill event to begin, commented, "Once upon a time they were sweet little girls, then something went wrong. They grew up and became downhill skiers. And here they are at Calgary." Speed skater Bonnie Blair, upon winning the first gold medal for the United States in the 1992 Winter Olympics, was referred to as the "typical girl next door with the pleasant smile, everyone's kid sister." In sports that traditionally have been seen as appropriate for females, such as gymnastics, we have been bombarded with the image of an adorable, "pixielike" competitor who is spunky and fearless, and who charms her way into our hearts forever.

Intelligent, sophisticated commentary about female athletes is rare. Women's team sports remain a threat to the power structure and male domination of sport. What has become one of the classic examples of sexist and racist broadcasting of women's sports occurred during a 1987 Pan-American basketball game. NBC commentators Billy Packer and Dick Stockton were commenting on U.S. player Jennifer Gillom as she brought the ball up court:

> B.P.: Doesn't she remind you of someone who is going to grow up and get married and have a large family and be a great cook? Doesn't she look like that? She's got just a real pleasant face.
>
> D.S.: Maybe she'll open a restaurant.
>
> B.P.: I'll bet her momma can cook.

In collegiate sports, references to the nicknames of college mascots as gender descriptors are often oppressive. Although the school mascot represents a tradition firmly entrenched long before the inception of competitive women's teams, educational institutions in the 1990s have not been sensitive to change. In an era in which "diversity education" is heralded, and combating racism and sexism is paid extensive lip service, the use of gender and ethnic descriptors reinforces the hierarchy and confirms prevailing biases. Women collegiate athletes are often co-opted into adopting alternatives even if the choice reflects a biological impossibility. The use of such contrived "feminine" descriptors as Ram"ettes," Ram"belles," "Lady" Rams, or WRams is inappropriate. Some schools adopt diminutive counterpart names for female athletes, so that, for instance, male athletes are called Bearcats and the females Bearkittens. Similarly, references to team nicknames, such as the "Redskins," become offensive when insensitivity is applied to a particular culture.

Measuring Progress

Television

Television is the most powerful medium of mass communication. In the past decade, the portrayal of women in a variety of roles on prime-time

TV has increased dramatically. Women not only coanchor most news programs, but their presence in dramatic roles has increased substantially as well. The proliferation of successful situation comedies with predominantly female casts has a profound effect on our interpretation of pop culture. Conversely, in sport, the lack of representation of girls and women sends a compelling message about the sanctioning of sport as a male preserve, and this message deters female participation (Duncan & Hasbrook, 1988; Kane & Parks, 1990). Given that females constitute 53% of the population and receive only 5% of the sports coverage (Duncan, Messner, Williams, & Jensen, 1990), the message is clear—the female sport experience is tangential to the male experience. This disservice has widespread ramifications in the socialization of our youth, who look to viable role models to confirm appropriate choices. With regard to televised sport, disparities between men's and women's coverage are usually manifested in three ways: (a) the construction of the events themselves, (b) the portrayal of the players, and (c) the quality of the production.

The *construction* of an event refers to the framework in which it is viewed. Men's games or contests are often presented as dramatic spectacles of historical importance, whereas women's events take on a flavor of recreational activities—fun and camaraderie are emphasized, rather than fierce competition (Duncan et al., 1990). Women's games are further trivialized through coverage that often focuses on upcoming men's events, creating ambivalence for the women's game as it takes on the role of "opening act" (Duncan et al., 1990). In the 1970s, women's coverage sometimes consisted of taped highlights of women's championship games being broadcast during the intermissions of regular-season men's games.

The *portrayal* of women athletes differs substantially from that of their male counterparts, in both the manner in which the women are addressed and the adjectives used to identify their competition. Women athletes in their 20s and 30s are frequently referred to as girls and young ladies, but male athletes over 18 are rarely referred to as boys; they are usually called men or young men, or even "the man of the hour." Researchers have reported that in sampled tennis commentary, women athletes were called by their first names 52.7% of the time, whereas such designations for the men occurred only 7.8% of the time. Women's games, contests, and sporting events are always gender specified; women compete in the Women's National Championships, whereas the men's equivalent is referred to simply as the National Championships (Duncan et al., 1990). Basketball and volleyball are the most frequently televised women's team sports. Adjectives used to describe competition in these games often reinforce the dominant theme of hierarchy. Physical prowess and such descriptions as "brilliant shot," "strategic placement," and "analytical ability" are blatantly omitted. Language is carefully selected to evoke gender distinctions. Aesthetic appeal predominates, and references to the action frequently employ such expressions as "graceful," "smooth," "easy to watch," and "beautiful" (Boutilier & SanGiovanni, 1983; Duncan & Hasbrook, 1988).

The *quality* of the production of women's sporting events differs substantially from that of men's events. Duncan et al. (1990, pp. 10-12) report

Athletes such as Christine Bannon-Rodriguez, a four-time World Karate Champion and Black Belt Hall of Fame inductee, compile press kit photos that demonstrate the strength, power, and form so often denied by the media's portrayal of the woman athlete. (Photo by Peter Cottrell)

that for men, sophisticated productions focus on superlative camera work, slow-motion and split-screen images, instant replays, multiple-angle views, and elaborate on-screen graphics. The production of women's games, however, is less technically sophisticated, less dramatic, tends to use flowery commentary and ambivalent visual images, and often contains errors in reporting. Further, the music used in women's sports telecasts is not as upbeat as that used for men's games.

Television's representation of male hegemony in sport is reinforced during men's competitions by the regular attention given to women in the stands, who serve as comical targets and objects of sexual innuendo as the camera zooms in on various parts of their anatomy. So popular is this practice that the term "honey shot" was coined back in the 1970s to describe it; such camera work remains standard fare in the production of men's sporting events.

Sport itself has no gender affiliation. A positive outcome of the increased television exposure of women in tennis and golf is the neutralizing effect the media have had on the notion of gender-specific sport. Interestingly, some recent studies have reported a shift in the nature of activities designated as "traditionally appropriate" for women. Tennis and golf have been classified as gender-neutral sports, and gymnastics and fast-pitch softball continue to illustrate the bipolar constructs (Buysee, 1991). Since both men and women compete in highly commercialized tours in golf and tennis, with sustained TV coverage, a neutralizing effect has developed. Imagine the potential opportunities available to everyone if the increased television exposure in other women's sports were quantified and qualified.

In women's collegiate sport, a slow but steady increase in coverage has occurred. In the early 1980s, the proliferation of cable networks devoted to sport (e.g., ESPN, HSE, Sportschannel, and Prime Ticket) increased opportunities for women dramatically (see Table 15.1). Television contracts are now easier to negotiate. The old guard persisted in preserving

TABLE 15.1 Televised Women's Collegiate Sports, 1989-1990

	Atlantic Coast	Big East	Big Eight	Big Sky	Big Ten	Big West	Eastern Collegiate Athletic	Pacific Ten	South-eastern	South-western
Championship competition										
Basketball	yes	yes	yes	—	—	yes	—	—	yes	yes
Gymnastics	—	—	yes	—	yes	—	—	yes	yes	—
Indoor track	—	—	yes	—	—	—	—	—	—	yes
Outdoor track	—	yes	yes	—	yes	—	—	yes	yes	yes
Swimming and diving	—	—	—	—	—	—	—	yes	yes	yes
Tennis	—	—	—	—	—	—	—	yes	—	yes
Volleyball	—	—	yes	—	—	—	—	—	yes	—
Regular season play (number of events)										
Basketball	3	10	4	—	7	4	—	6	4	5
Gymnastics	—	—	—	—	—	—	—	2	—	—
Softball	—	—	—	—	—	3	—	2	—	—
Volleyball	—	—	—	—	2	6	—	5	—	3

male exclusivity on the playing fields, but the new breed in management is more willing to negotiate contracts with women's leagues. In 1990, television coverage of women's basketball's "Game of the Week" became a reality. Current negotiating processes reflect women's active involvement. However, "to market women's sports today requires leveraging in order to attain the conference package" (P. Howlett, personal communication, March 3, 1991).

Print Journalism

A symbiotic relationship has evolved between contemporary sport and the newspaper industry. The rise in popularity of both provides a classic example of basic economics. Sport is consumed by the masses. In most major metropolitan newspapers, the sports section represents the most widely read part of the paper, attracting a larger readership than either business or political sections (Coakley, 1990, p. 282). In *USA Today*, the only national daily newspaper in the United States, sports coverage accounts for 25% of the entire paper.

Newspapers have never applied any systematic coverage to women's sports. Money dictates policy, and the lack of women's sports coverage is thus reflected. Exceptions have been made for major events such as the U.S. Open in golf and the U.S. Open in tennis, the Professional Figure Skating Championships, and the more commercialized marathon races. These events have substantial financial backing and are therefore perceived as newsworthy.

Duncan, Messner, and Williams (1991) studied recent trends in the coverage of women's sports by major daily newspapers. They utilized content analyses of the number, length, and placement of stories and the use of photographs. The results of this research were dismal, indicating a ratio of 23:1 for exclusive stories addressing men's sports compared with women's sports; 92% of the photographs in the sample were of men. However, some progress has materialized in the past decade with the inception and dramatic popularity of *USA Today.* This newspaper's coverage of women's sports is significantly broader than that found elsewhere, indicating that a paper targeting a broad constituency can accommodate women's sports without fear of reducing circulation or reader interest (Duncan et al., 1991).

In various pockets of American society, local papers have steadily improved the amount of coverage, length of stories, and placement of articles devoted to girls' and women's sports. Spotlighting both male and female "athletes of the week," "conference winners," and "all-star teams" has become commonplace.

The standardized format used by most newspapers and the ease of retrieval from the wire services have limited substantive changes in the material printed. As women's sports continue to grow, there should be an increase in the number of sports information directors feeding news into the system. This will create the much-needed data base from which news items are selected. Changes in a newspaper's format then become an issue involving social responsibility.

The Magazine Industry: Center Court or Centerfold?

Magazines provide unique opportunities for the development of feature stories through text, illustrations, and photographs. Unencumbered by the immediacy of rigid time constraints that limit other forms of media, magazines often showcase in-depth analyses.

Magazine coverage of women's sports is far more prolific than either television or newspaper coverage. However, the images portrayed fluctuate dramatically. In general, the focus frequently is on trendy, wealthy, upper-middle-class white women participating in individual and dual sports and in socially acceptable sports. Competitive team sports are usually placed on the euphemistic back burner.

The fitness explosion spawned a new dimension in the packaging and marketing of the healthy, physically fit woman. While female sexuality has been used to sell commodities for most of the twentieth century, the packaging of female athleticism is a relatively new phenomenon. The 1980s focused on a new dimension in the commodity market. Cosmetics alone do not suffice and will not hide or camouflage imperfections, so the physique itself has now become a commodity. Magazines such as *Shape* and *Flex* illustrate the current obsession with the ideal body, where image is central to the message and the "athletic look" has little to do with sport or athleticism. To survive, magazines such as *Women's Sports & Fitness* must target the larger market, where fitness, not athletics, means survival.

Because advertising rates are based on a magazine's subscribership, numbers of readers are important. To compound the problem, these magazines have no control over the highly sexualized images used by advertisers.

In recent years, a number of single-sport magazines have emerged, such as *Tennis, Volleyball Monthly,* and *Runner's World.* In a study of all 1991 publications of these magazines, feature stories exclusively addressed women 40%, 38%, and 37% of the time, respectively.[1] However, the trend toward heavier coverage of generic issues of interest to both men and women in these magazines demonstrates a more didactic approach to sports coverage.

Golf for Women, a bimonthly publication devoted to the female golf advocate, premiered in 1988. With a concentration on articles devoted to pedagogy, personalities, and feature stories, the magazine's regular fare is supplemented by items on such pragmatic concerns as dealing with travel, health issues, and equipment. The upscale approach is appealing to its constituency, and the magazine's success to date is reflected by women's increased participation in golf.

Alternative journalistic ventures with a modest "back to basics" look have materialized in the past few years. *Women & Sport* (formerly the *Women's Sport Pages*) premiered in 1988 as a monthly newsletter targeting individuals genuinely concerned about women's sport. Issues relating to high school, collegiate, Olympic, international, club, and recreational sport are presented in a format that informs, educates, and supports the female sports experience.

Sports Illustrated (SI) is considered the leading weekly sports publication in the United States. Since its inception in 1954, innovative advertising and marketing campaigns have revolutionized sales. *SI*'s superlative photography and striking advertisements are appealing and dramatic, and its in-depth analyses of sports personalities are heavily skewed toward men's football, basketball, and baseball. In general, portrayal of the woman athlete in *Sports Illustrated* has served to confirm the traditional stereotypical ideology about women competing in the "male preserve." Blatantly sexist terminology persists in much of the reporting (Lumpkin & Williams, 1991). As recently as the mid-1980s, the top-ranked women's basketball team in the country, the Texas Longhorns, were featured with the headline "The Women: The Best Little Scorehouse in . . . " (November 20, 1985).

The continued success of *SI*'s annual swimsuit issue, even after a decade of feminist condemnation, demonstrates the effectiveness of "soft porn" in promoting sales (Sabo & Jansen, 1992, p. 176). The 1992 issue, using an Olympic motif set in sunny Spain, to contrast "model to athlete" and "gold sequins to gold medals," was exceptionally demeaning to our women athletes.

Lumpkin and Williams (1991) report a significant increase in the number of *Sports Illustrated* articles featuring athletic women, although African American women receive less coverage that their white counterparts, even in sports where they dominate. Asian and Hispanic women are seldom mentioned in the context of American sport, but are occasionally featured in global reporting, such as the "Sports in China" special report (August

15, 1988) or the case of Argentina's tennis star Gabriela Sabatini. Conversely, superlative images of women athletes can be found in recent full-page *SI* cover photos: "Julie Krone, the Best Woman Jockey Ever" (May 22, 1989); "Wonder Woman! Martina Navratilova Wins a Record Ninth Wimbledon" (July 16, 1990); and "Solid Gold—U.S. Speed Skater Bonnie Blair" (February 24, 1992). These pictorial messages convey the power, drive, and determination we associate with athleticism.

A precursor of *Sports Illustrated for Kids*, the monthly magazine *Young Athlete*, was founded in 1975. Although considered more enlightened in its treatment of female athletes than other traditional magazines, its editorial policy reflected a conservative ideology that was self-destructive. Although the magazine reported 40-50% female readership, the editor, Dan Zandra, noted that "when male athletes are featured on the cover, both boys and girls buy the magazine, but when females are featured, some male readership is temporarily lost. The solution is to limit covers featuring females athletes" (quoted in Rintala & Birrell, 1984, p. 247).

The recently conceived *Sports Illustrated for Kids* (*SIK*) appears to mirror its parent publication. This is very problematic, because children are not as likely to participate in sports if visible role models do not exist (Duncan & Sayaovong, 1990; Rintala & Birrell, 1984). When *SIK*'s managing editor, John Papanek, was asked by researchers why female athletes were so underrepresented, his response echoed that of the editor of the now defunct *Young Athlete*: "It is reasonable to think that a cover featuring only females would be repugnant to those people who are most likely to buy the magazine, and there were only a very limited number of recognizable female athletes to draw from" (quoted in Duncan & Sayaovong, 1990, p. 103).

The importance of magazines targeting the children's market should not be underestimated. The responsibility of the media to serve as socializing agents should not be construed as a mandate to act as conservators of the status quo. That ideology eliminates opportunities to foster real change, expand options for children, and tap potential new markets that represent more than 50% of the population.

Collegiate Media Guides

Although not technically magazines or publications for commercial consumption, collegiate media guides have created a unique opportunity to showcase athletic programs. The purposes of these brochures are twofold: (a) They provide essential background information and statistics for broadcast commentators to use during athletic competitions and for print journalists reporting on those competitions, and (b) they are used by colleges and universities as an advertising tool in the recruiting process.

Cover photographs used by college media guides carry powerful messages about how athletes are perceived at particular institutions and the images those institutions wish to convey. Gender differences continue to prevail. In a recent study of basketball media guides in NCAA Division I schools, "true athleticism," defined as depictions of team members in uniform on the court and in action or active poses, was portrayed by female athletic teams only 38% of the time, compared with 60% by the male teams (Buysee, 1991). Cover photos of women's teams were predominantly passive or ambivalent. They ranged from the obtuse and thoroughly demeaning depiction of the Northwestern State University of Louisiana basketball team as Playboy bunnies, complete with bust, waist, and hip measurements, to that of Minnesota's basketball team in action, in uniform, on the court, playing the game for which the guide was intended (Buysee, 1991).

Film and Literary Depictions
of the Woman Athlete

In nonfiction, a variety of books have emerged during the past decade. Most noticeable are the tennis autobiographies of Billie Jean King, Martina Navratilova, Chris Evert, and Pam Shriver. Their themes of dedication to their sport, personal sacrifice, triumph, and struggle provide insight into the lives of professional women athletes in a sports world dominated by men. These autobiographies represent our first look at the "public figure/private life" aspects of the careers of successful female athletes exposed to a decade of media attention. A similar trend is emerging with the publication of autobiographies by track and field stars Joan Benoit and Mary Wazeter, and a children's story by Jackie Joyner-Kersee.

For action-packed drama, Arlene Blum's (1980) poignant account of the first all-female ascent of one of the highest peaks in the Himalayas, *Annapurna: A Woman's Place,* is superb. Her depiction of triumph and tragedy represents one of the finest chronicles of mountaineering adventure available. Expedition leader Blum reflects on the "bittersweet victory" and the continued resistance among expeditionary climbers to the inclusion of women in high-altitude assaults.

On the lighter side, Yvonne Zipter's *Diamonds Are a Dyke's Best Friend* crosses all economic, age, race, political, and ethnic distinctions to focus on the lesbian subculture of summer softball. The author showcases the "lesbian athlete" to defuse the power of the term itself, which is often used against girls and women participating in sport. The eclectic approach incorporates philosophical ideology with personal reflections and humor.

The need to document critical issues facing contemporary sportswomen at both amateur and professional levels cannot be overemphasized. Climber Julie Tullis, gymnast Mary Lou Retton, and author Mariah Burton Nelson have all made contributions that have begun to fill the void. Women's stories must be told. For positive images of women in sport, the proliferation of nonfiction literary works has provided a beacon.

One might assume that the literary portrayal of girls and women in sport would reflect the recent explosion in athletic participation, but this has not been the case. The fictional portrayals of female athletes in novels and in films have appeared to be stagnated in the past decade. Entrenched in issues of homophobia and femininity, the literary construction of the athlete in the 1980s was often the victim of the same dogma that affected portrayals of women athletes in other forms of the mass media. A comparison of the films *Personal Best* (1983) and *Pumping Iron II: The Women* (1985) and the novels *Sudden Death* by Rita Mae Brown (1984) and *All Out* by Judith Alguire (1988) serves to illustrate this point.

Personal Best focuses on two women training for berths on the U.S. Olympic track team. Chris Cahill, portrayed by Mariel Hemingway, and Tory Skinner, played by former Olympic hurdler Patrice Donnelly, become friends, lovers, and competitors. The central theme depicts an experienced athlete showing a novice the ropes—toward strength, stamina, mastery of skill, and self-mastery. As the athletes mature, the lesbian relationship is denied, assuring the audience that conformity to the dominant social order will be maintained. In *Pumping Iron II: The Women*, characters Bev and Carla, both of whom demonstrate massive builds, want to redefine criteria for success in the sport of bodybuilding, but the coaches and judges maintain the traditional symbolic order. Once again, female athleticism as a commodity remains endemic to acceptable gender prescriptions. The women competitors in *Pumping Iron II* never challenge the definition of femininity. They continue to evaluate themselves in comparison to the norm as defined by the judges. In *Personal Best*, the women never question the manipulative powers of their male coach, as the women in *Pumping Iron II* never deal with the ineptitude of the male judges in the bodybuilding competition. The male caricatures aid in trivializing the women's efforts: Good coaches and competent judges would not bother with female athletes. While musculature is not the attribute that confirms femaleness, sexual orientation becomes the issue that defies convention. The women in both films are co-opted and can find success only through conformity. Bev dyes her hair, loses bulk, and competes in a pink bikini; Chris finds love with swimmer Denny Stites, played by Olympic marathoner Kenny Moore, and renews her "friendship only" status with her former female lover.

In *All Out*, author Judith Alguire provides an insightful look at the struggle and determination of the elite athlete in the individual sport of marathon running. Her heroine, Karen, a focused marathon Olympic contender, and her lover Tab, a professor in women's studies, create a potential for real breakthrough of stereotyped characterization, but it does not materialize (Tabor, 1991). The book raises pointed questions about the responsibilities of athletes as role models and the destructive nature of competition for women, but the issues are left unresolved. In comparison, Rita Mae Brown's *Sudden Death* is a most destructive work, using the heroines and villains vindictively to portray sport as corruption with no socially redeeming qualities. Thinly disguised as a fictional representation of elite tennis champion Martina Navratilova, the book attempts to showcase the perversion of female participation in sport (Tabor, 1991). Whereas *Personal Best, Pumping Iron II,* and *All Out* grapple with the social issues that confront the female athlete, *Sudden Death* uses the same issues to destroy women's right to pursue highly competitive sport.

Although the literary depictions outlined above fail to develop complex personal relationships devoid of stereotypes, they begin to address the struggle, power, and physical stamina so long denied the elite woman athlete. If art does in fact imitate life, maybe the recent strong showing in the nonfiction genre will have a positive effect on future fictional portrayals of female athletes, both in literature and in film.

Proactive Strategies to Effect Change

Effecting change in the portrayal of female athletes by the media requires active support of girls' and women's participation in sport. Organization begins at the grass-roots level. An initial objective should be feminist representation on athletic boards, in booster clubs, and in sports organizations at the public, private, community, collegiate, Olympic, and professional levels. Organized proactive campaigns designed to penetrate a hard-core infrastructure usually involve watchdogs, troubleshooters, a radical avant-garde, and more moderate liberals. However, it is easiest to begin modestly, with realistic goals, and work to effect change at the local level. Those who want to make a difference can do the following:

1. Network to get women appointed or elected to representative bodies (clubs, boards, and committees).
2. Make personal contact with print journalists and sports broadcasters and develop ongoing dialogue relative to concerns for coverage of girls' and women's sports.
3. Encourage prospective writers to develop sports stories to feed to the media. Focus on significant, newsworthy, and human interest stories.
4. Be vigilant in assessing media coverage of girls' and women's sports. Call or write to newspapers, magazines, and radio and television stations whenever coverage warrants approval or praise for the legitimate treatment of the female athlete or event.
5. Loudly voice protest when media coverage is offensive or trivializing, and when women's events are blatantly ignored.

Conclusion

The current very limited coverage of female athletes by the mass media is demeaning, and the entire social construction of female athleticism by the media warrants change. Editors and news directors must continually make decisions regarding which sporting events will be considered newsworthy. Story placement and treatment are scrutinized. Although this process is not left to chance, these decisions are "judgment calls."

How do journalists, broadcasters, and reporters guard against their own prejudices? Who should be held responsible? The real tragedy here is that social consciousness with regard to "sexism" has not begun to elicit the immediate condemnation that negative ethnic or racist statements generate. When blatantly racist remarks target male athletes, the public response is immediate. Such comments are not tolerated on national television; when they do occur, they bring immediate apologies and loss of jobs, and spawn special live telecasts devoted to concerns for social change.[2] When individuals respond to similar social atrocities affecting female athletes, their concerns often fall on deaf ears. As Berger (1985) notes:

> News is not the presentation of reality . . . only the presentation of someone's perception of reality . . . and those perceptions are culturally determined. The media personnel are prisoners of their own, particularly American sense of reality and . . . we are their prisoners. (pp. 252-256)

It is not only a case of economics dictating policy or the selection of content tied to its revenue-producing capacity. What sells does not necessarily depend on demand. Marketing strategies that can create demand for Pet Rocks can certainly create sports heroines. Journalists are in constant search of instant heroes and villains and abandon neutrality in search of them (Miller; cited in Cohen, 1991).

The media have featured powerful dramatic stories as well as insightful documentaries on sports issues dealing with racism, violence in sport, the exploitation of collegiate athletes, and drug abuse in sport. The same ideology used to determine the appropriateness of these issues for public consciousness-raising should suffice in addressing gender inequalities in media coverage. Being feminine and athletic is not an oxymoron. It is a reality, and it should not be ignored or trivialized with sexual innuendo. The media have an ethical responsibility to address these issues, and the public has the responsibility to demand that they do so.

Key Words

television	magazine industry
cable sports networks	nonfiction
ambivalence	trivialization
sexual exploitation	film and literary portrayals
print journalism	proactive strategies

Discussion Questions

1. Bring in two visual images of women athletes portrayed by the media. Compare and contrast the techniques used in the social construction of the consumer's perception of that athlete.

2. What factors allow you to be optimistic that positive changes in media portrayals of women athletes can be expected in the near future? What factors indicate the converse or a backlash effect? What can you personally do to affect the outcome?

Notes

1. The content analysis compared women-only to men-only feature stories in the 1991 issues of *Tennis, Volleyball Monthly,* and *Runner's World.* When tabulations included women-only and

men-only stories with feature stories "unrelated to gender" or "inclusive of both genders," the proportions of women-only features dropped to 20%, 35%, and 25%, respectively.

2. Racist statements made by Al Campanis, then vice president and director of player personnel for the Los Angeles Dodgers, during a *Nightline* tribute to Jackie Robinson in 1986 prompted host Ted Koppel to devote a special telecast the next evening to the subject of racism in baseball. Featured were Harry Edwards, a sport sociologist; Peter Ueberroth, then commissioner of baseball; and Reggie Jackson of the Oakland A's. A follow-up program aired one year later to evaluate progress.

References

Alguire, J. (1988). *All out.* Norwich, VT: New Victoria.

American Newspaper Publishers Association. (1991). *Facts about newspapers: A statistical summary of the newspaper business.* Washington, DC: Author.

Berger, A. (1985). News, psyche and society. In D. Ungurait, T. W. Bohn, & R. E. Hiebert (Eds.), *Media now* (pp. 252-256). White Plains, NY: Longman.

Blum, A. (1980). *Annapurna: A woman's place.* San Francisco: Sierra Club Books.

Boutilier, M. A., & SanGiovanni, L. (1983). *The sporting woman: Feminist and sociological dilemmas.* Champaign, IL: Human Kinetics.

Brown, R. M. (1984). *Sudden death.* New York: Bantam.

Buysee, J. (1991, April). *Media guide portrayals of intercollegiate athletes in selected sports.* Paper presented at the annual meeting of the American Alliance for Health, Physical Education, Recreation and Dance, San Francisco.

Coakley, J. (1990). *Sport in society* (4th ed.). St. Louis: Times Mirror/Mosby.

Cohen, G. (1991). Media and international sport: Ethical issues. *Journal of the International Council of Health, Physical Education and Recreation, 27*(2), 14-17.

Downing, J., Mohamnadi, A., & Sreberny-Mohamnadi, A. (Eds.). (1990). *Questioning the media.* Newbury Park, CA: Sage.

Duncan, M. C., & Hasbrook, C. A. (1988). Denial of power in televised women's sports. *Sociology of Sport Journal, 5,* 1-21.

Duncan, M. C., Messner, M. A., & Williams, L. (1991). *Coverage of women's sports in four daily newspapers.* Los Angeles: Amateur Athletic Foundation of Los Angeles.

Duncan, M. C., Messner, M. A., Williams, L., & Jensen, K. (1990). *Gender stereotyping in televised sports.* Los Angeles: Amateur Athletic Foundation of Los Angeles.

Duncan, M. C., & Sayaovong, A. (1990). Photographic images and gender in *Sports Illustrated for Kids. Play and Culture, 3*(2), 91-116.

Halpert, F. (1988, October). You call this adorable? *Ms.,* pp. 36-39.

Jencks, C. (1987). Should news be sold for profit? In D. Lazere (Ed.), *American media and mass culture: Left perspectives* (pp. 564-567). Berkeley: University of California Press.

Kane, M. J., & Parks, J. B. (1990). Mass media images as a reflector of historical social change: The portrayal of female athletes before, during and after Title IX. In L. Vander Velden & J. H. Humphrey (Eds.), *Psychology and sociology of sport: Current selected research 2* (pp. 133-149). New York: AMS.

Lumpkin, A., & Williams, L. D. (1991). An analysis of *Sports Illustrated* feature articles, 1954-1987. *Sociology of Sport Journal, 8,* 16-32.

Powell, W. (1987). The blockbuster decades: The media as big business. In D. Lazere (Ed.), *American media and mass culture: Left perspectives* (pp. 53-63). Berkeley: University of California Press.

Rintala, J., & Birrell, S. (1984). Fair treatment for the active female: A content analysis of *Young Athlete* magazine. *Sociology of Sport Journal, 1,* 231-250.

Sabo, D., & Jansen, S. C. (1992). Images of men in sport media. In S. Craig (Ed.), *Masculinity and the media* (pp. 169-185). Newbury Park, CA: Sage.

Tabor, C. (1991, April). *Literary portrayals of women in sport.* Paper presented at the annual meeting of the American Alliance for Health, Physical Education, Recreation, and Dance (AAHPERD), San Francisco.

16

The Olympic Games
Our Birthright to Sports

ANITA L. DeFRANTZ

Sport belongs to all human beings. It is unique to the human species. Other animals, like humans, engage in play. Other animals, like humans, engage in setting aside and protecting their territory. But only the human species takes part in sport. We are the only ones on earth who set up barriers and try to jump over them to see who can get to the finish line first. We are the only ones who compete for the sheer satisfaction of winning.

Sport is our birthright. Sport provides an opportunity for individuals to set their own goals and accomplish those goals, whether to run a mile in four minutes or to jump eight feet. It allows a person to take on a personal challenge and to succeed. And yet, at the revival of the world's most enduring and important sporting event, the Olympic Games, 51% of humanity was excluded.

The founder of the modern Olympic Games, Baron Pierre de Coubertin, was not in favor of women participating in the Games, or in sports in general. Writing in *Revue Olympique* in 1912, de Coubertin defined the Games as "the solemn and periodic exaltation of male athleticism, with internationalism as a base, loyalty as a means, art for its setting, and female applause as reward" (quoted in Leigh, 1974, p. 76). According to Leigh (1974), he believed that "a woman's glory rightfully came through the number and quality of children she produced, and that as far as sports were concerned, her greatest accomplishment was to encourage her sons to excel rather than to seek records for herself" (p. 72). With such strong feelings on the part of de Coubertin, it is not surprising that women were excluded from the first modern-era Olympic Games, held in Athens in 1896.

Even though women were excluded from the 1896 Games, a woman named Melpomene trained secretly for weeks and asked to enter the marathon. Despite being denied by Olympic officials, she ran the distance from Marathon to Athens, with followers on bicycles to chronicle the event, in four and a half hours.

But times were changing. At the end of the nineteenth century and during the beginning of the twentieth century, industrialization and the impact of social reform through the women's movement changed the passive role of women to an active one. This change also was slowly becoming evident in sports.

The International Olympic Committee (IOC) always has had exclusive control of the program of the Olympic Games. Nevertheless, the IOC looks to international sports federations to propose the sports and events. Unless a sports federation supports women's sports, the IOC will not act on inclusion. Currently, Rule 52 of the Olympic Charter sets out the requirements for inclusion of a sport discipline or event in the Olympic Games. Basically, for women's competition a sport must be practiced in 40 countries on three continents. For men, the requirement is 75 countries on four continents. This rule was adopted in 1991. In fact, until 1968 there were no criteria for inclusion except the proposals made by the international sports federations.

Women competed in golf and tennis in 1900, and archery was added for women in 1904. Archery stayed on the program through 1908, and tennis continued on the program through 1924. But the International Swimming Federation was the first to promote women's involvement actively; it voted to include women on the Olympic Games program in swimming for 1912. This opened the way for other international governing bodies to follow, but they followed extremely slowly.

The story of track and field is very enlightening in this regard. In response to the exclusion of women from track and field in the Olympic Games, Alice Milliat of France founded the Federation Feminine Sportive de France (FFSF) in 1917 to oversee national women's athletic competition. Four years later, she established the Federation Sportive Feminine International (FSFI) to include international competition. The FSFI conducted the first Ladies Olympic Games in 1922 in Paris. The FSFI conducted similar games every four years until 1934, and the schedule of athletic events rose as high as 15, with 19 countries participating in the program of the 1934 games in London. In fact, the 1924 Women's International and British Games were attended by 25,000 spectators.

Naturally, when it became apparent that the Ladies Olympic Games were successful in terms of competition and participation, the men's international governing body, the International Amateur Athletic Federation (IAAF), became interested in absorbing the FSFI (much as the NCAA moved to take control of women's collegiate sport from the AIAW in the late 1970s). The struggle between the IAAF and FSFI went on for 14 years. During the struggle, the IAAF decided to offer women an opportunity to compete in the 1928 Olympic Games in Amsterdam. But the women were offered only five events, and the press (still a male-dominated institution) was decidedly against participation by women in the Games.

At the center of the 1928 controversy was the women's 800-meter run. The male administrators, members of the IOC, and the all-male media apparently had decided that women were too frail to compete in a race as long as 800 meters. As a result, the reports from the 1928 Games not only distorted the results of that race, but in some cases completely fabricated facts to support

Reported by the media as the "wretched 11," in fact only 9 women started the ill-fated 800-meter race in the 1928 Olympics. (Photo courtesy of the Amateur Athletic Foundation of Los Angeles)

their viewpoint. The tragic result was that the event was removed from the Olympic program and was not reinstated until 1960.

John Tunis (1929), a prominent sportswriter of the day, portrayed the 800-meter event as follows: "Below us on the cinder path were 11 wretched women, 5 of whom dropped out before the finish, while 5 collapsed after reaching the tape" (p. 213). Unfortunately for Mr. Tunis, the camera had been invented by 1928, and photographs, as well as Olympic Games records, clearly indicate that only 9 women started the race, *not* 11 (Abrahams, 1929; "Athletics," 1928). Furthermore, all 9 of the women finished the race. The winner, Lina Radke of Germany, set a world record. She and a few of the other competitors were understandably spent after racing at world-record pace. Some of them lay down beside the track, but none of them dropped out or collapsed from exhaustion. This report was made by Dr. Messerli, one of the officials of the race: "The journalists believed them to be in a state of exhaustion. . . . I can . . . certify that there was nothing wrong with them; they burst into tears, betraying their disappointment at losing" (quoted in Leigh, 1974, p. 333).

Harold Abrahams, the famous sprinter, saw the race and supported Messerli's view. Abrahams (1929) wrote that the "sensational" press accounts were "grossly exaggerated." He added:

> I myself witnessed no sign of collapse such as have been described. It is perfectly true to say that two or three of the competitors . . . showed signs of mild discomfort, but I incline to the view that this was more psychological than physical, and entirely to be accounted for by the natural disappointment of being beaten. (p. 147)

And yet, members of the press chose to write what would suit the purpose of the male-dominated administration, and effectively prevented women from competing in any race longer than 200 meters in the Olympic Games for the next 32 years.

It is interesting to compare a report on men's events from earlier Games. The men's 800-meter race at the 1904 Olympic Games was described as follows:

> Thursday afternoon at the finish of the 800 meter run, two men fell to the track, completely exhausted. One man was carried to his training quarters helpless. Another was laid out on the grass and stimulants used to bring him back to life. (quoted in Leigh, 1974, p. 333)

Apparently the men were allowed to collapse following 800 meters, but the women were not. It is interesting that no one used this race to prevent men from running that distance in subsequent Olympic Games.

The point, of course, is that anyone, male or female, has the right to be fatigued as a result of giving his or her all in a race. But in that 1928 women's 800-meter race, fatigue was used to limit the events in which women would participate in future Olympic Games.

Of course, we know today that the decision makers were wrong in denying women athletic opportunities equal to those enjoyed by men. We also know today that, given the opportunity to participate, women will excel and improve. The 800-meter event in 1928 challenged the ability of women to excel. Women have met that challenge. In fact, the improvement in women's athletic achievements since then has been remarkable. The gender gap is shrinking rapidly in sports events shared by men and women. For example, the women's world record in the 800 meters set by Lina Radke in the 1928 Olympic Games was 26 seconds slower than the men's world record. Today the difference between the men's and women's world records has shrunk to a mere 12 seconds. In the marathon, the current women's world record of 2:21.06, set by Ingrid Kristiansen, would have defeated all of the men in Olympic Games competition up to 1960, including the legendary Emil Zatopek, by 4 minutes. Kristiansen would have beaten the male winner of the 1928 marathon by a full 12 minutes.

The growth of women's participation in track and field in the Olympic Games following the 1928 incident was painstakingly slow. By 1936 the IAAF had managed to absorb the women's organization completely. Leaders of the IAAF promised increased participation and support for women's sports at all levels, but the record suggests that they have been slow to fulfill that commitment. It was not until 1960 that women were once again permitted to race the 800 meters. In 1964, the 400 meters was added, and in 1972 the 1,500 meters. By 1984 in Los Angeles the women had lobbied successfully for inclusion of the 3,000 meters and the marathon, and finally in 1988 the 10,000-meter race gained acceptance on the program. There is still no 5,000 meter run, although there was a 10,000 meter race-walk event for the first time in 1992 in Barcelona. It has taken more than 60 years, since that first 800-meter race, for women to approach parity with men in terms of the number of events on the Olympic Games track and field program, from just 5 events in 1928 to a slate of 19 events in Barcelona.

In sports other than track and field, the shrinking gender gap comparisons are even more remarkable. For example, in swimming, the 800-meter world record held by Frenchman Jean Taris in 1930 was a full 2 minutes faster than Yvonne Goddard's women's record. But in 1989, the diminutive Janet Evans's world record trails the men's time by only 27 seconds, and her time of 8:17.12 is more than 2 minutes faster than Mr. Taris' 1930 world record. At the 1932 Lake Placid Olympic Winter Games, in speed skating there was a 14.6-second difference between the times of the men's gold medalist in the 500-meter race and the winner of the women's 500-meter demonstration event. By 1988 in Calgary the margin between the male and female gold medal winners at 500 meters had decreased to 3.65 seconds.

Despite the impressive performances of female athletes in this century, women continue to see their athletic accomplishments distorted by the sporting press, just as they did in 1928. Study after study during the past 15 years has shown a clear pattern of underreporting and trivialization of women's sport by both print and electronic media (Duncan, Messner, Williams, & Jensen, 1990).

In addition to the problems of media coverage, girls and women are hindered by lack of input from women at the administrative level. Women are conspicuously absent from the upper-level management positions where policy is determined worldwide. A recent informal survey undertaken by the Amateur Athletic Foundation of Los Angeles revealed some disturbing evidence. The study discovered that of the nearly 13,000 administrative positions available in North American sports and the international Olympic movement, a mere 5% were held by women (DeFrantz, 1989). This is in stark contrast to the fact that women constitute more than 51% of the world's population.

It is disturbing for me, as an International Olympic Committee member, to acknowledge that, of the 167 presidents of National Olympic Committees (NOCs) worldwide in 1992, only 6 are women. And only 5 of the 167 secretaries general for those same NOCs are women. The six women presidents are Sophia Raddock, Fiji; HRH Princess Salote Ilolevu Tuita, Tonga; Princess Nora, Liechtenstein; Carol Anne Letheren, Canada; Lia Manoliv, Romania; and Vera Caslavska, Czechoslovakia. The five secretaries general are Eileen L. Parsons, British Virgin Islands; Nour El Houda Karfoul, Syria; Gunilla Lindberg, Sweden; Myriam Margarita Quezada De Rodriguez, El Salvador; and Nadejda Olkhova, Republic of Kazakhstan.

Even in the United States the record is not good. Since 1976 there has been only one female officer of the U.S. Olympic Committee (USOC). For the quadrennial leading to the Barcelona Games in 1992, not one woman was elected. There are many women who could serve as excellent officers, but none was proposed on the slate of officers.

Perhaps more important is the membership of the International Olympic Committee. There are only 7 women among the 94-member IOC. But prior to 1981 there was none. President Juan Antonio Samaranch has been

Anita DeFrantz has lifetime membership on the International Olympic Committee and is the only American woman on the IOC. Of the 94 committee members, only 7 are women. (Photo courtesy of the Amateur Athletic Foundation of Los Angeles)

a strong advocate for women's participation in the Olympic movement. He has ensured that women have become involved in the decision-making process. Now it is up to us to provide opportunities for women to take responsibility at every level of sport. There are indications that progress is being made. The election of Carol Anne Letheren as president of Canada's NOC is one example. But such instances are all too rare.

So where can girls and women go to develop their skills in sports and administration? Title IX of the Education Amendments of 1972 and the Civil Rights Restoration Act of 1987 make it clear that women are to have opportunities equivalent to those of men in the educational environment to take part in sports. This means on the playing fields, in coaching positions, and in administration. Where this is not occurring, it is up to women to bring complaints against offending organizations. The Women's Sports Foundation is an excellent source of information on opportunities for women in sport as well as information on Title IX issues. In addition, WSF provides grants to girls and women to support their travel and training.

The Amateur Sports Act of 1978 requires the U.S. Olympic Committee and its constituent organizations to provide sports opportunities without regard to sex or race. The USOC relies on volunteers to a very large extent. And of course, the tradition in this country is that volunteers support sport. However, the majority of USOC volunteers are men. Women are desperately needed. The USOC is headquartered in Colorado Springs, Colorado, and sport governing bodies for the various sports are located throughout the nation. The USOC can help persons who are interested in becoming involved in sports to contact the various sports bodies. Getting involved may take persistence, but that is what it takes today to be an administrator or athlete. The Ziffren Center Library at the Amateur Athletic Foundation of Los Angeles is also an important source of information on all aspects of sport and can provide the addresses and telephone numbers of numerous sports organizations.

As you can see, the source list is very short. Of course, there are women working throughout the United States in academic institutions, a few in professional sports, sports medicine, and international sports, as well as those in voluntary positions in sport. But these few are not enough. For sport to be available to everybody, we need an enormous increase in the number of women participating at all levels of sport.

The proving ground for upper-level management in sports is often the playing field. The future of women in leadership roles begins with today's young girls. They need to be encouraged to participate in sports and learn how to coach as well as to play. To encourage women to seek leadership roles, we need role models or examples for them to emulate. Without women in positions of responsibility, we have no role models. Certainly we must make every effort to take advantage of the few examples of successful women we do have in sports leadership.

Women must be allowed to move from the field of competition to the upper levels of management. They must be encouraged to do what Ms. Letheren and others are doing in an effort to ensure the rights of equal and fair competition for women worldwide. Sport belongs to us all, and women must continue to insist on our birthright to take part in sport. If, in fact, only 5% of all available leadership positions are held by women, that means there are still 95% of them available to women. The opportunities are many. Community-based organizations need women coaches and administrators. Sports clubs need parental involvement at all levels. For every opportunity women take advantage of, the universe of opportunities is expanded for all people to participate in sports.

Sport and the Olympic movement have long been held in high regard for their ability to appreciate and celebrate human excellence. The Olympic movement has been responsible for bringing together nations of the world. And, despite a rather slow start, the Olympic movement has been instrumental in spreading opportunities for women in sports throughout the world. The challenge for all of us is to keep the effort under way. The 1990s have brought enormous change in the political environment of the world. This environment of change should be used by all of us who care about sport to ensure that women and girls truly exercise their right to participate fully in the world of sports.

Key Words

Baron Pierre de Coubertin	Melpomene
International Olympic	International Amateur
Committee	Athletic Federation
Federation Sportive	sport records
Feminine International	administrative positions

Discussion Questions

1. Explain the significance of the media's reporting on the women's 800-meter race in the 1928 Olympics. Could (or does) this kind of thing happen today?
2. Contrast the strategy of the Federation Sportive Feminine International with that used by Billie Jean King and others from 1970 to 1973 to increase the prize money in women's professional tennis (see Chapter 24).

3. Women's representation in administrative positions related to the Olympic movement is dismal. What can you personally do to help create change?

4. What resources are available to you if you want to increase opportunities for girls and women in sport?

References

Abrahams, H. M. (1929). *The official report of the IXth Olympiad Amsterdam 1928.* London: British Olympic Association.

Athletics. (1928). In G. Van Rossen (Ed.), *Ninth Olympiad: Being the official report of the Olympic Games of 1928 celebrated at Amsterdam* (pp. 368-480). Amsterdam: Netherlands Olympic Committee.

DeFrantz, A. L. (1989, Summer). The sky is the limit. *Headway,* pp. 1,9.

Duncan, M. C., Messner, M. A., Williams, L., & Jensen, K. (1990). *Gender stereotyping in televised sports.* Los Angeles: Amateur Athletic Foundation of Los Angeles.

Leigh, M. H. (1974). The evolution of women's participation in the Summer Olympic Games, 1900-1948. *Dissertation Abstracts International, 35,* 5098A-5099A. (University Microfilms Number 75-3121)

Tunis, J. R. (1929, July). Women and the sport business. *Harper's Magazine,* pp. 159, 211-221.

17

Homophobia in Women's Sports
The Fear That Divides Us

PAT GRIFFIN

T he crowd was quiet as the players lined up for the free throw. The 10 young women athletes were poised, eyes focused on the basket, waiting to spring into the air for the rebound. The shooter bounced the ball once and settled herself by taking a deep breath and exhaling slowly. In the silence as spectators and players waited for the shot, someone in the stands yelled out, "You're all dykes!" A nervous titter rippled through the stands and people turned to look toward the cluster of young men who sat laughing at their joke. The game continued, and our team won 72-68, but what I remember most about that game was that moment of silence when the word *dyke* was hurled at the women on the court with the intention of ridiculing them. Why is it that despite the progress made in women's sport over the past 20 years, the association of athleticism with lesbians and the use of the lesbian label to intimidate women in sport is still so powerful? Why would a young man call a group of women "dykes" with such malicious intent when he probably knows nothing about them or their sexuality?

The answers to these questions are embedded in the larger social context of a culture in which women have yet to achieve equitable status in work or pay; are the targets of sexual, physical, and verbal assault; and hold few positions of power in government, law, or other major social institutions. In addition, we live in a culture that attaches extreme stigma to homosexuality. In this social context, lesbians and gay men are perceived to be severely deviant and alternately dangerous or comical.

There are several underlying assumptions that support the perspective on homosexuality reflected in this chapter. Readers should be cognizant of these assumptions.

1. We all have some degree of discomfort with the topic of homosexuality because we live in a culture that teaches us to fear or condemn lesbians and gay men and makes it difficult for us to gather accurate information about homosexuality.
2. This discomfort with homosexuality has negative effects on all of our lives, regardless of our sexual orientation. It affects friendships, family relationships, and personal choices as we try to avoid association with homosexuality.
3. No sexual orientation (heterosexual, homosexual, or bisexual) is inherently any more natural, normal, or acceptable than any other.
4. Not all readers will agree with the first three assumptions.

Homosexuality is a controversial issue and there is no social consensus about the status of lesbian and gay people. That is precisely why discussions about homosexuality are important.

Although this chapter addresses homophobia in women's sport, it is important to note that homophobia also affects men's sport and that gay male athletes and coaches are a part of the athletic world.

Homophobia is the fear or hatred of homosexuality. In a society where intolerance of homosexuality is enforced by religious, legal, and psychological stigma, it is not surprising that many of us grow up learning to fear or hate lesbians and gay men. Many of us have learned to accept lesbian and gay stereotypes and are uncomfortable discussing homosexuality or being around lesbian and gay people. Discomfort with homosexuality is manifested in many different ways. Examples include making jokes about gay people, using antigay slurs, avoiding association with people thought to be lesbian or gay, and avoiding personal behavior perceived as characteristic of lesbians or gay men. More extreme examples of homophobia include physical or verbal harassment and discrimination directed at lesbians or gay men. Homophobia also discourages us from speaking out against homophobic actions by others, even when we do not support such behavior.

In a heterosexist society (one in which heterosexuality is the only accepted sexual orientation) accurate information about homosexuality is difficult to come by, because of culturally enforced silence. Sport as a social institution in this cultural context reflects the values of a sexist and heterosexist society.

Despite attention to expanding opportunities for women in American society over the past 20 years, the enforcement of traditional gender roles and fears about homosexuality still have the power to intimidate and discourage women from participation in sport. Sport is viewed by much of the American public as a male activity. Women's sport is perceived by many people as a second-rate imitation of the real thing: men's sport. This perception reinforces the sexist notion that successful women athletes are masculine. All of the traits of successful athletic performance are defined as masculine. Traditional feminine expectations do not encompass such qualities as physical strength, aggressiveness, independence, tough-mindedness, and muscularity. In a sexist society, women who have these qualities are suspect because they challenge social norms that depend on the acceptance of socially constructed differences between men and women as biologically determined.

An effective way to prevent women from challenging these social norms is to stigmatize sport participation by women. Accusing women athletes of being masculine is one way to stigmatize women in sport. Another, even more effective, mode of intimidation is the use of the lesbian label. Because lesbian stereotypes are so severe (sick, evil, abnormal, predatory), most women are loath to be associated with them. Consequently, calling women in sport lesbians effectively marginalizes women's sport. In this way the sexist status quo in sport is maintained. Women in sport are afraid to challenge their low status because stepping out of line in this way brings intensified accusations of lesbianism and masculinity. As a result, all women in sport, not only lesbians, are affected by homophobia. As long as the lesbian label can be used to intimidate and divide heterosexuals and lesbians, women's sports can be trivialized and controlled.

Some coaches, athletes, and administrators attempt to purge from women's sport anyone they think is lesbian. In naming lesbian participation in sport as the problem, however, they fail to address the underlying motivation for using accusations of lesbianism—to control women's sport participation. Even if there were no lesbians in sport at all, the lesbian label would still be used to intimidate and control women's athleticism in a male-dominated society. Antilesbian policies and actions may appear to be directed at lesbians, but all women are victimized by homophobia in sport.

When a young male calls a group of women athletes "dykes" he is playing out the sexist expectation that "normal" women who accept traditional feminine roles are not athletic. His action serves as a warning to women athletes (or other women who defy traditional gender roles) that they are stepping out-of-bounds. In this way sexism and homophobia combine to marginalize and intimidate women in sport by imposing societal expectations of what is appropriate and acceptable sport participation for women.

Sport as a social institution in our society reflects the larger social issues that we grapple with outside of the sports arena. Unfortunately, coaches and athletes do not leave their prejudices and ignorance at the gym door. Racism and sexism as well as heterosexism and homophobia are problematic. Part of the athletic experience should be learning to respect such social diversities and to understand how people from different races, religions, and cultures can work together.

Why Homophobia in Sport Needs to Be Addressed

Many of the problems related to homophobia in women's sport are made worse because open discussions about homosexuality are rare. Most schools avoid discussions about homosexuality because it is a controversial topic. The issues need to be addressed.

1. It is generally accepted that 10% of the population is lesbian or gay. Therefore, coaches, athletes, and teachers can safely assume that they will work with lesbian and gay teammates, coaches, and colleagues throughout their careers.

2. Athletes bring their fears and prejudices with them when they join teams. Coaches must be prepared to help them unlearn their prejudices.

3. Violent hate crimes directed at many minority groups are on the rise. Lesbians and gay men are among the most frequent targets of violence and harassment. Young men of high school and college age are among the most frequent perpetrators of this kind of violence.

4. A U.S. Department of Health and Human Services study reports that up to 30% of teen suicides are lesbian and gay youth who are so isolated and unhappy that they kill themselves.

5. High school- and college-aged young adults are beginning to explore their sexuality and sexual identities, whether heterosexual, bisexual, or homosexual.

6. Coaches and teachers are responsible for teaching more than sport and fitness skills and teamwork. They also have a responsibility to set examples for athletes and students about social justice and appreciation of social diversity.

7. The fear of being called lesbian or gay keeps young women and men from choosing to participate in activities outside of traditional gender roles.

8. Discrimination against lesbian and gay teachers, coaches, and school administrators often goes unaddressed either because there is no legal protection or because victims are afraid to protest unfair treatment.

9. Because so many schools are silent about homosexuality and homophobia, and because there are few lesbian or gay coaches and teachers who believe they can reveal their identities without risking their careers, many educators and students have no accurate information to contradict destructive stereotypes of lesbians and gay men.

10. Unless teachers and coaches act to address homophobia on their teams and in their classes, the next generation of young people will inherit the same prejudices and fears.

11. It is the right thing to do to speak out against injustice and prejudice based on stereotypes and ignorance wherever we encounter them—in our students, our colleagues, and ourselves.

Research on Homophobia and Lesbians in Sport

Another consequence of homophobia is a lack of research focusing on these issues. Many researchers who might be interested in these topics are reluctant to pursue their interests, either because of their own fear of association with homosexuality or because their interests are discouraged by educational institutions, graduate committees, or journal editors. Despite these effects of homophobia, a few researchers have investigated either homophobia or lesbians in sport.

Guthrie (1982) was the first researcher to investigate homophobia in physical education. Her study examined and compared homophobia among women physical education majors and nonmajors and among women athletes and nonathletes. Hall (1985) edited a special issue of *Women's Studies International Forum* on women's sport in which several of the articles discuss heterosexism and homophobia in women's sport. Woods

(1989/1990) interviewed lesbian physical education teachers about their experiences in schools. Thorgren (1991) studied the pressures and stresses that college coaches experience and reported that homophobia had a significant impact on the coaches' experience. Blinde (1990) investigated pressure and stress among college women athletes and found homophobia to be a contributing factor. All of these studies support the contention that homophobia has a profound impact on women in sport and physical education.

Questions About Lesbians and Sport Participation

Because so few coaches or athletes have had the opportunity to participate in educational programs examining homophobia in sport or to address questions they have about homosexuality, myths abound about lesbians in sport. Typical questions asked about lesbians in sport are based on a few deeply entrenched and often contradictory stereotypes about lesbians.

Does participating in sports cause women to become lesbians? Anyone associated with women's sport would agree that although it is true that some women in sport are lesbians, many women in sport are not. In any case, scientists do not fully understand how sexual orientation develops, because many complex factors determine a person's sexual orientation. Defining a causal relationship between genetic, biological, or social factors and sexual orientation is complicated by the social prejudice that identifies homosexuality as abnormal. Most researchers would agree that linking sexual orientation to participation in sport or any other single activity or experience is associated more with gender role stereotypes and misunderstanding about sexual orientation than with accurate information.

Does playing on sports teams with lesbians cause women to become lesbians? There is no evidence that association with people whose sexual orientation is different from one's own will influence personal identity. People do not become lesbian or gay merely because they play on teams with, or are coached by, lesbian or gay people. Sexual orientation is more than behavior. It is an integrated sense of identity that is deeply rooted in a person's sense of being. While some women first acknowledge that they are lesbians while playing on athletic teams, their sports participation does not cause them to become lesbians.

Why do women athletes look so masculine? In answering this question it is important to define what is meant by "masculine" and to understand that many so-called masculine characteristics are socially defined, not biologically determined. Characteristics such as aggressiveness, strength, bravery, independence, and toughness are associated with being masculine in North American culture. Boys and men in this culture are taught to value these traits in themselves and other men. Yet these traits are not inherently male. Women may also possess these characteristics. Unfortunately, women (and men) who do not conform to traditional feminine (and masculine) gender roles are often thought to be imitating the other gender. This perception applies not only to personality traits, but to physical appearance and interests or talents as well. Women who are serious and talented athletes or coaches are not masculine; they are simply serious and talented athletes and coaches.

A tremendous variety of traits exist among women athletes. To call this group masculine arbitrarily is to ignore the wide range of differences in physical appearance, personality, and skill. Success in some sports is directly related to specific physical attributes. Weight events in track and cross-country running call for distinctly different body types. Unfortunately, large, strong women are more likely to be called masculine merely for having the characteristics necessary to succeed in their sports.

Another assumption underlying the masculine image of women athletes is that masculine women are lesbians. This assumption reflects two misunderstandings about gender roles and sexual orientation. In addition to the acceptance of traditional gender roles as appropriate and natural, this association assumes that all lesbians look or act in ways that lead others to believe that they want to be like men. Assuming that athletically talented lesbians want to be like men reflects an unrealistic and limited view of the range of female interest and talent. To assume that lesbians have a common appearance or personality is as oversimplified as assuming that all African Americans or all Latino Americans look or act the same way.

Are lesbian coaches more likely to seduce or sexually harass women athletes? Most educators would agree that sexual involvement between students and teachers or between coaches and athletes violates professional ethics, regardless of the sexual orientations or genders of the people involved. There is no reason to expect that lesbian coaches (or athletes) are more likely to sexually harass women athletes than are other people. The sexual predator stereotype, though without basis in fact, is one of the most destructive images of lesbians in sport. Although sexuality is part of lesbian identity (as it is for heterosexual identity), winning games, getting along with teammates, performing well in games, and taking care of injuries are far more likely to occupy lesbian athletes' thoughts in the athletic arena.

It is ironic that lesbians in sport have been targeted as a sexual threat to other women in sport. Statistics on sexual harassment and rape indicate that women athletes should worry more abut unwanted sexual advances from heterosexual male coaches and athletes than from lesbian coaches or athletes.

Why do lesbians in sport have to "flaunt it"? Can't they just keep it to themselves? Most lesbians in sport carefully hide their sexual orientation because they fear discrimination and harassment. These fears are justified in a culture where lesbians and gay men are considered to be unfit to work with children and young adults. Maintaining secrecy, however, takes a tremendous psychological toll. In addition, when respected and successful lesbian and gay coaches are forced to hide their identities, lesbian and gay stereotypes are left unchallenged.

Imagine never feeling free to talk about your personal life. Think about having to lie about your personal life to colleagues and teammates. What would it be like to fear losing your coaching job or being asked to leave a team, not because of anything you have done to violate standards of conduct, but solely because of your sexual orientation?

Heterosexual athletes and coaches, on the other hand, introduce their romantic partners to the rest of the team and talk about their relationships. They talk about weekend plans with romantic partners. Sometimes romantic partners are included in team social activities. News stories about professional athletes who are married may include pictures of spouses and children. If a lesbian coach or athlete expects the same privilege, she is perceived as flaunting her sexual orientation. If a lesbian coach or athlete claims her sexual orientation, she is called a bad role model. Because homosexuality has been wrapped in silence and secrecy, when lesbians and gay men claim the same privileges of openness and visibility that heterosexuals enjoy, they are accused of flaunting their identities.

Why are lesbians in sport so secretive and cliquey? Are they ashamed of who they are? There are several reasons lesbians in sport might be secretive. Women thought to be lesbians do lose their coaching jobs and are asked to leave teams, not because of any unethical behavior, but solely because of their sexual orientation and the stereotyped expectations that are associated with being lesbian. As a consequence, many lesbians in sport are secretive and protective of their identities.

Some lesbians in sport do not feel comfortable with their sexual orientation. Growing up in a culture that teaches everyone that lesbians and gay men are abnormal, sick, or disgusting affects everyone. Many young lesbians and gay men internalize these negative messages and must overcome feelings of self-hate. In the absence of visible role models and support from coaches, teammates, friends, and family, young lesbian and gay athletes or coaches look to each other for support and friendship. All minority groups, whether racial, ethnic, or religious, seek out others like themselves for affirmation and companionship. Lesbians and gay men are no different.

Why is talking about homophobia and lesbians in sport so difficult? Homosexuality is a controversial topic in our culture. As we grow up, most of us learn that homosexuality is such a taboo that silence is the only appropriate response. In this silence, enforced by cultural norms, stereotypes and ignorance flourish. Most of us learn that being associated with homosexuality, having a lesbian friend, or participating in an activity thought to attract lesbian or gay people is to be avoided because we will be assumed to be gay by our associations. Contrary to popular opinion, it is difficult to identify lesbians or gay men by appearance. Unlike racial identity or gender, sexual orientation is not so obvious. Consequently, many people are afraid of being associated with lesbians or gay men because they might be mistaken as gay. Speaking out about homophobia in sport or acknowledging a lesbian and gay presence in sport intensifies these associations. Most people are afraid to break the silence for fear of rejection or reprisal.

Because women's sport is associated with lesbians already, openly acknowledging lesbians in sport or addressing homophobia calls attention to issues many people would rather not discuss. Unfortunately, silence about homophobia and lesbians in sport allows discrimination and fear to thrive.

Aren't lesbians in sport bad role models? There are already lesbian coaches and athletes who are highly regarded in the sport community. These women set high standards for academic, athletic, and ethical performance; they are good role models. Unfortunately, they feel forced to hide their sexual orientation so that their lesbian identities go undetected. Most of these women fear that despite their excellent performances and exemplary conduct, their reputations would be irrevocably tarnished if their sexual orientation were made public. Due to the perversity of prejudice and ignorance, lesbian coaches or athletes could lose their credibility or their jobs. In this silence, the invisibility of highly regarded lesbian athletes and coaches promotes the unfair perception that lesbians are automatically and universally bad role models. A coach's or athlete's ability to be a good role model should be assessed by her professional conduct, not by her sexual orientation.

Can you tell who is a lesbian by appearance? Many of the stereotypes of lesbians and gay men are related to gender role expectations. Consequently, lesbians are expected to look and act in ways we associate with men. There are two problems with this assumption. First, there is as much diversity among lesbians as there is among heterosexual women. We often become trapped by our own stereotypes, so that we only suspect that someone is a lesbian when she fulfills our stereotype of what a lesbian should look or act like. Then we think we can tell by appearance or action who is or is not a lesbian. When our stereotypes limit our perceptions in this way, we do not acknowledge lesbians who do not fit our stereotyped expectations or the heterosexual women who do fit our stereotype whom we have mistakenly identified as lesbians. Not all women with short hair and athletic physiques are lesbians, and not all women who have long hair and wear makeup are heterosexual.

The association between lesbian stereotypes and traditional male gender role expectations illustrates how homophobia and sexism are interconnected. Attaching a masculine label to an activity or personal characteristic and intimidating women who pursue these activities or exhibit these personal characteristics with the lesbian label maintains the gender inequity that traditional gender roles reflect.

Alternative Sport Opportunities for Lesbians

Because there is so much fear and discrimination directed toward lesbians in high school, college, and professional sport, many lesbian

Athletes assemble for opening ceremonies of Gay Games III in the Vancouver, British Columbia, Stadium. (Photo by Joe Caputo)

athletes have chosen to participate in alternative sport experiences. Lesbian and gay sports leagues flourish in many large cities around the United States. In these leagues, lesbians and gay men compete locally and nationally in such sports as softball, volleyball, rugby, bowling, soccer, basketball, and rodeo. Unlike in traditional sports leagues or school teams, in these organizations lesbians and gay men can openly acknowledge their identities while they enjoy sports participation and the accompanying social activities.

In 1982 the first Gay Games were held in San Francisco. This international event, modeled after the Olympic Games, was founded by a gay man, Tom Waddell, who competed for the United States in the 1968 Olympic Decathlon. Waddell wanted to create a sports festival dedicated to, but not restricted to, lesbian and gay athletes who could celebrate their athleticism and their sexual identity. The week-long event includes competition in several team sports, swimming, track and field, triathlon, the marathon, weight lifting, tennis, and several other sports. The original organizers intended to call this quadrennial event the Gay Olympics, but they were successfully sued by the U.S. Olympic Committee to prevent the use of the word *Olympics.* Though other groups have used the word *Olympics* with no objections from the USOC—notably the Police Olympics and the Special Olympics—the association of the word with lesbians and gay men aroused the USOC's homophobia.

Nonetheless, Gay Games III was held in 1990 in Vancouver, British Columbia. More than 7,000 athletes from 30 countries around the world participated, making Gay Games III the largest international sporting event that year, eclipsing the Goodwill Games held the same year. Gay Games IV will be held in 1994 in New York City. Organizers expect more than 14,000 athletes to compete.

Alternative sport experiences such as the Gay Games provide lesbian and gay athletes and coaches opportunities to enjoy sport competition without the fear of harassment and discrimination most have experienced in the traditional sports world.

How Can We Address
Homophobia in Women's Sport?

Education about and action against homophobia are crucial to creating a more hospitable sports environment. Education about homophobia should be included in professional preparation programs for physical education teachers and coaches. Discussion groups, workshops, and readings on this topic can assist young sport professionals in overcoming their prejudice and misinformation about lesbians in sport and understanding how homophobia and sexism limit women's sport experience. Athletic teams can participate in programs that encourage respect for differences and provide information to counteract stereotypes. Professional conferences can also provide coaches and sport administrators with strategies for working with athletes to help them address their homophobia.

Silence has surrounded the issue of lesbians in sport. In that silence, innuendo, rumor, and outright discrimination perpetuate fear and ignorance. One of the most important ways to address homophobia in women's sport is for coaches, athletes, and administrators to speak out and act against homophobia and the discrimination and prejudice it causes. We must voice our objections to antigay jokes or comments among teams and coaches. We must address harassment and discrimination directed at lesbians or women thought to be lesbians. Athletic departments must adopt nondiscrimination policies that include sexual orientation, to provide institutional support for the tolerance of diversity.

Women in sport should be judged not on the basis of their sexual identities, but by their athletic talents and performance, personal integrity, and character. Everyone associated with women's sport should take some responsibility for working toward that goal. Until we understand the consequences of homophobia for all women in sport, our athletic accomplishments will be tainted by the prejudice that homophobia encourages and the fear that divides us.

Key Words

homophobia
heterosexism
homosexuality
lesbian

bisexuality
discrimination
Gay Games

Discussion Questions

1. How does homophobia stigmatize all women in sport?
2. How do certain sports get labeled "acceptable" sports or "dyke" sports? What is the implication of such labeling? How can it be stopped?
3. Is the existence of gay and lesbian leagues and the Gay Games an affirmation of an individual's right to be his or her own person, or is it an example of flaunting sexuality? Explain your position.

References

Blinde, E. (1990, March). *Pressure and stress in women's college sports: Views from athletes.* Paper presented at the annual meeting of the American Alliance for Health, Physical Education, Recreation and Dance, New Orleans.

Guthrie, S. (1982). *Homophobia: Its impact on women in sport and physical education.* Unpublished master's thesis, California State University, Long Beach.

Hall, A. (Ed.). (1985). The gendering of sport, leisure, and physical education [Special issue]. *Women's Studies International Forum, 10*(4).

Thorgren, C. (1991, April). *Homophobia and women coaches: Controls and constraints.* Paper presented at the annual meeting of the American Alliance for Health, Physical Education, Recreation and Dance, San Francisco.

Woods, S. (1990). The contextual realities of being a lesbian physical education teacher: Living in two worlds (Doctoral dissertation, University of Massachusetts, Amherst, 1989). *Dissertation Abstracts International, 51*(3), 788.

18

The Minority Experience in Sport
Monochromatic or Technicolor?

R. VIVIAN ACOSTA

As the United States becomes more culturally diverse, attention needs to be paid to the multiethnic makeup of the population. According to the *melting pot* metaphor, diverse cultures become blended into a uniquely homogenized American culture. The *stew* metaphor, on the other hand, has diverse cultures blending their flavors but remaining identifiable within the rubric of an "American" culture. Either way, awareness of similarities and differences is essential for us to appreciate the ingredients that make up the final product.

On a planet that is only one-fifth Caucasian, discussion of the "minority" experience becomes relative. However, in the United States of America, the dominant culture remains Euro-American. Using that perspective, this chapter focuses primarily on females who identify as being within the general minority classifications of African American, Latina American, and Asian American.[1] General references target those experiences held in common by all women not holding power or policy-making positions.

Women in general are subject to discriminatory treatment in education and employment. Women face inadequate legal protection of their economic and civil rights, and when they have children, they are usually the primary caregivers for those children. Minority men and women in general are subject to discriminatory treatment in education and employment. Minority men and women face inadequate legal protection of their economic and civil rights. Given that all *women* are at a disadvantage and all *minority* group members are at a disadvantage, *minority women* are affected in both regards.

Access to the Educational Process

Generally speaking, the better one is educated, the greater one's options for employment. It is widely accepted that minorities are generally not full participants in the educational structure; therefore, significant limitations may affect their employment options. Much emphasis has been placed on the value of obtaining an education as a means of improving one's quality of life. However, many young minority group members are not convinced they should attend college or even complete high school. To understand the unique circumstances minority students face, consider the following factors: (a) cost of education, (b) time constraints, (c) economic impact, (d) educational discrimination, (e) role models, and (f) psychological effects.

Cost of Education

Middle-class is a term that applies to a diminishing segment of American society, as more families struggle with increasing financial pressures. Because their parents have felt the impact of less education and resulting low-paying jobs, it is not surprising that minority students often come from families in which financial resources are extremely limited. Because single-parent families are more common among some minority groups (U.S. Department of Commerce, 1990), and because minority family units may include larger numbers of children than nonminority families, their financial options are even more limited. The schools chosen by minorities reflect these limited options.

Time Constraints

In becoming educated, school attendance and out-of-class preparation are very time-consuming. In a typical minority family structure, the philosophy concerning female children is that they should be at home to help with the day-to-day chores and care of younger siblings. Minority parents, particularly those who have not had educational opportunities beyond grammar or junior high school, have no experiential basis for understanding the need to spend long hours at school. When students are at home, they may not have adequate space or time in which they can fully concentrate on the task of studying. Female minority students often feel a sense of guilt for staying away from home for long periods, knowing that their presence is needed to relieve the pressure of home responsibilities ascribed to their mothers. When female students do fulfill home responsibilities, they are often too tired to spend the necessary time with their studies.

Economic Impact

Because of the limited financial resources of many minority families (U.S. Department of Commerce, 1990), it is extremely important for children who are able to work to contribute financially to their families' support. Often minority parents look forward to the day when their offspring are capable of finding work, even at minimum wage. A child with wage-earning capacity who postpones employment by attending school full-time for an extended period places a financial hardship on the entire family. Although that child's obtaining a college degree may benefit everyone in the long run, immediate family needs may be more compelling. The high school graduate has a difficult choice to make; deferring valuable income-producing years by attending college has an immediate economic impact.

Holding a part-time job, in addition to creating financial options, may help a student to become more focused. Further, working part-time can help the student learn to set realistic goals and to budget limited resources; a job can also give a student an appreciation for the work ethic and an opportunity to acquire diversified experiences. While opportunities for sport-related part-time positions exist and some students work in recreational facilities, at summer camps, and as lifeguards or swimming instructors, higher-paying jobs are usually found in housepainting, on fishing boats, in construction work, and in waitressing or tending bar.

Educational Discrimination

The American Association of University Women (1992), in its report *How Schools Shortchange Girls*, demonstrates how girls and boys are treated differently in the public schools. Girls are shortchanged by the quality and quantity of education they receive. Gender inequities begin at a very young age, and play activities also conform to traditional stereotypes that leave fewer options for girls.

Conversely, boys learn that sport participation and achievement are both good and desirable. They provide instant acceptance and approval by the dominant culture. The minority female has a double dose of cultural pressures to deal with. All of the "Americanized" cultural mores apply to her and, in addition, because she is part of a minority group, the cultural traditions of that minority group also apply.

Many communities include vocational high schools as part of their educational options. Although trade and vocational schools serve a laudatory purpose, students are often channeled into specific vocational programs without having any say in the decisions, which are frequently based on stereotypical perceptions of what vocations are "appropriate" for members of particular minority groups. For instance, a counselor's unconscious perception that Latinas make good secretaries or that black males have good futures as mechanics may influence the counselor's placement of minority students in specific vocational programs. Such a decision-making process is patronizing to minority students, who may be unaware of the many options available. What may appear as supportive actions by a counselor may in fact be nonsupportive, discriminatory, destructive to self-esteem, and severely limiting.

In recent years, many colleges and universities have made efforts to increase the cultural diversity on their campuses by recruiting minority students. According to Carter and Wilson (1991), from 1986 to 1988 minority student enrollment in the nation's colleges and universities increased 7.2%, outpacing a 4.3% gain in total enrollment. Latina enrollment in colleges increased by 10%. However, minority recruitment programs have not been as successful as anticipated.

A significantly larger number of African American college students are enrolling in black colleges and universities, finding more sameness and perhaps more comfort there than in other institutions. Between 1987 and 1989, black college enrollment increased 9.9%, far exceeding the 3.8% gain elsewhere. The distribution of bachelor's degrees in 1991 included 84.3% to Caucasians, 5.8% to African Americans, and 3.1% to Hispanics (Carter & Wilson, 1991).

The same recruiting methods used to attract Euro-Americans to attend prep schools and special high schools are often used to attract minority and low-income students. However, these methods do not always work well when applied to minority students, because school counselors may unconsciously preselect students they believe will be successful in college programs as opposed to vocational programs. Cultural biases often remain intact. When recruiters arrive at some high schools, very few minority students are available for interviews (Sullivan, 1989).

In rural communities, there is a reluctance to let children travel to out-of-state institutions. The fear that the young will seek employment elsewhere and not return to the rural homeland is a very real problem. This is true for all youth, and not confined to minority populations.

When minority students attend college, they enter a whiter, more monochromatic environment where fewer persons who share their ethnic backgrounds are present and where support systems have a smaller pool of participants from which to draw.

Role Models

The particularly low percentage of female minority group members serving as leaders in education in general, and in sport in particular, is unrepresentative of the population as a whole (Acosta & Carpenter, 1992). According to Smith (1991), "Five percent or less of all physical education teachers, coaches and sport administrators are multicultural minorities" (p. 39). Therefore, female ethnic minority students receive the message that educational institutions undervalue their ability to contribute professionally. All young people need to see examples of cultural diversity in education and in sport. Both education and sport are mirrors of society, and the reflections they cast are clear indications of the problems that exist.

Psychological Effects

All students, regardless of gender or ethnicity, must cope with the issue of achievement. Some students are more motivated than others, have set goals, have financial resources, enjoy relatively stable family life, and receive encouragement and support from family. However, many minority students may experience additional stress. Familial expectations among some minority groups continue to provide the greatest obstacle to higher education. Other minorities stress academic achievement, sending diametrically opposed messages to their female children.

Issues associated with upward mobility are very prevalent sources of stress, particularly in families with lower economic status. Academia may appear to be a foreign environment where one is forced to adjust to a white middle- and upper-middle-class society. For instance, minority students' attempts to comply with prevailing social mores may create fixations that erode self-confidence and self-esteem.

Because of poor preparation in high school and, in some cases, lack of facility with English, remedial courses are included in many minority students' college programs. Although necessary for some students, such remedial courses can slow minority students' progress toward degrees and jobs, thus contributing to the stress associated with feelings of incompetence and inferiority in the educational environment. Students' mastery of their own native languages and understanding of their own cultures are seldom viewed as accomplishments.

Minority Females and the Sporting Experience

Being female is hard enough when it comes to sport participation, but being female and a minority group member is doubly difficult. The minority woman has to be very determined to be a full-time participant in sport, because for the most part her heritage and birth culture speak loudly and forcefully against her involvement with most forms of sport. She is often expected to fulfill traditional roles as wife, mother, and homemaker. Departing from tradition marks her as disobedient, strong willed, strange, and much too different from the norm to be accepted by her family and other members of her minority group.

When minority girls and women do make the effort to participate in organized sports programs, it is important to realize that they bring their cultural values to the sporting arena. Many minority girls have not assimilated into the middle class of

This tree of tires invites children to play regardless of ethnicity or gender, but these Latinas often find discrimination when they pursue sport. (Photo by Carolyn Watson/ PLAN International)

mainstream white America. Their values relating to ethics, fair play, and winning may be very different from those of the dominant culture.

Further, many coaches are totally ignorant of cultural differences in expressiveness, of the differences between cultures in how emotions are exhibited (or not exhibited). The style of play that an individual adopts is often influenced by cultural values and customs. When one understands the variety of styles that exist among any group of individuals, it becomes easier to appreciate cultural pluralism.

The mature minority woman is in triple jeopardy; she faces discrimination based on gender, ethnicity, and age. These women did not have a variety of sports opportunities as children or young adults. Contemporary attitudes regarding the health benefits of physical activity and fitness were unheard of when they were young. Recreational and competitive opportunities for mature women are only marginally developed in this country. Currently, activities with the greatest visibility include swimming, usually as part of public agency programs for seniors; road racing, in events that have designated seniors' or masters' divisions; bowling, in leagues for seniors; and folk and square dancing, often sponsored by public agencies or private clubs. For minority women, underrepresentation in such activities is even more pronounced for seniors than for those in other age classifications.

Research Findings

A major research project sponsored by the Women's Sports Foundation (WSF, 1989) looked at the effects of varsity sport participation as related to African American, Hispanic, and white youth. The researchers focused on male and female athletes and nonathletes from their sophomore years in high school to four years beyond high school. A total of 14,000 youngsters from throughout the United States attending public and private high schools were included in the investigation. Pertinent findings germane to this topic are outlined below.

Minority athletes are socially involved. Compared with minority nonathletes, minority athletes report being more popular in school, more involved in extracurricular activities, and more receptive to taking on leadership positions in their communities after leaving high school (WSF, 1989).

The dumb jock stereotype is a myth. The notion that athletes, including female minority athletes, are "dumb jocks" has no basis in fact. The WSF study demonstrates that minority student-athletes are more likely to work harder than their nonathlete peers simply because they have a sense of loyalty to their school and because many schools impose academic eligibility requirements on students who wish to participate in sport. Thus sport involvement could very well be a motivator for academic success. In rural schools, for example, Hispanic athletes are three times less likely to drop out of school than are their Hispanic nonathlete peers (WSF, 1989).

Compared with whites, the upward mobility of minority athletes after high school is limited. Sport involvement should be pursued for its social and academic rewards during high school rather than as a guarantee of upward mobility after high school. The notion that success in sports will assure wealth, fame, and glory as a professional athlete is unrealistic. Statistics show that there is a greater probability of a black high school athlete becoming a doctor or a lawyer than a professional athlete (WSF, 1989).

Girls benefit from sports much as boys do. The study found that Hispanic females, particularly those from rural high schools, are more likely than their nonathletic peers to score well on achievement tests, to report high popularity, to stay in high school, to attend college, to seek a bachelor's degree, and to make progress toward that degree (WSF, 1989).

Females, whether members of minority groups or not, have discovered that excellence in sport brings feelings of self-worth, self-esteem, and pride. The lessons learned through sport, such as the value of risk taking, teamwork, courage, perseverance, self-discipline, and the work ethic, all help the female athlete succeed in life in much the same way as they help her male counterpart.

High school athletes stay involved as young adults. "Compared to [minority] former nonathletes, [minority] former athletes of both genders were two to eight times more involved with sports during the four years after high school" (WSF, 1989). Although the WSF study provides insight into the effects of sport participation on minority group members, the impact of culture on the decision to participate was not addressed. Traditionally, sport participation by females has been strongly frowned upon by society in general as not being a suitably feminine activity. However, in the past two decades, society has been more accepting of the athletic female, and minority athletic females are sharing in that greater acceptance.

Ethnicity and Stereotypes

A new layer of discrimination has been added. Participation rates are often directly manipulated by a form of preselection to various positions or sports based upon ethnicity. For example, in team sports, positions considered spatially central to the action are considered to be "thinking" positions. Stereotypes abound as coaches invoke a form of "predestination." The concept of *stacking* describes the assumption that minorities possess certain sets of skills appropriate to certain positions on teams (or to specific sports or events), and they will compete among themselves for those positions. Other playing positions or sports are not even considered viable options. Such problems have existed in men's sports for decades, but the full effect of a similar trend among minority women has only recently materialized.

When Eitzen and Furst (1988) analyzed playing positions in women's Division I collegiate volleyball, they found that black Americans, who represented 6% of the overall sample, were significantly underrepresented at the setter position (2.3%) and overrepresented at the hitter position (7.4%). These researchers characterize the setter position as a thinking position requiring leadership and intelligence, whereas the hitter position requires physical power (cited in Figler & Whitaker, 1991, p. 295).

In general, African Americans are concentrated in the sports of basketball and track and field, and are seldom represented in such sports as field hockey, gymnastics, and swimming. Asian American girls are often encouraged to pursue the sport of volleyball, with complete disregard to their interests or talents. Socialization into certain sports and away from others may be the result of a combination of factors, such as lack of opportunity, exclusionary clubs, financial outlay, lack of role models, rural/suburban accessibility to facilities, and availability of private coaches. The myths that equate racial superiority or racial inferiority with sports participation still influence some coaches, educators, and media personnel. It is important that these notions be exposed as false, and that they be eliminated.

Strategies for Change

Minority females in sport face obstacles that may be perceived as overwhelming. The barriers are both external and internal. Components of the external barriers include such things as societal acceptance, sex role stereotyping, and the attitude that female minorities lack competence. Internal barriers may consist of low self-esteem, fear of failure, fear of success, and the three-way conflict among the traditional female role, the newer liberalized roles of females in American society, and adherence to culturally defined ethnicity.

The external barriers limiting involvement of female minority group members in sport and sport leadership are difficult to deal with on an individual basis. However, progress toward overcoming them, or at least in dealing with them on an individual basis, is predicated on the individual's awareness that the barriers exist and that they can generate internal barriers. For instance, the attitude that female minority group members lack competence can all too easily be internalized, resulting in frustration, anger, and self-defeating bitterness. In the face of these emotions, some individuals simply choose to walk away, whereas others dig in their heels and overcome the odds.

Overcoming internal barriers is especially difficult for a woman who is physically isolated from her peers. In isolation, she has no access to positive reinforcement, mentoring, a support network, open discussion of issues, role models, and recognition of the double-whammy effect of being female and a minority. Although it is desirable to have role models, supporters, and mentors who are like oneself, it is perhaps more useful to have these functions fulfilled by any empathic person of goodwill. Such people don't always ring the doorbell. The minority woman sometimes needs to take the initiative to knock on doors. Everyone needs mentors to help open doors, point the way to opportunities, introduce networking, and warn of hazards along the way.

As minority women are underrepresented in sport leadership positions, they are both rare and valuable commodities. Therefore, if job market dynamics function unimpeded by discrimination, their salaries and perquisites should reflect the supply/demand relationship. If, as athletic directors often claim, female minority group members are being sought for sport leadership positions but not found, perhaps ineffective recruiting is the cause. The effective recruiting strategy for any underrepresented population, including female minority group members, recognizes the supply/demand relationship. If supply is perceived as low and demand is high, salaries and perks should rise accordingly. If this does not happen, the job market dynamics should be investigated, because it is likely that discriminatory practices prevail.

Ultimately, the responsibility for an individual's education, and for the quality of his or her life, belongs to that individual. The following comments made by Harry Edwards (1988) when advising black athletes are applicable to all minority students:

> [Black] athletes must insist upon intellectual discipline no less than athletic discipline. . . . If you fail to take a conscious, active, informed role in changing the course and character of [black] sports involvement, nothing done by any other party is likely to be effective or lasting—if for no other reason than the fact that *slaves cannot be freed against their will.*

Every individual, regardless of age, disability, or ethnicity, has the right to participate in sport. Are your sports experiences monochromatic or technicolor? Are the participants being manipulated or exploited? Are viable opportunities accessible to everyone? Insist on it! Multiculturally diverse experiences improve everyone's quality of life.

Key Words

discrimination	Asian American
diversity	economic impact
Latina	role model
African American	stacking

Discussion Questions

1. What factors make education and sports participation more difficult for female minority students?
2. What can be done to increase the representation of female minority group members in sport and in sport leadership positions?
3. Explain the concept of stacking, provide examples, and discuss the ramifications.

Note

1. Categorization of minority affiliation reflects a recent sensitivity to cultural heritage. Our evolution from archaic descriptors to categories such as Latino/a (Mexican American, Puerto Rican, Cuban) and Asian/Asian American/Pacific Islander reflects this transition. The terms employed in this chapter in reference to previous research reflect the terminology in use at that time.

References

Acosta, R. V., & Carpenter, L. J. (1992). *Women in intercollegiate sport: A longitudinal study— fifteen-year update 1977-1992.* Unpublished manuscript, Brooklyn College, Brooklyn, NY.

American Association of University Women, Educational Foundation. (1992). *How schools shortchange girls.* Washington, DC: Author.

Carter, D. J., & Wilson, R. (1991). *Ninth annual status report on minorities in higher education.* Washington, DC: American Council on Education, Office of Minorities in Higher Education.

Edwards, H. (1988). The single-minded pursuit of sports fame and fortune is approaching institutional triple tragedy in black society. *Ebony, 43,* 138-140.

Eitzen, D. S., & Furst, D. M. (1988). *Racial bias in women's collegiate sports.* Paper presented at the meeting of the North American Society for the Sociology of Sport, Cincinnati, OH.

Figler, S. K., & Whitaker, G. (1991). *Sport and play in American life.* Dubuque, IA: William C. Brown.

Smith, Y. (1991, March). Issues and strategies for working with multicultural athletes. *Journal of Physical Education, Recreation and Dance, 62*(3), 39-44.

Sullivan, M. E. (1989, November 8). Colleges need new tactics to recruit minority students. *Chronicle of Higher Education,* p. B2.

U.S. Department of Commerce, Bureau of the Census. (1990). *Current population reports.* Washington, DC: Government Printing Office.

Women's Sports Foundation. (1989). *The Women's Sports Foundation report: Minorities in sports.* New York: Author.

VI

Psychological Perspectives

Males are socialized to use their bodies to please themselves, while females are socialized to use their bodies to please others.

—*Dorothy Harris*

No one can make you feel inferior without your consent.

—*Eleanor Roosevelt*

*Sport holds a mirror to
a woman's life . . .
she learns not only how she moves,
but how she feels,
and thinks, and struggles,
how she is tormented, triumphs, and
then finds peace.
As she absorbs the mood, drama and
emotion
which are the essences of her sport
so she discovers
all the inward stresses that move her
being.*

—*LaFerne Ellis Price*

19

Competition
Perceived Barriers to Success

MIMI MURRAY
HILARY MATHESON

Sport historically and traditionally has been a male domain. Males have demonstrated their physical prowess and achievement motivation in sport. According to Oglesby (1983), sport is the "sexual signature of masculinity." Women participating in sport are thus threatening to both males and females. Men compete, women watch. Certainly, gender role violations are not welcomed. It is our contention that throughout this century myths and fallacies have been promulgated to preclude female sport participation. These fallacies abound, and the resulting consequences for women who ardently pursue sport participation are dire. The fallacies concerning women in sport are both physiological and psychological in nature. Until these fallacies are denied, and the rebuke accepted, girls and women in sport will continue to face barriers and inequities.

The Female Athlete as a Player

The increasing numbers of girls and women in sport have heralded a new age. Until the past 15 years, the social, psychological, physiological, and biomechanical research and information in sport was all about males, related to males, and for the purpose of improving the performances of males. Those coaching females have assumed, in many cases, that the information on males in sport was directly applicable to females. Consequently, girls and women have been coached in the same manner as boys and men. In reality, the similarities between males and females in sport are much greater than the differences. Yet, the differences are worthy of

AUTHORS' NOTE: Portions of this chapter are adapted from Mimi Murray, "The Female Athlete," in Greta L. Cohen (Ed.), *Sports Psychology and the Coach*, copyright 1988 by the Institute for International Sport. Used by permission.

note. Understanding these differences should help the female in sport maximize performance in this new age. Further, this knowledge is essential for better appreciation of the sociocultural restraints that impinge on participation and performance outcome.

Defining Terms

There is growing concern that some of the confusion arising from discussions about similarities and differences of males and females in sport may be directly related to a misunderstanding of appropriate terminology. *Sex* is biological. One's sex is determined by genes and chromosomes that directly relate to genitalia, hormones, and secondary sex characteristics. Sex is what one is born with. *Gender* is socially or culturally determined. Gender is how one develops after birth. *Role* refers to a series of expected behaviors. *Sex role* refers to what a given sex is able to do biologically, such as, for females, bearing children. *Gender role* refers to a series of behaviors deemed appropriate for a certain sex in a given society. Gender roles are culturally learned and include attitudes, values, and expectations, such as women may cry, men may not; women may knit, men may not; men may play football, women may not.

In this chapter, we emphasize gender role implications that affect women's sport participation. We address the sociological factors and physiological differences that have a psychological impact on the female in the sport milieu.

Gender Role and Sport

It would be most difficult and inappropriate to attempt to differentiate the sociological and psychological influences on girls and women and their sport participation; therefore, these will be presented together. These influences are directly related to gender roles or behaviors that our society has prescribed as acceptable for females.

How is gender learned? Gender identification is a function of the socialization process. Social institutions serve to teach society's values. The institutions through which we learn the values of our culture are the family, education, religion, polity, economy, and sport. The family, through the process of child rearing, appears to be the most influential and pervasive institution for enculturation. Further, for males the institution of sport in our society is probably one of the strongest reinforcers of the male gender role for boys who participate.

The Ramifications of Socialization

All societies have codes or regulations that are designed to control behavior. These mores take years for a child to learn and understand, and

TABLE 19.1 Differences in Childhood Socialization of Boys and Girls

	Girls	*Boys*
Discipline	withdrawal of love, leading to guilt	physical punishment or denial of privileges or property
Aggression	not condoned and not demonstrated	permitted except with siblings
Tasks assigned	washing dishes, making beds	emptying trash, mowing lawn
Educational expectations	lower	higher
Hobbies and social relationships	constructive	power oriented
Games (6-year-olds)	"feminine" occupations	aggression, speed
Emotionality	okay to cry and show fear	suppress fear, control emotions

the process of this learning and understanding is *socialization*. Many of the behaviors learned early through socialization persist throughout one's life. Child training or child rearing is a viable means of socialization.

American society has traditionally assigned differing gender roles to boys and girls. As a result, there have been dramatic variations in the socialization experiences of boys and girls. In recent years, movement away from traditional approaches has led to the teaching and acceptance of more similar child-rearing practices for boys and girls; however, differences still exist. Table 19.1 shows the areas in which these differences are likely to be found.

Achievement Motivation

The personality differences between the sexes seem to be cultural rather than biological in origin; thus they are potentially susceptible to change. Achievement as a personality characteristic is more strongly stressed and reinforced in the training of boys than in that of girls. Achievement training attempts to orient boys' behavior toward seeking excellence in performance, whereas on the distaff side, obedience, nurturance, and responsibility training are performance objectives. In many primary grades there is a wide variety of achievement motivation manifested for boys. When boys do achieve, their behavior is reinforced. Boys achieving in athletics often receive desired love and affection from their parents. Further, there appear to be relationships among independence, self-reliance, and motivation to achieve, and these traits are acquired early by boys.

Are the male/female differences found in achievement motivation the result of the fact that achievement has traditionally been measured on a standard of male excellence? Achievement in sport is not traditionally associated with female gender expectations. Consequently, if more valid measures of achievement were available to researchers, differences between the sexes might not be as dramatic as they currently appear.

This point is strongly suggested by the fact that highly successful athletes, whether male or female, have high need to achieve. Is there a causal relationship between sport and achievement? Do successful athletes become more achievement oriented because of and through sport participation, or do those who have or possess a high need to achieve enter sport to act out or demonstrate this need? Philosophers have said that sport is one of the few areas in our society in which young males can demonstrate achievement. Achievement, as is the case for so many other topics of sport psychology, is situationally specific. For example, an individual's academic achievement orientation does not imply that he or she also wishes to achieve in sport. Those women who seriously enter sport are usually high in need to achieve and enjoy being challenged.

"I didn't know girls could be so good, try so hard, have so much dedication." How many of this coach's athletes were never challenged because this coach had an attitude of the female in sport as inferior?

It has been shown that gender classification has a major impact on the motivational orientation of females. It is apparent that females who are psychologically classified as more masculine or androgynous are more likely to show higher levels of achievement motivation than those who are considered highly feminine. It may be that perceived gender role plays a part in a female's decision to participate in competitive sports, which in turn contributes to levels of achievement motivation noted in successful athletes.

Attributions

Related to the study of achievement is attribution theory. Attributions are the individual's perceptions of the causes of the outcomes of his or her behaviors; that is, attribution theory is concerned with to what the individual attributes his or her successes or failures. Interestingly, there is a strong need for children to take personal credit for success, which would be attributions to ability and effort, or those things that are internal. At the other extreme, children tend to externalize failures with attributions to luck and task difficulty. These attributions combine to form a "self-serving bias," which tends to protect the individual's ego and self-esteem, just as prejudices do.

There are gender differences in attributions. Women, compared with men, tend to evaluate their abilities as lower or lesser. Women often consider their own sex inferior, and those who do so have lower expectations for success. Whether successful or not, women generally attribute the outcomes of their performances to luck and task difficulty, which are external. Relative to men, women frequently see success as less important. Women consider their tasks to be easier than men's, and consequently they have much greater shame for their failures. This continues to compound, for there is greater shame associated with failure at an easier task, and with this shame goes guilt. For women who make such attributions, it is extremely difficult to flow, "let go," and play with confidence. They are too concerned with their mistakes and the shame and guilt associated with those mistakes.

"I coach 'em just like I coach boys. There are no differences." How many of this coach's players never achieve because he never identified the

Women who have positive internal attributions know that their skills and physical abilities are responsible for their success. The body language says it all! (Photo by Doug Gamage; courtesy of University of Rhode Island Sports Information)

male/female differences in incentive, motivation, attributions, gender expectations, and physiological concerns?

This vicious cycle compounds itself into *learned helplessness,* wherein the individual begins to make a response, the result of which is never contingent on that individual. This then leads to further adoption of the female gender role, including greater dependence, lower self-confidence, lower assertiveness, and lower expectations. Coaches can expect to find some female athletes fitting the above description who have the needed physical skills but cannot maximize performance because of social psychological problems. Females who demonstrate these responses cannot be "yelled at," humiliated, and denigrated by their coaches, and then be expected to perform well. Such athletes feel bad enough about their performance without any "help" from coaches or overly involved parents.

Recently it has been suggested that these differences between males and females and the attributional process are changing. Females now appear to be attributing positive outcomes to their own skills and abilities as opposed to luck. This may be a consequence of Title IX and the increased exposure of women to sports activities at all levels from an earlier age. However, in a pilot study of causal attributions of undergraduate physical education majors, women attributed success externally and failure internally. The converse was true for men. If the results of this study are replicated it may highlight why it is so difficult for some women athletes to get past their mistakes or failures.

Attributions cause some female athletes to get stuck on errors. An example of a player who cannot get past a mistake is the volleyballer who is aced on serve receive by a server who uses that very deceptive, and difficult to return, float serve (it has no spin, so it dances around like a knuckle ball). She then begins to think about her error and how "bad" she looked while missing that "easy" serve. Her thoughts then go to "Please don't serve again to me, please, please don't." Instead of thinking about and having a plan for how to get the next serve up, she is concentrating on the incorrect element, the mistake. Any server worth her salt will recognize that panicked look in her opponent's eyes and again serve to the same player, who will fail again. A perceptive coach would help this athlete by offering lots of positive reinforcement, changing her thought focus, and helping her establish a plan.

In such a situation the coach must know the individual athlete and her needs. Some athletes might prefer to be substituted to give them time to refocus their attention. Others, however, would rather "work it out" while playing. The worst thing a coach can do in this situation is yell at the athlete, as this just compounds a very small error and makes it a gigantic mistake fraught with shame and guilt.

Successful women in sport have a high need for the traditional achievement model. Their consequent attributions thus are similar to those of males; they attribute success internally and failure externally.

A woman who had coached national championship teams and was one of the "winningest" coaches in her sport was interviewed. Her response to the question, "To what do you attribute your success?" was "Being very lucky!" This is a typical female attribution. Her success was a result of her hard work, determination, skill, and talent. It is to be hoped that the typical attributions that women make will change as their contributions and abilities become viewed as valuable in our society.

With this paradigm it is a lot easier for athletes to find success. Their feelings of self-worth are enhanced by their successes and are not destroyed by failures. It would be better for athletes to make internal attributions for both success and failure. In so doing, they would assume the complete responsibility for their performance, whether good or bad. However, the ideal would be for athletes to be able to attribute success and failure accurately to internal or external causes as appropriate.

Attribution theory in practice is observable in a typical squash class for physical education major students. A characteristic response when the scores of a match are reported to the instructor is "Hey coach, I won, BIG," from a very loud-voiced male who has beaten another student, male or female. When a woman beats a man she quietly tells, if she reports it at all, that she won, usually after the instructor has repeatedly asked about the outcome. Often, the men who have lost will slink off the court or make a point of telling the instructor that they were injured or have never played squash before. These responses support the typical attributions of males and females when competing.

In an interesting study with fourth graders, boys who lost to girls did not attribute their losses to their opponents' ability, as they did when they lost to other boys (Iso-⟋ ... ·chers in the early 1980s found that male performances ...₀uted to effort and female performances were attributed to luck.

Self-Efficacy

A very positive finding of several studies is that there is definite psychological value accrued for women as a result of participation in sport. In the classic study on this topic, Snyder and Kivlin (1975) found that there is a strong relationship between women's athletic involvement and three measures of psychological well-being: better body image, higher energy levels, and better perceptions of health compared with women not involved in sport. Their results have since been replicated by other researchers. Self-efficacy is the sense or perception of one's own competence. It is situationally specific. Psychological well-being influences self-efficacy as related to sport.

Current levels of performance are said to be affected by past experiences and the success or failure associated with those experiences. Bandura (1977) indicates that an individual's feelings concerning present performance, or expectations of performance, are closely linked to self-efficacy. Low self-efficacy is generally accompanied by poor performance levels, whereas high self-efficacy is associated with better performance. Therefore, self-efficacy can be the key to optimal performance under stressful conditions.

In sports such as gymnastics or ice skating, where risk may be a big factor, high self-efficacy results in less performance avoidance behavior. In other words, if an athlete has low self-efficacy she is less likely to attempt new or risky skills than is an athlete with higher self-efficacy, because she feels that she may not be able to succeed. This may be the result of previous failures by that athlete when asked to perform similar skills in the past. Such a reaction is also more likely to occur in female than in male athletes.

Lower levels of self-efficacy may be recognized not only in an athlete's reluctance to perform certain skills but also in heightened emotional arousal, evidenced by jitters, nervousness, or excitability. An athlete low in self-efficacy is also more likely to set easier goals to attain because the likelihood of failure is lower. Such a state may have a continuing downward spiral of performance levels if the goals set are too low to show improvement. An athlete with a high sense of self-efficacy will set higher motivational and performance-enhancing goals, which in turn will further strengthen and magnify self-efficacy.

Because females are more likely than males to admit fear and anxiety in stressful situations, it is important for coaches and parents to recognize and accept this as an integral part of the female athlete's makeup. In doing so, they will be better able to build support, confidence, and self-efficacy throughout the skill-learning process. The female athlete can then build upon positive past experiences.

Competence

Gender differences in expectations of success have been related to the socialization process of females, and females frequently attribute success to situational factors that are not under their control. Lower expectations of success result in lower levels of perceived competence, or the feeling that a task/skill can be successfully completed.

Harter (1978) suggests that individuals possess a desire to demonstrate personal competence. Experiencing positive affective outcomes, such as success, pride, and enjoyment, is crucial for continued striving toward competence. A high level of perceived competence and feelings of personal control over the outcomes in achievement situations increase the likelihood of continued participation. Lower levels of perceived competence or control may result in negative affective experiences, which may surface in the form of frustration, shame, or anxiety. The greater the number of negative outcomes experienced, the lower the possibility of an athlete's wanting to continue with that activity. Parents and coaches can have direct influence on the competence levels of children and athletes by providing for successful experiences, positive reinforcement, and belief in the individual.

How a parent and/or coach reacts to competitive outcomes can determine the promotion of attitudes about self-worth, personal competence, and the value of intrinsically motivated behavior. Such perceptions can influence subsequent levels of achievement. When a child and or athlete perceives that she or he has not met required performance expectations, feelings of competence are lowered. Consequently, pride and enjoyment in accomplishment are reduced. However, it has been shown that athletes with high levels of perceived competence demonstrate higher expectancies, persist at a task longer, and have better performances than do athletes with lower levels of perceived competence.

Also, young athletes are not overly concerned with outcomes of competition; rather, they are more interested in enjoyment and being a part of a team. Awareness of this factor and redefinition of success and failure can be most positive. Effort and personal performance are more likely to enhance competence levels of athletes than is focusing on winning or losing.

Competitiveness

The numbers of women and girls participating in sport have risen dramatically over the past 10 years, but there are still more males participating than females (30%). Thus there is an assumption that males are more avid competitors. However, recent research indicates that although males do score higher on levels of competitiveness, females are just as goal oriented. Several studies by Gill and her colleagues indicate that females reflect a noncompetitive achievement orientation rather than a win orientation to sports (see, e.g., Gill & Dzewaltowski, 1988). Females are just as likely as males to value achievement and to enjoy sport.

An individual's perception of self-competence is directly related to her successes and failures in sports participation. (Photo by Alex Alexio; courtesy of Providence Journal Co.)

Females appear to concentrate more on personal goals and performance than on interpersonal comparison and winning. It also appears that successful elite athletes are more performance oriented, and thus coaches may not need to try to make females more win oriented. It may be that emphasis placed on goals and performance will serve to encourage them to achieve at higher levels.

Moral Sport Reasoning

Gender differences in moral reasoning have been studied by Oglesby (1983), who found that athletes have lower levels of moral reasoning than do nonathletes. Within the nonathletic population there are no significant differences in the moral reasoning of females and males, whereas in the athletic population females have higher levels of moral reasoning than do males. This may imply the need for a more ethical sport model for women; for example, winning at any cost is not a viable approach.

More recently, investigations by Bredemeier (1985) have indicated that athletic aggression may be looked at as a moral issue and that morally mature athletes accept less aggression in sport than do less mature individuals. Silva (1983) found that females regard injurious sports acts as less legitimate than do males. Similarly, athletes who compete at lower levels of sport for less time also think that aggression on the field is less acceptable.

Bredemeier, who interviewed female high school and college basketball players, endorses Silva's findings, but also indicates that research is needed in regard to the long-term effects of sport participation on moral reasoning. Perhaps the longer females are involved in highly competitive sports the more likely it is that their moral perceptions of potentially injurious sport acts and sport aggression will change to be more similar to those of their male counterparts. Also, it should be remembered that moral reasoning and game reasoning may not be the same. An athlete may have a high level of moral reasoning but still condone sport aggression. The influence of coaches and parents can be pervasive in the thinking of such an athlete.

Patty Sheehan, LPGA golfer, has been quoted as saying, "I have a real problem with the winning-is-everything attitude. I was brought up to really appreciate and enjoy the sporting event I was in. I don't think it's going to be a problem keeping that in perspective." Prior to making that statement, she had left the tour for five weeks to gather herself together, because golf wasn't "fun" anymore. She felt pressure to be the best representative possible for the LPGA. Even the most competent, successful, talented athletes must constantly work on their attitudes and keep sport in perspective.

Androgyny

Androgyny is a gender identity; thus it is a psychological rather than a physiological unisex construct. Individuals who are high in both instrumental (traditional masculine) and expressive (traditional feminine) qualities are considered androgynous. Individuals who are high in instrumental and low in expressive qualities are considered masculine. Those low in instrumental and high in expressive qualities are considered feminine. In revising her original theory, Bem (1974) has since added a fourth category, "undifferentiated," which describes individuals who are low in both expressive and instrumental qualities. Frequently, adolescents are undifferentiated in gender role.

Androgynous child rearing would appear to be an ideal format for psychological well-being. Androgynous individuals demonstrate greater intelligence, higher creativity, and more behavioral adaptability than do other individuals (Duquin, 1978). Typically, those high in androgyny have the highest self-esteem, followed by masculine, feminine, and undifferentiated individuals, in that order (Bem, 1974).

The problem with the acceptance of the concept of androgyny is well summarized by Steinem (1983):

Androgyny also raises the hope that female and male cultures could be perfectly blended in the ideal person; yet because the female side of the equation has yet to be affirmed, androgyny usually tilted toward the male. As a concept, it also raised anxiety levels of conjuring up a conformist, unisex vision, the very opposite of the individuality and uniqueness that (*humanism*) feminism actually has in mind. (p. 158)

Oglesby (1983) has suggested that the expressive orientations in sport be emphasized as well as the traditionally stressed instrumental functions.

The expressive values are often viewed as feminine, but they should be valued by males as well as females. These expressive values in sport are passivity (after injury, light workouts, psyching down, attention to coaching instructions), subordination (accepting one's role, changing habits and skills), dependency (giving control to the coach), naturalness (creativity in new skills, equipment, and strategies), and chaoticness (free-lance play). The appreciation and adaptation of the expressive would make sport a more positive environment for both males and females and would help change our limiting gender roles and stereotypes.

Homophobia

"I don't want my daughter playing that sport. Most of the girls who play that sport are lesbians. They are not going to get my daughter and make her a lesbian. No way. I don't care how much she likes the sport."

"I don't care what anyone says, you are not born a lesbian. They will be your best friend; they will wait for a moment of weakness and then they seduce you. You can't be too careful. They are very dangerous."

Homophobia is the irrational fear and/or intolerance of homosexuality. The two statements above are examples of two of the myths surrounding homosexuality and sport. Athletes, coaches, and administrators make judgments about others based on nothing more than appearance, hearsay, and their own homophobia. It is a myth that participation in certain sports will influence the sexual preference of an athlete, just as it is a myth that masculine-appearing females are all lesbians, that highly feminine-appearing females are all heterosexual, and that feminine-appearing males are all gay. Making such assumptions can result in decrements in self-concept and self-esteem for both heterosexual and homosexual athletes. Another common misconception is that gay athletes will "hit on" straight teammates. Some straight athletes perceive signs of friendship by gay athletes as "being hit on." This is erroneous thinking. It should be recognized that some homosexual athletes feel ostracized from their teams because of their sexual preference, and that some may intentionally lower their performance levels in an attempt to assure that their sexual preference is not discovered. Homosexual athletes may quit a preferred sport because of the emotional stress of dealing with their sexual orientation among teammates or coaches who are homophobic.

The acceptance of others as individuals first and then athletes would help in alleviating prejudice. Also, if the telling of homophobic, racist, and sexist jokes is not condoned, all athletes might be able to enjoy and profit from playing the sport they love.

Physiological Issues

It is well known that the mind and the body cannot be separated into two distinct entities. Maximal sport performance requires appropriate psychological coping skills as well as physiological capabilities. Early phys-iological research on women was limited and utilized women who were relatively untrained by comparison to today's sportswomen. Because of the increased participation of women in sport and higher levels of competition and training, the physiological and performance differences that existed between men and women several decades ago have diminished and may no longer exist. Current research shows that earlier sex differences in physiolog-ical characteristics were at least partially caused by the cultural bias that discouraged women from participating in sport and physical activity.

Despite new information, archaic beliefs, fallacies, and myths regard-ing girls and women in sport still exist. Concerns about potential negative effects of strenuous exercise on physiological functions of women have been presented as barriers to preclude women from participating in cer-tain sports. Physiological myths that have in turn had negative impacts on girls' and women's psyches include misconceptions related to body composition, muscle mass, endurance, menstruation, and nutrition. (For more detailed information on the physiology of women as it relates to sport, see Chapters 11 and 12 of this volume.) The fallacies associated with these variables must be exposed. Education is imperative if we are to address physiological concerns intelligently and eliminate the effect of these myths as psychological barriers to achievement.

Role Models and Leadership

Female role models are needed in all aspects of sport. The "herstory" of sport should provide guidelines for the future and prevent our repeat-ing mistakes of the past. Female role models in sport should be identified for younger athletes. It is important to encourage, not discourage, desir-able characteristics in women, including androgynous behaviors. One can only hope that encouragement of such behaviors will become a part of widespread child-rearing techniques. Sexist behavior and language should be eliminated. Use of crude names for female genitalia directed at boys who are perceived as not playing aggressively enough, along with such comments as "You run like a girl" and "She's pretty good, she shoots just like a boy," should no longer be tolerated.

People need to encourage and insist upon the hiring of women—or, if none is available, at least "qualified" men—as coaches for both women's and men's teams. High school and college administrators should be en-couraged to appoint female athletic directors and to hire female officials. The hiring of women as coaches, administrators, professional athletes, and sports media representatives needs to be advocated for and effected.

Coaches should coach humanely, through an understanding of attri-bution theory and its implications. Further, they must recognize and appre-ciate female athletes as women who have their own identities, and under-stand that to treat them only as athletes is to see them as one-dimensional. Coaches must be aware of the fact that girls and women (as well as boys and men) show caring and affection for each other and for their coaches, and that these behaviors are healthy and positive, not sexual. Coaches must be sensitive to differences related to ethnicity, sexual preference, race, and economic status, and emphasize accepting differences in others while celebrating similarities. It is our hope that the future will provide females with increased opportunities and possibilities for attaining their fullest potential. When the psychological obstacles are eliminated, the perceived barriers to success will no longer exist.

Key Words

gender role	androgyny
sex role	homophobia
achievement motivation	physiological myths
self-efficacy	barriers to success
attribution theory	

Discussion Questions

1. How can attribution theory negatively affect the female athlete? What changes are needed to reverse the outcome?
2. Explain the manner in which physiological myths about girls and women constitute perceived barriers to achievement.
3. A coach says, "I coach 'em just like I coach boys. There are no differences." What possible impact can this have on an athlete's self-efficacy?

References

Bandura, A. (1977). Self-efficacy: Toward a unifying theory of behavioral change. *Psychological Review, 84*, 191-215.

Bem, S. (1974). The measurement of psychological androgyny. *Journal of Consulting Clinical Psychology, 42*, 155-162.

Bredemeier, B. J. (1985). Moral reasoning and the perceived legitimacy of intentionally injurious sport acts. *Journal of Sport Psychology, 7*, 110-124.

Duquin, M. (1978). Attributions made by children in coeducational sport settings. In D. Landers & R. Christina (Eds.), *Psychology of motor behavior and sport* (pp. 462-469). Champaign, IL: Human Kinetics.

Gill, D. L., & Dzewaltowski, D. A. (1988). Competitive orientations among intercollegiate athletes: Is winning the only thing? *Sport Psychologist, 2*, 212-221.

Harter, S. (1978). Effectance motivation reconsidered. *Human Development, 21*, 34-64.

Iso-Ahola, S. (1979). Sex-role stereotypes and causal attributions for success and failure in motor performance. *Research Quarterly, 50*, 630-640.

Oglesby, C. (Ed.). (1983). *Proceedings of the New Agenda Conference*. Reston, VA/New York: National Association for Girls and Women in Sport/U.S. Olympic Committee.

Silva, J. M. (1983). The perceived legitimacy of rule violating behavior in sport. *Journal of Sport Psychology, 5*, 438-448.

Snyder, E., & Kivlin, J. (1975). Women athletes and aspects of psychological well-being and body image. *Research Quarterly, 46*, 191-197.

Steinem, G. (1983). *Outrageous acts and everyday rebellions*. New York: Holt, Rinehart & Winston.

20

The Coach's Role

PATRICIA A. SULLIVAN
DEBORAH J. WILSON

The role of the coach in the athletic environment is a complex and powerful one. The coach has tremendous influence over the development of the athlete's identity and feelings of self-worth. Coaches select teams and determine who competes on those teams. They are primary facilitators of the individual's skill learning, understanding of strategies, and general personal advancement in sport. They are responsible for challenging and leading teams in the pursuit of excellence. Clearly the power of the coach's role requires that each coach have an understanding of and a commitment to the responsibilities of that position.[1]

A coach's personal philosophy is underscored by his or her own ethics or values. These values are implicit in day-to-day actions as they are reflected in behavior. With a philosophy of fairness, a coach may proceed with some confidence that opportunities are being provided for each athlete to develop in a safe and encouraging environment. It will also help ensure that the coach's behavior is characterized by consistency, integrity, expertise, and thoughtful respect.

Each coach must understand that relationships within the team organization (coach-coach, coach-athlete, athlete-athlete) are the basis of team functioning and the avenue of motivation and influence. A philosophy of coaching should include the following basic behavioral components:

1. Accept responsibility for the power inherent in the coach's role.
2. Demonstrate respect for the dignity and worth of each individual in the team organization.
3. Be committed to enhancing the athletic performance of each athlete.
4. Uphold the ideals of athletic competition and fair play.
5. Try to prevent the misuse of power by others in the team organization.
6. Demand of oneself an attitude of inquiry, self-reflection, and self-evaluation.
7. Act in the best interests of athletes, staff, sponsoring organizations, and society.
8. Cooperate with the governing bodies of the sport.

Coaching a Division I team today is not unlike running a small business. Once a coach has mastered the sport pedagogy, the skills she or he has learned in physiology, psychology, management, finance, and communications become invaluable. (Photo by Pam Lee; courtesy of the National Softball Coaches Association)

With a commitment to these standards in place, coaching behavior can be effectively guided. Each athlete's experience, in turn, can be as positive and rewarding as possible. Understanding and integrating the philosophy behind these behaviors is a dynamic process. Those interested in coaching must take the time periodically to reexamine their behaviors to ensure that they are, in fact, supported by sound philosophy and principles and, indeed, that their actions accurately reflect their particular values. A point-by-point examination of the elements listed may be helpful for an understanding of their applications.

Issues of Power

Relationships within the team organization (coach-coach, coach-athlete, athlete-athlete) are the basis of team functioning. Each coach must accept responsibility for the power inherent in that role.

Coaches coach people. Athletes work with other athletes to create a team unit. Relationships in sport must be understood if the effectiveness of the group is to be maximized. A primary example of this is that coaches must understand the power inherent in their role and accept responsibility for this power. Coaches must maintain the highest standards of their profession and accept responsibility for the consequences of their actions. Coaches need to be aware that their recommendations and professional actions may change the lives of their athletes, assistant coaches, or others. They should be alert to situations and pressures that might lead to misuse of their influence.

To understand the power inherent in the role of the coach, consider the following situation. Tryouts are held for a high school soccer team. Chris, a junior, has trained hard in preparation for this year's tryouts, having not made the team last year. Although Chris's performance has improved, in the eyes of the coach the improvement is not enough for Chris to make the team. The coach has the power to put Chris on the team and the power to cut Chris from the team. In this case, the coach must recognize that cutting Chris from the team may have a tremendous impact on Chris's self-image. Not only should the decision to cut Chris be delivered with respect for Chris's efforts, it should also minimize messages of rejection or discouragement. Perhaps the coach's suggesting some alternatives for Chris might be helpful. Examples of alternatives might include additional or different training, a nonplaying role within the team organization, or opportunities to be on other teams or even to compete in a different sport.

Respect for Diversity

Head coaches must demonstrate respect for the dignity and worth of each individual in the team organization. Coaches need to recognize differences among people such as those associated with age, sex, race, socioeconomic, and ethnic backgrounds. When necessary, they should obtain training, experience, and/or counseling to assure that they can treat individuals equitably. They should remain open to change in expectations and values over time.

Head coaches need to be aware that their personal values may affect the manner in which they present information to others. When dealing with sensitive topics, they should recognize and respect the diverse attitudes members of the team may have toward such topics.

Coaches must not engage in or condone practices that are inhumane or that result in illegal or unjustifiable actions. Such practices include, but are not limited to, those based on considerations of race, ability, age, gender, sexual preference, religion, and national origin.

Confidentiality of information concerning members of the team unit must be respected by coaches. This means that whenever possible coaches should reveal information about a team member to others only with the prior knowledge of the individual concerned, and only when such revelations would help the individual or are necessary to preserve the integrity or welfare of the team or sponsoring organization.

An example of understanding the nature of respecting confidentiality follows. Leslie, a third-year player, and the coach have a very good working relationship and have established good rapport. The coach is aware that Leslie has been troubled by something lately. During a scheduled player-coach conference, Leslie requests that the coach not reveal any part of a conversation they are about to have, indicating that the coach is the only person Leslie can really trust. In fairness to the player and the organization, the coach indicates that every attempt will be made to respect the player's confidence. However, the coach goes on, depending on the nature of the information, Leslie must understand that it may be necessary to share some or all of the information with the athletic administration, the athlete's parents, or perhaps even representatives of the law.

The coach has shared these limits of confidentiality before the player has made any disclosures. The coach may also offer the player a referral to a professional, such as a social worker or psychologist who may offer the player more confidentiality.

Skill Development and Expertise

Coaches should be committed to enhancing the athletic performance of each athlete. They need to recognize the boundaries of their competence and the limitations of their knowledge, and make every reasonable attempt to maintain current knowledge of information related to their sport. Coaching should be based on careful preparation, so coaches should make an effort to ensure that their instruction is current and relevant and that they incorporate new procedures and changes over time. Coaches must recognize a primary obligation to help others acquire knowledge, skills, and appropriate training.

A good example of a coach's commitment to enhancing the athletic performance of each athlete follows. Coach Allen has coached for only two years, and as she enters her third year she still considers herself to be a "fledgling" coach. Her team was very successful this past year and many of the team members went to a sports camp over the summer. Camp was a terrific experience for the team members and they were very enthusiastic about the upcoming season. One day, as the team members who attended camp were sharing some of the things they learned with the coach, she told them that the new ideas were overrated. Conversation about sports

An effective coach must be able to stay focused, to perceive subtle changes in performance, and to suggest alternative strategies that will work to the team's advantage. (Photo courtesy of Tollgate High School, Warwick, Rhode Island)

camps was cut off. During the course of the season, as Coach Allen became more confident in her own abilities, she realized that perhaps she stifled the team members who had some good information to share. Late in the season she suggested that they all look into attending a camp the next summer—including Coach Allen.

Ethics and Values

Head coaches must be committed to upholding the ideals of athletic competition and fair play. Coaches remain accountable as individuals for upholding the highest standards of their profession. In the world of sport, *fair play* is considered to be a baseline standard against which we measure and judge the behavior of others. What is fair play? How can a coach ensure that the team is competing fairly? Consider the following situation. During a volleyball match, a player touches the net with her arm as she blocks a ball. She immediately raises her hand and indicates to the first referee that she has committed a net violation. The current rule in volleyball indicates that it is the responsibility of the referees to determine if a player has touched the net, which is a violation of the rules resulting in a point or side out. After the match is over, Coach Diaz explains to the team that in any competition, the rules define allowable behavior on the part of the athletes. In this case, it is *fair* for both teams to expect that the officials would make any and all decisions pertaining to the rules. It is inappropriate for the athletes, in this case, to "call their own fouls." In other sports, the role of the official may be different and it may be defined as appropriate for an athlete to assist in or to make a judgment call.

In a separate situation, during a conference championship tennis match, doubles partners Terry and Lynn discover that one of their opponents is an illegal player. The opponents are members of the team that will undoubtedly win the conference championship regardless of the outcome of Terry and Lynn's match. If Terry and Lynn report this information to their coach, the opposing team will be disqualified from competition and unable to advance to the NCAA tournament. In this case, it is the responsibility of the athlete to report the illegal player, even though the consequences of this action may be serious. Terry and Lynn's coach has an obligation to support and reinforce their actions.

Good Intentions: Misdirected Behaviors

Coaches must not knowingly allow the misuse of power by others in their organizations. Although head coaches cannot constantly monitor the behaviors of all the professionals in their organizations, they have a responsibility to guide and educate those individuals regarding the limits of their power. They must also respond to any specific concerns that may be brought to their attention. Emphasis should be on preventing the

misuse of power. Therefore, head coaches must provide appropriate training to clarify role expectations and limits.

Consider the following example. Lee is a key player on the basketball
team. The game to determine first seed in the conference championship
will be played on Saturday. On Thursday, two days before the big game,
Lee's chemistry instructor asks to speak to the head coach. The instructor
indicates that the assistant coach, who is responsible for the academic
performance and progress of the athletes, has requested that a major exam
scheduled for the day before the big game be postponed one week so that
Lee will not have to worry about the exam. The chemistry instructor is a
strong supporter of the basketball program and is happy to contribute to
the team's effort in this manner. In this case, the head coach has a responsibility to help the assistant coach and the chemistry instructor understand
that student-athletes should be treated the same as other students in the
school. Providing academic guidance, encouragement, and support has
limits in regard to how much and what type of intervention is appropriate
on behalf of the student-athlete. Student-athletes should be encouraged to
develop good working relationships with their instructors and to negotiate on their own for any special considerations.

Privacy and Professionalism

Head coaches must demand of themselves an attitude of inquiry,
self-reflection, and self-evaluation. Coaches need to recognize personal
problems and conflicts that may interfere with their professional effectiveness. They should not participate in any activity that could lead to personal problems that may affect the performance of their duties or create
potential harm to others. If they become aware of personal problems
interfering with their work, they should seek out competent professional
assistance to determine if they should suspend, terminate, or otherwise
modify their involvement with the team.

For example, Coach Smith is experiencing a lot of personal distress in
a current relationship. Outside of school, Coach Smith is preoccupied with
this problem. It has been extremely difficult for the coach to maintain
concentration, and radical mood swings seem to be easily triggered. In
this case Coach Smith must evaluate whether this situation is affecting the
performance of coaching duties. The coach may find it helpful to conduct
this evaluation with a trusted colleague. The evaluation may lead Coach
Smith to several possible conclusions. The coach may decide that this
personal problem is not affecting professional performance, and therefore
the coach may appropriately continue to work with the team. The coach
may also decide that, with the additional support of a professional to
address these personal issues, coaching responsibilities may continue. A
conclusion that is perhaps more difficult to face is that for the coach to
continue coaching at this time is inappropriate. In any case, it is not
appropriate for the coach to share or burden team members with problems
of a personal nature.

Coaches must be aware of their own needs and the potential use of their influential position to meet those needs. They must avoid exploiting the trust and dependence of others. They should make every effort to avoid relationships that could impair their professional judgment or increase the risk of exploitation. As a specific example, sexual intimacies with student-athletes are not acceptable.

The Big Picture: A Matter of Perspective

Head coaches must act in the best interests of their athletes, staff, sponsoring organizations, and society. Coaches need to understand the areas of competence related to their profession, and make full use of all the professional, technical, and administrative resources that best serve their athletes. These may include participation in sports camps, clinics, and seminars as well as visits to elite-level training facilities. Head coaches who employ or supervise other professionals or professionals in training accept the obligation to facilitate the further professional development of those individuals; thus, they must provide appropriate working conditions and opportunities for continued professional growth. To initiate this process, the head coach must first consult with the coaching staff on an individual basis to determine their professional goals. The opportunities and limitations on opportunities should then be explained. For example, a coach may indicate an interest in attending a particular clinic, but other professional responsibilities or lack of financial support from the institution may prohibit attendance. At this point the most helpful options among the possibilities should be agreed upon and a course of professional action should be planned.

Conclusion

The power and significance of the coach's relationship to each member of a team organization and, in particular, to each athlete must be emphasized. The significance of that relationship is magnified when one considers the developmental needs of student-athletes or other athletes who, because of particular circumstances or characteristics, are especially vulnerable to a coach's influence.

Because the coaching role in its most influential aspect is a powerful relationship with each athlete, it is of paramount importance for coaches to consider carefully the ramifications of their behaviors. They must strive for an understanding of the ethical and professional issues related to their role. They must also consider how their philosophies and the principles they espouse are reflected in their daily behaviors. Athletes often demonstrate respect and adulation for their coaches. The responsibility to provide a role model worthy of such respect is substantial.

With the acceptance of a coaching position, the coach assumes the responsibility of putting the welfare of others foremost, of demonstrating commitment to the ideals of competition, and of accepting personal accountability to players, fans, sponsoring organizations, and the governing bodies of the sport.

Key Words

team organization	values
power	coaching responsibilities
respect	professionalism
ethics	relationships

Discussion Questions

1. Discuss acceptable and unacceptable ways for a coach to demonstrate frustration and/or stress during a game. How does this behavior affect the team?
2. Think of a coaching dilemma that involves conflict, distress, or confusion for a coach and an athlete or athletes. Describe what principles or underlying values are at issue. Explain an option the coach might have in resolving this dilemma that is in keeping with principles of a good coaching relationship.

Suggested Reading

Bird, A. M., & Cripe, B. (1986). *Psychology and sport behavior.* St. Louis, MO: Times Mirror/Mosby.

Cox, R. H. (1990). *Sport psychology: Concepts and applications.* Dubuque, IA: William C. Brown.

Sabock, R. J. (1991). *Coaching: A realistic perspective.* San Diego, CA: Collegiate Press.

Williams, J. (Ed.). (1986). *Applied sport psychology: Personal growth to peak performance.* Palo Alto, CA: Mayfield.

Note

1. We would like to acknowledge that this chapter draws heavily on the American Psychological Association's (1990) "Ethical Principles of Psychologists."

Reference

American Psychological Association. (1990). Ethical principles of psychologists. *American Psychologist, 45,* 390-395.

21

Women With Disabilities

CLAUDINE SHERRILL

> Women with disabilities face double discrimination—discrimination based on gender and discrimination based on disability. Women of color who are disabled face yet a third type of discrimination. . . . The limited available statistics suggest that economically, socially, and psychologically, women with disabilities fare considerably worse than either women who are non-disabled or men who are disabled. (Women and Disability Awareness Project, 1989, p. 20)

Little is actually known about women with disabilities, and still less about those who engage in sport. Women athletes who overcome disability barriers are seldom featured in the national news. Notable exceptions are Wilma G. Rudolph, a 1960 Olympic gold medalist in track, who had polio as a child; Kitty O'Neal, a famous race car driver and Hollywood stunt woman who is deaf; and Linda Down, the first woman on crutches ever to compete in the New York City Marathon (1982) and to receive television coverage.

Universities seldom honor their female athletes with disabilities or give them much notice. Exceptions are the University of Illinois at Champaign and Wright State University in Ohio, which sponsor women's wheelchair basketball teams. Another exception is Texas Woman's University, which bestowed its coveted alumnae award on Sue Moucha, Paralympic gold medalist, just as it honored Olympic gold medalist Louise Ritter several years earlier, thereby giving equal recognition to its two athletes (cerebral palsied and able-bodied) who had achieved international acclaim.

Special Olympics, Paralympics, and Deaf Sport are international movements that contribute to awareness of the potential of female athletes with disabilities. Each follows the able-bodied Olympic model in conducting international summer and winter games every four years. Special Olympics, which serves only athletes with mental retardation, holds its games in the United States in the year prior to the regular Olympics. The Eighth International Summer Special Olympic Games in 1991 provided competition for 6,000 athletes from 100 countries and was heralded as the largest sporting event in the world. In contrast, Paralympics serves athletes who

Paralympic gold medalist (1984 and 1988) Sue Moucha, who has cerebral palsy, prepares for competition in Barcelona. This kind of flexibility in a cerebral palsied individual requires extensive training. Photo courtesy International Olympic Academy.

are physically disabled or blind and holds its games in the same year and in the same country as the regular Olympics. Deaf Sport serves people with a hearing loss of 55 decibels or greater who see themselves as a separate cultural and linguistic community rather than as disabled (Stewart, 1991). Their international games are held the year following the regular Olympics, and most athletes use sign language. Press and media coverage of these events is gradually improving.

Books on women's studies and women's sport seldom mention female athletes with disabilities. Exceptions are descriptions of Wilma G. Rudolph (Guttman, 1991) and Sydney Jacobs, a Paralympics swimmer from 1975 through 1980 who currently enjoys one-up/one-down mixed doubles tennis (Nelson, 1991). (One-up/one-down doubles tennis is competition in which one partner plays standing and the other plays in a wheelchair.) Textbooks and journals on sports psychology and sociology also largely ignore disability. Television commercials have begun occasionally featuring athletes with disabilities, but the models chosen thus far have been males. On the positive side, Roberta Abney and Dorothy Richey (1992) of Slippery Rock University of Pennsylvania have established the precedent of equal coverage for ethnic minorities and athletes with disabilities when describing opportunities for minority women in sport.

How do people with disabilities see themselves? What disabilities are women most likely to have? Does gender bias enter into diagnosis? How do the life experiences of women with disabilities differ from those of others? Do women with disabilities face double and triple discrimination? The following pages are designed to help answer these questions.

People With Disabilities: A Diverse Minority

Approximately 43 million Americans (17% of the population) have disabilities severe enough to entail documentation, special services, and legal protection of rights. This includes about 10% of all children and adolescents, about 30% of young and middle-aged adults, and about 50% of persons beyond the age of 65. While 17% of the American public could constitute a powerful political, economic, and social minority if it were cohesive and organized, persons with disabilities are so diverse that they do not identify with each other. A child with severe asthma, for instance, has little in common with a wheelchair basketball player or a senior citizen who is gradually losing sight or hearing. A woman informed that she has breast cancer feels little affinity with someone who is mentally retarded or who is recovering from a heart attack or stroke.

Nondisabled persons generally perceive three categories of human beings (like me, unlike me and nondisabled, and disabled), whereas persons with disabilities tend to categorize themselves only with others who have specifically the same functional loss. This practice is evident in the fact that the United States has eight major sport organizations for athletes with disabilities that are analogous to the U.S. Olympic Committee (USOC), which governs sports for the nondisabled. These organizations and their dates of founding are as follows:

- American Athletic Association for the Deaf (AAAD), 1945
- National Wheelchair Athletic Association (NWAA), 1956
- National Handicapped Sports (NHS), 1967
- Special Olympics International (SOI), 1968
- U.S. Association for Blind Athletes (USABA), 1976
- U.S. Cerebral Palsy Athletic Association (USCPAA), 1978
- Dwarf Athletic Association of America (DAAA), 1986
- U.S. Les Autres Sports Association (USLASA), 1986

The first seven of these organizations are represented on the Committee on Sports for the Disabled (COSD), which is a Group E member of the USOC in Colorado Springs and thus receives support under the Amateur Sports Act of 1978. USLASA, which serves *les autres* (a French term, literally "the others," for those with other mobility impairments who are not served by existing organizations), has applied for COSD membership. Although forced politically to interact in decision making regarding Olympic-level competition, these disabled sports organizations have little in common other than the shared cultural experience of people who are perceived as a minority and treated as different and often as inferior.

Since 1988 international policy has required that all disabled athletes, except for the deaf and the mentally retarded, compete at the same time and place. Psychologically, this has been very hard for many athletes who have had little experience with disabilities other than their own and have the same apprehensions, anxieties, and prejudices as nondisabled people. In essence, most athletes want to be perceived as individuals with specific strengths and weaknesses rather than lumped together into a two-category system (disabled, nondisabled). Most would like to have their events a part of the regular Olympics rather than relegated to a separate time and place.

Gender and Disability

What disabilities are females most likely to have? Historically, being female has been linked with nervous disorders, depression, mental illness, and fragility (Hymowitz & Weissman, 1978; Rosenberg, 1992; Showalter, 1985). This stereotype of women was particularly prevalent during Victorian times and the early 1900s, when social, economic, and cultural conditions stifled women's potential for self-actualization. Women in 1800 bore an average of eight children; Queen Victoria (the model for women in both England and the United States during her reign, 1837-1901) bore eight children and feminist Elizabeth Cady Stanton (1815-1902) bore seven. Some historians suggest that one method of controlling frequency of intercourse and hence family size was "for women to take to the beds, alone, suffering from ailments which may or may not have been imaginary" (Hymowitz & Weissman, 1978, p. 72).

The ability to bear and rear eight children suggests robust physical and mental health and/or the money to pay large household staffs. Frequent pregnancies, however, may help explain why few married women athletes emerged before the era of birth control. Frequent pregnancies also are associated with weakened resistance to tuberculosis and other infectious diseases, often resulting in death, delicate health, and depression.

Disability throughout history has been closely associated with poverty, poor nutrition, inadequate health care, lack of opportunity for exercise and socialization, and various kinds of stress. Regulation of family size, divorce, meaningful life-style, and wage-earning ability commensurate with need have always been sources of stress. Early women leaders who did not marry (either by choice or lack of opportunity) experienced considerable stress, and reports of "nervous breakdowns" were common (e.g., Jane Addams, Catharine Beecher, Frances E. Willard, Florence Nightingale).

Today statistics show that women are twice as likely as men to seek help (and therefore to be diagnosed) for depression. The gender distribution for other types of mental illness (e.g., schizophrenia, bipolar affective disorders) is equal. Research shows that vigorous daily exercise and active sport participation deter depression, creating a strong rationale for women's developing healthy attitudes toward physical recreation. Women with disabilities particularly need guidance in this area, because depression is a common outgrowth of disability and ill health, both of which make an individual culturally different in undesirable ways.

Some of the most prevalent disabilities are summarized in Table 21.1, which shows that physical disabilities, except for arthritis and osteoporosis, are *less* common in females than in males. This helps to explain why so few women are seen in wheelchairs and why this minority has so much difficulty in finding companionship and challenge in sports such as wheelchair basketball, tennis, and track. These statistics also help explain why sports organizations for athletes with disabilities serve larger percentages of males than females, and why disabled female athlete role models are so rare.

Gender distribution of disability also varies by age group. In the school-aged population, only one of every three students receiving special education is female. In adulthood, the distribution is more equal. In old age, because women live seven to eight years longer than men, the preponderance of those with disabilities appear to be female.

The diagnosis of some disabilities (e.g., mental retardation, conduct disorders, specific learning disability) is partly political, economic, and cultural. Sex role bias is sometimes cited as a contributing factor in the male:female ratio disparity in these disorders (Women and Disability Awareness Project, 1989). In the school-age population, society seems able to tolerate a greater amount of subnormality in females than in males. This is particularly true in specific learning disability and emotional disturbance, the two special education disability categories with the greatest prevalence. Another factor in the gender distribution disparity is that official diagnosis of a disability by a school system means that extra money must be found to finance special services.

In times of economic hardship, society tends to spend money on the people and programs it values most. Central to this issue may be subtle and unconscious beliefs that males make better use of educational opportunities in that they are more likely than females to be heads of households and responsible for supporting others.

Life Experiences of Females With Disabilities

How does it feel to be a woman with a disability? The answer depends partly on whether the condition was present at birth or acquired. Persons born with cerebral palsy, mental retardation, and/or visual or auditory impairments are likely to be overprotected and thus socially immature because of impoverished play experiences. Whereas nondisabled children are typically socialized into sport by family members, athletes with disabilities emphasize the importance of self-motivation and friends in learning sports and becoming athletes (Sherrill, 1986). In general, the life experiences of persons born with disabilities are very different from those of their peers.

In contrast, persons disabled in adult years by accident or illness have already acquired sport and fitness attitudes, beliefs, and skills. If they

TABLE 21.1 Common Disabilities: Ratio by Gender

Disorder	Male		Female
Cardiovascular			
coronary heart failure	1.5		1
coronary artery disease			
under age 45	1.5		1
age 45-64	3		1
age 65-74	1.8		1
75 and over		equal	
stroke			
75 and under	H		
75 and over		equal	
Respiratory			
asthma		equal	
Neurological			
Alzheimer's disease			H
autism	3		1
cerebral palsy	3		2
epilepsy		equal	
muscular dystrophy	H (80%)		
traumatic brain injury	2		1
Metabolic			
diabetes			
type I		equal	
type II			H
Cancer (deaths)			
age 55 and over	H		
age 30-55			H
Musculoskeletal			
amputation (from)			
trauma	10		1
disease	2		1
congenital and tumor	1.2		1
osteoarthritis		equal	
osteoporosis	1		8
rheumatoid arthritis			
age 50 and under	1		3
age 50 and over		equal	
spinal cord injury	H (80%)		
Psychological			
anorexia			H (95%)
bulimia			H
attention deficit disorder	10		1
conduct or behavior disorder	4		1
depression	1		2
mental retardation	2		1
schizophrenia		equal	
specific learning disability	3		1

SOURCE: American Psychiatric Association (1980), Long (1992), and Sherrill (1993).
NOTE: H = higher incidence.

were athletes before the onset of disability, the probability is strong that they will resume pursuit of sport. The larger the community of residence, the more likely disabled peers will be available for sports practice, competition, and support.

Compared with nondisabled women, women with disabilities are less likely to marry or to have spouse-equivalent partners, more likely to divorce, and more subject to risk in childbearing (Fine & Asch, 1988). Many feel that the high premium our society places on physical attractiveness puts them at a particular disadvantage. Whereas men are typically judged on the basis of both competence and appearance, women more universally are successful when good-looking, slender, and fashionably dressed. Women with disabilities are often perceived as asexual—as not capable of "good sex"—or as not worthy of attention. Overprotective parents and siblings often further complicate issues of sexuality.

Women with disabilities are also more likely to live with parents or siblings than with friends, spouses, or alone. This is related partly to overprotective parenting, but is also influenced by such culturally determined feminine characteristics as passivity, dependence, and low rate of risk taking. It is also an economic phenomenon, because living at home saves money. For elite women athletes who need a lot of money for travel, special coaches, and the like, this is an important consideration. Living at home may also be a time saver, with parents continuing to take care of food preparation, laundry, and other chores, thus freeing the female athlete to concentrate on sports excellence.

Employment opportunities and fair salaries are major problems for people with disabilities, especially females. Only 32% of working-age adults with disabilities work, compared with 79% of nondisabled peers, according to the U.S. Bureau of the Census's March 1988 *Current Population Survey* (cited in Bowe, 1990). The percentage for women is lower, with only 27% of women with disabilities in the labor force, compared with 69% of nondisabled women.

Overall, the mean earnings of people with disabilities are 35% less than those of nondisabled peers. Males and females who hold year-round, full-time jobs earn approximately $24,000 and $16,000 a year, respectively; only about one-third of those in the disabled working-age population, however, hold such jobs. Part-time employed males and females with disabilities average $15,500 and $8,000, respectively. These salary levels are partly related to the undereducation of people with disabilities. Of the persons surveyed, only 9% had college degrees, compared with 23% of all Americans in the same age range. More than 40% of the adults with disabilities in the survey lacked high school diplomas (Bowe, 1990).

Reactions to People With Disabilities

Do females with disabilities face double and sometimes triple discrimination? The facts speak for themselves. The more severe the disability, the more a disabled person is treated in different and undesirable ways. A 1991 nationwide Harris poll of public attitudes toward people with disabilities revealed that most Americans still worry about how to relate to individuals who are different from themselves. Following is an account of how Americans surveyed said they relate to people with disabilities:

- admiration, because people with disabilities overcome so many barriers, 91%
- pity, because of their situation, 74%
- awkwardness or embarrassment, because of lack of knowledge about how to behave, 58%
- lack of concern, because of belief that disabled persons can manage okay, 51%
- fear, because of possibility that similar disabilities can happen to oneself, 47%
- anger, because disabled people cause inconvenience, 18%
- resentment, because disabled people get special privileges, 9%

Moreover, 30% of the people surveyed said that they would be concerned if a coworker had a serious disability, and 23% would be concerned about having a supervisor with a disability. More than half said that they would be uncomfortable with their child's dating a person with a disability, and 25% would be uncomfortable with their child's bringing a disabled friend home.

The everyday reactions that people with disabilities face make them a social minority bound together first and foremost by the stigma of their undesired "differentness." People with disabilities do not want admiration or pity. They want merely to be accepted and liked as individuals who are diverse and thus defy stereotyping. The psychosocial differences between males born with disabilities and females born with disabilities are perhaps less pronounced than those between nondisabled persons and persons with acquired disabilities. This is because many males born with disabilities are treated in much the way society has traditionally treated females; they are overprotected and their parents assume they will not be high achievers in sports and vocations that require aggressiveness for success. Many males with disabilities, like many females (both disabled and nondisabled), develop low self-concepts as they come to realize that families, teachers, and communities expect little of them.

Persons with disabilities who become leaders say the major difference between them and other disabled people is parents who encouraged them to take risks. Persons disabled later in life talk also about the support of teachers, coaches, friends, spouses, and associates, who serve the critically important function of conveying high aspirations and insisting on the individual's full use of his or her potential.

Athletes With Disabilities

Numerous athletes with disabilities are featured in journals such as *Sports 'n' Spokes*; *Palaestra: The Forum of Sport, Physical Education, and Recreation for the Disabled*; and *Deaf Sports Review*.[1] These specialized journals, however, do not take the place of equal-opportunity coverage in sports sections of local newspapers and in popular magazines such as *Sports*

Illustrated. Athletes with disabilities want to be known as athletes, recognized for their sport achievement as other athletes are, and watched by spectators who appreciate their sport, not their disability or their ability to overcome barriers.

Although increasing numbers of athletes with disabilities are competing at local, regional, national, and international levels, they continue to receive little attention from the public. Likewise, research (especially on psychosocial dimensions) has been minimal. Most of the research on female athletes with disabilities has been generated by a handful of studies using two inventories: the Profile of Mood States (POMS) and the Personal Orientation Inventory (POI) (Sherrill, 1990).

On the POMS, all disabled athletes (except blind females) exhibited the iceberg profile, which is associated with good mental health and elitism among nondisabled athletes. The iceberg profile occurs when persons score above 50 on vigor and below 50 on tension, depression, anger, fatigue, and confusion. There were no statistically significant gender differences among cerebral palsied athletes, but significant differences did occur on the fatigue and confusion scales among blind and spinally paralyzed athletes. In both instances, males demonstrated better mental health than did females.

Jan Wilson, winner of four gold medals in swimming at the 1988 Paralympics, also enjoys ski racing. She is seen here with former U.S. skiing champion Billy Kidd.

The POI measures self-actualization, yielding a total score as well as individual scores for 12 scales. Research on self-actualization of disabled athletes has revealed no gender differences, regardless of whether the condition is cerebral palsy, spinal paralysis, or visual impairment. In general, athletes with disabilities are self-actualized to the same extent as the general nondisabled population. Moreover, they tend to score higher than the general population on the Self-Regard Scale. When interviewed, athletes with disabilities emphasize that sport is a means of affirming their competence. Sport focuses attention on their abilities rather than on their disabilities.

It takes many years, however, to acquire the skill and expertise to be an athlete. Girls with disabilities need special nurturing in school and community physical education and sport programs. The Individuals With Disabilities Education Act of 1990 (P.L. 101-476) is the update of P.L. 94-142, enacted in 1975, which requires that all children and youth diagnosed as disabled be given physical education instruction. The setting for this instruction must be regular, mainstream physical education unless an individualized education program documents the need for a separate or special environment. Equal opportunity for girls with disabilities to learn and participate in sport thus rests mainly with mainstream teachers, their ability to adapt, and their aspirations for helping all students to achieve their potential.

Key Words

athletes with disabilities	Paralympics
Deaf Sport	sex role bias
disability	sexuality
discrimination	Special Olympics
employment	wheelchair sports

Discussion Questions

1. Contrast the diverse social minorities served by Special Olympics, Paralympics, and Deaf Sport. What are some of the probable life experiences of women associated with each of these international movements?

2. Discuss or debate sex bias in relation to the diagnosis and treatment of disabilities. Consider historical, social, economic, and political factors.

3. Identify different kinds of discrimination and brainstorm ways nondisabled people can help people with disabilities to overcome barriers.

Note

1. Addresses for ordering these journals are as follows: *Deaf Sports Review*, AAAD Deaf Sports Review, Subscription Department, 1052 Darling Street, Ogden, UT 84403; *Palaestra*, Challenge Publications, P.O. Box 508, Macomb, IL 61455; *Sports 'n' Spokes*, 5201 North 19th Avenue, Suite 111, Phoenix, AZ 85015.

References

Abney, R., & Richey, D.L. (1992). Opportunities for minority women in sport: The impact of Title IX. *Journal of Physical Education, Recreation and Dance, 63*(3), 56-59.

American Psychiatric Association. (1980). *Diagnostic and statistical manual of mental disorders* (3rd ed.). Washington, DC: Author.

Bowe, F. (1990). Employment and people with disabilities: Challenges for the nineties. *Office of Special Education and Rehabilitative Services (OSERS) News in Print, 3*(3), 2-6.

Fine, M., & Asch, A. (Eds.). (1988). *Women with disabilities: Essays in psychology, culture, and politics.* Philadelphia: Temple University Press.

Guttman, A. (1991). *Women's sports: A history.* New York: Columbia University Press.

Hymowitz, C., & Weissman, M. (1978). *A history of women in America.* New York: Bantam.

Long, J. W. (1992). *The essential guide to prescription drugs.* New York: Harper Perennial.

Nelson, M. B. (1991). *Are we winning yet? How women are changing sports and sports are changing women.* New York: Random House.

Rosenberg, R. (1992). *Divided lives: American women in the twentieth century.* New York: Noonday.

Sherrill, C. (Ed.). (1986). *Sport and disabled athletes.* Champaign, IL: Human Kinetics.

Sherrill, C. (1990). Psychosocial status of disabled athletes. In G. Reid (Ed.), *Problems in movement control* (pp. 339-364). New York: Elsevier Science.

Sherrill, C. (1993). *Adapted physical activity, recreation, and sport: Crossdisciplinary and lifespan* (4th ed.). Dubuque, IA: William C. Brown.

Showalter, E. (1985). *The female malady.* New York: Penguin.

Stewart, D. A. (1991). *Deaf sport: The impact of sports within the deaf community.* Washington, DC: Gallaudet University Press.

Women and Disability Awareness Project (1989). *Building community: A manual exploring issues of women and disability.* New York: Educational Equity Concepts.

VII

Economics of Sport

We don't have time for centuries of slow evolution. The specter of computer-rule is all too near. And women have waited long enough.

—*Barbara Starrett*

The feeble tremble before opinion, the foolish defy it, the wise judge it, the skillful direct it.

—*Jeanne Manon Roland*

22

Equity
What Price Equality?

CHRISTINE H. B. GRANT
CHARLES F. DARLEY

Demeter's Grief

Demeter, goddess of grain, who caused the earth to be fertile and crops to flourish, had a beautiful daughter, Persephone. Persephone was known as the goddess of the young shoots, the new growth. While gathering flowers in a meadow, Persephone was attracted by a large, glorious flower. As she bent to admire it, the earth opened, and from it emerged Hades, god of agricultural wealth, keeper of the earth's rare and precious minerals. Hades swept Persephone into his horse-drawn golden chariot and abducted her to the underworld. Hearing Persephone's cries, Demeter rushed out but could not find her. She searched for days in grief. When she discovered that Persephone was with Hades, she decreed that nothing would grow on the earth until Persephone was returned to her.

The resulting famine reached such proportions that Zeus commanded Hades to return Persephone. He decreed that she could remain with her mother only if she had eaten nothing in the underworld. Persephone had touched not a morsel, but in her excitement at leaving, she swallowed some pomegranate seeds given her by Hades. Demeter's joy at being reunited with her daughter was tempered by the news of the seeds. A compromise was soon reached with Zeus that Persephone would return to the underworld as its queen for half of each year, during which time the earth would produce no crops, and remain with Demeter the remainder of the year, when the earth would bear fruit.

AUTHORS' NOTE: We would like to thank Susan Birrell, Sally Hickerson, Sam Becker, N. Peggy Burke, Jennifer Hanson, and Helen Smith for their helpful suggestions during the preparation of this chapter.

The Return of Persephone, by Lord Leighton. (Reproduced by permission of Leeds City Art Galleries, U.K.)

A Case for the Feminine
in Intercollegiate Athletics

Those women who have labored to implement a vision of sport for women that incorporates the ideals of nurturance, cooperation, and broad participation may find the Persephone myth a familiar story. This myth carries within it significant revelations that apply directly to intercollegiate sport in the United States. The precarious circumstance for women in intercollegiate athletics is intimately connected with the troubled state of that institution. The present structure of intercollegiate athletics both causes and suffers from the exclusion of a feminine viewpoint. The Persephone myth may be used as a touchstone to develop a strategy designed to accomplish the following:

1. Relieve the current ethical and economic crises in intercollegiate athletics and thereby advance the process of melding intercollegiate sport with the educational mission of our colleges and universities.
2. Infuse intercollegiate sport with those qualities traditionally thought of as feminine.
3. Secure the equitable representation of women in administrative and coaching positions within intercollegiate athletics.
4. Enlighten people regarding gender stereotyping and the power such assumptions have to oppress women.
5. Attack directly the physical consequences of women's motility and myths relating to gender inequality.

The Nature of the Ethical and Economic Crisis in Men's Intercollegiate Sport

Intercollegiate sport has the capacity to lift athletes to great heights of excellence. It often serves to unite and inspire the communities those athletes represent. These benefits notwithstanding, unethical and illegal behavior in intercollegiate sport has concerned the university community and the public for decades. These abuses include illegal payments to students, fixing of students' grades, inattention to the quality of students' academic programs, unsporting behavior including violence on the playing field, improper responses to athletes' injuries, insensitivity to and abuses of minority students and women, encouragement of performance-enhancing drug use, and excessive time demands on students.

To illuminate the causes of such abuses, Sage (1990) argues that social reality, including institutions such as sport and the beliefs about it, are socially constructed. Second, social structure profoundly affects human behavior. This is at variance with the popular notion that individuals are free agents who have total control over their experiences and choices. Finally, dominant groups in society often create and promote certain beliefs favorable to them so that those beliefs are accepted as "the natural order of things" by the groups or individuals they wish to influence and control. Sage applies Antonio Gramsci's concept of hegemony, which reveals how dominance may be exercised by consent rather than force, using persuasion, negotiation, concession, and compromise. The mass media, schools, religious organizations, public ceremonies, sport, and other seemingly apolitical or unbiased sources are often vehicles for maintaining hegemony.

Working from these underpinnings, Sage traces the development of men's intercollegiate sport in the United States from its beginnings in the late nineteenth century as an informal, student-run institution to its current state as a highly commercial, corporate enterprise. According to Boutilier and SanGiovanni (1983), corporate sport, as distinguished from informal sport and organized sport, is

> dominated by the demands of profit and power and is controlled by large bureaucracies. These organizations, such as the AAU, NCAA, IOC, and professional sports organizations, use their economic power to enhance their own survival and growth. They devote themselves less to the desires and needs of the participants and more to the demands of owners, alumni, sponsors, fans, and other vested interest groups. (p. 97)

The dramatic changes in men's intercollegiate sport reflect the economic changes occurring in the United States during the nineteenth and twentieth centuries. As technology advanced, entrepreneurial capitalism and its small, localized businesses evolved to monopoly capitalism, with relatively few large corporations controlling industry. The goal of industry was to achieve an optimal cost-efficiency ratio—to produce "the most goods and services at the lowest price with the highest profit margin" (Boutilier & SanGiovanni, 1983, p. 28). To reach this goal, businesses became increasingly bureaucratic. Their success depended on an expanding mass consumer market.

Urbanization and the emergence of leisure time as a valued retreat from increasingly alienating work environments created demand for new forms of recreation. Conditions were ripe for an explosion of commercial spectator sport. Athletic competition began on most university campuses in response to students' desire for recreation and some faculty members' belief that the university should promote the values inherent in sport and competition. These positive motives have endured, but they provide something of a smoke screen for other, less righteous ones. Although their mission is ostensibly educational rather than commercial, universities were lured by the potential of spectator sport for gaining loyalty and financial support from a populace ambivalent about the value of postsecondary education (Chu, 1989).

In response to financial pressure from business-oriented governing boards, many university presidents began to relinquish their role as overseers of academic quality and integrity. Instead, they became public relations liaisons to external constituencies such as alumni, corporations, government agencies, pressure groups, and potential benefactors. In that capacity, they became image makers, acquiring prestige for their institutions in an environment where "a school's success may depend less on the actual job it is doing than on others' perceptions about the job it is doing" (Chu, 1989, p. 31).

Men's intercollegiate sport began to assume the character of its corporate industrial setting:

> Sports and its values are a microcosm of the society itself. The values of the society are mirrored in its sporting rites and its rituals, habits, language,

goals, and passions. Competitive, aggressive, individualistic societies structure their sports to emphasize the glories of winning and the disgrace of losing. Cooperative, serene, and group-centered societies play their games to enhance the communal, playful, and joyful traits of their social life. (Boutilier & SanGiovanni, 1983, p. 24)

In the United States, men's intercollegiate sport moved away from an unfettered world of play toward a structured and commodified one in which winning and making money were central goals.

Given our recent governmental and corporate history, it should not surprise anyone that ethical abuses occur in a system where power, money, and competitive success are the driving forces (Etzioni, 1985). For commercialized intercollegiate sport, university athletic teams and student-athletes are often treated as products to be packaged and marketed. Undoubtedly most faculty, administrators, and coaches would contend that they direct their efforts toward the personal welfare and educational development of student-athletes. They would deny conceiving of or treating students as commodities. Nevertheless, the commercial factor can be insidious; it often catches in its subversive net basically honest and well-meaning individuals along with more willing, unethical captives. As focus shifts from What is the university's obligation to this student? to How can this student further the success of the university? doors open for the types of abuses detailed earlier.

In order to compete with each other, corporations and government entities often sacrifice long-term financial health for short-term profit. By following the religion of unlimited economic growth, many have spent and borrowed themselves into deep financial holes. Universities have not been spared. They have invested precious capital in unnecessary athletic equipment and buildings, elaborate recruitment procedures, high salaries for prominent "power" coaches, and assorted perks and bonuses for staff members (e.g., bowl game trips). In doing so, many universities have neglected their educational infrastructures—instruction, student services, libraries, student development, maintenance of existing facilities, and the creation of a real academic community. The result is an immediate economic crisis with little material or spiritual equity to draw upon. More than 70% of Division I athletics departments are in the red. Several of our most affluent institutions have cut sports.

In an effort to alleviate the ethical and economic crises these institutions face, the NCAA and its Presidents' Advisory Commission have engaged in a renewed wave of reform efforts. From the perspective of a hegemonic model, it is predictable that these reforms—higher academic standards, reduced coaching staffs and scholarships, and increased compliance efforts—largely affect the individuals with the least power, the student-athletes. Some reforms address student concerns over time demands and segregation from the nonathlete student body. Nevertheless, a statement made by Sage in 1990 prior to yet another wave of NCAA legislation still appears to be valid: "The structure of big-time, commercial college athletics—a structure that is largely responsible for the pervasive corruption and abuses—has been left intact, with no substantive changes" (p. 182).

Women and Intercollegiate Athletics

For decades, women did not enter the mainstream of intercollegiate athletics in the United States. To some degree this was a conscious choice made by the women physical educators who controlled women's intercollegiate sport. They detected the contradictions between men's intercollegiate sport and their own philosophy of sport for recreation rather than competition or commercialism. They constructed player-oriented (rather than spectator-oriented) events called play days, in which women of varying skill levels participated in multiple activities. Although their philosophy represented a clear alternative to the commercial model, they perhaps unconsciously accepted certain limiting conceptions regarding women's physical and psychological capabilities and inclinations.

Purported inadequacy in qualities such as aggressiveness, psychological adaptability to competition, and strength has been used to exclude women from sport. The assumption that there are innate and immutable gender differences helps justify this inequity. Contributing to women's exclusion is a definition of "true sport" promulgated by a male-dominated sports culture that incorporates traditional male qualities such as "power, strength, virility, endurance, and courage" (Boutilier & SanGiovanni, 1983, p. 18). But if gender and sport are socially constructed, and as such are redefinable and reconstructable, then any rationale for such exclusion disappears.

Unfortunately, if excluding women serves the male sports establishment's needs, that establishment has the resources to try to maintain such exclusion. There are many means of persuasion. For example, media depictions of women athletes that focus on their "feminine" qualities rather than their performances serve to reinforce entrenched notions of gender difference; hints and allegations about the sexual preferences of athletic women divert attention from the reality of women's physical competencies; comparing levels of performance for male and female athletes in the same sports perpetuates notions of innate difference, when in fact a history of oppression and exclusion accounts for most discrepancies in performance.

Women have made strides throughout the twentieth century in establishing themselves as popular and capable athletes within amateur and professional sport. For the most part, however, they have distinguished themselves in those individual sports typically thought of as requiring feminine qualities such as grace and fluidity. Opportunities for team play at a highly competitive level have been minimal. In 1971 the Association for Intercollegiate Athletics for Women (AIAW) was founded. Its purpose was to provide collegiate women athletes with opportunities to develop their skills to a greater degree and compete in national championships, as men had traditionally been enabled to do. However, rules were constructed to embody an approach very different from that of men's intercollegiate sport. "According to the AIAW, the real value of the sport experience lay within the student-athlete's ability to extract from sport knowledge of self and values that pertained to self" (Grant, 1984). This "educational model" was reflected in the transfer, recruiting, financial aid, and participation rules, and perhaps most profoundly in the Student-Athlete's Bill of Rights. Procedures were developed to allow broad participation in postseason competition while running educationally sound and fiscally prudent programs.

Although some people have argued that the AIAW was a dangerous move toward an elitist, competition-based corporate model for women's intercollegiate sport, others contend that it was a major step toward removing inequities for women. It also presented a model of female athletic excellence that could counteract negative attitudes toward females as athletic performers. Unfortunately, the AIAW's resounding success presented either too great a threat or too attractive a target, or both. At its 1981 convention, the NCAA voted to begin Division I women's championships. This eroded the AIAW's financial base, and 18 months later the organization had been put out of business.

Although opportunities for women to compete in intercollegiate sport have increased over the past 20 years, men have moved into many positions in both the coaching and administration of women's athletics. Women's opportunities to provide role models in intercollegiate sport and to determine the philosophical direction their sports will take have declined precipitously (Grant, 1992). No less troubling is that those women still holding positions of influence in intercollegiate athletics must operate within a structure they did not create and with which most philosophically disagree. As a final blow, the current financial crisis threatens to disadvantage women further. Many institutions have recently made across-the-board cuts in budgets and coaching staffs. These cuts disproportionately reduce budgets for women's sports and women's already diminishing coaching opportunities.

Demeter, Persephone, and Hades

The coercive, alienating, and self-defeating aspects of corporate intercollegiate sport arise from a materialist/dualist worldview. That view produces the abuses we observe. It is embodied in the Persephone myth by Hades, god of the underworld, holder of agricultural and mineral wealth. He has captured the nurturing essence of women's sport, embodied in myth by Persephone and in real life by the AIAW. Demeter symbolizes the women of the AIAW and their ideals of cooperation and care. They grieve the loss of their daughter.

Here the parallels of myth and reality diverge slightly to let pass a touch of poetic justice. Whereas Demeter had the power to withhold fertility from the land, women in intercollegiate sport have no comparable power. Ethical and financial woes have arisen as a natural consequence of the male establishment's suppression of a feminine model of sport. Hades still holds Persephone underground, but he must release her to restore abundance to the earth.

Women's Dilemma, Women's Choice

Most women and men who long for the infusion of a feminine, organic worldview into intercollegiate sport have sought reform "within the system." This approach includes working through national and conference committees to enact reform consistent with an educational model of sport. Liberal feminists have pressed for legislation to prohibit sex discrimination in educational institutions. Working within the existing system in this way has been criticized as a liberal approach that makes two dubious assumptions: first, that those in power will yield or share their power if they can be brought to see the justness of the case presented them; and second, that equality and justice within a corrupt system are worth attaining. Hegemonic theory exposes the fallacy of the first assumption. The diminishing presence of women in coaching and administrative positions should be enough to demonstrate that hegemony inhibits justice for women in intercollegiate athletics. As for the second assumption, for the sake of maintaining a presence in intercollegiate sport and sharing its riches, do women risk being co-opted by a system they decry? Will feminine values be compromised by Hades' pomegranate seeds?

Some feminists advocate separation of women's institutions from men's as a means of ensuring their control over the construction of those institutions. According to Birrell (1984), "Two factors are essential in evaluating the viability and the possibility of separatism: whether separatism is chosen or dictated; and whether the separate structures include distinctive ideologies" (p. 27).

If given the choice, many women in intercollegiate athletics would return to the AIAW, with its separate structure and distinct ideology. This alternative appears hopelessly idealistic. The NCAA has a monopoly that financially cannot be challenged. The removal of the separation option places women in a double bind. They have no alternative national organization into which to retreat, and they are being systematically excluded from governance positions within the NCAA and decision-making positions at their own institutions.

Faced with this dilemma, it appears that women in intercollegiate sport have one choice: to continue to work within the existing organization, resist surrendering their values, and effect change based on those values. Although this direction is dictated by the current power structure, it may have certain positive benefits. Hargreaves (1990) argues that only by working with men for their mutual benefit can women bring about significant changes. Separatism may provide an environment safe from co-optation, but it has limited utility for changing prevailing conceptions about gender and sport. It also fails to address the ways men are oppressed in sport.

> Sex-role stereotyping in sport impoverishes both men and women: few of either sex have a wide and fulfilling range of movement experiences—those that are energetic, powerful, skillful and exciting and those that are more expressive and sensuous, using the body with delicacy and flexibility. (Hargreaves, 1990, p. 300)

Hargreaves favors "a cooperative venture with men for qualitative new models in which differences between the sexes are unimportant" (p. 302).

Birrell and Theberge (in press) provide direction for implementing Hargreaves' approach. They suggest that to effect change an action must be either resistive or transformative. Resistance occurs when "disempowered groups of individuals refuse to submit fully to their disempowerment," and transformation (social change) involves "a fundamental change in the structure of relations of power and ideologies that hold those structures in place."

Informed by the viewpoints of Hargreaves and Birrell and Theberge, women and men seeking change in intercollegiate sport should take an eclectic approach: Whittle away at the existing structure to make it fit the ideal, work politically to bring more women into positions of power, and create new directions for intercollegiate sport that can someday supplant the destructive elements of the present system.

Getting Persephone Back: Strategies for Change

In her discourse on gender equity, Janet Chafetz (1990) states that equal access to elite roles is the most difficult to achieve yet most crucial aspect in the battle for the acceptance and implementation of feminist agendas. She suggests that the assistance of male elites can be invaluable in this endeavor. Help is most likely to be offered by those who perceive it as economically prudent or self-rewarding. Where elite factions contend for power, women's support may be perceived as vital for victory. Such a power struggle is taking place on university campuses. Presidents are attempting to establish powers of oversight regarding personnel and budget issues in athletics departments. In many cases they are fighting both athletic directors and "power" coaches. Owing to excessive media coverage of intercollegiate sporting events, these coaches in particular have become the most readily identifiable members, or symbols, of their universities. Virtually anyone with an interest in sport knows who coaches basketball at Indiana, Duke, or Georgetown. How well known are the presidents of those schools? Is it any wonder that when conflicts arise regarding hiring, firing, contract extensions, and appropriations for new facilities and operating expenses, the president often comes out the loser?

The time is ripe for women to intervene. Universities may soon be required to comply with Title IX's strictest interpretation: that female student-athlete participation rates should reflect the percentage of women in the undergraduate population. Most schools have far to go to comply. Since it is clear there will be no additional monies available for athletic programs in the 1990s, money needed to establish equity for women must come from the elimination of current expensive and excessive practices. The aforementioned conflicts can only intensify over the ramifications of strict compliance with Title IX. If presidents knew that women as a group might support them in their power struggles with administrators and power coaches in men's programs, would it not be prudent for the presidents to secure that support by pursuing policies consistent with a feminine model of sport?

How should policies change to bring intercollegiate athletics in line with a feminine model? The AIAW had some excellent ideas. Some of what follows comes straight from that organization's policy manual.

1. Support measures designed to create equity at all levels of governance in intercollegiate athletics.
2. Eliminate all off-campus recruiting except for a limited number of trips for talent evaluation. Rescind the NCAA Division I rule prohibiting campus auditions. This would create an economic windfall and provide relief for overstressed coaches.
3. Carry the current NCAA financial distribution plan to its logical conclusion, severing completely the link between winning basketball games and money.
4. Ask Congress to allow the NCAA to take control of television scheduling, and severely limit coverage per school.
5. Cut football rosters and scholarships by at least one-third. This would discourage specialization, create an economic windfall, and bring participation rates closer to Title IX requirements.
6. Push the NFL and NBA to establish minor leagues like those in professional baseball, so that young men interested only in training for professional football and basketball may do so immediately after high school.
7. Restructure conferences based on a principle of regionalism. This would eliminate diffuse conference structures that produce excessive travel costs and unreasonable time demands on student-athletes and coaches.
8. Automatically award scholarship athletes tuition aid only, with the proviso that they may receive additional aid based on need.
9. Prohibit coaches from receiving money from sports equipment and shoe manufacturers. Any such income should go to athletics departments.
10. Require that all expenditures for new athletic facilities at an institution be approved by a majority of its faculty.

For inspiration regarding programs that can take intercollegiate athletics in a new direction, we turn to an economic treatise offering an alternative to the entrenched gospel of unrestricted growth. In *Small Is Beautiful: Economics as if People Mattered*, E. F. Schumacher (1991) espouses an organic, holistic version of economics based on optimal rather than ever- increasing consumption, smallness rather than giantism, and decentralization rather than concentration. He believes our management of the land (and, by extension, all natural resources, including human bodies and minds) must be oriented toward three goals: health, beauty, and permanence. "The fourth goal—the only one accepted by the experts—productivity, will then be attained almost as a by-product" (p. 112). Schumacher proposes a broadening of the industrial landscape, with people returning to more direct contact with their products in smaller workplaces. Growth is given a qualitative dimension as an alternative to the quantitative basis for most corporate industrial standards of "success."

Schumacher decries the illogic and waste of a system that relies upon goods being imported from distant locations while local resources go untapped. This conception is consistent with the organic, educational model for intercollegiate athletics.

By translating Schumacher's model to athletic programs, coaching time saved by recruiting cutbacks can be reallocated to local sports programs for school-age children and adults. Given the necessary NCAA rule changes, student-athletes interested in supplementing their tuition scholarships could be paid to assist with these programs. As conferences regionalize, universities can work together on clinics, workshops for high school coaches, and programs at the state and regional levels. Legitimate criticisms of class and racial elitism leveled at athletics departments can be addressed by subsidizing programs for those unable to pay. An example is the U.S. Tennis Association's Local Excellence Programs (LEPs). These are intended for children with special talents and an interest in tennis who may not have programs available to them. This is fertile ground for university athletics departments. Aside from the intrinsic ethical value in such involvement, it would bring athletics departments into congruence with universities' educational mission. It would also provide a close-to-home crop of well-trained athletes, reducing the need for national and global recruiting. Coaches should be encouraged to receive continuing education credits and become certified within their sports' governing bodies. Such advanced training would include not only technical knowledge in their sports, but also teaching methods, sport science updates, and self-enrichment endeavors. It appears that coaches' free time is so limited now that in some senses they are dying on the educational vine.

Whereas political action and persuasion will provide some progress toward gender equity, athletics departments can do much toward directly neutralizing gender as a source of women's oppression. Young (1980) describes how many women's oppression is expressed, and perhaps reinforced, by the way they use their bodies:

> Women in sexist society are physically handicapped. Insofar as we learn to live out our existence in accordance with the definition that patriarchal culture assigns to us, we are physically inhibited, confined, positioned, and objectified. (p. 152)

Similarly, Henley (1977) examines the effects of power and dominance on nonverbal behaviors such as gestures, posture, use of space, pitch of voice, and touch. She finds that inequalities of power between individuals are correlated with distinctive patterns of nonverbal behavior from each party.

When interpreting observations such as these, it is imperative to recognize the danger of falling into a "blame the victim" mentality. Nevertheless, it may be helpful for women to examine the ways in which their behavior reinforces gender bias. Some believe that whatever the original source of women's oppression, it continues to the degree that men perceive they have physical power over women. Not only are men often bigger and stronger, but the way women have been socialized to use, or not use, their bodies reinforces these perceptions. Most women's potential for quick, powerful movement is virtually untapped. Courses in movement training directed at full use of body parts, learning to experience explosiveness, and shedding the restraints of inhibition would have a positive effect on women's self-image and on gender bias. Coaching staffs should direct clinics specifically for untrained girls and women in order to liberate them from these handicaps. In the same manner, boys and men could be encouraged and shown how to develop the expressive component of movement. To complement this personal approach toward gender issues, we should press the mass media to provide greater coverage of women athletes and to reject material that perpetuates feminine and masculine stereotypes.

Conclusion

> In the end we can never know if we truly are acting in our own best interests or if the subtle tools of pleasure and deception are enfolding us even more deeply into relationships which favor the dominant group. (Birrell & Theberge, in press)

We should remember that Demeter's agreement to allow the earth to bloom did not guarantee her joy throughout the year. Persephone swallowed Hades' pomegranate seeds, which compelled her to visit the underground six months of the year as its goddess, Hades' wife.

Birrell and Theberge stress that whether an act qualifies as either resistive or transformative is always open to question. With regard to the strategies proposed here, one may ask: Can fundamental change be brought about by working "within the system"? Given the lack of options for women in intercollegiate athletics, the question is moot.

Still, there is cause for optimism and resolution rather than cynical resignation. The very act of rethinking philosophies and policies is liberating, if only from our own complacency and rigidity. And we must believe that, given our nurturance, viable new ideas will take root and grow.

Key Words

Persephone	hegemony
intercollegiate athletics	corporate sport
economic crisis	Association for Intercollegiate
ethics	Athletics for Women
gender	

Discussion Questions

1. What parallels do the authors draw between the Persephone myth and the dilemma facing women in intercollegiate sport?

2. What factors contribute to the ethical crisis in intercollegiate sport?
3. What arguments support a strategy of "working within the system" rather than separation?
4. In your opinion, which policies and new programs proposed by the authors stand the greatest chance of creating significant changes in intercollegiate sport?

References

Birrell, S. (1984). Separatism as an issue in women's sport. *Arena Review, 8,* 21-29.

Birrell, S., & Theberge, N. (in press). Feminist resistance and transformation in sport. In S. Guthrie & M. Costa (Eds.), *Womensport.* Champaign, IL: Human Kinetics.

Boutilier, M. A., & SanGiovanni, L. (1983). *The sporting woman: Feminist and sociological dilemmas.* Champaign, IL: Human Kinetics.

Chafetz, J. S. (1990). *Gender equity: An integrated theory of stability and change.* Newbury Park, CA: Sage.

Chu, D. (1989). *The character of American higher education and intercollegiate sport.* Albany: State University of New York Press.

Etzioni, A. (1985). Will a few bad apples spoil the core of big business? [Editorial]. *Business and Society Review, 55,* 4-15.

Grant, C. H. B. (1984). The gender gap in sport: From Olympic to intercollegiate level. *Arena Review, 8,* 31-48.

Grant, C. H. B. (1992, February 7-8). *The legacy of and options for women in sport.* Paper presented at the National Girls and Women in Sport Symposium, Slippery Rock University of Pennsylvania.

Hargreaves, J. A. (1990). Gender on the sports agenda. *International Review for the Sociology of Sport, 25,* 287-308.

Henley, N. M. (1977). *Body politics.* Englewood Cliffs, NJ: Prentice-Hall.

Sage, G. H. (1990). *Power and ideology in American sport: A critical perspective.* Champaign, IL: Human Kinetics.

Schumacher, E. F. (1991). *Small is beautiful: Economics as if people mattered.* San Bernardino, CA: Borgo.

Young, I. M. (1980). Throwing like a girl: A phenomenology of feminine body comportment motility and spatiality. *Human Studies, 3,* 137-157.

23

The New Competition
Sports Careers for Women

MARJORIE A. SNYDER

Until 20 years ago, no one paid much attention to women in sports. Along with the military, sport was thought of as one of the last great bastions of male supremacy. And then, in 1972, along came Title IX. The opportunities for females in high school and college sports multiplied during the years after Title IX was passed. By 1978 there had been a sevenfold increase in the numbers of girls playing high school sports (see Table 23.1). Similar gains were made in intercollegiate sports, where athletic scholarships for women were almost nonexistent before Title IX. Now there are more than 10,000 scholarships for women athletes. According to the National Sporting Goods Association, women now outnumber men in participation in fitness activities.

Attitudinal changes accompanied the increases in participation rates. Parents now believe sports are equally important for girls and boys, and nearly all agree that sports and fitness activities provide important benefits to girls who participate (Women's Sports Foundation, 1988). Women are gaining greater acceptance on the golf course and in the locker room. This chapter examines how these changes have affected women's share of the employment pie in sports, identifies ways women can increase their share, and surveys the range of opportunities available in sports-related careers.

TABLE 23.1 Participation Rates of Girls and Women in High School and Intercollegiate Sports

Level	1971-1972	1977-1978	1990-1991
High school	294,015	2,083,040	1,892,316
College	31,852	64,375	92,778

SOURCE: High school data are from the National Federation of State High School Associations; college data are for National Collegiate Athletic Association institutions only.

Painting the Picture of Opportunity

Where Have We Been?

If you were a young woman interested in translating your passion for playing or watching sports into a career opportunity in 1972, what kinds of options would you have had? Unless you were fortunate enough to have a professional tennis instructor as a father (like tennis champion Chris Evert), you had few alternatives. Only a handful of women made their livings as professional athletes. Opportunities were generally limited to golf and tennis. There were several failed attempts to operate professional leagues for women in baseball, basketball, softball, volleyball, and other sports. Fewer still made their living as sports broadcasters (Donna de Varona and Phyllis George), marketers, or physicians. Not surprisingly, this was a reflection of societal conditions for women as a whole. In general, women were not doctors, lawyers, or executives either. And women of color were even less likely to translate an interest in sport into a career opportunity.

Teaching physical education, coaching, or athletic administration offered the greatest chances for women who wanted to pursue sport-related careers. Women found a niche in educational institutions—the segment of society men did not view as an attractive career option because it offered low pay, few benefits, and little status.

Where Are We Now?

According to the February 1992 *Economic Report of the President*, 40 years ago, 31% of U.S. women over the age of 20 worked full-time (U.S. Department of Commerce, 1992). Today, the proportion has grown to almost 60%. The purchasing power of women is fertile new territory for the sporting goods industry. Women who want to play sports can now buy equipment and clothing designed exclusively for women. Women are also demanding access to facilities and equal pay for equal work, and are poised to use the force of law to back them up.

Sport has grown to be a more than $60 billion industry, bigger than the auto, petroleum, lumber, and air transportation sectors of the U.S. economy. Along with this growth, there has been an explosion in opportunities for sport-related careers (see Table 23.2). If a woman wanted a career in sport 20 years ago, she became a coach or physical education teacher. Many universities now offer degree programs in sport-related fields from sport psychology to exercise science to sports nutrition. More than 100 colleges and universities offer sport management degrees.

Although male domination in sport-related careers is still the norm, there are some inklings of change. There are exciting women at the top of many fields. For example, women own major league baseball teams and sporting goods companies, head major college athletics departments, serve as sports reporters at Wimbledon and the Super Bowl, and race in the Indianapolis 500. Women establish "first time ever" accomplishments

TABLE 23.2 Sports Career Opportunities, 1992

Career Opportunity	Number of Jobs	Percentage of Total Jobs
Sports marketing	1,457,500	32
Sports entrepreneurship	1,155,000	26
Athletic administration	496,000	11
Athlete representation	370,000	8
Sports journalism	301,000	7
Other sports-related careers	720,000	16

SOURCE: Data are from the *Sports Careers Newsletter*, 1992.

nearly every day. A woman has now served as the chief medical officer of the U.S. Olympic Committee; the International Olympic Committee has its first black female member; the NBA has its first female club president; and a female has been president of the NCAA. While women still may be scarce at some levels and in some areas of sports, they are no longer oddities. By 1990, 5 of the 41 national governing sports bodies had women as executive directors. A handful of women appear regularly on network sports television. By 1988, one-third of the members of the American College of Sports Medicine were women.

Although career opportunities for professional women athletes are still quite limited and highly competitive, they are greater than they were 20 years ago (see Table 23.3). In the United States there are professional opportunities in auto racing, beach volleyball, billiards, bowling, cycling, equestrian sports, figure skating, golf, racquetball, skiing, sled dog racing, sports climbing, squash, surfing, tennis, triathlon, and waterskiing. Even though U.S. universities produce many of the world's finest women volleyball and basketball players, there are no U.S. leagues in these sports for women. Players must go abroad to Northern Europe, Italy, Japan, or New Zealand.

Ironically, the increase in sport participation opportunities for girls and women has been paralleled by a corresponding decrease in the numbers of women coaching and administering sports (see Table 23.4). In 1972, women held almost all the coaching and administering positions in women's intercollegiate sports. By 1992, less than half of the coaching positions were filled by women, and only about one in eight women's college athletic programs was headed by a female. As in the past, representation of women of color in

TABLE 23.3 The Growth of Women's Professional Golf and Tennis

	Golf		Tennis	
	Early 1970s	*1992*	*Early 1970s*	*1992*
Number of players	60	326	70-80	1,000
Number of tournaments	30-40	41	17	65
Prize money	$1,500,000	$21,750,000	<$50,000	$25,000,000

SOURCE: Golf data are from the Ladies Professional Golf Association; tennis data are from the Women's Tennis Association.

A variety of careers in sport were represented at a recent meeting of the Board of the President's Council on Physical Fitness and Sports. Left to right: invited speaker Dr. Doris Corbett, Howard University physical educator and president of the American Alliance for Health, Physical Education, Recreation and Dance; Arnold Schwarzenegger, bodybuilder, film star, and President's Council chairman; Chris Evert, former tennis professional turned sports commentator. (Photo courtesy of the President's Council on Physical Fitness and Sports)

coaching and administration is poor. For example, Acosta and Carpenter (1992) estimate that there is a minority group member (male or female) in only one out of five of the athletic administrative structures of NCAA member institutions, and overall they estimate that less than 5% of all physical education teachers, coaches, and administrators are minorities.

Where Are We Going?

The challenge now is to achieve equity in the sport-related work force. Even though it appears that growth in the industry as a whole will continue, women will have to be armed and ready to gain their fair share. In the words of Anita DeFrantz, we have to "stop believing we have no role in sports past the playing field." We need to go beyond the assumption that the lessons of sport—teamwork, goal setting, confidence building, risk taking, and so on—are enough to prepare women for career success. Women must learn the rules of the sports career game and then play it with enthusiasm. They must be prepared to fight for and take advantage of laws that prohibit

Where are they now? This photo was taken at a 1977 World Series game between the Orange Lionettes and the Connecticut Falcons. The catcher, Rayla Allison, is currently executive director of the National Softball Coaches Association; the batter, Donna Lopiano, is now executive director of the Women's Sports Foundation. (Photo by Joan E. Chandler)

discrimination in the hiring process and on the job. They must be willing to serve as role models and mentors for younger women. And, regardless of career choice, they must take the steps necessary for career success.

Self-evaluation and exploration of career options. Loving sports is not enough. Women must assess their skills and determine how to translate those skills into careers in sport. The appendix to this chapter lists professional organizations that can provide information about many different sport-related careers. Women can contact these organizations and talk to people

TABLE 23.4 Status of Women as Coaches and Administrators in Women's Intercollegiate Sports

	1971-1972	*1977-1978*	*1991-1992*
Percentage of women coaching women's teams at the college level	90+	58.2	48.3
Percentage of women administering women's teams at the college level	90+	not available	16.8

SOURCE: Data are from Acosta and Carpenter (1992).

who are already in the fields that interest them. They can find applicable journals and other publications in their libraries (see the appendix for a partial list) to find out more about particular careers. Table 23.5 provides a partial listing of sports-related employment, leadership, and career options.

Goal setting. Women who want careers in sport should think about what they want in terms of salary, responsibilities, location, and advancement opportunities, and about the talents they have to offer and the interests they want to pursue. Career planning is a process—one may not know exactly what one wants right away, but the better defined the goal, the easier the rest of the process becomes.

Education. Almost every career has bottom-line educational requirements. Career research and the advice of guidance counselors can be helpful for women who want to design programs to fit their needs.

Experience. Internships, work-study, and part-time and summer jobs are all good sources of experience that can help prepare an individual for a career. Almost any real-world job experience will gain job seekers some points by showing that they can tackle projects, take on responsibility, and deal with people and deadlines. As with education, however, the more directed this sort of experience is, the more connected it is to one's goals, the more impressive it will be on a job application or résumé. Work experience is also useful as a laboratory for testing career goals and adding information to job research files.

Entering the job market. After completing the needed education and gaining some experience, job seekers must take the next step—more research. They should look for entry-level positions that can be paths to their career goals. They need to talk to contacts and let them know they are looking for work. They should also check standard job listings—newspapers, professional journals, placement services.

Job seekers need to prepare résumés—lists of their educational and work experiences designed to emphasize their best attributes. The ideal résumé is short, simple, appealing, and directed as specifically as possible toward the desired job.

Women seeking employment in sport-related fields, like most job seekers, need to be aggressive; they must follow every lead. They should send their résumés to all the possible job sources their research has unearthed—whether or not jobs are known to be available. Getting a job is sometimes just a matter of being in the right place at the right time, and one should do everything possible to make sure the odds are in one's favor.

Networking. Women interested in sports can join professional organizations, attend conferences, start contact lists, and find out how to gain access to key decision makers. They are also wise to seek out mentors.

TABLE 23.5 Selected Career Opportunities

Occupation		Description	Professional Preparation/Requirements	Earnings Range per Year	Outlook
Athlete	professional athlete	receives compensation for competing in a sport, must be willing to travel, seasonal; sports include auto racing, basketball, beach volleyball, bowling, figure skating, golf, horse racing, racquetball, rodeo, surfing, tennis, waterskiing	athletic talent, many years of training, high school and college experience, sponsorship, some have qualifying events	$10,000-$1,000,000+	poor
Communications/ journalism	public relations	creating positive and exciting images for sports personalities and organizations, promotion of amateur and professional athletics and sports organizations	undergraduate to master's degree in business/sports management, communications or journalism preferred	$15,000-$100,000+	fair
	sportswriter	editing, research, and writing on sports-related events for magazines and newspapers	undergraduate degree in journalism/liberal arts required; sports experience and knowledge helpful	$11,000-$50,000+	fair
	photographer	photographing events and athletes for print or broadcast media	portfolio is a must to demonstrate abilities; experience and knowledge of sport and personalities helpful	$9,500-$75,000+	fair
	broadcaster	reporting sports news to television/radio audience; color commentary during games	undergraduate degree; good communication skills	$12,000-$1,000,000+	fair
Education	teaching—P.E., teaching professional	teaching and developing "the art and science of human movement," teach sport skills or design P.E. programs for schools, community programs, social agencies and clubs	undergraduate to doctorate required	$17,000-$65,000+	good
	coaching	teaching, developing, and overseeing development of sport skills and competitive strategies, guiding team in competition and tournaments as well as recruitment for amateur and professional sports	undergraduate to master's degree in physical education/sports management, emphasis in coaching, some states require certification at community and high school levels	$18,000-$50,000+	high school and college, good; professional, poor
	athletic administration	development and management of athletic programs in colleges and schools	undergraduate degree to doctorate in physical education, sports management or athletic administration required; coaching/teaching and sports background helpful	$25,000-$50,000+	good

270

Category	Job	Description	Requirements	Salary	Outlook
	officiating	performing the duties of an official at all levels of athletic events	certification in sport; knowledge of rules and regulations	$25.00 a game-$90,000+ a year	community officiating, good; professional, poor
Health/fitness	personal trainer	structuring a fitness program for individuals, taking into consideration habits, work schedule and goals of the individual, and working with them to meet the goals	no educational requirements, but training in exercise and nutrition helpful	$25-$500+ a session	fair
	exercise physiologist	analysis and improvement of cardiopulmonary endurance and capacity, muscle power and joint flexibility	master's degree to doctorate in exercise physiology/biomechanics required	$17,000-$65,000+	good
	aerobics instructor	leading exercise and aerobic classes; developing routines for sessions	no formal requirements, exercise and dance familiarity helpful; certification available	$11,000-$31,000+	excellent
	corporate fitness	implementing and maintaining in-house or out of house fitness programs for individuals or groups of employees	master's degree in exercise physiology, physical education, or a related field	$15,000-$75,000+	fair
Medicine/science	athletic training	prevention and rehabilitation of athletic injuries for clinics, educational institutions, hospitals, professional teams, and research centers	undergraduate degree; certification from National Athletic Trainers Association; continuing education	$16,000-$85,000+	good
	physician	examining and diagnosing injuries; prescribing treatment and rehabilitation for sport injury	medical degree	$40,000-$100,000+	good
	physical therapist	rehabilitation of athletic injuries primarily through the design and supervision of exercise programs	undergraduate to master's degree in physical therapy; state certification	$19,000-$48,000+	excellent
	psychologist	studying and teaching human behavior in sports and physical-activities situations; doing research/writing on this subject	master's degree to doctorate in sports psychology or in physical education with emphasis in sports psychology; certification available	$417,000-$65,000+	good
Recreation/leisure	outdoor recreation—camps	development and management of recreational/sports programs and facilities in public parks and industry	undergraduate degree in recreation, P.E. or sports management required; experience through entry-level jobs/internships important	$15,000-$75,000+	fair

continued

TABLE 23.5 Continued

Occupation	Description	Professional Preparation/Requirements	Earnings Range per Year	Outlook
community recreation—YWCA, parks and recreation departments	development and management of multi- or specific-sport camp programs for children, adolescents, and adults; supervise instructors; facilities management	undergraduate degree in recreation or physical education preferred	$15,000-$75,000+	fair
Sports business				
marketing	mixing the fundamentals of marketing with athletics in an effort to promote a product or service	undergraduate degree in business or related field and knowledge of athletics helpful	$25,000-$95,000+	poor
special events	handling all aspects of planning and execution of a sports event	undergraduate degree; experience in event management helpful	$18,000-$85,000+	fair
athlete agent (also law)	representation of athletes, coaches, or officials to secure the best financial situations for clients	undergraduate degree in business or sports management; law degree helpful	normally a % of the athlete's contract; $200,000-$750,000	fair
sporting goods manufacturing	management, marketing, research and development, and promotion of numerous product lines	undergraduate degree in business or related field with general sports knowledge	$12,000-$85,000+	excellent
sporting goods sales	management of businesses that sell sporting goods; development, marketing, and promotion of product lines	undergraduate to master's degree preferred; sports experience helpful	$10,000-$35,000+	excellent

SOURCE: Data are from Field (1991) and Reith (1991).

272

Risk taking. It is often worthwhile for individuals to apply for jobs even if they lack a few of the listed qualifications. They may have other strengths that employers want more than their missing skills.

Conclusion

Although it is clear that career opportunities for women in sport-related fields have blossomed in the past 20 years, it is also true that women still do not have their fair share of the employment pie. Years ago the only sport-related career alternatives available to women were in coaching, teaching physical education, and athletic administration. The tremendous surge in the participation rates of females in sports, combined with the growth of the sports industry, should lead to a corresponding increase in the numbers of women employed in that industry. Women currently have at least nominal representation in a wide variety of sport-related careers, but there are still many hurdles to clear before equity is achieved.

Key Words

Title IX	professional preparation
career planning	earnings
job opportunities	sport-related resources

Discussion Questions

1. What factors have contributed to increases and decreases in sport-related career opportunities in the past 20 years?
2. Pick a career, identify a network, create a contact list, make a résumé that fits the career, and find out how jobs in the field are advertised.
3. Identify and profile a successful woman in a sport-related career.

Appendix

Organizations With Professional Development Emphasis

Aerobics and Fitness Association of America, 15250 Ventura Boulevard, Suite 310, Sherman Oaks, CA 91403; (818) 905-0040

American Alliance for Health, Physical Education, Recreation and Dance, 1900 Association Drive, Reston, VA 22091

American Coaching Effectiveness Program, P.O. Box 5076, Champaign, IL 61820; (217) 351-5076

American College of Sports Medicine, 401 W. Michigan Street, Indianapolis, IN 46202; (317) 637-9200

American Volleyball Coaches Association, 122 Second Avenue, Suite 201, San Mateo, CA 94401; (415) 342-7828

Association of Women in Sports Media, P.0. Box 4205, Mililani, HI 96789

Business Opportunities for Women in Sports, Pam Magee, Director of Marketing/ Advertising, Brooks Shoes, Inc., 9341 Courtland Drive, Rockford, MI 49351

International Dance Education Association, 6190 Cornerstone Court E, Suite 204, San Diego, CA 92121-3773; (619) 535-8979

National Association of Collegiate Women Athletic Administrators, University of Minnesota—Twin Cities, 516 15th Avenue S.E., Minneapolis, MN 55455

National Softball Coaches Association, 215 E. Del Norte Street, Colorado Springs, CO 80907; (719) 444-8826

National Sporting Goods Association, 1699 Wall Street, Mt. Prospect, IL 60056; (708) 439-0111

National Sports Law Institute, 1103 W. Wisconsin Avenue, Milwaukee, WI 53233; (414) 288-7090

NCAA Professional Development Program for Women and Ethnic Minorities, 6201 College Boulevard, Overland Park, KS 66211; (918) 339-1906

Sporting Goods Manufacturing Association, 200 Castlewood Drive, North Palm Beach, FL 33408; (407) 842-4100

Women's Basketball Coaches Association, 4646 B Lawrenceville Highway, Lilburn, GA 30247-3620; (404) 279-8473

Women's Sports Foundation, 342 Madison Avenue, Suite 728, New York, NY 10173

Other Resources

Aspire Higher: Sports Careers for Women (1989). Video (available from the Women's Sports Foundation for $19.95 plus postage and handling).

Cylkowski, G. (1992). *Developing a lifelong contract in the sports marketplace.* Little Canada, MN: Athletic Achievements.

Filippell, B. G., & Lipsey, R. A. (1991). *The directory of women in sports business.* Princeton, NJ: Sportsguide.

Lipsey, R. A. (1992). *Sports marketplace.* Princeton, NJ: Sportsguide.

Prine, M., & Rosenbaum, J. (1986). *Opportunities in fitness careers.* Lincolnwood, IL: VGM Career Horizons.

References

Acosta, R. V., & Carpenter, L. J. (1992). *Women in intercollegiate sport: A longitudinal study— fifteen-year update 1977-1992.* Unpublished manuscript, Brooklyn College, Brooklyn, NY.

Field, S. (1991). *Career opportunities in the sports industry.* New York: Facts on File.

Reith, K. M. (1991, September). Playing the career field. *Women's Sports & Fitness,* pp. 64-65.

U.S. Department of Commerce. (1992). *Economic report of the president.* Washington, DC: Government Printing Office.

Women's Sports Foundation. (1988). *The Wilson report: Moms, dads, daughters and sports.* New York: Author.

Women's Sports Foundation. (1992). *A woman's guide to coaching.* New York: Author.

24

Tennis
Hard Work Paying Off

CHRISTINE M. SHELTON

Women's professional tennis is one of the great success stories of the modern sports world. Its evolution from an exclusive, elite beginning to an international professional game has been phenomenal. The women's tennis tour, as we know it today, did not come about easily. Its evolution involved a lengthy and intense struggle that a small group of female players and supporters endured to gain credibility, financial solvency, and equality in professional tennis.

For many years the central issue in tennis focused on the status and privileges of professional and amateur players. How would they compete together? Was the elite establishment of tennis willing to change its negative attitude toward the concept of "professional"? Would tennis prove to be a popular professional sport with a substantial public following? If this proved to be the case, would corporate sponsorship follow?

The most dramatic change over the course of the past 25 years has been the influx of money invested in the world of professional tennis. Paralleling this process have been endorsement contracts for players, sponsorship of tours with large prize money, and the promotion of tennis spectaculars. The prizes at first were minimal for men and even smaller for the women, but as tennis participation and tournaments grew in popularity, the purses increased and the push for financial equality intensified.

Economic Impact: A Historical Overview

The history of women in tennis dates back to the reign of King Henry III, when 30-year-old Mademoiselle Margot was considered to be one of the best players in France. Margot of Hainault, the first great woman professional champion, appeared in 1427 and played "the best tennis any man had ever seen." She was said to have used her bare hands rather than gloves when playing and hit the ball "very powerfully, cunningly and skillfully as a man could" (Gillespie, 1975, p. 15). Margot was considered a professional because she competed with the men and there were always handsome bets put on her matches. From the time of the famous Margot until the eighteenth century, there is very little mention of women as tennis players in the literature of sport, and certainly there is no indication that women were able to earn a living playing tennis.

Mary Ewing Outerbridge is given credit for bringing tennis to the United States in 1874. The story goes that she had seen some British officers playing in Bermuda and purchased a set of rackets, balls, a net, and the directions for the appropriate setup of the game. She introduced the game to the "smart set" in Staten Island. Lawn tennis was picked up immediately by wealthy men on the East Coast, who tried to take credit for introducing tennis into the United States; however, historians have substantiated that it was Outerbridge who brought Wingfield's game across the Atlantic (Lumpkin, 1981).

In 1880 the United States National Lawn Tennis Association (USNLTA) was formed for amateur players and was opened to men only. Tournaments were organized for men by the USNLTA, but by 1889 women demanded recognition. On February 2, 1889, 15 years after Mary Outerbridge introduced the first rackets to this country, the USNLTA extended the right of membership to women players (see United States Lawn Tennis Association [USLTA], 1972). The wealthy of America played tennis and recognized amateurs, not professionals, as the true tennis players until the 1920s. The definition of *professional* during this era was as follows: "one who is paid directly or indirectly, for playing, engaging in, or teaching the game of tennis or any other form of athletic exercise or sport or who has competed in any game or sport for a stake, or purse, or for gate money" ("Annual Meeting," 1928, p. 163). This definition was highly restrictive compared with the definition of *amateur* in other sports.

Professional sports were growing in popularity in the 1920s. A tennis professional was limited to teaching. Amateur tennis players did receive money under the table, a practice referred to as "shamateurism." Shrewd promoters were looking for gate attractions. Although boxers and wrestlers were routinely showcased, Charles C. Pyle, also known as "Cash and Carry" Pyle, felt there could be financial return from staging exhibition matches between well-known tennis players. He offered France's Suzanne Lenglen, the top woman amateur in 1926, $50,000 to go on a professional tour. As Billie Jean King (1988) notes, Suzanne Lenglen was not the first woman tennis player to earn wages for playing. Women such as the Sutton sisters, Violet and Florence, were professionals who earned wages as teachers of the game. Lenglen was the first woman to agree to accept payment for playing. Mary K. Browne, the sixth-ranked player in the United States at the time and an American champion from 1912 to 1914, signed with Pyle's tour as Lenglen's opponent. These two women, along with some male players, became part of the first pro tennis tour. The first series of exhibitions were held at Madison Square Garden on October 9, 1926 (USLTA, 1972). The French Tennis Federation called Lenglen's turning professional "deplorable." She lost her social status, because at that time *professionalism* was considered a dirty word. Lenglen stated her reasons for turning professional in her souvenir program of 1926:

> In the twelve years I have been champion I have earned literally millions of francs for tennis and have paid thousands of francs in entrance fees to be allowed to do so. . . . Where did all this money go? . . . Why shouldn't the players get something out of it? It meant years of practice and a life's work for most of us. . . . The owners of these clubs at which I so often played were mostly shrewd businessmen and they saw to it that these tournaments netted them a handsome profit. . . . Under these absurd and antiquated amateur rulings only a wealthy person can compete. . . . Is that fair? Does it advance the sport? Does it make tennis more popular or does it tend to suppress and hinder an enormous amount of tennis talent . . . whose names are not in the social register? (quoted in Little, 1988, p. 83)

Lenglen's view was remarkably progressive and prescient. She foreshadowed modern feminism in her call for equity with regard to class and exposed many of the "shamateur" policies in the game.

The first U.S. professional tour drew substantial crowds and was considered a financial success, with the players receiving extra money for endorsing clothes, equipment, and, in Suzanne Lenglen's case, perfume (Little, 1988). Ted Tinling, a friend of Lenglen's, declared that her tour was so successful that Pyle should double her wages. Lenglen was "an early leader in the fight against the establishment's stranglehold on tennis—a battle that took players forty years to win" (King, 1988, p. 41).

In 1927 the Professional Lawn Tennis Association (PLTA) was formed. Its purpose was to obtain "a proper and recognized status in the tennis world" (USLTA, 1972, p. 59). During the same year the United States Lawn Tennis Association passed a resolution allowing clubs to have matches or tournaments open either to professionals only or to amateurs and pros with the permission of the USLTA. The governing body of American tennis wanted to have strict control over the interaction of professional and amateur tennis players. In 1933, the USLTA gave permission to the Germantown Cricket Club in Philadelphia to have an open championship, a tournament open to amateurs and professionals. This decision caused chaos on the international level, and the International Lawn Tennis Federation (ILTF) vigorously objected to this format of play between amateurs and professionals. The controversy over open tournaments would continue for many years, with the elite leaders and players condemning the concept of professionalism as crass and detrimental to the sport.

Bill Tilden had organized Tilden Tours, Inc., in 1930 and tried to convince top amateur players to turn professional with him. Unfortunately, the public kept losing interest in Tilden's pro tour because the stars had little or no competition. The answer to this problem was for Tilden to lure the top amateurs into the ranks of the pros. Between 1940 and 1941, Alice Marble and Mary Hardwell played pro matches all over the United States. In 1947 they were joined by Pauline Betz. Before 1960 the controversial Gussy Moran, a woman who revolutionized tennis dress for women, had also joined the pro circuit. The USLTA wanted to open some of its tournaments to professionals, but did not dare go against the firm policy established by the ILTF.

On March 30, 1968, the ILTF finally sanctioned open tournaments, but still insisted on distinguishing between amateurs and professionals. The result of this extremely conservative policy on the part of the ILTF and the USLTA was that amateurs received expense money under the table for their travel to tournaments, waivers of entrance fees, money for food and housing, and sometimes they were paid just to show up and participate in a certain tournament. The pros, on the other hand, were playing for straight wages and had to fund their travel, food, and lodging from tournament earnings. In the 1960s many players turned professional and actually took salary cuts of $40,000 to $50,000. Rosemary Casals, Anne Haydon Jones, and Francoise Durr were some of the first to turn pro after the open concept was ratified. They signed $25,000-$30,000 contracts for two years and helped to usher in the new hope for women in professional tennis.

The differences among pros, registered players, and amateurs were minimal. The pros took their money openly and publicly, the registered players negotiated their prize money with the tournament officials and remained "untainted," and the amateurs received their money under the table in various forms. Open tennis was operational when 12 tournaments in four nations (Britain, France, Australia, and the United States) sanctioned amateurs and professionals to compete against one another. During this transitional period, competitive tennis players were classified as amateurs, professionals, registered players, and shamateurs by tournament directors and governance structures such as the ILTF. At that time, the ratio of men's prize money to women's prize money was 2 to 1. In 1969, only one year later, that ratio reached 5 to 1. By 1970, it reached an astonishing 12 to 1 (Long, 1990). Other equity imbalances also existed. Bud Collins, one of the first sports journalists to cover women's tennis, stated that women tennis players in the late 1960s were treated as second-class citizens. They received the leftover courts, the leftover court times, and less money under the table during the shamateur years than men, and, finally, they did not receive nearly as much press coverage as the men (Long, 1990). Outraged at this treatment, the women on the tour became more and more aware of the importance of taking a stand on this issue.

Meanwhile, the "old boy network" of the tennis world was laying the groundwork to limit the tournament winnings for women, based on three assumptions. First, men played the best three out of five sets in the Australian, Wimbledon, French, and U.S. Open championships, while the women played two out of three sets. Second, the men could beat the women; therefore, the public must be more interested in seeing the men play. Finally, the men believed that few people would actually come and watch women's tennis. What they failed to recognize was that athletes do not get paid according to the length of time they are on the court or the playing field. The women argued that they were just as exciting to watch as the men, and they were willing to fight to be given a chance to prove this. By the 1970s women tennis players united and forced a male-dominated sport to notice them and to accept their premise that women professionals could add color, excitement, emotion, and high quality to the game of tennis.

The Battle Begins

In August 1970, thousands of women were speaking out at meetings and going on strike to celebrate the new feminism and the first Women's Rights Day. At the same time, two female tennis professionals, Ceci Martinez and Esme Emanuel, were talking about how dissatisfied they had become with the low prize money women received. These two women distributed questionnaires to the fans on the issue of lower prize money received by women at the 1970 U.S. Open Tennis Tournament at Forest Hills (Lichtenstein, 1974). The fans were appalled at the disparity in men's and women's earnings. This consciousness-raising activity moved the women players to take action against the czar of pro tennis, Jack Kramer.

The final blow came in 1970 when word got out that Jack Kramer, promoter of the Pacific Southwest Championship, was offering prize money at a ratio of 12 to 1 in favor of the men. The men's prize money totaled $12,500, whereas the women would compete for a piece of a meager $1,500 in prize money. Women who failed to reach the quarterfinals would not get a cent (King, 1988). With Billie Jean King at the forefront, a handful of women threatened to boycott the event unless Kramer worked out a prize scale that would be more evenly awarded (Lichtenstein, 1974). Upon his decision to hold firm with the original 12 to 1 ratio, Kramer stated, "If they don't like it, I won't give them *any* prize money" (G. Heldman quoting Kramer; in King, 1988, p. 123). Incensed at this, Gladys Heldman, a smart, aggressive businesswoman and founder of *World Tennis* magazine, decided to take a stand. She organized the first all-women professional tournament, an alternative to competing in the Pacific Southwest Championship. Players wishing to compete signed a $1.00 pro contract with Heldman in an effort to protect the tournament site from retribution. Gladys Heldman took it upon herself to lay the groundwork. She had to find a tournament location and, most important, a sponsor. She made site arrangements with the Texas Lawn Tennis Association and the Houston Racket Club. She arranged sponsorship with Philip Morris, Inc., maker of Virginia Slims cigarettes, through a longtime friendship with Joseph F. Cullman III, then president and CEO of the company. It is hard to believe that a tobacco company, the producer of a product scorned by health-conscious persons, would help usher in the success of the athletes who made up the Women's Pro Tennis Tour. But that is exactly what happened, and the Virginia Slims advertising slogan, "You've come a long way, baby," would become the theme of this tour through the 1980s.

Eight players chose to sign the $1.00 contract and compete in the first-ever Virginia Slims Tournament with a purse of $7,500 in prize money. These women became known as the Houston Eight or the Emancipated Eight of 1970. They included Billie Jean King, Rosemary Casals,

Judy Dalton, Peaches Bartkowicz, Valerie Ziegenfuss, Kerry Melville, Kristy Pigeon, and Nancy Richey. A ninth player, Julie Heldman (daughter of Gladys), also signed the contract but was unable to compete because of an injury. Casals went home the winner of this historic event, beating Judy Dalton in the final and taking home $1,500 (Collins, 1974). This rebellious action, a sign of the women's unwavering dedication to pay and prize equity, did not go unnoticed by the officials of the USLTA. All who signed the symbolic $1.00 contracts were suspended by the USLTA, which meant that the women would not be eligible for ranking and thus their futures in tournaments such as the U.S. Open and Wimbledon would be uncertain. Yet they remained united in their stand.

The Virginia Slims Tour, with its promising future, posed a threat to the USLTA. Therefore, along with the suspensions, the USLTA created and sponsored 23 new additional tournaments for women, offering competition for women such as Chris Evert and Evonne Goolagong, who remained loyal to the USLTA.

In 1970 two Virginia Slims tournaments were held. The first was in Houston and a similar one took place in Richmond, Virginia. From these eight-player events with $7,500 in prize money, the tobacco company created the Virginia Slims Circuit, a multievent tour, which enjoyed rapid growth and success from 1971 to 1978 (Smith, 1989). Growth was so rapid that within a year the prize money had increased from $7,500 to $40,000 (Smith, 1989). In 1971, the Slims held tournaments in 19 cities, with a total of $309,100 in prize money. In 1972, another city was added to the list and the purse grew to $501,275. By 1973, there were 22 host cities and total prize money of $775,000. At that time the men's professional circuit was playing for $1,280,000 (Lichtenstein, 1974). Along with increased prize money, the Slims tour also increased its player membership. As of 1973, 69 of the world's best female players were participating in the tour under the tutelage of Gladys Heldman.

The conflict continued between the Virginia Slims organization and the USLTA for a number of years. The conflict was especially harmful when one considers the bigger picture. With talented and motivated female athletes taking sides, the women were unable to find new sponsors or to expand the tours for the satellite players. The women began to recognize that there was power in unification. While the progress they made separately was significant, solidarity was now essential.

According to King (1988), "The year 1973 was a momentous one for every woman in tennis" (p. 142). In April of that year, the International Lawn Tennis Association (counterpart to the Men's Association of Tennis Professionals) declared that the women must either submit to the national association or be banned from the Grand Slam tournaments (Australian Open, French Open, U.S. Open, and Wimbledon) forever. The threat of this drastic action forced the groups to compromise. The competing factions united under the USLTA, but retained the Philip Morris Company as the primary sponsor featuring the Virginia Slims. Gladys Heldman, the driving force behind the creation of the Virginia Slims Tour, was dismissed from her post.

Billie Jean King: A One-Woman Show

Pleased but not satisfied with only a merger, Billie Jean King felt the need to do more. She recognized a need for the women of professional tennis to form a group, a union that would act to improve the conditions of their profession, that would speak out in the players' interests, and that would continue to carry the torch. In June 1973, only days before King beat Evert in the Wimbledon finals, a new organization was formed. It was called the Women's Tennis Association (WTA), later changed to the Women's International Tennis Association (WITA). Billie Jean was elected the organization's first president. Three months after the inception of the WTA, a milestone was reached. The U.S. Open offered equal prize money to the men and the women. This was the first time a major tournament offered an equal payoff (King, 1988, p. 144).

The year 1973 also brought the famous "Battle of the Sexes" tennis match between Billie Jean King and Robert (Bobby) Larimore Riggs, a 55-year-old man who challenged King to a $100,000 winner-take-all match. Riggs had previously beaten top-ranked Margaret Court with ease. King accepted partly because she disliked the fact that the public reacted chauvinistically to the annihilation of Court. Politically speaking, Billie Jean King was a woman with a mission: She would prove to the world that women are competitive—in fact, competitive and talented enough to beat men.

Once the stage was set, the event was publicized as no other event in tennis history ever was or has been since. Riggs went on record boasting that he was a male chauvinist. He proclaimed, "Women belong in the bedroom and the kitchen, in that order," and "I can see her coming apart at the seams already." His sexist clichés were seen on T-shirts and in the headlines of newspapers all over the country. After handing Margaret Court her embarrassing loss, Riggs advised Court to "go home, be a good girl and make dinner. She was such a nice lady, she should have stayed home to take care of her child" (Lichtenstein, 1974). The gender battle found its way into homes all over the country. Husbands and wives were making bets on Bobby and Billie Jean, with the losers to do household chores for a week (Lichtenstein, 1974). The hoopla continued steadily until September 20, 1973, the

In 1990, Billie Jean King became the only female athlete named by Life *magazine as one the 100 most important Americans of the twentieth century. She shared this distinction with athletes Babe Ruth, Jackie Robinson, and Muhammad Ali. (Photo by Russ Adams; courtesy of the U.S. Tennis Association)*

date set for the "best three out of five sets" match. The *Washington Post* (1973) reported the match to be "Texas big, Hollywood showbiz and Madison Avenue slick. It's a fun time, a social event and a crusade for women's liberation. It's Bobby Riggs vs. Billie Jean King in the tennis event of a lifetime."

King prepared herself well. She studied the Riggs versus Court match for hours and formulated her strategy:

> My plan was not to play fast and furiously and not to hit my serve too hard. I wanted Bobby to generate all the pace, and I wanted to hit plenty of balls to his backhand. I also decided to stay in the backcourt and prolong the rallies to test his conditioning, even when I had a chance to put the ball away. (King, 1988, p. 145)

The extravaganza was viewed by 30,472 at the Houston Astrodome, with another 50 million watching from their living rooms all over the United States. In her book, *We Have Come a Long Way: The Story of Women's Tennis*, King (1988) writes, "I thought about my career and my dreams as a child. I thought about women and low self-esteem, and I thought about athletics and acceptance. . . . I was at top throttle as I awaited the biggest match of my life" (p. 145). She also recalls the moment when that tension and anxiety transformed into exhilaration. It happened as she was carried onto the court on an Egyptian litter, "This was what I always wanted: arenas, sequins, and nighttime tennis" (p. 145). Billie Jean King emerged victorious in this historic event, outplaying Riggs 6-4, 6-3, 6-3. This monumental win provided women in occupations ranging from housewife to corporate executive with a new sense of pride and strength.

King has recounted numerous stories of the ripple effect created by women who felt empowered by the victory. Women working as secretaries for a newspaper in Philadelphia surrounded her a few days after the match and told her that they had wanted to ask for salary increases for many months, and after she beat Riggs they got the courage to ask. King was pleased that this action had taken place, but wanted to know the outcome. The women got their raises! Her accomplishments questioned traditional assumptions about gender definitions. She proved to men and women alike that women could play a "man's game"—and the victorious attitude that prevailed gave women a whole new outlook on their worth. King (1988) explains:

> The symmetry of those years was impossible to escape. We began our quest in Houston in 1970, rebels with a cause and an uncertain future. And we came back to Houston in 1973 after proving we could make it on our own. We began our quest in Houston in 1970 because a man, Jack Kramer, underestimated our value as athletes and entertainers. And we came back to Houston in 1973 because another man, Bobby Riggs, dared to make the same mistake. (p. 146)

Economic Parity: At What Price?

In the early 1970s, women initiated changes that have shaped modern-day tennis. In creating equity for themselves, they addressed two important concerns. First, the strategic role of "temporary separatism" was employed. The Virginia Slims Tour was separate from the men's tour and was successful. It provided the players with opportunities to develop a successful strategy. The women's tour stood on its own merits rather than riding on the coattails of the men's programs.

The second concern involved a more introspective assessment of themselves as professional athletes. The players found in themselves personal qualities: courage, self-esteem, drive, and dedication. To secure the gains they had made, players such as Billie Jean King created opportunities for empowerment. King used part of her earnings to start a satellite tour for new players called the Ms. America Tour. She was the driving force behind the creation of the Women's Sports Foundation, and she founded *WomenSports* magazine to expand opportunities for women in all areas of sport. Martina Navratilova followed her example, donating the seed money to start a campaign called Aspire Higher that would focus on creating sport opportunities for underprivileged girls.

Tennis is booming. The professional women tennis players of today have been described as "the gum-popping, pastel-outfitted, pony-tailed brigade" (Women's Sports Foundation, 1986). The sport continues to be identified with the white, wealthy, and elite, and the young female players have been described as selfish, with little understanding of or respect for the game (Feinstein, 1991). The players on the women's circuit have achieved a degree of success. After all, a one-hundredth-ranked tennis

Martina Navratilova, through both her advocacy of women's sports and her exemplary career, has provided a strong role model for a generation of women. As a proponent of gay and lesbian rights, she lost numerous contracts for product endorsements, even though she set new standards of excellence in technique and physical fitness. (Photos © Carol L. Newsom; courtesy of the Women's Tennis Association)

player can make about $30,000 a year and may be only 14 years old. Of the top 40 money winners in professional sport during 1991, 4 were women and all 4 were tennis players (*USA Today*, 1991). Players of the 1990s are a part of professional tennis, which is a business that brings in more than $13 million annually (Women's Sports Foundation, 1986). Tennis is ruled by sponsors, agents, and promoters who focus on marketing and image making.

Economically, the female tennis pro has been co-opted. Unless she conforms to the media image of traditional "femininity," she will not reap the monetary benefits of endorsement contracts. Corporate sponsors love legs and cleavage, and they reward select players such as Steffi Graff and Gabriela Sabatini with big contracts. Players who do not fill the "appeal" bill may have outstanding rankings, but their opportunities to expand their incomes through product endorsements are few and far between.

Some people would argue that the women who struggled for pay equity and recognition of women's physical ability have mistakenly adopted the male model of success, accepting the sexism and excessive competition so often associated with tennis. While there may be some validity to this claim, one must also appreciate the significant achievements and strategic lessons learned.

The brief history recounted here suggests that the key factors in the success of the women who sought equity with men included the following:

1. belief in themselves, their skill, their talent, and their worth as tennis players
2. ability to mobilize, organize, and work together to achieve common goals
3. ability to compromise, adopt new strategies, and accept change

Professional tennis was blessed with players who were willing to invest their time and financial resources to expand women's access and opportunities in tennis. They were pioneers with a clear commitment to guaranteeing equity, not only for themselves, but for future generations of women. Billie Jean King could discern, despite the media hype and glitz, the symbolic importance of beating Bobby Riggs before a national audience. In doing so, she demonstrated that women are not simply the economic pawns of corporate sponsors, but can adroitly use such events to advance a greater cause.

Key Words

amateur	Jack Kramer
professional	Billie Jean King
shamateurism	Virginia Slims Tour
Suzanne Lenglen	Women's Tennis Association
United States	Bobby Riggs
Lawn Tennis Association	temporary separatism

Discussion Questions

1. The 1970s were a significant decade for change in women's tennis. What were the economic and political factors that influenced this change?
2. How has the definition of professionalism changed in tennis and how has it affected the women's game?
3. How did women pioneers in tennis help achieve equity in their sport?
4. What impact has the fight for economic parity in women's tennis had on other women's sports? Can similar tactics be implemented in other sports?

References

Annual meeting of the United States Lawn Tennis Association. (1928). *Spalding's Tennis Annual*, pp. 162-165.

Collins, B. (1975, May). Who's afraid of Virginia Slims? *WomenSports*, pp. 29-31, 56-58.

Feinstein, J. (1991). *Hardcourts*. New York: Villard.

Gillespie, N. (1975, May). Love through the ages. *WomenSports*, pp. 15-18.

King, B. J., with Starr, C. (1967). *We have come a long way: The story of women's tennis*. New York: McGraw-Hill.

Lichtenstein, G. (1974). *A long way baby: Behind the scenes in women's pro tennis*. New York: William Morrow.

Little, A. (1988). *Suzanne Lenglen: Tennis idol of the twenties*. Wimbledon, UK: Wimbledon Lawn Tennis Museum.

Lumpkin, A. (1981). *Women's tennis: A historical documentary of the players and their game*. Troy, NY: Whitson.

United States Lawn Tennis Association (USLTA). (1972). *USLTA official encyclopedia*. New York: Harper & Row.

VIII

Changing Times

*Praise our choices, sister, for each doorway open to us was taken by squads of
fighting women who paid years of trouble and struggle, who paid their wombs,
their sleep, their lives, that we might walk through these gates upright.*

—Marge Piercy

*By integrating our fragmented selves, and by inverting the patriarchal order
and worldview, we work to create a new paradigm, . . . a new dream, a new web,
a common language.*

—Judy Grahn

The door itself makes no promises.

—Adrienne Rich

25

One Future for Sport
Moving Toward an Ethic of Care

MARY DUQUIN

> If people are surrounded by nurturant institutions, i.e. institutions that are nurturant to people and that reward people for being nurturant, then people will tend to become nurturant; if people are surrounded by institutions that are exploitive, i.e., if people are exploited and are rewarded for exploiting others, then people will tend to become exploitive. (Love & Shanklin, 1983)

Sport and the Ethic of Care

Ethics surrounding sport are a primary concern for many women. Mariah Nelson (1991), in her book *Are We Winning Yet?* notes that women often prefer to engage in sport and physical activities that are nurturant and supportive of participants. She describes the development of the partnership model of sport, where participants practice sport guided by values emphasizing the ethic of care for self and others:

> Teammates, coaches, and even opposing players view each other as comrades rather than enemies. Players with disparate ability levels are respected as peers rather than ranked in a hierarchy, and athletes care for each other and their own bodies. . . . athletes are motivated by love of themselves, of sports and of each other. . . . partnership athletes maintain that sport should be inclusive; in balance with other aspects of life; cooperative and social in spirit; and safe. (p. 9)

The structure and ideology of these partnership sport models that emphasize the ethic of care offer alternative options for the future of both women and men in sport. Fundamental to developing an ethic of care is the value of nurturance. Nurturance involves an interest in the protection, growth, health, and well-being of self and others. An ethic of care also emphasizes the importance of developing a sense of emotional empathy and responsiveness to others. Response to human needs, fulfillment of interpersonal responsibilities, and commitment to maintaining relationships are integral aspects of an ethic of care. Ethical behavior is learned in relationships with others.

In our society, the responsibility for nurturance has been socially constructed to reside primarily with mothers and other females. Thus the ethic of care is often associated with maternal beliefs, attitudes, and practices (Ruddick, 1983). However, in a humane society the practice of the ethic of care is the responsibility of all members of society. In professions and disciplines that require caring, such as healing, teaching, and parenting, practicing an ethic of care involves demonstrating an interest in the protection, growth, health, and well-being of others. Caring involves developing a sensitivity to and identification with others. As Noddings (1984) states, "When we see the other's reality as a possibility for us, we must act to eliminate the intolerable, to reduce the pain, to fill the need, to actualize the dream" (p. 14). The potential for developing powerful relationships in sport between coach and athlete and among athletes gives those participating in sport rich opportunities to experience the practice of caring.

Approaching sport from the perspective of an ethic of care means that a priority is established in relation to all the myriad motivations that might prompt engagement in sport as a leader or participant. That priority is to act in such a way so as to preserve and reinforce oneself as a caring person. The ethic of care grounds moral behavior in nurturance and values the importance of needs and emotions, of social relationships and responsibilities.

Respecting the Body, Heart, and Soul of the Athlete

Bodily Health

Many sport practices today put the health of the athlete at substantial risk. An insensitivity to bodily well-being is evidenced not only in training and dieting regimens but in the valorization of athletes' willingness to sacrifice bodily health for victory. This socialization toward bodily sacrifice has contributed to an increasing rate of sport injuries among youth: annually more than 1 million in basketball, 900,000 in baseball, 500,000 in football, 110,000 in gymnastics, and 105,000 in soccer (Arnheim, 1985). Statistics also show more fatalities and serious injuries ending in permanent disability, higher surgery rates, greater incidence of anorexia and diet-related illnesses, more chronic injuries related to overuse, higher rates of drug abuse, and increased stress-related psychological and emotional problems among young athletes than among other youth ("Study Shows," 1989). More and more sportswomen are asking hard questions about the relationship of sport to their bodily well-being and the well-being of others. As Nelson (1991) reports, women are asking,

> Must we play as the men play? . . . Should we celebrate women boxers? Should we take drugs? Must college athletes suffer so many injuries? What are we doing to ourselves in the name of winning? Are sports still fun? (p. 8)

The ethic of care reflects a respect for the integrity of embodiment, that is, a respect for the athlete's physical and mental health. Caring for the body of the athlete is evidenced by instituting sport structures and engaging in sport practices that protect and enhance the athlete's health and safety.

Emotional Receptivity and Responsiveness

The ethic of care confirms not only the integrity of the body but also the importance of emotional receptivity and responsiveness. Part of caring involves attending to emotions, being attentive to the individual needs of another. Becoming skilled in the ethic of care requires the cultivation of the caring response, of empathy, of engrossment, and of a willingness to extend to others. Development of emotional receptivity is crucial to the development of the moral self and the ethic of care.

Most females are given extensive socialization in caring behavior. However, sport environments that desensitize females to their own feelings, or to the feelings of others, sabotage the ethical process. Although sport is a place for the expression of strong emotions, it also teaches a systematic harnessing of certain kinds of emotions. Emotions that might negatively affect competitive performance, be they fear, pain, or empathic identification with an opponent, are often actively discouraged. Disassociation from one's body is a technique suggested by some sport psychologists to block the pain associated with training and sport performance. By not paying attention to their pain, athletes not only repress emotional sensitivity to their bodies but also increase their chances of serious injury.

For many years women emphasized and celebrated the relational nature of sport by sponsoring social events with competing teams (Lee, 1978). This practice may still be endorsed in recreational sport. However, more and more often females participate in sport environments that value sport and winning over athletes and their relationships. In such environments social distancing between teams is practiced and one's opponents may be viewed as antagonists rather than as cooperating participants. The practice of social distancing between athletes, or between coach and athletes, reduces the emotional impact of human relations and obscures the moral obligation to care. Coaches often engage in social distancing from athletes. Anshel's (1990) summary of research on coaches indicates that coaches are often more interested in giving than in receiving information, are selective in soliciting feedback, tend not to view athletes' feelings as valid, are not comfortable allowing athletes input, do not feel obligated to meet certain needs of players, and often do not have personalities conducive to healthy relationships with athletes. This account of coach-athlete relations may indicate the presence of unhealthy leaders, an unhealthy sport system, or both. When sport environments suppress emotional responsiveness, when leaders and participants become emotionally insensitive, and when athletes are desensitized to their own feelings and the feelings of others, the moral climate of sport is diminished and the ethic of care is put at risk (Blinde, 1989; Duquin & McGinnis, 1992).

Moral Reflection

An ethical sense of self is formed through moral reflection, moral dialogue, and moral practice. The automatic obedience to authority expected in many sport contexts undermines the athlete's developing sense of moral reflection. Athletes' obedience in sport is largely a function of their social powerlessness. Athletes obey not only because they have been socialized to do so, but also because they have so little legitimate power to negotiate the conditions under which they experience sport. The autocratic structure of sport suppresses moral questioning and inhibits coach-athlete communication about moral relations and moral issues in sport.

Sport can also undermine the ethical ideal of caring by insisting on loyalty to the organization, creating in-groups and out-groups, and demanding obedience to rituals and rules that separate and divide people into hierarchies. Obedience to rules tends to diminish genuine caring because responses to others become ritualized, formalized, and rationalized (Noddings, 1984). In addition, coaches' rules in sport are often applied invariantly, without consideration of individual circumstances. Moral reflection and moral practice involve considering individual needs, abilities, material conditions, and situations. Responding from an ethical ideal of care requires attention to the concrete and respect for connection, particularity, complexity, and ambiguity.

Weaving an Ethic of Care Into Sports

What we teach young people to value and the experiences that form their moral character will have profound effects on the quality of life we will experience when they come of age. The goal of developing ethical human beings is not confined to the home and school. The education of youth regarding ethics is the responsibility of the entire community. However, coaches and other

The development of an ethic of care starts with the very young. (Photo by Pam Mellor-Deslorieux)

recreation leaders have a special opportunity to work with young people in constructing, maintaining, and enhancing ethical ideals.

There is no one structure that will guarantee to promote caring relations in sport, just as there is no one way to demonstrate care. However, sport leaders can structure programs and engage in practices that either enhance or diminish caring relations. While the ethic of care in sport is strongly related to the practices of sport leaders, an ethic of care also stresses the importance of the responsiveness of athletes in helping leaders maintain caring relations. In order to fulfill the caring relation, athletes must recognize and respond to caring behavior on the part of leaders. An ethic of care may be supported in sport in the following ways:

1. Coaches and athletes reflect a respect for the body. Coaches and athletes engage in practices that demonstrate concern for the health, welfare, protection, and enhancement of all athletes.

2. Coaches and athletes confirm the importance of emotional responsiveness by attending to individual needs and emotions and by exemplifying an awareness of the interconnectedness of human relations.

3. Coaches and athletes honor individual responsibility in developing ethical ideals through moral reflection, moral dialogue, and moral practice in the exercise of sport and leisure.

The Coach-Athlete Relationship

Coaches enter into a special relationship with athletes. Both coaches and athletes have ethical responsibilities in maintaining this relationship. Coaches have the responsibility to be models of caring, to help athletes develop ethically, and to be proficient in the art and science of education. Athletes have the ethical responsibility of responding to the care shown by coaches through questions, effort, commitment, and cooperation. When coaches model an ethic of care, they teach the value and importance of social relationships and responsibilities. A good sport leader is an admirable model of both learning and caring. Coaches enhance the ethic of care when they do the following:

- Show respect and regard for the interests and goals of athletes.
- Demonstrate expertise in helping athletes achieve competence.
- Act on the belief that the athlete is more important than the sport.
- Behave as models of both learning and caring.
- Demonstrate responsiveness to individual needs and feelings.
- Reflect the best possible image of each athlete, finding something admirable in each and communicating this information to the athlete.
- Maintain an open dialogue with athletes.
- Select tasks and engage in practices that maintain or enhance the ethic of care for self and others.
- Support athletes in developing and maintaining an optimal level of health and well-being.

- Communicate the belief that all relationships have ethical importance and consequences.
- Engage in practices that promote caring relations among athletes.
- Work with athletes to establish rules that offer support to and promote caring relations.

The Instructional Program

The ethical development of participants in sport, recreation, and exercise/fitness programs is affected by both what is offered and how the instructional program is conducted. Although reference is made to coaches, the following guidelines may apply to any leader in a sport or physical recreation program. The instructional and programmatic aspects of sport and recreation work to enhance the ethic of care when the following conditions apply:

- Practices or activities that diminish the ethic of care for self or others are rejected (e.g., sports, such as boxing, that require the infliction of pain or injury on others; practices that involve physical exercise as a form of punishment).
- The sport, recreation, or exercise program is diverse, allowing for individual interest and selection.
- Groups or teams are small, thus enhancing the opportunity for responsive athlete-coach relationships as well as a greater opportunity for participation.
- Coaches and athletes have the opportunity to work together over a number of years.
- The sport program encourages links with parents and other members of the community.
- Opportunities for athletes to practice caring skills are provided (e.g., tutoring less skilled or younger athletes, aiding disabled or injured athletes, maintaining equipment or facilities, officiating, peer teaching).
- The sport program is sensitive to and inclusive of multicultural diversity.
- The sport program allows for coach-athlete discussion of ethical issues and conflicts as they arise in the practice of sport.
- The sport program provides the opportunity for joy and delight in learning for the athlete.
- The activities selected promote the lifelong health and well-being of athletes.
- The sport program allows athletes multiple chances to learn as well as the necessary time to develop mastery in skills needed for competence.

Ethical Areas of Concern

A commitment to an ethic of care requires that each teacher, coach, team, and athlete engage in an ongoing evaluation of how the operating social structures and behaviors of people in that particular sport context affect the physical, ethical, and emotional welfare of participants. A commitment to an ethic of care requires that physical, moral, and emotional abuse be resisted and that sporting activities promote health, growth, and the development of people who are able to care. The following list highlights some of the ethical areas of concern for the future well-being of people in sport.

- *nurturing the athlete's health and safety*

  promoting athlete-coach dialogue regarding the use of both performance-enhancing and recreational drugs

  restructuring sport programs to avoid violence and physical abuse

  instituting policies and procedures that reduce injuries in sport

- *promoting positive emotional experiences for athletes*

  creating a safe and nurturing environment in which athletes can learn; showing sensitivity to athlete concerns with body image and self-concept

  encouraging peer acceptance and sensitivity

  encouraging athletes to take risks but not attempting to coerce or control them

- *fostering an appreciation of human diversity; understanding the role of sport and play in bridging diversity*

  discussing how caring relations are affected by cultural diversity, including the areas of race, ethnicity, religion, physical/mental ability, age, gender, and sexual orientation

- *developing positive gender relations*

  exploring how sport and physical activity relate to the development of gender relations in our society

  promoting and modeling of nonsexist attitudes and language by coaches and sport administrators

  making possible the experience of coeducational sport activities in a mutually caring and supportive environment

- *improving the quality of the environment*

  encouraging athletes to explore the relation between caring for one's health and caring for the environment, especially in relation to land, water, and air pollution

  discussing nondestructive creative leisure and lifelong health

Conclusions

Institutions are not ethical; only people are capable of moral action or inaction. All relations are moral relations, and moral relations are reproduced and created anew everyday in the practice of sport. It is ethically crucial that athletes develop the ability to question, on moral grounds, the formal rules and informal norms of sport and that they have the courage for disobedience when institutional authorities threaten the ethic of care. The ethic of care is diminished when sport practices violate the integrity of embodiment, discourage emotional sensitivity to self and others, and block the development and practice of caring relations. Sport structures and practices promote the ethic of care when they preserve health, promote well-being, permit moral dialogue, develop emotional receptivity, and encourage caring relations.

Key Words

ethics   health
caring behavior   well-being
sports participation

Discussion Questions

1. Do an ethic of care and the burning desire to win represent conflicting values or ideologies? Explain.

2. If an athlete wants to maintain an ethic of care in her life, what actions might she need to take in relation to her sport, her coach, her teammates, other competitors?

3. How do we create an ethic of care when violence in sport is normalized? Is it possible to maintain an ethic of care and still really enjoy participating in physically aggressive contact sports?

4. Do you believe females are socialized more than males toward an ethic of care? If so, is this good? How would sport change if males adopted an ethic of care for self and others?

References

Anshel, M. (1990). *Sport psychology: From theory to practice.* Scottsdale, AZ: Gorsuch Scarisbrick.

Arnheim, D. (1985). *Modern principles of athletic training.* St. Louis: Times Mirror/Mosby.

Blinde, E. (1989). Unequal exchange and exploitation in college sport: The care of the female athlete. *Arena Review, 2,* 111-123.

Duquin, M., & McGinnis, N. (1992, February 7-8). *Cutting our own throats: Bleeding for the father.* Paper presented at the National Girls and Women in Sports Symposium, Slippery Rock University of Pennsylvania.

Lee, M. (1978). *Memories beyond bloomers.* Washington, DC: American Association for Health, Physical Education and Recreation.

Love, B., & Shanklin, E. (1983). The answer is matriarchy. In J. Trebilcot (Ed.), *Mothering: Essays in feminist theory* (p. 282). Totowa, NJ: Rowman & Allanheld.

Nelson, M. B. (1991). *Are we winning yet? How women are changing sports and sports are changing women.* New York: Random House.

Noddings, N. (1984). *Caring: A feminine approach to ethics and moral education.* Berkeley: University of California Press.

Ruddick, S. (1983). Maternal thinking. In J. Trebilcot (Ed.), *Mothering: Essays in feminist theory* (pp. 213-230). Totowa, NJ: Rowman & Allanheld.

Study shows 23% of high school basketball players injured. (1988, Fall). *National Athletic Trainers Association News, 1*(1), 15-16.

26

Women's Sport and the Feminist Movement
Building Bridges

NANCY BAILEY

Picturing representatives from the feminist movement and from the women's sport movement standing together on the same bridge is not easy. Competition is fundamental to sport, whereas a cooperative model is espoused by feminism. The two groups appear to be worlds apart. When feminists see women athletes as sometimes self-absorbed, narrowly focused, single-minded, and male identified, it is safe to assume that they are not going to be pounding on the gymnasium doors, inviting sportswomen to get on board, even if they do see active, energized personalities. Grass-roots liberation groups looking for alliances find groups of kindred spirits, more politically motivated groups who might share their vision, such as the National Association for the Advancement of Colored People or the Mexican American Political Association. These politically motivated groups have developed strategies very different from the booster clubs of America so often associated with sport.

Women in sport and physical education need to organize and be active in their own feminism as they build bridges with the women's movement. Since the days of Title IX activism and the early work of the Association for Intercollegiate Athletics for Women (AIAW), where have we seen women in sport organized and moving around feminist issues? Which wave of feminism are we going to catch? We share goals, but that is not sufficient to form an alliance. We need to take action on our own issues. We cannot build alliances with the women's movement if we have nothing to bring to the table. It should be our collective feminist activism that we take to the women's movement. That activism is necessary to build bridges.

The majority of women in physical education and sport are feminists at heart, although many may not subscribe to that label. Most of these women

AUTHOR'S NOTE: Sincere appreciation is extended to Drs. Lois Sprague and Gwen Guibord for their contributions to this chapter.

are not actively involved in the feminist movement. In like manner, feminist activists have demonstrated little or no interest in the oppressively male-dominated world of sport. Finding ways to mobilize ourselves for action requires overcoming the stigmas that prevent us from speaking out. Sportswomen have worried for too long about the consequences of speaking out, and the focus has been negatively directed. The fear of retaliation and loss of ground already gained is very real. Instead, the focus requires a 180-degree turnaround. The women's movement can teach us a great deal about the empowerment necessary to accomplish our goals.

The Feminist Movement:
Strategies, Tactics, and Resources

A great portion of our foremothers' work and writings has only recently been uncovered and published (Spender, 1988). Contemporary feminist writings relative to the women's movement are prolific. These works document and describe strategies used by the contemporary women's liberation movement. The ideology is inspiring. Together these works provide firm footing; the interconnection is well grounded. Each generation must build on the work that was accomplished by those who came before us. Documented evidence to this effect is nicely illustrated in Charlotte Bunch's (1987) "A Broom of One's Own: Notes on the Women's Liberation Program."

In the women's movement there was an awakening, a raised consciousness, a discovery of the universal experience of women: a motivation, a pride in rejecting oppression and in finding strength in sisterhood. There was a resurgence of feminist literature that was nurtured in consciousness-raising groups and in diverse forums. By overcoming resistance to change, women found a shared exhilaration in identifying the personal-political connection. Previously, each individual imagined that personal pain was uniquely her own. Personal and private remedies were prescribed.

Focus was directed toward major institutions, such as the family, religion, education, and government, that perpetuated women's status as inferior, or that of victim. It was labeled "the patriarchy," and some women became survivors. Self-help services and groups were organized, new skills for self-caring were learned. Women organized for reproductive control, holistic health care, and family services. They developed a strong political ideology and focused on assertiveness training. They infiltrated the political scene and developed women's publishing companies. A new sense of self-worth and self-esteem was necessary to end the psychological dependence on men. Gaining this sense of control over one's own body was fundamental to the acquisition of control over one's own person and the immediate environment. A great deal of activity focused on perceived weaknesses that arose from internalizing sexism.

Activist Maggie Kuhn founded the Gray Panthers, a group that fights against ageism against women. (Photo © Bettye-Lane)

Women organized locally and nationally to challenge the system. They documented discrimination and pressured for remedies: equal access to employment and social services, job time sharing, and child care. They exerted pressure to abolish "men-only clubs," even as they created "women-only space" for inspiration, safety, and developing women's culture. In finding that inspiration, they began speaking out wherever they worked or studied, in places such as schools, labor unions, the black civil rights movement, professional organizations, and churches. National organizations were formed, with local or regional chapters. Caucuses, task forces, collectives, and kindred-spirited groups were organized, setting agendas that women identified and felt about passionately. Someone once asked if the women were going to talk themselves to death in this movement, or if they were ever actually going to *do* something.

Strategies were developed for moving the feminist agenda. Sit-ins, fasts, marches, boycotts, letter-writing campaigns, demonstrations, and noncompliance of all sorts illuminated and moved the agenda forward. Women's studies programs became the academic arm of the movement, nurturing a feminist scholarship and education. Activists worked for social change to end sexism, ageism, racism, and compulsory heterosexism and to end female dependency on males. The object was to challenge institutions where sexism and women's oppression were perpetuated.

In short, women became feminists: people who believe in equality and are willing to work to make it a reality. Some women became radical feminists: women who believe that our institutions require fundamental change, and that merely gaining access to a patriarchy without changing the ideology does not benefit anyone (Boutilier & SanGiovanni, 1983). Feminists see the connections among sexism, racism, heterosexism, and ageism. These are not separate and distinct problems, but parts of an intricate web strongly tied to the patriarchy. Albrecht and Brewer (1990) provide insight concerning this topic in their text, *Bridges of Power: Women's Multicultural Alliances*. The vision expanded. Feminism became more than a constellation of women's issues, it became a perspective, a philosophy, a political ideology. Women developed an understanding of the issues that formed the bedrock of the patriarchal system and male hegemony. And women found men who professed feminist ideologies, working to liberate both men and women from their circumscribed options. The research of men such as Donald Sabo (1987) and Michael Messner (1990) provides excellence references.

Women's Sports Organizations and Goals

The new feminist consciousness transcended disciplines. Feminist women in physical education and sport brought this ideology to their own professional organizations. In the late 1960s and throughout the 1970s, political issues focused on two important developments: the formation of the AIAW and the passage of Title IX.

Members of the National Association for Girls and Women in Sport (NAGWS), a subdivision of the American Alliance for Health, Physical Education, Recreation and Dance (AAHPERD), recognized a need for a structure that would increase opportunities in competitive sport at the collegiate level. Surrounded by a sport environment in which male hegemony prevailed, the founding mothers were able to design, create, and implement a working organization that met their needs and goals. Created by women for women, the AIAW represented "a place of their own."

With the passage of Title IX, separate departments for men and women in physical education at both the secondary (public education) and collegiate levels became obsolete. The merging of curricula that had espoused very different philosophies was no simple task. Women brought a new feminist agenda to the bargaining table, but viable compromises could not always be effected. With the implementation of Title IX, avenues for protest were created. The U.S. Department of Health, Education and Welfare as well as the Equal Employment Opportunity Commission and the Human Rights Commission became conduits through which sex discrimination cases could be heard.

Organizations such as the Amateur Athletic Union, the U.S. Olympic Committee, and the International Olympic Committee, as well as local departments of recreation, represent sport governing bodies unrelated to our educational system. However, their policies also affect opportunities for girls and women in sport. Attaining membership on these governing boards has been difficult for women. Strategies to infiltrate the infrastructure have been painstakingly slow. With no law to address inequality, such as Title IX of the Educational Amendments Act, mobilization techniques had to be redefined.

Issues in Women's Sports

There are many concerns relating to the quantity and quality of opportunities available to women in sport. Women struggle with issues related to sexism, ageism, and racism. The socioeconomic status of women in general is low; women are paid less than their male counterparts in like occupations, which denies them equal buying power and/or access to certain sports. Within their own sport organizations, women address these topics with determination. Strong feminist leadership from organizations such as the National Organization for Women has helped considerably.

Until very recently, issues related to homophobia in women's sport have not been addressed, nor has lesbian presence been acknowledged. Lesbians in sport and physical education cope with the pervasiveness of homophobia by remaining silent. They have become so adept at coping that for many individuals it is easier to remain silent than to risk disclosure of a lesbian identity. The heterosexual male majority that dominates women's sport sometimes "tolerates" lesbian presence as long as that presence is inconspicuous or "discreet." Heterosexual women in sport and physical education often defend themselves from the lesbian label by joining closeted lesbians in denying that any of this occurs, or that it has any political significance. Women are quick to point out that there are no more lesbians in sport and physical education than in the population at large. The implication is that shame and discredit would descend on the profession if someone discovered that lesbian presence is something greater than the national average. The actual percentage is inconsequential compared with the pervasiveness of heterosexism and homophobia.

Underlying issues of homophobia are the political ideologies of heterosexism that go unnoticed, promoting misogyny and keeping the patriarchal system alive. Even if lesbians in sport knew all of this, and most do not (Bunch, 1978), communicating it from the closet is next to impossible. Many athletes, teachers, and coaches express fear and anguish over their inability to act in their own behalf or on behalf of their students who are just learning to deal with homophobia (Bailey, 1989). However, women who were once paralyzed by fear are now speaking up. The wave is swelling dramatically. Meetings, workshops, and lectures addressing homophobia and gay and lesbian issues in sport are now regular features at the national AAHPERD conventions.

Achieving parity with their male counterparts remains an uphill battle for many women committed to providing viable opportunities in girls' and women's sport. Hard work and continual vigilance are essential. The following "activists' agenda" is a work list for use in countering inequities facing girls and women in sports programs:

- implementation of actions that challenge sexism, racism, ageism, and homophobia
- expansion of programs for girls in recreational leagues, girls' clubs, sports camps, and individual sport federations
- presentation of challenges to overt employment discrimination against women in the hiring of coaches, teachers, administrators, and athletic trainers, as well as in recruiting student athletes, research assistants, and work-study students
- implementation of actions that challenge salary discrepancies where equal work exists
- funding of programs and attraction of corporate sponsorships
- expansion of public relations opportunities, sports information personnel, and media coverage

- promotion of the need for feminist analysis of sport programs that have become institutionalized via their governing bodies
- promotion of more comprehensive historical analyses, not limited to the "wealthy white man's version of history"

A Plan of Action

Strategies for political action provide the necessary tools to effect change. These strategies can be applied at the local level to begin bridge building. The following "instructions" track a generic action plan for activists with an agenda:

1. Choose an issue or project you want to initiate, support, or fight and find other people who agree with you.
2. Spread the word and amass support from each individual for your project.
3. If they agree, find out what kind and what level of support they are willing to give. (For example, will they sign a petition, testify at a hearing, write letters, or speak out publicly?)
4. Make a careful list of your supporters and their talents or contributions. Finding those who support the issue is part of the process of building alliances.
5. Meet with individuals in the chain of command and articulate your plan. Informing people in advance prevents them from being blindsided once the plan is initiated. People appreciate advance knowledge; it has an "inclusive" sound to it.
6. When someone directs you to stop, you must evaluate and measure the risk of continuing.
7. Document everything. Make notes of your discussions with people, including dates, statements made, and witnesses who were present.
8. Tell everyone what you are doing and why. Carry out the plan and broadcast it widely.
9. If you are harassed, you have options: Dialogue around it, file grievances, call in your supporters, compromise, create alternatives.
10. Plan your negotiating strategies in advance so that you will be ready for confrontation at any step.

The basic underlying tactics of this plan of action are twofold: (a) People sometimes underestimate the great latitude individual rank-and-file workers can exercise, and (b) although it is easier to imagine that the "boss" has the power to remedy a situation, there are often instances when it is really in the worker's own hands.

In reality, there are always at least two ways of looking at an issue. Even after conducting a major campaign to effect change, we may discover how incredibly difficult it is to change policy substantially. Stability and resistance to change are inherent characteristics of our major institutions. Because sport in America has many institutional qualities, effecting change is no simple matter.

Building Alliances

Bridges come in all sizes, depending upon estimated use and traffic patterns. A variety of structures are needed; large freeways are needed to build clout for major projects, and small foot-traffic bridges are needed for quick action at the local level. The task forces and caucuses, committees, and subcommittees from both the feminist movement and the organizations supporting and governing women's sport form the work force that constructs these bridges. Through networking, what started as a small footpath becomes a multilevel web of intersecting roadways.

Networking should be initiated at the level on which one already has access. A few examples might include student clubs and senate organizations, professional organizations at the local level, unions, and athletic advisory boards. Locally, public recreation departments provide many opportunities for sport-related programs. This grass-roots approach provides a starting point for the action earmarked to create change.

Women need to engage in dialogue about their sports experiences, their work, and feminist ideas, identifying issues they feel strongly enough about to work for change. Men who are coaches, trainers, and teachers should be part of the grass-roots movement in women's sport; this movement cannot afford separatism.

Conclusion

The opportunity for extending the goals of the feminist movement to the world of women's sport belongs to those individuals intimately connected to it: the students, athletes, teachers, coaches, researchers, representatives, and administrators of sport programs. Issues that have stunted progress in women's sport must be challenged. Building alliances with the feminist movement will increase the power base for both sport and feminist organizations. The sportswomen have gained the footholds necessary to showcase the feminist ideology the movement espouses. It is time to build bridges; the tools needed to accomplish the goal are readily available.

Although action is needed, essential components in this bridge-building effort include understanding of each group's strengths and weaknesses and a willingness to compromise. To achieve real change, there must be commitment to the cause. Women in both the feminist movement and sport know that only they can provide these ingredients. In the face of overt discrimination causing anguish, fear, and rage, the women must stand together on that bridge.

Key Words

feminist movement	ageism
political tactics	homophobia
building alliances	racism
sexism	organizational structures

Discussion Questions

1. How can a feminist women's movement help women in sport fight discrimination in the areas of sexism, homophobia, and ageism?

2. Imagine you are teaching and coaching in a local public high school. You have just been warned by the administration to stop actively crusading on issues to end the sexist treatment of girls' participation in sports and the homophobic graffiti in the school. What would you do? How would you accomplish your goals?

3. Some educators have argued against separate courses in women's sport that espouse a feminist ideology, insisting instead that such content should be mainstreamed into other existing courses. What are the advantages and disadvantages of this approach?

References

Albrecht, L., & Brewer, R. (Eds.). (1990). *Bridges of power: Women's multicultural alliances*. Philadelphia: New Society.

Bailey, N. J. (1988-1989). Lesbians in physical education and sport: Perceptions of risk. In *Perspectives: Journal of Western Society for Physical Education of College Women, 9*, 87-88.

Boutilier, M. A., & SanGiovanni, L. (1983). *The sporting woman: Feminist and sociological dilemmas*. Champaign, IL: Human Kinetics.

Bunch, C. (1978). Lesbian-feminist theory. In V. Vida (Ed.), *Our right to love* (pp. 180-182). Englewood Cliffs, NJ: Prentice-Hall.

Bunch, C. (1987). A broom of one's own: Notes on the women's liberation program. In *Passionate politics: Feminist theory in action, 1968-1986* (pp. 27-45). New York: St. Martin's.

Messner, M. (1990). Men studying masculinity: Some epistemological issues in sport sociology. *Sociology of Sport Journal, 7*, 136-153.

Sabo, D. (1987). *Opening the closet door: Some political implications of doing controversial research*. Paper presented at the annual meeting of the American Alliance of Health, Physical Education, Recreation and Dance, Las Vegas.

Spender, D. (1988). *Women of ideas and what men have done to them*. London: Pandora.

27

Sport in the Global Community

GRETA L. COHEN

The global community is constantly changing; the political dynamics have created opportunities not believed possible just a few years ago. The ease of travel and sophisticated communication options have increased interaction among women cross-culturally. Exciting things are happening worldwide in women's sports. At various levels of participation, at different age levels, and in a variety of sports, games, and physical activities, women are actively involved. Women in academia, organized sports programs, and recreational and agency affiliations are developing sports programs worldwide. The women's movement has empowered feminists, and the groundswell is reaching out to every continent.

In a sense, some women have created their own brass ring and are now thoroughly immersed in the process of catching that ring. Images of change are abundant. Women around the world are developing programs involving sports and physical activities. These programs are in various stages of development, but this does not in any way diminish the nobility or the aggressiveness with which these women pursue their targeted goals.

This chapter addresses four issues that affect the global perspective: access to sport in diverse cultures, competitive opportunities, educational programs, and the sisterhood of sport. Providing an overview of such an expansive topic constitutes a most challenging task.

Access to Sport in Diverse Cultures

Sport, like music, is a language that transcends culture. Interest in play, games, and sport is universal. Sport exists in a social context. For centuries,

AUTHOR'S NOTE: I would like to thank the following women for their contributions, candidly provided during phone conversations: Cheryl Aaron, Kathy Arenson, Doris Corbett, Jackie Hansen, Darlene Kluka, Diane Palmason, and Chris Shelton. The assistance and comments of Marjorie Smit were invaluable to the final revisions of this chapter.

Cross-cultural influences are apparent as school girls at Tiekunu Primary School in Kenya play netball in the school yard. (Photo by Carolyn Watson/PLAN International)

the trappings of caste have led the working class to replicate the sports and games of the wealthy; will the trappings of gender lead to similar emulation? In many cases sport is intricately related to politics. The popularity of sport has created a unique phenomenon whereby winning is often equated with prestige, acceptance of a particular nation's political ideology, or a symbol of a country's culture or dignity. What impact does this have for women— a population that has been excluded from decision making in world politics? Is the male model shaping competitive sport for women? What impact do these social and political considerations have on women's access to sport?

As we look at sport in a global context, we must consider a variety of factors. Various cultures create their own, often distinct, social constructions of sport that reflect multiple or diverse heritages. Apart from race, class, gender, and sexuality are the indigenous traditions, religious ideologies, and Western practices that shape the development and popularity of sport.

For example, colonial powers such as Great Britain brought games such as cricket, hockey, and rowing to their colonies in Africa, South and East Asia, the South Pacific, and North America (Stokvis, 1989). Merchants, missionaries, soldiers, teachers, and industrialists transplanted modern sport worldwide as developing countries shed their traditional customs and modernization took place. Attempts are just now getting under way to retrieve and preserve the indigenous sports, customs, dances, and games that are part of the cultural heritages of people in countries such as Yemen, Japan, and Thailand, as well as those of Native North Americans.

Religious fundamentalism, whether traditional or revived, has had a severe impact on sport participation, particularly for women. Stevenson (1989) reports that in keeping with Yemeni Islamic tradition, women should not appear in public without face veils and concealing body covers; therefore women cannot play sports in any public forum. This religious tenet holds true for women in many countries in the Middle East and on the African continent.

In colonial Malaya, women educators (American Methodists, French and Irish Catholic nuns, and British Anglicans) were sent as missionaries to devote their lives to helping emancipate Asian girls and women from centuries-old traditions and customs (Brownfoot, 1990). These women, acting in the spirit of sisterhood, were able to get close enough to the Asian women to gain their trust and to effect change. Historian Janice Brownfoot (1990) believes that sport became the conduit through which the "multi-racial society of Malaya effected interracial harmony." These missionaries also believed that sport was wholesome and would "provide positive alternatives to the Asian vices such as prostitution, concubinage, opium smoking, and gambling" (Brownfoot, 1990, p. 68).

As developing countries emulated Western practices, their traditional sports became obsolete. Animal sports were actively repressed by the colonial and state authorities, because they appeared uncivilized by Western standards (Stokvis, 1989). The popularity of modern sports was advantageous because they possessed standardized rules at both national and international levels. In some countries, however, one can observe people willing to embrace Western practices, but who still maintain allegiance to their own traditional sports.

In sport, women are underrepresented in general throughout the African continent. Although restrictions are not as limiting as those of their Muslim counterparts, the level of Westernization is not as pronounced for women as it is for African males (Mazrui, 1987):

> Compared to the Muslim world, where women are relatively spared physical labor and denied physical skills, black African women often do more work than their men. In some African societies they walk longer distances, carry heavier loads and have to learn a greater variety of balancing skills than their men. (Mazrui, 1987 p. 220)

According to Mazrui, these traditional chores condition women for sport, and more attention should be given to developing sports based on the indigenous activities in which women excel—marathon walking, weight lifting, and balancing skills, as demonstrated by the

> enormous bundles of firewood strapped on their backs while they carry baskets laden with farm produce or water balanced on their head and hands free to carry cassava or baskets of fruit. The graceful carriage and balancing skills could be developed into more than one sport and would turn these skills into proud, competitive feats of triumph and honor, developing champions, and may even lead the men into honorable chores. (p. 221)

In Western industrialized countries, sport opportunities for women are much more extensive. However, American women have difficulty finding sponsorship, network television coverage, and support for professional ventures because of a perceived saturation of men's sports as well as deep-rooted prevailing sexism and homophobia (Rounds, 1991). Interestingly, women do enjoy successful professional team sports programs in Western Europe, Japan, South America, and Australia. In countries such as Australia, New Zealand, Holland, Finland, and West Germany, club systems are extensive and provide lifelong opportunities for the pursuit of sporting activities, unlike the U.S. concentration on high school and collegiate systems. While sport options are certainly not uniformly available worldwide, many more girls and women have increased their opportunities to pursue numerous sport and recreational activities in Western industrialized countries.

It is important to remember that sport is a luxury. It is often easy to ignore the vast populations that are totally removed from such activities. They live in poverty, where their days are spent in hunger and work is directed toward fulfilling basic needs for family. The women of Bangladesh, Somalia, and Ethiopia face lives where high rates of infant mortality and starvation are commonplace. In other, less devastated countries, Westerners have established clubs and extensive sports facilities that are often restricted. Many indigenous inhabitants do not have the time or the financial means

This young girl carries millet while leading a child and goats through the dusty harmattan weather near the village of Mogodin in Burkina Faso. (Photo by Carolyn Watson/PLAN International)

to engage in these sports. In some cases they would not be welcome even if time and money were not controlling issues.

Gender Discrimination

Gender bias long served to exclude women from certain sports, and the rationale was universally accepted. According to Mazrui (1987), "Nothing in human history has been more responsible for the political subordination of women than their demilitarization" (p. 225). The notion that fighting was the responsibility of males automatically excluded females from warfare. Banishment from the battlefield ensured banishment from the gladiator's arena, and this translated into banishment from the playing fields—women were judged unfit for such "combat." As Sir William Fraser (1889) noted, "The battle of Waterloo was won on the playing fields of Eton." This roughly translates to the adage that sport is the training ground for war. How could women be considered unfit for war and be judged fit for sport? Various nations have used this rationale to prohibit women from participation in certain sports, a right reserved for the "warrior." In Britain, women were excluded from rugby, soccer, and even cricket (Mazrui, 1987). In the United States it was football and baseball; bullfighting in Spain, Mexico, and Tanzania; and so on throughout much of the global community. While some sports enhance the traditions of warriors, attitudes regarding women's ability to compete in the world of sport remain diverse. In some cultures, little or no movement has been made, whereas other societies reflect dramatic advances in social and political receptiveness.

Competitive Opportunities

Global Competitions

The largest, most dramatic single event on this planet remains the quadrennial display of Olympic sports competition. The Olympic movement has had a profound effect on the development of sport worldwide. Traditionally, developing countries have looked forward to the day when they can join the Olympic opening ceremonies procession behind their symbols of nationalism and compete with the major Western powers. If some countries interpret this commercial enterprise as a commodification of sport, many developing countries see it as a means to foster national unity, integration of internal dissenting factors, international recognition, and the emancipation of women (Riordan, 1986).

The Olympic movement has particularly affected opportunities for women in China. In a society with a history reflecting thousands of years of feudal culture, men and women are now treated identically in the pursuit of athletic honors. "Women are paid the same daily stipends when they take time off from work to practice and women are equally encouraged to excel" (Deford, 1988, p. 42). Why? With so many medals in international competition available, excluding women in a country that wants to win is counterproductive. This practice is not unlike that of the former USSR or the former East Germany.

Because most Chinese women marry late and the government limits births to one per family, women are not severely hindered in keeping up their training schedules and tend to stay with their sports longer (Deford, 1988). This has created a unique phenomenon: The success rate for Chinese women is substantially higher than that of their male counterparts in international competition.

> The saying "women can hold up half of the sky" gives full expression to the confidence of the Chinese women today in challenging a traditional patriarchal society. In the past ten years, the rate between women's sports that have reached world class levels and those of men is approximately 18:7, which, obviously, indicates the importance of women in China's sports circle. (Hua, 1989, pp. 98-99)

In many countries, women are not encouraged to excel in sports unless they participate in the Olympics. However, the International Olympic Committee continues to limit women's involvement in Olympic competition, and the sanctioning of some events has been painstakingly slow.

Examples include the 5,000- and 10,000-meter races and sports such as softball, soccer, and the biathlon.

World championship competition exists in a variety of women's sports that include both individual and team competitions. For example, world championships are regularly held in sports such as figure skating; fast-pitch softball; Alpine, Nordic, and freestyle skiing; gymnastics; cycling; and athletics (track and field events). In 1990, world competition in ice hockey was added. In 1991 the first World Cup championships in the sport of soccer were held for women. It is particularly interesting to note that the U.S. women won this event, because soccer has not been embraced by the U.S. patriarchy and lives in the shadows of the male-dominated triumvirate—American football, basketball, and baseball.

Regional Competition

Most people are familiar with such global events as the Olympic Games and the World Cup championships in designated sports. But regional competitions also exist throughout the world, and women compete in a variety of sports offered. The examples cited here only *begin* to illustrate the diversity of athletic pursuits and the number of regional competitions considered "standard fare."

The Arctic Winter Games involve athletes from the Northwest Territories, Alaska, Greenland, and the Russian Arctic. The mushers have made incredible gains in this sport over the past decade. In the Southeast Asian Games, Thailand's women's team won 9 of the 10 gold medals awarded in women's shooting (Anderson, 1989). Regional African Games provide qualifying competition for the All-African Games. Zaire's women's basketball team has created something of a dynasty for more than five years on the African continent (Lema, 1989). Only individual sports are contested in the Commonwealth Games. For women, competition exists in athletics, lawn bowls, cycling, diving, gymnastics (artistic and rhythmic), shooting (which is coed but will be contested separately after 1994), swimming, synchronized swimming, and judo (which will be omitted after 1994). It is interesting to note that bids have been made to add weight lifting and wrestling. In the Pan-American Games, the U.S. women's basketball team has dominated, and volleyball competition has seen hotly contested battles between Cuba and the United States.

National and Local Competitions

More latitude exists on national and local levels to pursue a broad spectrum of sporting activities. Countries such as Canada, Norway, New Zealand, and Australia have government-funded programs to promote women's sport. In the Netherlands, federal money was set aside to develop league competition and to build broad-based competitive sports programs for people of all ages. Women now enjoy lifetime participatory sports programs, with competition at the local and district levels (M. Smit, personal communication, April 1992).

The United States does not fund at the federal level, but does endorse private corporate sponsorship models. For example, the New York Road-runners Club organizes the corporately sponsored Advil Mini-Marathon, which attracts 3,000-8,000 women runners annually. On the West Coast, San Francisco's famous Bay to Breakers 12K race has attracted 100,000 participants, making it the largest participatory sporting event in the world. The race is sponsored by the *San Francisco Examiner*, and proceeds are distributed to a variety of Bay Area charities. The race features every-one from elite runners to party goers in the costume division. Various corporations help sponsor the festivities that follow.

Worldwide, recreational pursuits have created an infrastructure that ranges from the very informal to highly sophisticated programs. The case of Martha Aupaluktuq, related recently by Laura Robinson (1992) in *Ms.*, is just one example of the sheer love of sport that personifies women's pursuit of their own brass ring. An Inuit woman living in a village of 1,400 in the Canadian Arctic, Aupaluktuq organized women from isolated communities for the first women's ice hockey championships in the North-west Territories. Women arrived at Rankin Inlet with their infants on their backs and toddlers and hockey sticks in their hands. The new ice rink on which they were to play had no ice-clearing equipment, so the players cleared the ice themselves by skating across it holding a sheet of plywood between them. "Almost 90% of the players had children; those not old enough to watch the game were cared for by women relatives or other players." Aupaluktuq's commitment to this endeavor and the difficulty in pulling off such a feat constitute a "triumph of legendary proportions" (p. 16).

Educational Programs Promoting
Girls' and Women's Sports Internationally

A variety of North American professional organizations have been working on other continents with the express purpose of promoting and developing opportunities in sports for girls and women. Many programs have incorporated a Peace Corps model, implementing educational pro-grams that are self-sustaining. These opportunities include physical edu-cation programs as well as recreational activities and intensive sport experiences to develop skill and expertise at the international level.

The educational programs usually follow one of three formats: (a) intensive two-week conferences in which exchanges focus on philosophy, pedagogy, or practical self-help workshops; (b) long-term residence, in which educational programs are actively implemented and hands-on training is available for the local practitioners; and (c) goodwill tours involving informal competitions and clinics. In all cases, cultural ex-changes form the basis for personal interactions that promote and develop opportunities in sports. Language barriers may be problematic, but the interest in sport fosters the mutual respect essential in developing bonds of friendship. The love of sport transcends culture.

The Inter-American Commission

Physical educators interested in promoting more global opportunities for women as teachers, coaches, and administrators created the Inter-American Commission for Girls and Women in Sport. Since 1978, women have engaged in developing programs designed to promote interest in sport, physical education, and fitness for children in the Caribbean and Central and South America. By establishing affiliations with the National Association for Girls and Women in Sport, the Caribbean/Central America Action Group, the International Council of Health, Physical Education, and Recreation, and sponsorship from UNESCO, the Inter-American Commission has actualized a variety of projects. Teams of clinicians have been sent to Jamaica, Haiti, and Barbados to conduct seminars in a variety of sports and sport-related theory courses. A series of international conferences on girls and women in sport were subsequently held in Pennsylvania, USA (1982); Caracas, Venezuela (1983); Curacao (1984); Costa Rica (1986); and Guatemala (1987). Conferences in El Salvador and Mexico were canceled because of political unrest. Plans to expand the commission to increase global representation are under review (C. Shelton, personal communication, October 1991).

Canadian Paradigms

In Canada, two educational models for developing girls' and women's sports have expanded internationally. A program designed in Vancouver, British Columbia, by Betty Baxter focuses on a coaching school run by women for women to develop coaching skills and a support system. Having piloted this program in Canada, Baxter took the hands-on experiment to Norway, where she remained for six months to assist in developing a similar model. The program focuses on practical and theoretical aspects of coaching. This model was then promoted at the international conference in conjunction with the Commonwealth Games in Aukland, New Zealand, in 1990 (D. Palmason, personal communication, April 1992).

A girls' sports program was created and funded by the City of Ottawa Community Recreation Department. An alternative to the competitive model, this program was developed for girls ages 9-15 and designed to keep girls from dropping out of sport by emphasizing participation, instruction, recreation, and social aspects of sport rather than high levels of competition. The success of this program has spawned a more competitive aspect to the recreational format. Sport Canada provided support and informational packets for other communities who wanted to develop similar programs. Like the previous model, this program was also presented at the international conference held in conjunction with the Commonwealth Games in Aukland, New Zealand, in 1990 (D. Palmason, personal communication, April 1992).

Institute for International Sport

Although not operating exclusively on behalf of girls' and women's sport, the Institute for International Sport does promote international programs that have had significant impact on the quality of the female sport experience. The institute, operating independently from the University of Rhode Island campus, was founded in 1986 for the express purpose of promoting peace and understanding through sport worldwide. The Institute has developed both an internship program and a Sports Corps program. Opportunities exist for interns to establish residencies abroad and to work with local practitioners in organizing and administering sport programs for young athletes, particularly disadvantaged children.

The Sports Corps programs have enabled high school and college teams to travel abroad to participate in goodwill tours. Women's sports teams at both high school and collegiate levels have had the opportunity to travel to foreign countries to work with community groups teaching the sport in which they specialize, to compete with local community teams, and, when practical, to work with physically challenged youth.

A Worldwide Women's Sports Coalition

At the 1992 annual conference sponsored by the Women's Sports Foundation of the United States, representatives from Japan, Australia, New Zealand, Canada, the United States, and Great Britain met in Colorado and formed a coalition of all international organizations demonstrating a focus on women in sport at the international level. The mission of this coalition is "to achieve gender equity in and through sport and physical activity" (Brackenridge, 1992). The objectives are fourfold:

1. to raise awareness of the need for equitable opportunities for all women in sport, at all levels, in all societies
2. to facilitate communication and build a network of support among national and international sport organizations for women
3. to develop and maintain a worldwide data base detailing women's sports organizations
4. to facilitate the sharing of information about practices, programs, and resources that concern women (Brackenridge, 1992)

The newly formed coalition is actively seeking support and participation from interested organizations. A series of national and international conferences and meetings covering a three-year span has already been planned.

Promoting World-Class Competition

Cross-cultural exchanges involving highly competitive sports teams provide a different dimension to educational programming at the international level. One of the classic examples in U.S. history involves the illustrious professional softball team the Connecticut Falcons (now the Raybestos Brakettes), who, in 1977, proposed an exhibition series of friendship games with the women of China. In 1979 the request was granted and the U.S. players traveled to China to compete against all-star teams from a variety of provinces who came to Peking (now Beijing) and Lanzhou for

The Connecticut Falcons and a Chinese all-star team enter a packed stadium with 40,000 spectators in Peking for an exhibition series of friendship games. (Photo by Joan E. Chandler; courtesy of the Kathy Stilwell Collection)

the competition. As it turned out, the Americans completely outclassed the Chinese. According to Eva Auchincloss (1979):

> The Chinese took a giant step in gaining parity in the sport when they invited the Falcons. The team wasn't asked to China on a mere whim; they were invited to display skills and to teach those skills to the Chinese women. . . . The U.S. players graciously obliged and instructional sessions including the pitching techniques of Joan Joyce, batting by Willie Rose, and catching techniques of Jackie Ledbetter were meticulously filmed by camera crews for future use. The Chinese were most gracious, accepting instruction and advice eagerly. (p. 51)

Three years later, in 1982, the International Softball Federation sponsored the Fifth World Championship Games in Taiwan. The Republic of China team defeated the United States twice to make it to the finals against New Zealand. The worldwide popularity of big-time women's fast-pitch softball has been growing steadily; it will make its Olympic debut in 1996 as a medal sport.

As women enter the international sports arena as educators, it is particularly interesting to note that their programs are multidimensional. In all of the educational programs described above, distinctions are made among programs designed to promote sport for health, fitness, and recreational purposes, programs designed to foster international goodwill, and programs designed to showcase high-level competitive sport. Women working internationally appear to have no difficulty making such distinctions, and are comfortable with both a recreational model to promote health, fitness, and well-being and the physically intensive competitive ethic. Regardless of the level of competition, promoting friendship and cross-cultural sensitivities does not appear to be mutually exclusive.

The Sisterhood of Sport

Is competition among feminist women a contradiction in terms? Some feminist theorists believe that aggressive behaviors fueled by competitive athletics are antithetical to the cooperative-supportive model that feminists espouse. The success of the feminist movement is in part a reflection of cooperative efforts. In this paradigm sport becomes counterproductive to feminist ideology and creates adversarial positions among women that prevent bonding. These feminists see the reward structure in sport as nothing more than a form of tokenism—rewarding a few at the top at the expense of their competitors, while ignoring the problems that fester underneath, feeding an already corrupt sports system.

Conversely, the more popular theory embraces the notion that the competitive ethic fosters drive, determination, perseverance, and the will to succeed. Aggressive behavior is applauded; power, strength, and endurance become enviable goals. Are these skills not essential? The very act of competing creates a process in which decision making and processing of ideas and testing of strategies are inherently addressed. With each success, an individual becomes more capable, self-assured, and assertive, and these traits strengthen the psyche. Competition creates opportunities to master the very skills feminists find essential when creating a cooperative model.

An interesting dialectic emerges. Is competition a feminist taboo or does the fabric of sport, the "competition," provide the substance by which feminism is refined? A competitive ethos has been encouraged and even nurtured in many cultures throughout the world. According to Lichtenstein (1987), "Competitiveness seems to evolve regardless of culture. Otherwise how could Rosa Mota, world class marathoner, have emerged from the Latin chauvinism of Portugal; Gabriela Sabatini, Argentine tennis sensation; or Nawal El Moutawakel, the Olympic medalist runner from Muslim Morocco?" (p. 52). In Algeria, Muslim runner Hassiba Boulmerka became both a heroine and an outcast after winning the women's 1,500-meter race at the World Track and Field Championships. As a symbol of the antifundamentalists, she finds herself caught between competing factions struggling for power in her native Algeria, and a safe and welcoming return to her homeland depends on which group rises to power. She has offended Muslims because it is illegal for her to wear running clothes in public ("Veiled Threat," 1992). For all of these women the desire to compete was somehow nurtured despite cultural bias, and their success created additional opportunities to pursue higher levels of competition. Their talent, determination, and drive enabled them to achieve championship status.

Competition, the Fabric of Sport:
Socialization, a By-Product

Strong bonds of friendship exist among sportswomen everywhere. "Sports oriented women know that the game is nothing more than a game . . . anything but a life and death struggle" (Lichtenstein, 1987, p. 53). Every sport is set within boundaries. That is why Chris Evert and Martina Navratilova, fierce competitors throughout the 1980s, could sit together and share a bagel in the locker room just prior to an all-out competitive effort at Wimbledon's center court (Lichtenstein, 1987). Track superstar Heike Drechsler (Germany) comforted her injured rival Jackie Joyner-Kersee (USA) at the 1991 World Championships in Tokyo. Long jumper Joyner-Kersee feared she had broken her leg, ending her career. Drechsler stayed with her until both women were reassured that the injury was not serious, even though Drechsler still needed to jump 1¼ inch further to defeat Joyner-Kersee (Moore, 1992).

Former marathon world record holder Jackie Hansen relates the following story. A French woman living in Morocco was assigned to the American team as the translator at an International Amateur Athletic Federation 15K championship race. Her job as interpreter did not include the invitation she extended to the Americans to visit her home, or the sightseeing trip around town, or even the ride up to Nice in her own car. But, Jackie believes, "women athletes look out after each other—we are all in this together" (personal communication, November 7, 1991).

Joan Benoit, the first Olympic marathon winner in 1984, in a commencement speech to the graduating class of 1990 at Colby-Sawyer College, remarked that it was her heroine, Jackie Hansen, who applied the pressure for more than 10 years—from her glory days in the 1970s—until the marathon race was finally sanctioned for women competitors. "The pioneer women in our field . . . put the world within our reach and asked us to take from it what we need" (Samuelson, 1991, p. 48). In stories such as these, we are reminded that we each stand on the shoulders of those who came before.

Raybestos Brakettes softball pitcher Kathy Arenson, 13-time all-American, was selected as the pitcher on the World All-Star Team in 1986, the last year such a team was assembled. She remembers the fun she had learning to bond with teammates on a team with no common language. Her catcher and third basewomen were Japanese, a New Zealander played first base, an American played second, the shortstop was from Chinese Taipei, and three women from the Republic of China were in the outfield. The real differences were unrelated to speech—they were in the ways the team members viewed competition and sport. The game, Arenson says, "was a piece of cake compared to the Japanese warm-up, which was more strenuous than the game and required total synchronization" (personal communication, April 1992). Americans, Arenson contends, are not nearly as disciplined as her Asian teammates. Fairness and ethics are valued traits; the obsession with winning was American, and the disgrace directed inward at losing was internalized by the Chinese.

The countries of Ireland, England, Scotland, and Wales have created an annual event involving their international girls' and women's teams at each of four levels: ages 13 and under, 15 and under, 19 and under, and open ladies' division. Each country hosts the round-robin competition at one of the four levels, and the event rotates among the countries annually. The competition takes a backseat to the accompanying mixers, in which not only players but families, organizers, and officials participate. The hosts rent out a ballroom at a local hotel for dancing or some form of activity after each basketball game. Following the last game, everyone participates in the closing banquet featuring awards ceremonies for everything from "best spirited team" to "best uniforms" (C. Aaron, personal communication, February 1992).

Our Global Village

The global community is more readily accessible than ever before. Nationality is ignored as individuals who desire to improve skill level and expertise travel extensively to seek the ideal programs, climates, and environments for their training. Athletes from all over the planet train and compete in countries other than their own. Some return to their homelands for Olympic competition; many vie for positions at club, collegiate, and professional levels in countries other than their own.

For example, the internationalization of NCAA volleyball is pervasive, as women around the world select the United States so that they can play college volleyball while earning academic degrees (Kraft, 1991). In the 1991-1992 season, the top 20 teams listed in *Volleyball Monthly*'s preseason rankings included 22 players from foreign countries, including Brazil, Australia, Russia, Scotland, Czechoslovakia, Finland, and Germany (Kraft, 1991). In like manner, many American women travel to Europe and Asia to extend their sport careers in the professional volleyball and basketball leagues. Lucrative contracts, product endorsement contracts, and stardom in foreign leagues are as enticing to American athletes as the collegiate opportunities in the United States are to other women.

Conclusion

On the playing fields, women are not isolated, nor are they kept divided from one another. By traveling to the worlds of others, we can identify with them; we begin to understand the kinds of lives they lead and how they perceive us. Athletes also experience firsthand the obstacles that some players have to overcome for the opportunity to compete. Sometimes they find themselves exposed to competitive ethics that are very different from their own. The challenge may very likely have no bearing on skill performance or physical expertise.

In a world that divides us by race, class, religion, age, ethnicity, and sexual orientation, we are bound together by gender and share in our sisterhood a common oppression that is universally understood. Through sport we are developing a partnership model to promote peace and under-standing in the global village. This unobtrusive mobilization is being nurtured by our inherent love of sport itself.

Key Words

indigenous sports	competitive opportunities
religious fundamentalism	educational programs
Westernization	coalitions
discrimination	sisterhood of sport

Discussion Questions

1. Select distinctly different cultures and contrast their social construction of sport and the sports opportunities available to girls and women.
2. Are global competitions such as the Olympics a commodification of sport or a means by which women are emancipated?
3. Support or refute each of the following statements: (a) Competition is a feminist taboo; (b) Competition provides the substance by which feminism is refined.

References

Anderson, W. W. (1989). Sport in Thailand. In E. A. Wagner (Ed.), *Sport in Asia and Africa* (pp. 121-146). Westport, CT: Greenwood.

Auchincloss, E. (1979, September). From China with glove. *WomenSports*, pp. 34-38, 51.

Brackenridge, C. (1992). Women's International Sports Coalition. In *Proceedings of the first meeting of the Women's International Sports Coalition*. Unpublished manuscript, Women's International Sports Coalition, Sheffield, UK.

Brownfoot, J. N. (1990). Emancipation, exercise and imperialism: Girls and the games ethic in colonial Malaya. *International Journal of the History of Sport, 7*(1), 61-84.

Deford, F. (1988, August 15). An old dragon limbers up: Sports in China, a special report. *Sports Illustrated*, pp. 36-43.

Frazer, W. (1889). *Words on Wellington*. London: J. C. Nimmo.

Hua, T. (1989). Movement and sport in Chinese women's life yesterday, today and tomorrow. In *Proceedings of the Jyvaskyla Congress on Movement and Sport in Women's Life, August 17-21, 1987* (pp. 91-106). Jyvaskyla, Finland: University of Jyvaskyla.

Kraft, D. (1991, November). Invasion: The collegiate volleyball ranks feature players on a world-wide scale. *Volleyball Monthly*, pp. 51-53.

Lema, B. (1989). Sport in Zaire. In E. A. Wagner (Ed.), *Sport in Asia and Africa* (pp. 229-247). Westport, CT: Greenwood.

Lichtenstein, G. (1987). Competition in women's athletics. In V. Miner & H. Longino (Eds.), *Competition: A feminist taboo?* (pp. 48-56). New York: Feminist Press.

Mazrui, A. A. (1987). Africa's triple heritage of play: Reflections on the gender gap. In W. S. Baker & J. A. Mangan (Eds.), *Sport in Africa: Essays in social history* (pp. 217-228). New York: Africana.

Moore, K. (1992, July 22). Head to head. *Sports Illustrated*, p. 66.

Riordan, J. (1986). State and sport in developing societies. *International Review for the Sociology of Sport, 21*, 287-303.

Robinson, L. (1992, January-February). Canadian hockey: Inuit style. *Ms.*, p. 16.

Rounds, K. (1991, January-February). Why men fear women's teams. *Ms.*, pp. 43-45.

Samuelson, J. B. (1991, July). To dream, to dare, to create . . . *Runner's World*, pp. 46-48.

Stevenson, T. B. (1989). Sport in the Yemen Arab Republic. In E. A. Wagner (Ed.), *Sport in Asia and Africa* (pp. 27-49). Westport, CT: Greenwood.

Stokvis, R. (1989). The international and national expansion of sports. In E. A. Wagner (Ed.), *Sport in Asia and Africa* (pp. 13-23). Westport, CT: Greenwood.

Veiled threat. (1992, January 27). *Sports Illustrated*, p. 12.

Author Index

Subject Index

About the Authors

R. Vivian Acosta, Ph.D., past president of the National Association for Girls and Women in Sport, is a Professor of Physical Education at Brooklyn College. She has been active in work on equity issues, and one of her primary activities includes research on women and minorities in sport leadership.

Nancy Bailey, Professor of Physical Education, is currently Chairwoman of the Department of Physical Education and Athletics at California State University at Bakersfield (even though her vita is thoroughly infused with feminist and antihomophobia work). Her research specialty is concentrated in issues relating to lesbian and feminist ideology.

Marjorie Caldwell is Professor in the Department of Food Science and Nutrition at the University of Rhode Island. Her current teaching and research interests are in the areas of diet, exercise, and weight control, international nutrition, and clinical nutrition.

Linda Jean Carpenter, Ph.D., J.D., serves as Professor of Physical Education at Brooklyn College, where her research focuses on the status of women in intercollegiate athletics. She is also an attorney and is a member of the New York State and U.S. Supreme Court Bars.

Kathleen Cerra-Laquale is Head Athletic Therapist at Rhode Island College. A lecturer, clinician, and author on subjects relating to sport medicine and nutrition, she currently chairs the National Council of Athletic Trainers for the American Alliance for Health, Physical Education, Recreation and Dance.

Carol L. Christensen, Ph.D., is Professor of Exercise Physiology in the Department of Human Performance at San Jose State University, California. Her research has been presented at regional, national, and international conferences. Her specialty is women's response to training and exercise, weight control, sports nutrition, and exercise physiology.

334

Greta L. Cohen is Professor of Physical Education and Women's Studies at the University of Rhode Island. She is the former editor of the monograph series for the Institute for International Sport. In her field of sport sociology, her research on women in sport has been presented at regional, national, and international conferences.

Charles F. Darley received his doctorate in cognitive psychology from Stanford University. A former Head Women's Tennis Coach at the University of Iowa, he is currently Coordinator for Special Resources in the Women's Athletic Department. He is a member of the Department of Physical Education and Sports Studies faculty at Iowa, and the Head Coach for the U.S. Tennis Association's Iowa Area Training Center.

Anita L. DeFrantz is a member of the International Olympic Committee and President of the Amateur Athletic Foundation of Los Angeles. A former Olympian, she won the bronze medal in rowing in the 1976 Games.

Mary Duquin is an Associate Professor at the University of Pittsburgh. She received her Ph.D. from Stanford University in 1975, specializing in the psychosocial aspects of sport. She and her life companion of 20 years have two girls, ages 7 and 3. Thus her interest in creating a strong ethic of care in sport is both personal and professional.

Christine H. B. Grant is currently Women's Athletic Director and Associate Professor at the University of Iowa. She is former President of the Association for Intercollegiate Athletics for Women and the National Association of Collegiate Women Athletic Administrators. She served as expert consultant to the HEW Office for Civil Rights Title IX Task Force.

Susan L. Greendorfer is a Professor in the Department of Kinesiology at the University of Illinois, Urbana-Champaign. A specialist in sociology of sport, widely published in gender issues and sport, she is considered the leading authority in female sport socialization. She is cofounder of the North American Society for Sociology of Sport, a member of the Advisory Board of the Women's Sports Foundation, and a staunch supporter of women's right to participate in whatever sporting activity they choose.

Pat Griffin is Associate Professor in the Social Justice Education Program at the University of Massachusetts at Amherst. Her research, teaching, and writing interests focus on sexism, racism, and heterosexism in education. She is considered the leading designer and facilitator of developmental programs addressing homophobia in sport.

Betty Hicks, a golf champion, was selected Associated Press Woman Athlete of the Year in 1941, and won the Women's National Amateur Championships of Golf that same year. She was runner-up to Babe Didrikson in the 1940 and 1946 Women's U.S. Open Golf Championships. She has recently retired from full-time teaching and as Chair of the Aviation

Department at Foothill College in Palo Alto, California. She can now devote more time to her golf game and to her writing.

Donna A. Lopiano, Ph.D., is the Executive Director of the Women's Sports Foundation and former Director of Intercollegiate Athletics for Women at the University of Texas at Austin. Her involvement in sport as athlete, activist, author, speaker, and administrator has established her reputation as a leading authority on women in sport.

Mary C. Lydon is currently Director of Physical Education and Health for the Quincy, Massachusetts, Public Schools. Her professional career includes teaching physical education, health, and coaching at the elementary, secondary, and college levels. She has been actively involved in women's sport equity for many years and, since its inception, has served as Chairperson of New Agenda: Northeast for the advancement of girls and women in sport and for the Massachusetts celebration of National Girls and Women in Sport Day.

Hilary Matheson completed her undergraduate training at Warwick University in England, her master's degree at Iowa State University, and her doctorate degree at Springfield College with an emphasis in sport psychology. She has taught in England, Hong Kong, and the United States, has coached field hockey and gymnastics at each post, and currently lectures at Wolver Hampton Technic in England.

Helen T. McCarthy, Ph.D., teaches classes in the principles of nutrition at Brown University in Providence, Rhode Island. She is also a Supervising Public Health Chemist for the Rhode Island Department of Health, where she is involved in research and in the testing of foods and water for their conformance to public health standards.

Michael A. Messner, Ph.D., is an Assistant Professor of Sociology at the Center for the Study of Women and Men in Society at the University of Southern California. He is coeditor, with Donald Sabo, of *Sport, Men, and the Gender Order: Critical Feminist Perspectives* (Human Kinetics), and he and Dr. Sabo also write the column "SportsMen" for *Changing Men*, a profeminist magazine about gender issues. He recently published *Power at Play: Sports and the Problem of Masculinity* (Beacon, 1992).

L. Leotus Morrison recently retired from the position of Associate Director of Athletics at James Madison University in Harrisonburg, Virginia. She has served as President of the Association for Intercollegiate Athletics for Women and the National Association for Girls and Women in Sport, and has been a member of the U.S. Olympic Committee for eight years. She has been a speaker and official delegate to numerous national and international conferences, including a UNESCO Conference on Sport and Physical Education and the First Pan-American Conference on Women in Sport.

Mimi Murray, Buxton Professor at Springfield College in Massachusetts, has been the sports psychologist for the U.S. equestrian team and individual professional athletes. Her coaching successes include three Division I national championships in gymnastics, and she has served as coach of the U.S. gymnastics team. She is on the U.S. Olympic Committee Sports Psychology Registry and has served as President of both the National Association for Girls and Women in Sport and the American Alliance for Health, Physical Education, Recreation and Dance.

Joan Paul is Professor and Head of the Department of Human Performance and Sport Studies at the University of Tennessee. She has published a number of historical studies in refereed journals, and was elected President of the North American Society for Sport History.

Mary Pratt played in the All-American Girls' Professional Baseball League from 1943 to 1947. She pitched for the Rockford Peaches and the Kenosha Comets. A graduate of Sargent College, she taught physical education for 48 years at the secondary, collegiate, and elementary levels in her home state of Massachusetts. She currently works on behalf of women's sports programs such as the New Agenda Committee and the Massachusetts Interscholastic Athletic Association.

Donald Sabo, Ph.D., is an Associate Professor of Sociology at D'Youville College. He is coeditor, with Michael Messner, of *Sport, Men, and the Gender Order: Critical Feminist Perspectives* (Human Kinetics), and he and Dr. Messner also write the column "SportsMen" for *Changing Men*, a profeminist magazine about gender issues.

Christine M. Shelton is an Assistant Professor in the Department of Exercise and Sport Studies at Smith College in Northampton, Massachusetts. She has been inducted into James Madison University's Athletic Hall of Fame. She has served as President and acting Executive Director of the National Association for Girls and Women in Sport and has directed the NAGWS Latin American Project since 1979, heading the U.S. delegations to sport conferences in Barbados, Costa Rica, Guatemala, and Venezuela. She was a Junior Wightman tennis player, ranked nationally, and has competed in the United States, Canada, and South America.

Claudine Sherrill is Professor in the Kinesiology Department of Texas Woman's University. As a researcher and author, she has published numerous books, chapters, and articles and is considered a leading authority in the field of adapted physical education and recreation and sport for the disabled.

Marjorie A. Snyder, Ph.D., is the Associate Executive Director of the Women's Sports Foundation, a nonprofit educational organization dedicated to promoting and enhancing the sports and fitness experience for all girls and women. Prior to assuming her current position, she was a college coach and Professor of Physical Education at Hope College in Holland, Michigan.

Patricia A. Sullivan, Ed.D, is an Assistant Professor in the Department of Exercise Science at George Washington University in Washington, DC. Her departmental responsibilities include the coordination of the coaching education program. Previously, she served as Women's Volleyball Coach at the University of Nebraska and as Women's Volleyball Coach at George Washington University.

Paula Welch is Professor of Exercise and Sport Sciences at the University of Gainesville in Gainesville, Florida. She has coached basketball at the university level and is a sport history researcher and a member of the Education Committee of the U.S. Olympic Committee.

Deborah J. Wilson, Ph.D., is a counseling psychologist on the staffs of George Mason University in Fairfax, Virginia, and George Washington University in Washington, DC, where she specializes in working with student-athletes. From 1972 to 1980 she was the Women's Basketball Coach at The Ohio State University.